**CHILD
LEARNING,
INTELLIGENCE,
AND PERSONALITY**

CHILD LEARNING, INTELLIGENCE, AND PERSONALITY

Principles of a Behavioral Interaction Approach

Arthur W. Staats
University of Hawaii

Harper & Row Publishers
New York, Evanston, and London

Contents

Preface

A primary goal of mine has been the development of a general, unified conception of human behavior—child and adult, normal and abnormal, individual, group, and cultural—based upon the laboratory established principles of learning. This task must extend from the elementary principles to the subject matter of the social sciences and include methods ranging from laboratory experimentation to naturalistic and clinical observations.

In pursuing these interests in complex human behavior it became evident to me that traditional personality and social theories for various reasons would not be adequate. It also became apparent in the process that the traditional learning theories by themselves were also lacking—and in fact in their own realm required development and revision. Furthermore, the restrictive separatism of both orientations prevented productive unification.

It is necessary to break out of each tradition to make a combination of the productive elements of each. My previous books have been steps in the direction of unifying the findings and concepts of the study of man within the learning conception, and this book is intended similarly.

One of the schisms that must be eliminated as a contemporary obstacle is that between what is considered to be basic science and that considered to be applied science. Scientific theories, it should be noted, are valuable in great part because, in addition to providing conceptual understanding, they allow us to predict events we are interested in and because they allow us to affect those events. These products of science are frequently of practical significance. In the realm of human behavior it is no less necessary that a theory show its potential for producing the same products. The present work aims to build a structure that provides conceptual understanding as well as practical products.

Thus, the book includes a general conception of personality development —in the behavioral sense to be developed—and deals also with certain aspects of personality, especially with what is called intelligence. As indicated above, moreover, the book also deals with the development of aspects of behavior important to human adjustment—in terms of specific principles and conditions. The material presented aims to provide knowledge by which to affect the conditions of child development, as well as to provide a general conception. As such—and in the author's opinion this is a central aspect of psychological theory development—the present book intends to have practical applications at the same time it yields a theoretical conception.

In previous works I have dealt more extensively with basic principles and experimental methods in analyses of behavioral repertoires. However, I have written the present book not to emphasize the basic, but to indicate how how the principles can serve to understand and deal with human behavior. Thus, the book is appropriate for those who have neither special training nor special interests in basic learning, necessarily; rather, it is for those whose interests are in human affairs and in understanding human behavior development.

As has been suggested, the present book is conceptually oriented, in the sense that it aims to introduce general principles and concepts of personality development—as well as to describe types of determining conditions that are involved—rather than being primarily a review of the research literature in behavior modification. This aim is in contrast to much of the present behavior modification work, which generally concerns the demonstration of the prnciple of reinforcement, or classical conditioning, in treating various relatively simple behaviors in short term procedures.

It is hoped the book will prove productive for the student of child development and personality, for those with a behavior modification approach, for the psychological, psychiatric, pediatric, educational, or other professional who works with problems of human behavior, especially with children and their parents, and also—in a break with tradition—for the inquiring parent himself who can maintain his interest through an academic introductory section. The book is appropriate for the latter audience because of the specific and practical content of the book (stemming from the functional philosophy of theory construction involved).

I have been studying human learning of significant behaviors for over a decade and a half. Much of this has been unique research with the learning of children in various areas of behavior (including investigating and dealing with behavior development of my own children). A good deal of this work has appeared in scientific journals. However, following my above-stated philosophy, I have long felt that the principles of psychology should be made available to those who perform such a crucial role in determining the development of the child. The parent has almost no source of information concerning child learning, although the parent is a most central determinant of what the child learns. The needed information can be channeled through the professional to the parent with special problems. However, specialists themselves have had no source of information for understanding the principles and conditions by which children develop through learning, and of the important behavioral skills the child must acquire in this manner. The author has employed the types of principles and procedures described herein in both dealing with children's problems directly as well as in helping parents to do so with their own children. It is thus suggested that use of these materials can be expected to constitute preventive treatment of central problems of child behavior and child development. Moreover, the materials can be used as behavior modification methods by parents whose children have already developed problems of development.

This manuscript was completed in October of 1968, except for parts of Chapters 1 and 2 and later sections on stuttering and speech pathology— and was read by several individuals in the field of behavior modification. Wayne Holtzman also critically read this manuscript and made helpful suggestions, for which I am very grateful. I also thank Mrs. Carol O'Neill for her contributions in copyediting the manuscript; and to Mrs. Dorothy Powell, Mrs. Roberta Fong, and Miss Judy Miller for typing the manuscript.

Arthur W. Staats

part I
A LEARNING CONCEPTION OF HUMAN BEHAVIOR

chapter 1 / Introduction

The concerns, methods, facts, and technologies of the broad fields of physical, biological, and behavioral science are so vastly complicated that it would seem unlikely that general methodological principles could be abstracted that would be meaningful for everyday problems. Common to scientific endeavor in general, however, is a basic method that can be stated simply. The common basis is a reliance on observation. One begins obtaining knowledge about an event (or a realm of events) by observing it. When this has been done in detail, *then* one can look for determinants of the event, the causes of the event.

Having found an independently observed condition, which when it has occurred will be followed by the event we are interested in, we can predict the event of interest from knowledge of the prior condition. Such prediction is one of the powerful products of scientific observations and statements. In addition, if we can manipulate the causal condition, we can bring about or prevent the event in which we are interested. It is this possibility of affecting the events in which we are interested that is a unique product of scientific knowledge; this control of nature is another of the powers of science. Because of the enormous power of prediction and control, such knowledge has great potentially practical value for solving the problems of everyday life.

It is hard to think of characterizing present-day science in terms of such simple rules. Historically, however, whether or not to follow observational methods—versus methods springing from authoritative dogmas, for example—involved in many cases very sharp and significant contests. Actually, in almost any area of human concern there is always a body of folklore, dogma, mythology, and so on that is not based upon systematic observation. People ordinarily believe that they have in this body an account of the causes or explanations for the actual events. These accounts, which contain much that is false, mixed in sometimes with some observational statements, are usually held with great emotion and tenacity. Thus, a scientific approach may have to do intellectual battle before it is free to unrestrictedly pursue with objectivity its task of observational discovery.

A common path of a developing science has been for the science to retreat to the laboratory in the process of finding its basic principles. This is necessary in order to reduce the events dealt with so their relationships may be seen in the stark simplicity of laboratory experimentation—simplicity not ordinarily obtainable in the uncontrolled complexity of everyday occurrences. Perhaps the "retreat" to the laboratory, and the attendant artificiality of the events dealt with in experimentation, serve another purpose, however. That is, perhaps the scientist is more free to pursue the study of events seemingly removed from the passionate concerns of the world; more free than he would be if he attempted to objectively study matters that touched central matters of concern and investment.

To continue, most scientists are interested in the laboratory events they study and the laws of their relationships, and this study takes place in the laboratory. However, there are always a few who come to see the laws found in the laboratory to be of general significance in the realm of nature treated. These individuals are not only interested in the specific scientific law in its laboratory demonstration, but also in the possibility that the more complex events of the world "move" according to the same laws. These men are responsible for demonstrating the generality of the scientific laws in solving problems of the world. In the doing, however, an even fewer number of scientists may see that these laws and their demonstration in the laboratory and in worldly events actually constitute a conception. The conceptions of such men are likely to challenge the entrenched dogma and opinion that ordinarily dominate common-sense, generally accepted views.

By the time this realization of such a confrontation is made, however, the systematic observations and laws of the science, and the success of these laws in dealing with worldly events, may constitute such a powerful conception that it cannot be displaced by the common-sense view. Then the scientific conception begins to penetrate our common language, and it ultimately comes to be widely held on a common-sense level.

This is, of course, an oversimplified description—which has many variations in actuality. It will serve, however, as a means of considering briefly the area of scientific endeavor that is of concern to the present effort. That is, although the progression described is by no means complete, it is suggested that psychology as a science is slated for a similar process. Psychology, as the study of the behavior of organisms, especially man, began with naturalistic observations and with natural philosophy—as is the usual case. In its development psychology went to the basic laboratory in the attempt to isolate elementary principles. Moreover, the psychology of learning—which can justifiably be considered a science itself—made great strides in this endeavor. Men like Pavlov and Thorndike began the systematic observation and statement of the two main types of learning laws or principles. These principles have been available since the very early 1900s, and later researchers and theorists considerably advanced the findings. Some of this work was done by men whose interest was concentrated in the specific principles of learning. Other individuals were interested in a more formal statement of the learning principles to establish a more complete basic theory of learning. A few psychologists in the field of learning have seen the possibility that the psychology of learning could be used as a set of principles with which to consider aspects of functional human behavior. In recent years this number has increased greatly.

While this characteristic has not been evident to all in the field of psychology—even those who are interested in applying learning principles to aspects of human behavior—the methods and principles of the science can be integrated to provide a unified approach to man. In the author's opinion, moreover, it should be the goal of psychology to do just that: to extend its principles and methods to human concerns toward the goal of constructing a general conception of man that is basic to the social and behavioral sciences, to the professions that deal with man and his problems, and to man in general. Much of the author's work has been directed toward this goal.

It is to be expected that since the basic principles of such a conception are empirical principles, the conception will yield explicit statements concerning what should be done to deal with some of the problems of man. The types of prediction and control that have been mentioned should be the products of the general conception. It is suggested that the effort to develop the principles of learning as a conception of human behavior is important not only as a potential contributor to human welfare, but that the process is an essential feature in verifying the basic principles and demonstrating their generality.

These points of philosophy are being stressed in this introduction because in various areas of science there has been a denigration of work that deals with actual problems of the world. The word used to describe such work is "applied," in contrast to "basic" or "pure," and for some scientists the word is one of opprobrium. Some of this denigration is misdirected. While it is true that the most basic principles of a science are its most general statements—since they may apply to a multitude of specific events—the extension of such a basic principle to problems of the world is an aspect of the basic theory construction. That is, demonstration of the basic principle in the complex conditions of the world helps verify the principles. In addition, the generality of the principle is shown, and thus its significance is enhanced.

This statement indicates the strong "functional" philosophy of the present approach. This book will be concerned not only with general principles but also with knowledge that should have functional value in dealing with various types of behavior. Several other general aspects of the approach to be elaborated may be briefly introduced.

PERSONALITY IN A BEHAVIORAL INTERACTION APPROACH

Psychology as a science has made a great deal of progress in a number of directions. It has developed an advanced research methodology. It has sophistication in the logic of scientific method. It has a number of well verified cause-and-effect principles, especially in the area of learning. And it has explored various aspects of behavior. On the other hand, psychology has remained separatistic. It has developed competitive conceptions that prevent utilization of its findings and developments. There are deep and dividing issues that must be resolved in bringing the parts together to form a productive whole.

One of the major, unresolved schisms in psychology has separated learning theory (behavior modification or behavioristic) approaches from the personality oriented (psychodynamic, cognitive, developmental, or biological) approaches. Until this time the major modern conceptions of human behavior have been those of the latter type that consider the primary determinants of human behavior to reside within the individual. Psychoanalytic theory, for example, has inferred inner needs and personality processes and structures to account for human behavior. Developmental psychology, as another example, has traditionally considered the causes of child behavior development to come from biological growth. Other theorists have inferred inner processes such as the self, self-concept, perceptual field, cognitive states, personality traits, and so on to account for human behavior.

In contrast, a primary characteristic of behavioristic approaches has been to look for the determinants of human behavior in the directly observable principles of learning and in presently acting environmental conditions. This has meant an overt or implied rejection of the various concepts of inner determination of the personality theorists. This has also meant, in contemporary behavior modification, a general restriction to treatment of relatively simple or straightforward problems of behavior, with little analysis of general human behavior and its causes.[1] A weakness of behaviorism that has not been emphasized is that it has largely remained a suggested strategy rather than a fulfilled theory.

The present resolution of the behaviorist versus personality theory schism involves various points. One is that the elementary principles of learning do not themselves constitute a theory of human behavior or provide knowledge of the determining conditions for human behavior—knowledge that is necessary to deal with the various concerns of human behavior. It is suggested that

[1]The author's early work and concepts have constituted one of the foundations of what is now called behavior modification; that is, the use of reinforcement principles in treating specific problems of behavior. Although it was necessary to first deal with simple behaviors, progress necessitates extension to more complex human repertoires in greater depth and comprehensiveness than is characteristic of most present day behavioral efforts (see Staats, 1970, in press a).

while learning principles must be basic in the theoretical structure—not a secondary consideration as in some earlier treatments of personality—the principles require other elements to constitute a general theory of human behavior. The theorist must work in conjunction with broader conceptions of man; naturalistic (and clinical) concepts and observations must be incorporated along with extensive learning theory directed observations of human behavior.

In developing this conception, it is thus suggested that in addition to the higher-order (more elementary) basic principles of learning there must be a personality level of the theory. Rather than rejecting the concepts of personality—intelligence, self-concept, super-ego, traits (such as creativity or sociability), needs (such as achievement or imitation), purposes, goals, and so on—the present approach recognizes the explanatory importance of the behaviors referred to.

The rapprochement between traditional learning theory and traditional personality theory is possible when it is realized there are individual personalities. These "personalities" determine the individual's present and future behaviors. *But the personality characteristics, although general and enduring, are themselves learned.* It is suggested that man learns complex repertoires of interrelated types of behavior. These are learned in a hierarchical, cumulative way with the acquisition of one repertoire leading into, and sometimes becoming part of, a more complex repertoire. And repertoires learned through separate principles are fused into functional combinations. It is this possibility for long term, cumulative, hierarchical acquisition of personality repertoires that allows for the very great complexity and infinite variability that we see in individual and group human behavior. Because these personality characteristics are relatively enduring, and consistent in development, they help give the erroneous impression of internal psychodynamic causation.

It will be suggested that these personality constellations of behavior also give rise to other inferrences that have been the subject of issue. Behaviorists have insisted that human actions are determined by the observable environment, not by inferred processes that are not directly observed. Behaviorists have frequently stressed that this is the only view that coincides with scientific views of cause and effect determininsm. This has included a denial of free will, self-determination of one's behavior, or any type of spontaneity. These characteristics have led critics to reject behaviorism for representing human nature as passive.

In contrast, the present approach asserts man's self-direction, his "free will," creativity, freedom, and spontaneity—in a manner still in accord with scientific determinism and behaviorism. As the following chapters will develop, both views are correct. Man learns his personality behavior complexes in a deterministic manner, but these complexes in turn determine how he decides, plans, reasons, creates, and directs his own behavior—all giving the experience of freedom. These repertoires also determine how he will respond differently from someone else in the same situation. Intelligence, as one aspect of personality, will be treated in detail herein, as will the individual's cognitive, language, or symbolic processes. In addition, other aspects of personality such as imitation, the self-concept, the motivational system, and so on, will be considered. The focus will be on how the child acquires these aspects of personality, as well as on the manner in which these aspects of personality function in his further behavior, learning, and general adjustment.

OTHER PRINCIPLES
OF INTERACTION

In addition to the personality theory level of the approach, human behavior principles must also be added to the elementary learning laws. These human behavior principles are in concert with the basic principles and may be reduced to, or be capable of derivation from, those principles. But these human behavior principles arise from systematic observations of human behavior, not from the basic laboratory. A number of such principles will be introduced later. In fact, as may already be evident, the focus in the present book will be upon the personality level of description and the human behavior principles, rather than on the statement of basic learning theory.

One type of interaction principle has already been implied. There is an interaction between behaviors the individual has learned and what he will do in future situations, because the former have a cause and effect link with the latter. As one of a number of examples, Chapter 13 describes the manner in which the individual's thinking consists of learned behaviors. But his thinking will also determine what he does in many different situations and will characterize his later behavior. The same is true in many human actions. Complex cognitive, emotional, and social repertoires of learned responses (overt and covert) will directly elicit other acts of the individual himself. It is important to understand the principles and conditions for learning such repertoires as well as the manner in which they interact causally with the individual's general behavior.

Another type of behavior-behavior interaction occurs where repertoires the individual has learned do not directly elicit other behaviors. Rather, they determine the manner in which the individual will respond to an environmental situation. One example the author has referred to previously (Staats and Butterfield, 1965) is that of a culturally deprived child who has learned a motivational system that is inappropriate for the rewards available in school. He thus does not work and learn in this situation and develops behavioral deficits. A number of examples will be given herein of children who are able to learn new skills in a situation only if they have previously learned a basic behavioral repertoire requisite to the new learning. Their already acquired behaviors (personality) will ordinarily determine their future behaviors in a continuing succession of experiences and what is thus learned in the continuing personality development. As in the above example, one aspect of personality may affect the formation of a different aspect—the child's motivational system helped determine how his intellectual development would proceed. The example below will indicate that the reverse may also occur.

A third type of interaction occurs between the individual and the stimulus circumstances that his personality repertoires create for him. To continue the previously employed example, the culturally deprived child may not learn in school because of the mismatch of his motivational system with that of the school's. The deficits in cognitive skill he "acquires," however, will create social circumstances where further unfortunate personality development will occur. That is, his social failure will further adversely affect his motivational system—he will thereby learn negative attitudes towards school-related stimuli. Thus, in a spiraling process, his motivational system results in deficits that further affect his motivational system which produces further learning and so on in a downward cyclical interaction. In general, a child who displays desirable repertoires of behavior will create social environments that will further determine his behavior in a manner different from the child who displays undesirable behaviors. Much of this interaction between behavior and the social environment takes place between parent and child and affects both.

This introduction illustrates possibilities for a rapprochement between traditional personality approaches and a behavioristic approach. To achieve this goal, principles, concepts, and observations other than laboratory learning principles are necessary. The chapters to follow will elaborate these suggestions, beginning with a more detailed consideration of the general concept of intelligence.

chapter 2 / Intelligence: Personal Quality or Learned Skills?

This chapter is a general framework for later discussions. Some of the aspects of prevalent conceptions of intelligence and human abilities will be reviewed in general terms. Most of us, in fact almost all of us who have not had special training to the contrary, traditionally consider human behavior in terms of inner processes and forces that supposedly determine the overt actions displayed by an individual. For example, when we observe that a child has told an imaginative story—that is, has displayed imaginative verbal behavior—we assume that he can do this because he has lots of "imagination." We assume some inner process to be the "cause" of the overt behavior.

When we see that a child spends a great deal of time playing an instrument, we say that he does so *because* he has a great deal of interest, implying again an inner condition that accounts for the behavior. When a child will not do something no matter what the pressure, we say that this is because he has a "strong will," and thereby believe that we have explained his behavior. When we see that the child handles social situations very readily and seeks such relationships, we say that it is because he has a strong "sociability" trait, which is also considered to be some internal personality process.

A child who learns very well, who displays verbal facility, who solves problems well, and so on, is said to be able to do this because he is very intelligent. As in the other cases, it is commonly accepted that the observable behavioral skill of the child is a function of some internal personal quality—the intelligence of the child.

Let me say at the beginning that these common usages are all meaningless "explanations" of behavior, although they are part of general language usage and the logic is ingrained in our thinking. They supposedly account for the behavior in terms of certain processes, purportedly within the individual. But these processes have no status. They are never observed, in everyday life or with the special equipment of science. And what is not observed cannot in this case be considered a cause. Thus, concepts such as "will," "intelligence," "talents," "traits," and so on are merely terms in our language —a hangover from the past when less was known about human behavior than now. To explain behavior we must be able to state the conditions that lead to the behavior, the conditions under which it will occur or will not occur.

There are various forms of the conception that the individual's behavior is determined by internal, personal, usually organic conditions—which are always left unspecified. It will serve well in introducing the present conception to indicate some of the lines of this thought in the context of intelligence and human abilities.

THE COMMON CONCEPTION OF INTELLIGENCE

Our concepts of human behavior help determine the way we behave toward people in many different situations. Our conceptions actually constitute a social theory from which we derive our social actions toward social problems, our rules of everyday social intercourse, as well as our scientific actions in the study of human behavior.

The concept of intelligence has been a central one, both in the common language of lay people and the more technical language of professionals and scientists in the behavioral and social sciences, education, and the health fields. As such, the concept of intelligence has been a basic one from which social actions have been derived, and the conception has also heavily influenced a great deal of scientific investigation. As frequently happens in the development of knowledge, a conception that represents a step forward at one time later on holds back more advanced conceptions that would yield more positive contributions to knowledge and to human adjustment. It is suggested that intelligence has been such a conception— and it is thus worthwhile to examine briefly its nature and some of its effects, in the task of introducing a more advanced notion. Such an examination is important not only to the study of child learning but also to the understanding of overall human behavior.

Speaking generally, it may be said that the fundamental aspect of the common conception of intelligence is that it is a personality process of organic origin. However, in our common language the organic events are left unspecified. It is simply assumed that people have inherited in some measure an internal, personal, mental quality that enables them to do many things better or less well than others—depending upon the nature of their inheritance.

The term "intelligence" is not used merely to *label* the differences we see in the behavioral skills of various individuals. The term is used as a supposed *explanation* of why there are variations. The school child "explains" his relatively poor performance in school in comparison to a friend by saying it is because his friend is more intelligent. The parent accepts this explanation. The concept is part of the common language. As another example, the teacher feels that the varying performances of her pupils are due to their inherited intelligence—some pupils are fortunate and some not. Education in general accepts the concept, and the major effort is to discover the child's personal quality of intelligence. Once discovered, through testing, the children may be grouped and given training appropriate to their supposed respective intelligences. The child considered to be low in this internal, personal, inherited, and many times immutable intelligence is grouped with other low-level children. He thus associates with other relatively unskilled children and receives training in relatively less complex intellectual skills.

Moreover, in this general area there are closely allied concepts, also thought to be explanatory. Thus, exceptionally skilled behavior in some intellectual or artistic area—mathematics, art, music, writing, dancing, and the like—is explained by reference to a special talent. Talent is also commonly thought to be a personal quality of organic origin which, again, individuals have more or less of.

Similarly, the concepts of readiness and maturation are closely linked to that of intelligence, to use two additional examples. That is, it is felt that this internal, personal, quality of intelligence is organic in nature. Since children advance considerably in their behavioral skills with age, it is assumed that this advancement must be due to the growth of this organic entity or process. Differences in behavioral skill of young children are thus apt to be looked upon as differences in the rate of development of the organic entity. This variation in the rate of organic development is also thought to account for the variations in success that children have when presented with learning tasks. Thus, behavioral development is thought to be due to biological maturation, which it should be noted is always inferred, never observed. And the level of maturation is thought to determine the child's "readiness" for intellectual learning.

Basically, these views are held also by professionals and scientists in the behavioral and social sciences as well as in the health sciences. Moreover, these views play a role in many areas of investigation. Thus, for example, assuming there to be an internal, organically determined intelligence, many individuals have devoted their careers to the construction of tests with which they intended to measure this internal quality of the person. They were not interested in the human behaviorial skills *per se*, but only in the extent to which the skills would provide an index of the internal intelligence. This is not a criticism of the practical function of tests in comparing the relative skills of people. But the practical value of intelligence tests, it should be stated, does not corroborate the conception of intelligence held by the professionals in this field.

Other investigators of a similar orientation spent their scientific careers attempting to "prove" an organic conception of intelligence, *by showing that behavioral skills are not learned.* Some did this by attempting to demonstrate that a particular behavioral skill came about in the individual just through the passage of time—thus presumably due to biological development. That is, the central rationale of such studies was to rule out the possibility of learning. The assumption was that if learning was ruled out as a cause of the behavior development, it proved that organic maturation was the determinant of behavior development. As an example, Carmichael (1928) anesthetized pollywogs to prevent the occurrence of learning, and concluded they later swam just as effectively as pollywogs with normal experience. The same rationale underlay attempts to show that development of some simple behavioral skill took place as readily in a supposedly untrained twin as in a trained twin.

In theoretical endeavors as well as in experimentation, internal, organically based, alleged explanations have played a large role in conceptions concerning many aspects of human behavior. Currently, the major controversy in the study of language has been raised by the proposal, following the lead of Noam Chomsky, that language—a central behavior skill to the human—is given primarily by the individual's innate qualities. Language development is again thought to be determined by the child's organic-mental development. In this view, deficits and defects in language must be attributed to the personal defects of the individual. When it is understood that language development and intelligence development are largely overlapping behavioral skills, this proposed theory of language can be seen as another organic-mental conception of intelligence.

In summary, then, the organic-mental view commonly held is that the individual inherits some quality of personality process or structure (left unspecified) which determines the quality of his intellectual (and other) behavior. Names such as *intelligence, aptitude, talent, capacity, ability,* and the like refer to qualities of behavior, supposedly largely given in their pure state by the individual's biologically determined "mental" inheritance. Moreover, aligned with this conception is the corollary that the organic structures or processes that give the individual his qualities of behavior grow or mature during the child's growth. Thus, advances in the child's behavioral skill with age are taken as indications of maturation of the causal organic structures or processes. The human is thus thought to be in part a "preformed" organism who will display behavioral characteristics as the biological mechanism—whatever it is—advances toward maturity. As the "preformed" mechanism is completed by growth, the child will come to display his organically determined behavior. Concepts such as readiness, as well as stages and sequences of child development, include this principle, at least implicitly.

It should also be indicated that this common organic-mental conception of intelligence (and related terms) assumes that the internal quality has some unitary status. Intelligence is in this view considered, at least in part, to be a general quality that determines how well the individual will behave in many different specific situations. A frequent definition has been that intelligence is the individual's general ability to learn. Some psychologists, such as E. L. Thorndike, have suggested that there are several different kinds of intelligence, each of which is a unitary process that determines the quality of behavior in a particular area. It has also been suggested that there is a general, unitary intelligence, and many factors specific to different areas—a view that has been associated with Charles E. Spearman.

THE CONCEPTION OF INTELLIGENCE
AND SOCIAL DECISIONS

There is a long history of the development of theories of the determinants of human behavioral skill. In this history the organic-mental concept of intelligence once represented a step forward in terms of scientific explanation. That is, previous to the development of concepts that were consistent with science, it was thought, for example, that the person's behavioral skill depended upon divine inspiration of some type. Explanation of human behavior was sought in the inference of supernatural forces. Such conceptions also included a corollary of personal worth: The gifted person was the righteous person, the one favored by the divine force. In this view, then, the quality of the individual's behavior could be attributed to his internal, personal quality—as determined by divine force.

However, the accumulation of various sources of evidence over a long period of time brought the explanation of human behavior out of the supernatural and into the realm of natural events (still accepting, without direct evidence, internal quality as the cause of behavior skill). The conception involved was a huge step forward in terms of bringing the powerful weapons of scientific observations to bear upon the study. Whereas a theological conception tells us not to attempt to study the events through observation, a scientific concepion (even of an organic-mental nature) assumes natural causes and suggests that search for those causes will be productive.

As one example, the establishment of the concept of biological evolution by Darwin and others played a very important role in moving away from theological explanation within the biological and behavioral sciences. Evolution suggested that there are genetic variations in organisms that have adjustmental (and thus survival) value for the organisms. It was observed, for example, that species which at one time had biologically given characteristics that enabled them to adjust specifically to a particular environment died out when the environment changed and their special biological characteristics were no longer as adjustive as those of some other organism.

Moreover, the observations of Darwin and others demonstrated that in the course of history species have developed more and more complex biological structures. Individuals became interested in comparing the differences in biological structural complexity. Thus, one of the effects of the evolutionary conception was to stimulate interest in comparing species—

both in biological structure and in behavioral function. Comparative study of these aspects of the various species reveals readily that as the physical structure of the organism increases in complexity so does the complexity of the behavior of the organism. When the organism has a simple nervous system it is capable of simple, relatively invariable behaviors. Anatomical study of the nervous system indicates, for example, the relationship that the cortex of the brain increases in size systematically with the biological and behavioral advancement of the species. In man the fullest development of the brain is seen, as well as the most complex behavioral development.

It is an easy but significant extrapolation to conclude that the differences we see in the behavioral complexity within the human species have the same cause. That is, anatomical development produces behavioral development between species. It has thus been assumed, arguing in a backward direction, that the individual behavioral differences we see in man are also a result of anatomical differences in the brain. While it would be unjustified to make this jump as a *conclusion,* it is not an unreasonable hypothesis to test empirically. Actually, as an early example, the inference was once of central scientific interest, in the field of phrenology. The assumption was that different parts of the brain being more or less developed produced more or less developed behaviors in the individual. It was also assumed that the head contours followed the brain's strengths and weaknesses. The latter we now know is not the case, and it is rejected. Direct evidence relevant to the first assumption is not substantial enough to take it out of the hypothesis stage.

The important point in the present brief historical mention is to indicate how the conceptions that are held help determine what is done—in a wide variety of situations where the concept of intelligence is a relevant concern. In the realm of social events it will serve to illustrate the point by several examples of how social behaviors and decisions depend upon the prevailing conception of intelligence.

The Organic-Mental Conception in Medical and Psychological Diagnosis

One example occurs frequently in the context of medical and psychological diagnosis of children with behavior problems. Thus, it is common to have a physician diagnose a child as minimally brain damaged if the child does poorly in school and has very low academic achievement test scores, but does not evidence the more general behavioral deficits that lead to the label of mental retardation. The minimal brain damage or cerebral dysfunction diagnosis is more likely to occur if the child has several other additional behavioral characteristics, such as hyperactivity, temper tantrums, and so on. Sometimes the child may be given neurological tests (such as brain-wave recordings), which in some cases indicate some deviation from the usual— and these will also be used as evidence of cerebral dysfunction even though many children who behave normally will also evidence the same type of recordings. The main point here, however, is that the diagnosis of the child may be made entirely on the basis of the child's behavior—with no evidence of .unusual brain structure or function that has been causally related to the behavior in question.

Such a diagnosis is likely to lead to very different attempts to solve the problem than would an analysis that concluded that the problem was the child's past history of experience and his present environmental conditions. That is, detailed accounts of the child's behavior might reveal that the child has never paid attention in school, in the way that successful children do. It might be the case that since his very earliest schooling when the teacher began formal presentations of academic material, the child in question would not look at the stimuli presented, would not make the responses involved— at least in most cases—and would occupy himself with other matters. It might also be the case that the child would have had experience where his hyperactive behavior would disrupt such learning sessions and thus remove what for him was a boring, distasteful activity. Later on, as the case progressed, it might also have been seen that the child began to suffer various forms of social punishment for his backwardness. That is, when called upon in class the child would respond in ways that would make the other children laugh. Or other children would reflect disparagingly upon his performance in class, or upon his deficits in knowledge. At home, also, he would not meet with the same conditions of reward as would a more successful child—and likely he would meet aversive conditions of various kinds. The child might also have found that he could escape such aversiveness by behaving in an unusual or bizarre manner when in such aversive situations. Under these circumstances it would be expected that the child would acquire negative attitudes toward the individuals involved— especially toward the school situation and the school personnel—as well as some unusual ways of behaving. This type of learning could form the basis for the child acquiring a number of additional behaviors that would impede his learning as well as result in the appearance of undesirable behaviors usually termed "emotionally disturbed."

In this example, to continue, the organically oriented conception, and the organically oriented examination, would lead to organically oriented treatment. It is quite common, for example, to attempt to treat children with the problems described above with drugs to decrease the hyperactive behavior and other unusual behaviors. The analysis of the child's problems in terms of his learning history, on the other hand, would not suggest organic abnormality and the need for medical treatment. This analysis would indicate the need for reversing the child's aversive experiences at school, for ensuring his attention and participation in school learning, and for special training procedures to make up some of the learning deficits that have already occurred in the child's history. (For some examples of treatment procedures for such cases, see Staats and Butterfield, 1965; Staats, Minke, and Butts, in press; Ryback and Staats, in press.)

The Organic-Mental Conception
in Educational Placement

In the school the appraisal of the children will also involve the conception held of human behavior. The most dominant conception in our schools is also organically oriented. Thus, when a child is not doing well in his school work and when his achievement and IQ tests are low, the child will be considered mentally retarded, to have a low organically determined intelligence. It will be concluded that the biological deficit is the seat of the problem. This conclusion may occur even though the child clearly does not pay attention in class and participate in school work, does not study at home, and is not involved in academically related activities such as reading for pleasure. Under such circumstances, from a learning orientation, it might be expected that a child who has below-average learning circumstances in and out of school would score below average on intellective tests. The organically oriented conception, it should be noted, includes homogeneous grouping of children on the basis of personal "quality"—which is established on the basis of tests. In practice this means the child who is backward in learning is placed in a group of similar children, and thus receives training that is less rich than children who have already learned more. While this may make practical sense in terms of handling the backward child, in learning terms it also helps produce a cumulative decrement (retardation) in the child who was backward to begin with. It must also be remembered that much of the child's learning comes from his peers. Thus, the child who is backward behaviorally, who needs a superior learning situation, is instead associated with other backward children who provide him with an inferior learning context, and he again receives a less rich learning experience.

An actual example of the manner in which the conception that is held determines social decisions was provided in a community with which the author is familiar. The issue was whether or not to provide public schooling for four-year-olds, as many parents requested. A number of people, including professionals, suggested that most preschool children are not ready (organically) for formal learning. According to this organic-mental conception, if school was provided it should only be for those children who have demonstrated enough maturation or readiness. This advice was followed. Thus, the children who already were advanced over most other children, and who needed special training the least, were given extra preschool training that would further enhance their advancement.

In this example the organic-mental conception led to a social decision affecting human behavior which was quite opposite to that which would derive from a learning conception. That is, what is called readiness for learning could be seen not as a result of organic maturation, but of the behavioral skills the child has developed through learning. The important conclusion from a learning conception would be that the child who is backward in the development of these behavioral skills, rather than being excluded from learning opportunities, should be given extra learning opportunities in quantity and quality. This conception would suggest that it is the backward child who should be given special opportunities for going to school when he is four years of age. Furthermore, when the individual child fails to develop a particular skill when most other children do, rather than simply waiting for some supposed organic development to occur, it would be considered necessary to discover the training deficit that was responsible for the behavioral deficit, and to provide remedial training.

The Organic-Mental Conception and Racist Views of Ability

As another example of the effect of one's conception on social decisions, the organic-mental view of intellectual development has been a prominent aspect of racist conceptions in the United States. This conception interprets the poorer intellective test results of Afro-Americans in comparison to whites as being due to biological limitations. A good example of this conception was given several years ago on a television interview of one of the powerful parish leaders in Louisiana. This leader made a statement to the effect that the intellectual maturation of Negroes ceases by the age of twelve. Negroes were thus considered to remain mentally immature and not capable of advancing to the level of the white man. It would be expected that social decisions based upon such a conception, among other things, would provide a school program that would help ensure that intellectual advancement in Negro children would be limited.

The organic-mental conception of racial differences in intelligence as a way to "explain" differences in performance is not limited to the southern states, however (see Jensen, 1969). That is, it is quite well known that black children as a group do not do as well in school as white children. As a group, the intellectual achievements of black children are not as great in our society as those of white children. As a group black people do not attain the same levels of success as whites. As a group, moreover, black people do not do as well as whites on intelligence tests.

If we can infer organic-mental differences from differences in the excellence of performance for *individuals*, it is as reasonable to make the same inference for *groups*. This inference is commonly made explicitly or implicitly, and it is one of the most socially detrimental aspects of the organic-mental concept of intelligence. It may also be suggested that since this concept is common to our culture, it must be expected that the Negro group in the United States would hold the same basic view. This means, of course, that black people who hold the conception for individual behavior will hold it also for group behavior. Accepting the conception is derogatory in the extreme, for it suggests that if the group's performance is poor it follows that the group is inferior. The error here, as will be elaborated later, is in accepting differences in behavior, in performance, as indicating biological differences when there is insufficient evidence of any organic difference.

Black leaders in the United States are presently attempting to raise the self-appraisal and self-confidence of the black people. It is suggested that one of the obstacles within the Negro group to the achievement of a positive group identity is the concept that human behavior is organically determined—especially in the realm of intelligence. Such a conception leaves little hope for improvement and leads to a strategy of denial of performance deficits rather than positive action. On the other hand, to add here another brief precursor of the conception to be later introduced, if we consider that intelligence is learned, then inferior behavior of a group is simply a sign of the inferior environmental conditions to which the group has been subjected.

The Organic-Mental Conception and Child-Rearing Problems

Another of the effects of the organic-mental conception of human behavior occurs with parents in raising their children—and with practitioners who advise parents. It is true that parents can have such a conception of human behavior and yet be very good parents. Some parents because of their own fortunate histories of learning and fortunate life circumstances provide excellent (though perhaps not maximal) learning conditions for their children—irrespective of the conception of human behavior that they hold. In other cases, however, the parents have not been so fortunate and thus are not naturally good trainers of children, or their life conditions may be such that the training circumstances for their children have been disrupted. In such cases, when the child does not develop behaviors as he should, the organic-mental conception of behavior which the parent already holds, or receives from the practitioner he consults, may be an egregious handicap.

It may elucidate the possibilities here to give an example or two. The author is acquainted with a case of two parents who both worked, but at different times of the day. They did this so that one of them would always be home with their young child. However, they each slept during the waking hours of the child, who was left alone in a safe but asocial situation almost all the time. The first two years of the child's life were spent in this manner—and then he had additional training deprivations in the next two years through another set of circumstances. Needless to say, at the age of four this child exhibited glaring deficits in his behavioral skills. Among other things he did not score a point on an individually administered intelligence test. At this time he was considered, because of his behavioral deficits, to be brain-damaged. In the case under discussion the parents were not unconcerned about their child. They were as loving and conscientious as usual. However, they had a strong conception that a child grows through personal maturation. They believed that proper food, clothing, cleanliness, and so on provided an environment for that maturation. Of course, the conception was inadequate, and the child's learning experience was inadequate. It is interesting to note that although they consulted professionals regarding their child's behavioral retardation, they never received information concerning their specific actions in producing the child's behavioral development.

As another example, it is not unusual for the parent to take his child to a pediatrician because the child has not learned to talk when other children have already done so, because the child is not toilet trained, and so on. Frequently, the parents' own misconceptions will be bolstered by the advice of the practitioner, who will advise them to wait until the child advances into the appropriate stage of development. Practitioners who know only an organic-mental developmental conception will be more concerned that the parents do not attempt to push the child when he is not "physiologically" ready than they will with the actual behavioral deficit. The parent will be told to provide a warm, loving atmosphere, and to wait for the child to mature. It is concluded that maturation itself will bring about the necessary behavioral development. As will be suggested, however, maturation itself does not yield such development. If the parent actually does nothing but provide a generally loving atmosphere, his child will continue to display his behavior deficits. Child problems require more than waiting, or general warmth.

Thus, as an example, when the parent is interested in producing good toilet behaviors in the child he must know the training conditions by which to produce the behavior. The same is true when the child fails to develop language, will not respond to instructions, or has deficits in other skills. The parent then needs a conception of child development that tells him how to produce desirable behaviors in his child. On the other hand, when his child displays overly aggressive or selfish behavior, or cries too frequently, or has temper tantrums, displays bizarre behaviors, or spits or bites or whatever, the parent has to have a conception of child behavior that tells him how to decrease benignly the incidence of undesirable behavior. A passive approach frequently leads to a child who later has deep and persistent deficits in behavior, or undesirable inappropriateness of behavior that persist as the child grows older.

The Organic-Mental Conception and Science Styles

Finally, it may be indicated that the conception that one holds of human behavior and behavior development also effects science styles concerned with the study of this subject. The predominant conception held will contribute to determination of what is studied, what type of study has status, what research is supported, what type of work is honored, and so on. Thus, for example, it is definitely the case that biological science activities have much greater status and support in contemporary culture than do environmental (learning) science activities.

The generally held organically oriented conception of intelligence, for example, has influenced the type of research conducted and the type of research supported. Moreover, the conception that there is an internal, unitary, organic–mental quality or process or structure has had other effects. This conception has led to (1) a primary concern with measurement of the supposed internal process, and (2) many studies relating scores on intelligence tests to familial relationships. The conception has led away from the study of the specific skills involved in the child responding to the items on the intelligence test (or, in general, the study of the skills of which intelligence is composed). That is, the items have not been of concern themselves, since they were only considered to reflect the important process—the internal mental quality of intelligence. Thus, there are no studies of how to train a child so that he can successfully respond to specific items on an intelligence test. In fact, when one accepts the assumption that there is an internal mental quality of intelligence that is the important thing, the idea of studying how the child learns the skills involved in the test items becomes ridiculous.

This orientation is only the blindness of viewpoint, however. From another viewpoint, a conception would be considered erroneous that leads one away from an interest in the specific behaviors involved in one child being considered intelligent in comparison to another. As will be indicated further on, it is central to ask these questions: What are the behaviors composing intelligence? How are those behaviors learned? How do those "intelligence" behaviors contribute to the child's adjustment, to his ability to solve problems, and above all to his ability to learn new skills, intellectual and otherwise? It is time that scientific interest be directed toward this type of knowledge, and a conception that supports this interest is also to be valued for this reason.

NATURE AND NURTURE CONCEPTIONS

Thus, even in these few examples, it is clear that the conception one holds concerning intelligence will help determine important personal and social actions. The topic may be seen to be one of some moment. It is no doubt for this reason that concern with a conception of intelligence has attracted attention since antiquity. Aristotle has been said to have begun the empiricist or nurture (environmental) approach to the development of the "mind." According to one of his statements, the mind is in the beginning a *tabula rasa*, an empty tablet. The tablet of the mind is then written upon by the experience of the individual. What the individual becomes is thus a function of his experience.

The competition between the organic (nature) and experiential (nurture) conceptions of intelligence have occurred in one form or another as long as men were concerned with explanations of human behavior. The manner in which Darwin focused attention upon hereditary acquisition of adjustive characteristics has already been noted. In 1869 Darwin's half-cousin Francis Galton published *Hereditary Genius,* a book that recorded in careful biographical study the tendency for extraordinary accomplishment to occur in families. Galton was a confirmed hereditarian, and one of his major concerns was how intelligence could be increased in "racial" groups through intentional control of the people who have children (eugenics). Galton also began the interest in the relative contributions of nature and nurture to intelligence, as well as the use of twins to separate biological and learning effects. Galton was also interested in the measurement of intelligence, considered as an inherited quality. Since his time, of course, a great deal of effort has gone into the design of intelligence tests.

The competition between these conceptions (nature versus nurture) has utilized the testing technology for its studies and thus the conception on which the tests were based. In this pursuit there has been a multitudinous proliferation of studies that have attempted to show that test intelligence was a function of environmental conditions or of biological inheritance. There have been, on the one hand, studies that have correlated IQ with environmental circumstances such as parents' educational, occupational, and social class, and their rural-urban status. On the other side, there have also been studies that have correlated IQ test results with closeness of biological relationship—for example, the extent of correlation of unrelated children, siblings, twins, and identical twins.

NATURE NOTIONS

While it is not possible herein to consider the various studies that have been conducted on this issue, or to provide a detailed interpretation of these results, a few words may be said in the process of introducing the conception that is to be developed in the present book. First, it may be suggested that the studies conducted thus far from the organic-mental orientation do not provide a definitive basis for that conception of intelligence. Perhaps an example or two will help illustrate that studies accepted by one individual as definitively demonstrating the inheritance of intelligence can be interpreted differently from another frame of reference.

A very organically oriented interpretation of intelligence has recently been given by Jensen (1969) in an article that has attracted a great deal of attention because of its important social implications. Jensen sees intelligence as being 80 percent or so inherited. Moreover, he interprets the data to support this conception for racial differences as well as for individual differences. Thus, he accepts the poor performance of Afro-Americans on intelligence tests to be a very suggestive index of biological difference from Caucasians.

A central type of result upon which Jensen bases his conception of inherited intelligence concerns correlations between the IQs of people with varying closeness of relationship, when any environmental differences are supposedly controlled. For example, Jensen finds, "The conceptually simplest estimate of heritability is, of course, the correlation between identical twins reared apart, since if their environments are uncorrelated, all they have in common are their "genes" (Jensen, 1969, p. 51). He indicates that there are only three major studies of this type, which in total involved 116 pairs of twins. The correlations between the IQs of such identical twins ranged from .77 to .86, which means that from 60 to 70 percent of the variation in the IQs of the subjects was predictable from their relationship.

Placement Bias
and Familial IQ Correlations

The difficulty with interpretations of this type of data, however, lies in the assumption that their environments were uncorrelated. For one thing, it is common practice in our culture—which so strongly accepts a biological conception of individual differences—to attempt to give a child the same conditions that he would have had with his natural parents. This is done because it is felt that those are the conditions that are suited to the child, on the basis of his biological inheritance. This is a common, if sometimes implicit, aspect of child placement from institutions, which may have far-reaching effects. Because of the biological conception of human behavior that is commonly held, placement officials actually *try* to place a child in a home that coincides with the child's supposed biological inheritance. A case occurred several years back in New York where temporary foster parents were not going to be allowed to permanently adopt a child they had grown to love, with the child reciprocating the affection. The reason was that the parents were considered to be unsuited for the child. She was a blond, blue-eyed child of northern European descent, and the foster parents were dark-haired, brown-eyed, and of southern European descent. According to a biological conception of human behavior it would be important to provide the child with parents of her own "kind."

At any rate, it is suggested that the more similar two children are in physical appearance the more similar will be their placement. They should, if similar environments produce similar IQs, thus become similar through placement bias. It should be noted, moreover, that the children will also be placed in other ways that should produce a correlation between degree of biological relationship and similarity of IQ. That is, placement officials will examine the child's records and attempt to place him in accordance with his parent's religious, educational, and socioeconomic level. When the agency has two or more children from the same family, it can be expected that the officials will attempt to place the related children in similar homes *to the extent of the children's relationship and to the extent of the similarity between the children.* It would be expected that these factors would produce correlations between the IQs of identical twins, and to a progressively lesser extent in nonidentical twins of the same sex, nonidentical twins of opposite sexes, siblings of the same sex, siblings of opposite sexes, and unrelated children. The studies show that the correlation in IQ does vary with the degree of relationship in this order, but it is not possible to take into account the extent to which placement-determined experiential similarities play a part in the correlations.

Inherited Physical Similarities
and IQ Correlations through Learning

It is suggested that these possibilities have not been given adequate weight in such studies. Moreover, there are other experiential factors involved that have not been considered. For one, the experiences that a child has are to some undetermined extent a function of his physical appearance and physical characteristics such as beauty, strength, speed, stamina, and so on. A child who is short and fat and homely will not have the same social environment as a child who is very pleasingly built and very handsome. A boy who is robust and strong and large and who does not wear glasses will have a very different social experience from a child who is thin and small and weak and who does wear glasses. The first type of child will systematically if not invariably experience much more reward for physical performances of various kinds, including physical aggressiveness. Such a child will as a consequence tend to have greater opportunity for social interactions, and for the experience of positive social response in others. Children who are small, thin, weak, and wear glasses will systematically experience less reward for such behaviors. The closing off of these behaviors will tip the scales in the direction of the development of other behaviors, which will result in a differing experience for the children.

(It is interesting to consider in this context the recent debate about the relationship between so-called super males—men with two male chromosomes instead of the usual one—and criminally aggressive behavior. It is noteworthy that double chromosomes males tend to be unusually large. When one realizes the experiential effects this will have, consideration of any differences in aggressive behavior need not concern organic terms. Certainly, the smallest boy in a class will in a statistical sense be less likely to be rewarded for physically aggressive behavior than the largest boy.)

This suggests that there are physical characteristics that statistically will tend to produce behavioral characteristics in people. This is not to say that the action is invariable. A small, weak, thin child, for example, may be raised by a father who because of these characteristics provides the child with an extraordinary training experience that reverses the characteristic development. But, other things equal, physical characteristics are important for the social conditions they produce and for the learning experience they thus provide for the individual. The important point in the present context, however, is that these experiential factors will be correlated with the degree of relationship between two children. Identical twins will be most alike in physical characteristics, siblings less so, and unrelated children less so. The social effects of physical similarity through biological relationship can thus be expected to produce correlations in behavior, including IQ measures. It is interesting to note that in one of the studies of the correlation of twins' IQs, correlations were also computed for the height and weight of the children, which were .94 and .88, respectively. This simply quantifies the close physical similarity of the twins, not only in facial characteristics but in other physical characteristics that, as suggested, would also have similar effects upon the social experiences of the pairs of children.

IQ Similarities from Parental Conceptions of Intelligence

It may be added that the organic-mental conception of human behavior that is generally held can make for similarities in behavior between relatives in other ways. As an example, a case may be described within a family that was very well known to the writer. This involved a mother and son, with the father deceased. The mother was sure that the boy "took after his father," which meant to her that the boy would display the same behavior as the father. Over the years of the boy's childhood there were repeated allusions to the resemblance of the boy's behavior to that of the father. Most importantly, this was done in a manner of great approval for any action of the child that resembled the father. The principles of learning would state definitively that the child should come to display those types of behavior for which he received the rewarding approval from a beloved mother. One particular "characteristic" is of interest in the present context. The boy was continually rewarded for demonstrating interest in mechanical, mathematical types of activities—because that was like his father. This occurred although the boy actually demonstrated a much greater occupation with literature. The fact is the boy was raised in a family in which artistic, social, and unusual scholarly interests were more predominant. Nevertheless, the boy did become an engineer—and the effect of the mother's conception of behavior upon the development of the child was shown, although it was not clear that this was the most appropriate profession for the boy. It may be noted, making the example more general in the present context, that the biological conception of foster parents may also have the same effects on the behaviors of the children they raise—behaviors that result in the child having a behavorial resemblance to the biological parent and away from the foster parent. This process could be exemplified in various ways. For example, a working-class foster parent might go to unusual lengths to push a child academically because his "real" (biological) parents were college-educated.

Thus, as this discussion has suggested, there is a great deal of interpretational variation possible in the type of correlational study described. In this type of study the control of environmental circumstances is very gross. It is many times simply assumed that the environment is randomly distributed over the subjects. Or, when the environment is manipulated for the subjects, it is done on a gross basis of some variable such as educational level of parents, economic status, and so on. Such studies do not make specific observations of either biological variables or of the environmental variables actually involved in the child's learning. As a consequence such studies cannot produce understanding of biological mechanisms that could possibly be involved in behavioral development, or indeed of the learning conditions or learning principles involved.

BIOLOGICAL-BEHAVIORAL
RELATIONSHIPS

More will be said of this later, but here it should be noted, first, that there is no suggestion in the present approach that the brain is not the central mechanism for the acquisition of behavior and for the maintenance of behaviors once acquired. There is much biological evidence that directly indicates that the brain is one mechanism by which learning takes place. Thus, for example, there have been a number of experimental and clinical studies that show that if parts of the brain are removed or impaired, the organism will not be able to learn a type of behavior, or will show general learning loss. It has also been shown that in the organism that has already acquired a particular type of behavior, destruction of a particular part of the brain may result in the loss of that type of behavior. It has also been shown with individuals under-going brain surgery that stimulation of parts of the brain will produce certain types of responses. Depending upon the area of the brain stimulated, motor behaviors, verbal behaviors, sensory responses, and so on may be elicited. Furthermore, the recovery of human behaviors skills that have been lost may be effected by removal of conditions interfering with brain function, such as ablation of brain tumors.

Another aspect of this evidence is that there are certain identifiable biological conditions that rather definitely correlate with behavioral deficiency. Take for example cases of intelligence (behavioral skill) deficiency that are shown by children who are mongoloids, microcephalics, suffer from phenylketonuria (PKU), and so on. We can see clearly that the biological dysfunction (or dysformation) causes the behavioral deficiency. In such cases actual differences in the brain can be detected, if not yet specifically related to behavioral characteristics. In addition, in the case of PKU the mechanism of the difficulty is known—inability to utilize certain proteins—and can be treated by eliminating the proteins from the child's diet. It is important to note how necessary it is to isolate the particular biological mechanism that affects the behavior of the individual. This type of knowledge provides the basis for doing something about the behavior—quite different than correlations of grossly identified conditions.

Similar findings are available concerning drugs (or other toxic conditions resulting from fever, other illnesses, and so on). That is, there are drugs that when ingested will affect the individual's behavior. As an example, alcohol may have effects upon the individual's sensory-motor behavior, ease of social behavior, emotional states, and learning and retention.

Interpreting Findings
of Biological-Behavioral Relationships

Again, however, there are important problems of interpretation involved in treating this type of evidence. It appears clear that the evidence shows that the brain is necessary in the acquisition and maintenance of human behavior. Some individuals, however, also see the evidence as support for the organic-mental conception of intelligence in its fullest aspects; for example, that individual differences in intelligence are generally a function of biological differences in the brain (Jensen, 1969). It must be noted, however, that evidence that the intact brain is necessary for behavior acquisition is not the same thing as an interpretation that the brain is sufficient in itself for behavioral acquisition—that its development largely determines behavioral development. The evidence is also not sufficient for the interpretation that the differences we see in general behavioral skill (intelligence, aptitude, talent, and so on) are to be attributed wholly or partly to brain differences. The latter interpretations require additional evidence, evidence that would isolate brain differences that produce behavioral differences. This type of evidence is not yet available. Jensen (1969) cites only one study that lends itself to this type of interpretation (a study by Money, 1964, in which a genetic sex chromosome deviation is reported to be linked with perceptual difficulties and difficulties in mathematics learning). It is interesting to consider in this context the following statement of a scientist in brain research.

> You study the brain of a genius, and it doesn't show anything
> different from the brain of an idiot. Their tissue is the same, their
> brain waves travel in the same way. No chemical analysis, no electrical
> presence separates those two individuals. In a . . . [biological science]
> laboratory, you'll never discover why one person can write so well
> or paint so well or do mathematics so well, and another cannot (White,
> 1967, pp. 112–113).

To make statements that brain structure or function is responsible for individual differences in complex human behavioral characteristics will require a great deal of evidence that has not been found. It is thus important to indicate what interpretations the presently available evidence does and does not justify.

Interpreting Brain-Behavior Relationships
Among Animal Species

To continue, however, it may again be mentioned that much evidence is available that there is progressive development of the complexity and quantity of nervous tissues as one moves up the animal evolutionary scale— and brain development is associated with development in behavioral complexity and learning ability. Moreover, some animals that have developed certain special skills, like sensory skills, may show a corresponding development of the brain (Diamond and Hall, 1969). And there are studies that show with lower organisms that certain behaviors are given in the biological makeup of the animal. Migratory behaviors and other behaviors in birds, sex behaviors in some lower organisms, and so on may be seen as the result of biological variables, with learning well ruled out. Such studies, however, cannot be extrapolated in kind to the human level. These, and the preceding types of evidence, do provide a solid foundation of interest for investigating possibilities at the human level. However, the fact that species' differences in behavior can be attributed to biological processes does not support the interpretation that human differences have the same cause. For one thing, it is just that progressive increase in brain complexity that is associated with the progressive increase in the modifiability (learning potential) of behavior. (In this context it is interesting to note an inconsistency in logic. Many individuals who would attribute differences in intelligence to organic factors also interpret intelligence to be the ability to learn. If intelligence is the ability to learn, then learning must be important to the development of human behavior.)

NURTURE NOTIONS

By the same token, the nurture (environmental) approach to intelligence has been less than convincing. This approach has also accepted the concept of intelligence as a quality of mind—a unitary process of some kind. Thus, it has also utilized the tests of intelligence as the dependent variable, and has sought to show how environmental events can affect intelligence. In a manner characteristic of the gross manipulation of biological (familial) relationships, the environmental approach has also manipulated gross environmental events. Thus, such environmental variables as social class, education of parents, occupation of parents, and so on have been related to "intelligence." As with the studies of familial relationship, environmental studies have shown a relationship between experiential conditions and IQ.

In addition, there have been studies in which some type of environmental enrichment program has been given a group of young children (Dawe, 1942; McCandless, 1940; Peters and McElwee, 1944). Such studies have shown that IQ will increase as a consequence of special training. For the most part, however, such enrichment programs do not indicate the specific stimuli that were manipulated in the program, nor do they specifically show the changes in the children's behavior that were produced. The environmental manipulation is unclear, the behavior produced is unclear, the principles involved in the change of behavior to increase intelligence are unclear. The argument thus must remain on the level of whether the unspecified complex behavior of intelligence is a function of gross environmental conditions, in the same manner "nature oriented" conceptions have grossly manipulated biological conditions and employed gross behavioral measures. A similar criticism may be leveled at John Watson's early suggestion that he could produce any type of child desired, by environmental means. This conception must remain less than credible until the principles and conditions by which this can be done are specified.

Such a grossly stated environmentalist conception does not indicate (1) what intelligence or other human abilities are behaviorally, (2) specifically how and by what principles they are acquired, (3) the functions of such processes, or (4) the specific conditions to be provided to treat specific deficits in children. The conception is thus inadequate. Moreover, the conception does not advance principles and methods for additional scientific advancement.

NATURE AND NURTURE INTERACTION

A third position or conception regarding intelligence has taken a middle course. This position, called an interaction approach, eschews the unproductive controversy concerning whether nature or nurture produces the greatest effect upon intelligence. Interactionism simply accepts that there are determining conditions in both of the major areas. It presents a compromise, and states that heredity contributes to intelligence and environmental events contribute to intelligence. Again, since neither the postulated determining events, nor the intelligence that is to be explained are stipulated, and since the principles involved are not stipulated, this view also remains largely a philosophical conception.

The fact is that the several views have not been able to answer the kind of question that has been described: What are the behaviors of which intelligence is composed? What are the principles involved in the acquisition of those behaviors, if they are learned? Or, what are the mechanisms involved if the behaviors came about through biological conditions? And, importantly, how do those "intelligence" behaviors contribute to the child's adjustment, to his ability to solve problems in life, to his ability to learn new skills, and so on?

The interactionist approach is actually an attempt to sweep the issue under the rug. This is justified on the basis of the waste involved in the nature-nurture controversy. But nothing new in conception is provided in the interactionist approach. A new framework is needed to urge both the learning approach and the biological approach to consider intelligence in a new light —not as a unitary quality of the person—and to conduct research to establish what intelligence behaviors are, the specific determining conditions for the various intelligence behaviors involved as well as the principles by which the conditions have their effect. Part of the consideration of what intelligence *is* will involve indication of the specific skills that compose intelligence, as well as the effects of these skills on the child's further development. The broad correlational types of study in either the heredity or environmentalist camp will not provide this type of knowledge. It behooves both approaches to begin research attempting to describe specifically the causal conditions and the effects upon human behavior. This framework does not suggest a value of continued study to show that either gross biological variations (such as familial closeness) or gross environmental variations (such as educational level of parents) are relatively more important than the other to the development of intelligence. There is sufficient direct or indirect evidence to justify the conduct of specific research both from a biological as well as a learning orientation. The major function of gross studies can only be to encourage the more detailed, explanatory type of research—and there is already a surfeit of such encouragement in each area. The time for such general studies and arguments, it is suggested, is passed.

The present account will specify aspects of intelligence (and other aspects of personality) in learning terms and indicate the role that learning conditions can play in their development. In addition, the manner in which these aspects of intelligence function in the child's further learning and adjustment will be dealt with. This will be done in specific terms, both as to the intelligence behaviors themselves, and to the conditions and principles involved. Because of this, the conception will have practical value in dealing with the problems of raising young children who are "intelligent," as well as theoretical and heuristic value as a conception of intelligence. These are points that will be made clear in dealing with the topic, however. Here, a few points have to be dealt with in laying the general foundation for the work.

UNJUSTIFIED NOTIONS OF INTELLIGENCE

The manner in which conceptions of intelligence contribute to social decisions, as well as to individual actions toward other individuals and groups, has been exemplified previously. Moreover, it has been suggested that the nature and nurture research has been adequate only to encourage actual research in which the specific determinants of the specific behavioral skills called intelligence are isolated. Before introducing some of the general aspects of the present approach, this section will characterize some of the notions that commonly compose the widely held conception of intelligence—and to indicate that the evidence available does not justify acceptance of those notions. This is done because the notions are influential guides to action which, it is felt, are not justified by evidence in support of the notions.

The Notion That Brain Development Produces Complex Behavior Development

One of the central notions in some organic-mental conceptions of human behavior is that the child's behavior develops as his central nervous system (and other organs) develop. Certainly there are conditions involving the growth and maturation of muscle and bone tissue, and so on, that are necessary for the acquisition of certain behavioral skills. The child has to attain a certain level of strength to learn to walk, for example. Moreover, as another example, it has been shown that a few simple reflex behaviors change in the infant as some of his neural cells become better covered by insulating fatty tissue.

However, the developmental conception has been extended by analogy to include general behaviors for which there is no evidence that the child's biological growth is involved. There are also many behaviors considered to be largely (if not entirely) due to physiological development, that observations and behavioral analysis would indicate heavily involved learning conditions and the principles of learning. Thus, the skill of walking, when analyzed into its components, indicates clearly that a great deal of specifiable learning is involved. Moreover, if learning principles and procedures are employed, a young child can be trained to walk at an earlier age than usual (Staats, 1963, pp. 369–373).

An example of a realm of behavior that is currently being attributed to biological development in large part, at least in one theoretical approach, is that of language. Some linguists and recently some psychologists have come to believe that children have an innate predisposition to language. Thus, it is hypothesized that with only minimal contact with the particular rules of the parent's language, the already set predispositions of the child are activated. Such theorists would aver that the child does not acquire language according to known principles of learning in an extended learning process.

The author has indicated the inadequacy of this position in detail (Staats, in press b). A foremost problem with this position is that there has been no research to establish the existence of any neurological structures that, when present, are correlated with language development. The innate theory of language as originally espoused by Chomsky (see 1968) has rested upon observations of language behavior itself, which is an inadequate base.

In general, it is not possible to observe only behavior, albeit over time, and infer that the changes that occur in the behavior are due to some change in internal structure or physiological function. No matter how orderly the behavioral changes occur across the population studied, it is not possible to infer the causes to be orderly internal changes. This has frequently not been recognized. Thus, many of the early child developmentalists were sure that the longitudinal observations they made of behavior development from infancy through childhood represented indices of physiological maturation. Many people still regard as well-verified indices of physiological development the behavior development charts that show that a three-month old infant will do such and such usually, a six-month infant will ordinarily stand, and so on. These observations are very valuable and can serve as useful comparison standards in dealing with the behavioral development of individual children, it should be noted. But they should not be thought to indicate anything about the physiological maturational level of the child—or of children in general. This has not yet been established, and may well not be the case at all.

Notwithstanding, this conception has had great effect in making social decisions, as has already been indicated herein in part. It is useful to note that the maturational conception has affected educational policies very extensively. The conception states, in essence, that if most children develop a particular behavior at about the same time, then that age is the age when the children's biological equipment involving that behavior ordinarily matures. The inference is that the behavior occurs when the child is physiologically ready. Based upon this conception, the time when the child is taught certain subject matter has been fixed. For example, to attempt to teach the child reading before a certain age has been considered to be fraught with dangers at worst and to be useless or uneconomical at least.

As has already been indicated, until there is *direct* evidence of biological structures or processes that produce complex behavior development, or the readiness to acquire behavior development through learning, it is not justified to conclude that such exists. It is quite feasible, even with no further knowledge, that the behavior is entirely due to learning. The only function of age (time) may be to allow learning trials to take place. If there is considerable homogeneity in training practices in a culture, then many children will have a similar number of learning experiences at the same age and will demonstrate similar behavior development. Most children may not begin to learn to read until six because they do not receive the necessary training. It might be found—and indeed it has—that much younger children can be trained to read.

It is thus suggested that another interpretation of the norms of child behavior development is that they reflect cultural characteristics of child training. This conception, unlike the biologically oriented conception, leaves open the question of the most appropriate time to begin a type of training. It gives impetus to studies to determine possible learning conditions in behavioral development. It also gives impetus to the treatment of problems of behavior development, rather than to passively waiting for some alleged organic development. Rejection of the physiological maturation conception of child behavior development as unsubstantiated does not itself justify a learning conception. However, the rejection does open the way for study of learning conditions in this context.

The Notion of Inheritance of Specific Behaviors or Behavior Patterns

There has been a strong notion that specific behaviors or behavior patterns are inherited by individuals.[1] The common-sense notion is based mainly upon (1) anecdotal evidence, such as evidence of complex skills running in

---

[1]This section does *not* refer to the reflex behaviors of various kinds that are present in humans due to their biological structures. Rather, as the examples will indicate, the behaviors considered are of a more complex, variable type.

families, (2) analogical extension of evidence that specific behaviors and patterns of behavior are biologically determined in lower animals, and (3) the general cultural conviction that such determination occurs on the human level.

Anecdotal accounts, for example, frequently appear in the mass media. One example is the appearance of marvelous behaviors by someone in a totally different manner than would be expected on the basis of the individual's supposed gross environmental experience. Recently there was a report of a boy raised in a village in India where he supposedly had no access to mathematical training. The boy nevertheless developed a high degree of skill in mathematics. This type of common-sense description of both the boy's learning circumstances and of his behavior is taken as evidence that he must have come by his skill through his biological development. Such common-sense description is completely inadequate as evidence. Moreover, the evidence conflicts with clear demonstration that many learning trials are required for the acquisition of mathematical skills, by anyone.

Another frequently given type of evidence is that of very talented individuals and families. Thus, in families that have produced many very skilled members it will be implied that it must be due to heredity—although it could just as well be learning. To illustrate the possibility of family skills through learning, it was not uncommon in times past for the father to teach the son the skills of the trade, and there are many family lines of smiths, cartwrights, millers, and schumachers. There is no reason why special musical, artistic, or intellectual skills should be considered to be inherited, while more mundane, albeit complex, skills are readily seen as learned—except that the fine skill requires a longer course of training, is exotic, and is not as explicit. The difference in interpretation is probably because we see the smith teach his son the skills involved, but we do not see so readily the special tuition (formal or informal) that could go into the formation of the intellectual or artistic genius.

Newspaper accounts (the author has one in mind) will also cite as "evidence" cases of prodigies who in addition to their special talent also began reading at the age of three, or some such, supposedly on their own, with no special training. These cases are used to suggest that there really is exceptional biological endowment involved in genius-level skill, biological endowment which is of a general nature and which shows itself in early development. However, this type of evidence is not acceptable. A detailed learning analysis of the learning task will reveal, for example, that it is manifestly impossible to develop reading on one's own. To acquire this complex of skills requires that the child come to make a very large number of responses to letter, syllable, word, and phrase stimuli—which can only be learned with prompting. Learning to read *must* involve many, many, many, learning trials (see Staats, 1968a), no matter who is involved in the learning. The fact is that the great multitude of informally held interactions between parent and child are not normally considered to be training. If a child himself *requests* the parent to name a letter or word, for example, that is not considered teaching in the same manner as if the parent initiates the tuition. In principle they are the same, however.

Common-sense descriptions by parents of their training methods are quite faulty in general. Two children could receive greatly different types of training from the parent, without the parent labeling his training methods as being different. The author had a colleague, for example, who had an unusually advanced child, including reading skills at age three, and the parent insisted the talented behavior came about, in essence, through the child's own biological endowment, without special training. A tape recording of the child's reading talent at a very young age, however, revealed the type of training—which was informally conducted as an enjoyable interaction—that was producing the intellectual advancement. There are many other well-documented cases of extraordinary intellectual or artistic advancement that involved unusual tuition.

The author was acquainted with another case where an individual had what is called perfect pitch—any note presented could be correctly labeled by this individual. This is a very unique behavioral skill, and is commonly considered to be an innate talent.[2] According to the available account this particular "talent" came about with no special training. In this case, however, the author had an opportunity to inquire into some of the circumstances. It appeared quite evident that this individual's display of the rudimentary skill in childhood had received a great deal of social reward. Amount of reward for a behavior is, of course, an overwhelming determinant of the amount of time the child will spend in an activity, and thus of the amount of training trials that will take place. Obviously, as is the case with reading or any complex skill, in learning perfect pitch someone has to teach the child the names of the different tones. How many children receive this experience when they are only a few years old? It is suggested that cases of exceptional behavioral development, where analysis shows complex learning is required, must *include* exceptional learning conditions, in every case.

The notion of the inheritance of specific behaviors or behavior patterns is not acceptable in the present view for several reasons. For one thing, there is not sufficient evidence to that effect—evidence that indicates clearly that there are such biologically based behaviors, and evidence that isolates the biological mechanisms that produce such behavior—on the human level. Even more importantly, however, detailed analysis of the types of skilled behaviors that many people feel can come about through the individual's biological development reveal that much learning has had to be involved. It is not generally recognized that with every complex human skill a fantastically large number of different stimuli have to come to elicit a response, and a great number of complex combinations of responses must come under stimulus control. People tend to think of skills as coming from unitary, internal abilities.

2The following phrase illustrates the common conception: "[Ziggy Ellman was] born with perfect pitch. . . ." (*Newsweek*, 1968, p. 53.)

When one considers what is called perfect pitch, for example, one realizes that it involves the ability to respond with the name of the key to every reasonable auditory stimulus. This means a large number of responses have to be learned to a large number of stimuli. And it should be noted that the stimuli are highly similar, which makes the learning task more difficult and thus more demanding in terms of learning trials. One can imagine the demands of having to learn the names of a large number of reds (or any other type of color) so they could be named on individual presentation. The study of the difficulty in learning responses to stimuli that are highly similar has been shown clearly in the laboratory. Thus, the learning of perfect pitch would be expected to involve many, many learning trials. When scrutinized in detail, the learning of a functional reading repertoire—an area the author has studied intensively—can be seen to involve also a great, great number of learning trials. It takes a great learning organism to be able to accomplish the task. It is the same for all complex intellectual tasks. To produce a skilled mathematician takes learning trials that must number in the millions, beginning with the learning of number discriminations and counting and so on—which, incidentally, the author has also studied in detail with preschool children (Staats, 1968a; Staats, Brewer, and Gross, in press). It is no accident that the child progresses up to higher mathematics only over a period of twenty years or more, for it takes that long to get in the great number of learning trials involved.

The same is true of general intellectual "skills" such as intelligence. Consideration of the specific items on intelligence tests reveals quite readily that very complex areas of skill are involved. Even at the two-year level of an individual intelligence test, one can see that each item tests for the existence of a broad repertoire of specific skills, as will be indicated in greater detail in later discussions. Many of these repertoires of skill depend upon the prior acquisition of other complex repertoires of skill. Many, many learning trials may thus go into successful performance upon one item. It is in large part because of analyzing human skills in terms of the specific stimulus and response terms of which they are composed that the writer has been led to realize the great numbers of learning trials that must be involved. It is thus felt that the conception of the *development* of these intellectual skills must include knowledge of the learning tasks involved.

Inheritance of General
Behavioral Potentialities

It could be said that while humans do not inherit specific behaviors or behavioral repertoires, humans do inherit general potentialities. That is, while an individual might not inherit through his biological structure specific responses of a complex nature to multitudinous and complex stimulus conditions, it is commonly thought that some individuals inherit the *capability* of acquiring such repertoires of skill to a greater extent than do other individuals. This is a strongly held conviction—and it seems to be justified by such naturalistic observations as that some individuals do indeed acquire virtuosity in some skill areas clearly above that which even experts acquire. The singularity of such performances clearly suggests to many that the individual involved must in some way be different than other people. Moreover, it is assumed that training opportunities could not be *that* much different for the outstanding individual than for other highly trained people who are expert in the skill. A related type of naturalistic evidence is that a child may readily learn one type of material and not another. A person may develop extraordinary skills in one area and be quite ordinary, or less than that, in another area. It is assumed that this indicates that such an individual simply has a higher innate potentiality for acquiring skill in one area than he does in the other.

Another favorite piece of evidence interpreted as proof of biological determination of general area potential, or talents, is that given by so-called "idiot savants." These are cases where the child is retarded in general behavior but displays an unusual skill in some sphere. Thus, the child may be able to tell you the population in any city of the United States, or he may be able to tell the date of birth of any well-known figure of history, or some such thing. The implicit assumption is that while the brain of such an individual is generally defective, it has one "bright" spot that accounts for the special behavioral talent. Again, however, it is possible that detailed observation of the child's learning history would reveal just how he acquired his special skill. From such an orientation, it might be expected that such a child if he had also been subjected to the same social rewards in another area of learning could as well have acquired high levels of adjustive skills in the other area. At any rate, such examples of talented behavior in which the learning circumstances are undefined cannot be used as examples to justify a conception of talents. Moreover, there is no anatomical corroboration for the expectation that idiot savants have uneven brain development.

Thus, in the context of this notion, it must be remembered that evidence has not been found of special structures or processes in the brain which supposedly underlie cases of special skill acquisition. Moreover, one cannot accept a common-sense assessment of equality (or difference) in experiential opportunities as justification for ruling out learning as a possible explanation. The conceptual framework by which professionals, not to mention laymen, could assess learning conditions and their effects upon human behavior in the naturalistic situation have not been available. Human behavior has been too complex an affair to have been adequately treated by common-sense description. It has already been indicated how a parent (himself a research psychologist in the area of language) had not had a clear conception of what constituted learning trials for his child in reading in the naturalistic situation. Such shortcomings are common.

One other point should be made in the context of this discussion. It is generally believed that different types of abilities or talents are required in different areas of complex human skill. The areas of human skill are considered to be fundamentally different. It is thought that a child who learns to read early is different in his innate (organic) structure than a child who learns arithmetic and counting early. Analysis of the tasks into their specific elements, however, reveals no difference in kind. Abstract visual stimuli are involved—a great many of them—and a great number of responses have to be learned to the stimuli in both reading and arithmetic. Although it is commonly thought that different abilities or talents go into being very able in mathematics as opposed to literature or social science, there is actually no evidence in the tasks themselves to justify such a conclusion— except such facts as that people can come to be very proficient at one while remaining ordinary in the other. Thus, it is being suggested that it is possible—we actually know nothing to the contrary—that acquiring reading skills is no different in principle than acquiring mathematics skills than acquiring science skills than acquiring a musical skill (that is, in terms of the biological mechanisms involved). It is important to be aware of what we do not know. And although it is commonly assumed to the contrary, the actual fact is that we do not know that different internal "abilities" go into the acquisition of these various types of complex skills.

The example of perfect pitch may be employed in this context. It would ordinarily be thought that an unusual skill like perfect pitch would demonstrate an ability fundamentally different from the common skill of naming colors. However, a learning analysis of the two skills would suggest that there is no difference in principle in the acquisition of the skills—only a difference in the particular stimuli involved and in the particular responses the stimuli must come to elicit. (Actually, both types of responses are verbal responses.) The difference in the frequency of occurrence of the two types of skill, it would be suggested, results from such things as the number of stimulus-response elements involved (that is, the number of colors to be named versus the number of sounds to be named), the closeness (similarity) of the stimuli to one another, the manner of presentation of the stimuli (the ease of having colors presented alongside each other versus the greater difficulty with sounds), and so on. According to this analysis, as long as the child can visually discriminate the colors from one another, or the tones from one another, it should be equally possible for the child to learn to name the colors or tones to perfection, except for such differences as mentioned previously. What is being suggested is that there are notions connected to the common conceptions of human abilities that are not well justified by evidence. Moreover, the common conception may not agree with detailed analysis of the behavioral skill.

Naturalistic Examples of Unusual
Talents that Involve Unusual Training

It should be noted, in this case as with the others, that there are a number of documented cases of unusual intellectual development that have involved unusual learning conditions. The manner in which James Mill extensively and intensively trained his son John Stuart in various aspects of intellectual skill is a well-known example. John Stuart Mill was trained to read before he was three, at which time he began the study of Greek. At eight he began the study of Latin, geometry, algebra, and so on. The intensity of the training was remarkable. However, there are a number of other renowned men of intellect who also received intensive cognitive training from their earliest years—including Francis Galton who, notwithstanding, was strongly convinced of the inheritance of genius. It should also be borne in mind that generally most parents, who accept a biological conception, are eager to indicate that their child has a high intellectual quality. This means they customarily underestimate the importance that experience has had in the child's performance, and thereby stress the child's quickness, natural ability, ease of learning, and so on.

The fact that biological determinants of potentialities for the acquisition of skills in general areas have not been found does not mean that such do not exist. Nor does this mean that special skill development depends only upon special learning conditions. The latter statement also requires demonstration that learning experience can produce extraordinary skills. It is interesting in this context that there are other naturalistic observations in favor of the latter view. To illustrate, it is appropriate to describe the violin teaching methods recently innovated in Japan by Suzuki. Children taught by these methods apparently learn to play the violin at an early age in a manner previously thought impossible. But this is true also in a number of different areas. Children today standardly learn intellectual skills with which only the outstanding scholars were once acquainted. There is a great deal of naturalistic evidence of this type—certainly as much as the naturalistic evidence that supports the common-sense notions of the inheritance of specific behaviors or of general behavioral potentialities.

It should also be noted that the extrapolation of learning principles from successful demonstration with a less complex skill to a more complex skill is not such a great extension. That is, when one shows that a less complex repertoire such as counting can be produced according to strict learning principles, the extrapolation to more complex repertoires of skills can be made with some confidence. This is especially true if analysis of the more complex repertoire (number operations, algebra, and so on) can be made in terms of the same theoretical elements employed in the analysis of the less complex skill. For example, the author (see Staats, 1968a; Staats and Staats, 1962) has indicated previously that the complex repertoire of reading is based upon the same types of learning that are involved in the child's acquisition of language. For this analysis the author indicated that a child with normal language performance has shown all the capabilities necessary for the learning of reading—a suggestion markedly different from a conception that many cases of reading failure involve a specific inherited deficiency (medically called alexia).

Of course, demonstration of special skill development through specific learning conditions is necessary. The hypothesis that all normal children are capable of learning a complex intellectual repertoire such as mathematics can only be shown by specific demonstration. We should have studies that attempt the demonstration. Only positive results could accrue, since the recipients of the training would profit from the treatment. Nevertheless, at present the evidence that high level intellectual skills could be standardly produced through the institution of appropriate learning conditions is far from complete—although there are many suggestive studies.

The Notion That Personal Qualities Can Be Inferred from Observations of Behavior

Human behavior is the event that is of interest, the event that one wishes to explain in understanding and dealing with man and his problems. Explanation resides in the ability to indicate the other events that cause behavior to be as it is. In simplified terms, a true explanation of a type of behavior is the ability to indicate that when such and such preceding events occur, the behavior will follow—and without the occurrence of those prior events the behavior will not occur.

However, as was briefly mentioned in beginning this chapter, there has been a very prevalent tendency to infer inner, personality entities or processes to supposedly explain various types of human behaviors. We "explain" various human behaviors by reference to supposed inner mental qualities such as a "vivid imagination," "high intelligence," "strong interest," and so on. These are not explanations at all unless that supposed internal personality entity or process can be independently observed. If one has only one observation, that of the behavior itself, no matter how elaborately or abstractly the behavior is described, this does not justify the conclusion the behavior has been explained.

This is certainly the case in the areas of human behavior under special consideration herein. That is, let us say that we have only the observations that a child has been slow in developing intellectual skills such as language, has not developed sensory-motor skills as rapidly as other children, is very backward in his school learning, does not respond as quickly to various types of problems as others, and has a very low IQ score in comparison with other children his age. These observations by themselves would not justify the conclusion that the child was mentally retarded, in the sense that the explanation of the child's behavioral deficits would lie in the child's defective organic-mental qualities.

It is suggested that this is not a proper logical method. If it had been shown that these behavioral conditions would occur only in the case of certain organic conditions, then when the behavioral condition occurred it would be justified to infer the previous occurrence of the organic condition. However, many children who evidence the behavioral deficits that lead to the label of retardation exhibit no organic deficiency whatsoever. Moreover, a child seriously deprived in personal experience will not develop intellectual behaviors normally. In any case of behavioral deficit it is impossible to state what the cause was—because it could conceivably be either organic or experiential in nature.

Nevertheless, it should be realized that our language is absolutely loaded with words that imply internal personal causation to human behavior. This type of thinking is ingrained into our culture and is so natural that without calling attention to the fact one generally does not consider the topic. It is thus important to indicate that to provide explanations of human behavior requires the specification of the conditions that will produce the behavior. The catchall attribution of internal personal characteristics as an explanation of the individual's or group's behavior is always unjustified without such specification.

Conclusions

In order to allow new concepts to occur in a science, it is necessary to loosen up confidence in the set of concepts that have come to be commonly accepted. It is thus suggested that we generally need to explore the evidence for the common convictions that internal personality processes are the foundations for individual behavioral differences in areas of human skills. The purpose of the present chapter is thus in part to create that instability of conviction that will open up the conceptual field of other possibilities.

A BEHAVIORAL APPROACH
TO INTELLIGENCE

Intimately associated with the research done to establish an explanation of intelligence has been the conception that underlies the method of measuring or indexing what is meant by intelligence. The fact is that all researchers—whether they wished to see if environmental variables affect intelligence, or whether the purpose was to see if familial relationship was related to intelligence—have employed the same definition of intelligence as some unitary mental quality. This definition has affected the type of research conducted, it may be suggested, whether from a nature or nurture orientation. The measurement of intelligence has been of a gross, global type (or types, when several types of intelligence were posited). It appears that this conception of intelligence has in both cases inspired the same type of treatment of the possible determining factors. That is, when one deals with a specific skill, such as being able to name an object, one is likely to look for a specific determinant. When one deals, however, with an unanalyzed conglomerate of events, it is more likely that the same lack of specificity will be employed when seeking explanations.

It would be expected on this basis that a new definition or conception of intelligence would have heuristic value in stimulating research. There are several aspects to the manner in which intelligence is to be considered in this work that may be introduced here in outline form, for one of the purposes of the book is to provide such a conception, one arising from a behavioral theory. First, one of the central points is to indicate that what is called intelligence, and considered in global terms generally, can be seen when subjected to a behavioral analysis to be composed of many different specific behavioral skills. In this context it is edifying to examine the items on an intelligence test, and examples of such items will be employed later in various discussions of the behavior skills that make up what will be considered intelligence for children of various ages.

To continue, however, it is suggested that the types of individual intelligence tests that have served as standards in the field (for example, the Stanford-Binet) are composed of items, each of which involves one or more behavioral skills. The items ask the child to label various objects, imitate certain actions, draw or complete pictures, and so on. There is nothing in the behaviors themselves that indicates they should all be taken as an index of some internal quality. When such a conclusion is made, however, interest in the specific items for themselves wanes—one is interested only in whether the item correlates with other items, or with the child's success in school, or some such variable. *It is quite a different strategy to be concerned with what the intelligence items are, in and of themselves, as behavioral skills.* This strategy leads to concern with the conditions and principles by which such behaviors come about. The strategy also leads to the question of why the behavioral skill is important to the child's adjustment. And it also leads to an emphasis upon learning. Unless specific behaviors can be inherited, the behaviors must have been acquired through experience.

Notwithstanding current opinion to the contrary, it seems to this writer quite possible that there is no internal, unitary, mental quality that is reflected by how the child answers the items of an intelligence test. (This suggestion would exclude the small percentage of children with stipulable organic defects.) Rather, the child's performance on the test may be a function of the number of behavioral skills he has acquired.

Specific and General "Factors" in Intelligence

One may ask about the fact that there appears to be a general factor in intelligence tests. That is, the success of response to one item is correlated with success of response to other items. As will be described in greater detail further on, the relationship between items that seem to deal with different behavioral skills actually occurs, in part, because the items include overlapping or common behavioral skills: There are behavioral skills common to a number of items. If the child has the behavioral skill, he is in a position to respond to various specific items. If not, he will miss the various items. To give one example, a behavioral skill that has generality across various items involves the child's attention being under the control of the test examiner. In many items the examiner will verbally direct the child to look at something, do something, respond to certain words, and so on. If the words of the examiner do not control the child's attentional responses, the child will fail on each of the items. The attentional skills of the child thus are general. In addition, of course, each item would test for the presence of specific skills, the specific motor or verbal response involved—but the item would also test for the general skill. Additional processes that make for the correlation of seemingly diverse items, and thus the appearance of unity, will be described in the sections to follow.

Items Are Samples of Broad Behavioral Repertoires

On first glance it might seem to someone ingrained in the common conception of the intelligence test that considering such tests to be composed of distinct behavioral skills provides no general properties to the conception. One might parody what has been said so far by saying, "Well, if intelligence as tested consists only of specific behavioral skills, then let's make children intelligent by training them to respond to the intelligence test items." It should be noted, however, that generality is involved in the conception in various ways—including the type of general behavioral skills just mentioned that cut across various items. In addition, the specific items on a test are actually samples of much broader classes of behavioral repertoires. Thus, an item that tests whether or not a child can label a particular object involves more than this very specific response. The item may be considered to have sampled the child's repertoire of labeling responses—a class of behaviors that may have many, many members. Training the child on only the one item would leave him with glaring deficits in the other items in the repertoire.

The types of items that are included on intelligence tests have been arrived at empirically. That is, they have been selected because they correlate with school achievement, with performance on other intelligence tests, and so on. This means of selection of intelligence items, it is suggested, has guaranteed that the classes of behavioral skills on a valid intelligence test are important to the child's adjustment in school, his ability to learn in many situations, his ability to solve general problems relevant to his age group, and so on. It would be expected that various intelligence tests would vary in their ability to predict children's future performance in their life situations to the extent to which the tests sampled the various behavioral skills that were relevant to success in those situations. The fact that intelligence tests are correlated with such things as school success attests to the efficacy of the tests and the relevance of the behavioral skills tested. (It might be expected, however, that a detailed behavioral analysis of the skills the child required for success in the various situations would suggest additional types of items for inclusion on tests.)

At any rate, the suggestion is that intelligence tests deal with a dependent variable, the various behavioral skills sampled by the items, which the child has or has not acquired. Such behavioral skills are the result of previous conditions— whether one suggests learning or organic determinants—and in this sense the test is a dependent variable, a resultant or end product.

Intelligence, Rate of Learning, and the Basic Behavioral Repertoire

For many people, one of the types of evidence that there is an internal quality of intelligence involves the very apparent difference among individuals in rate of learning. One of the most ubiquitous definitions of intelligence that has been given is that of individual differences in ability to learn. In the present approach it is suggested that there are indeed individual differences in the rate of learning, but these differences, at least in part (and, by extrapolation, perhaps in full), can themselves be considered learned.

The learned mechanisms underlying the child's ability to learn in various situations will be the subject of discussion in various places in the present book. Central to the learning conception of intelligence, and other aspects of personality as well, is the concept of the basic behavioral repertoire. That is, it is suggested that the child early in life begins to learn different basic repertoires of skills. These skills are important in and of themselves for their adjustive value. They increase the adaptability, precision, and productivity of the child's behavior. They enable him to adjust to social and environmental situations. They are the basic elements in what constitutes becoming a human being, in what constitutes personality.

In addition, however, these basic behavioral repertoires constitute the foundations upon which the child makes further advances through learning. Aside from being adjustive in and of themselves to the child, these basic behavioral repertoires prepare the child for learning of a more advanced nature. As mentioned before, intelligence should not be considered as some gross learning ability, a personal quality that resides in some process or structure within the child. It is suggested that the intelligence of the child resides, at least in part, in the skills he has acquired that make him a good learner in the later learning situations he will face. Thus, intelligence-test skills may be considered to sample parts of basic behavioral repertoires the child begins to acquire at an early age and which, as the name implies, constitute a basic set of skills for the acquisition of further intelligence skills.

The preceding gives only a bare outline of the present conception. The central aspect of the conception comes in indicating what the basic behavioral skills are and, furthermore, in specifying the circumstances under which such basic behavioral repertoires are learned. In addition, the manner in which the basic behavioral repertoires determine the course of later learning requires specification. It will be the purpose of the second part of the book to outline some of these basic behavioral repertoires that are important to personality, as well as the manner in which these repertoires of skills are acquired and how they affect the later learning of the child. After dealing with these topics, it will then be possible to return to the conception of intelligence and to develop it upon a more complete basis. It should be remembered, however, that each of the areas of behavioral skill to be presented constitutes an aspect of what we have so grossly labeled in our common language as intelligence or some other aspect of personality.

Intelligence Is a Cause
as Well as an Effect

At one time there was considerable concern with producing a definition of what intelligence really was. A number of early psychologists considered it the individual's personal amount of learning ability. Another definition was that "intelligence is a general capacity of the individual consciously to adjust his thinking to new requirements" (Sten, 1914, p. 14). Another early example is that "intelligence seems to be a biological mechanism by which the effects of complex stimuli are brought together and given a somewhat unified effect in behavior" (Peterson, 1921, p. 125).

These are but examples of the various definitions, of which there were many. In fact, there were attempts to classify the definitions. For example, Pintner (1931) suggested that the various definitions could be grouped as biological, educational, faculty (an aspect of the mind), and empirical (concern with test construction for predictive purposes). On the other hand, the classification of Freeman (1939) categorized definitions of intelligence as organic (biological), social (those emphasizing the role of symbols and concepts of a cultural nature), and behavioristic (those emphasizing definition in terms of performance on a test). "What Pinter and Freeman have actually succeeded in doing is to play up the undubitable truth that general intelligence is a vague concept and that it may properly be considered from many different though by no means conflicting viewpoints" (Mursell, 1949, p. 79).

These passages are presented to indicate both the vagueness and variety of concepts of intelligence utilized by investigators in the field of intelligence testing. It was because of the uncertain nature of the concept that it was later proposed by some psychologists that "intelligence should be considered to be what intelligence tests measure," and be done with the attempts to define what it actually was. From this latter view the concept was not considered to have explanatory qualities to suggest determinants of human behavior. Intelligence tests were considered to be measurements of the quality of the individual's behavior (as indicated on the tests), not of internal processes of any kind. In these terms intelligent behavior can be considered as an *effect* of unknown variables.

In the latter case, however, the conception does not square entirely with the general finding that a child who scores high on a test will later do better in school, and so on. Such observations appear to give the intelligence test result the status of a cause, not just an effect. That is, if the child scores high on the test, whatever it is that is being measured appears to make the child a better learner in many situations.

The answer to the dilemma is that intelligence tests measure both an effect and a cause. This was implied in the preceding section in introducing the concept of learned basic behavioral repertoires that make possible, and accelerate, future types of learning. Thus, it is suggested that while the child's performance on intelligence test items is an effect of past learning, the behaviors measured on the test are a cause in the sense that they will determine at least in part how the child will behave in future situations. Moreover, the presence or absence of the skills measured on an intelligence test (as samples of larger repertoires of skills) will also be a determinant of the child's future learning in many situations. It is suggested that these functions of the behaviors on tests in part account for the validity of such tests. That is, if the child has the basic behavioral skills in good measure he scores high on the intelligence test. Moreover, the child will also do well in other learning situations because he has the basic behavioral repertoires in good measure. Thus, for example, intelligence test scores will be correlated with such things as school grades and academic achievement of various kinds.

It is suggested that the task of a conception of intelligence is to indicate the principles by which the specific behaviors measured on intelligence tests are acquired, as well as the learning conditions and procedures involved. Moreover, a complete conception must also indicate how the behavioral skills measured on an intelligence test are important in the adjustment of the child and in his further learning. These possibilities will be illustrated in later sections. Explication of the learning determinants and the behavioral consequences is necessary in theories of various aspects of personality.

BIOLOGY
AND LEARNING

It should be noted that the present approach is not in any way antagonistic to basic biological conceptions in general, or to the possibility that biological conditions could determine aspects of human behavior, including intelligence. It is felt that there is enough suggestive evidence from various areas of study to warrant research on this hypothesis, to seek to establish the actual biological mechanisms that affect human behavior. However, additional *suggestive* evidence—from studies that deal not with biological mechanisms but only with familial-intelligence correlations—cannot be the ultimate goal. Suggestive evidence can only encourage one to do direct biological research. It is necessary to find the specific biological mechanisms which, if they exist, actually determine the behavior involved. The same task may be demanded of a learning approach.

The fact is, on a hypothetical level there could be many biological mechanisms that could affect the human behaviors termed intelligence. It has already been noted that there are a number of types of evidence that indicate that the central nervous system is a primary mechanism in the organism's acquisition of behavior and in the continued display of that behavior once it has been acquired. It is conceivable that individuals differ in sensory acuity to stimulus inputs in ways that will affect the manner in which they can acquire certain complex skills. Certainly, being deaf makes it impossible to respond to sound stimuli—which markedly limits various types of learning. Increase in acuity over that which is general could conceivably have advantages also. It is also possible that there could be differences in speed of neural conduct that would affect behavior in some ways important to learning. Biochemical characteristics of the brain laid down in heredity could also affect the learning or retention of skills. There could also be differences in the total number of stimulus-response elements that could be acquired and retained, as a function of the complexity and size of the brain. Possibly, differences could also exist in the rapidity with which associations between inputs (stimuli) and outputs (responses) can be formed and retained through other mechanisms. Other possibilities for variations in neural structure or function exist that could affect the individual's acquisition and retention of behavioral skills.

Whether or not there are such structures or processes that do affect human learning and skill display will only be shown by research, which lies in the future. As will be suggested below, however, in the present opinion any such biological differences will be ones that affect general characteristics of learning and retention, rather than the presence or absence of specific behaviors or areas of behavior. Moreover, since there are such significant social issues that hinge upon the conception that there are individual differences in intellect based upon biological structures or processes, such a conception should be proposed definitively only on the basis of solid findings that do not permit alternative interpretation. Direct evidence of the biological mechanisms involved would of course be a primary ingredient.

The manner in which an extreme "nature" conception of intelligence has implications as a social philosophy can be seen clearly in the case of Jensen's (1969) recent suggestion that there are probably inherited deficiencies in Afro-Americans' intelligence.

> When the advancement of hypotheses by a scholar with standing is bound to have a great impact on the resolution of current social and political issues of enormous magnitude, I am suggesting that scholarly responsibility dictates care in advancing those which are highly speculative. The bare fact that they might be true does not, I suggest, justify advancing them with the full panoply of scientific validation when they do not in fact have a sufficient degree of firmness. . . . [A] sensitivity to the social problems of our day requires a clear showing of the high probability of their truth before hypotheses are advanced which reinforce the stereotypes on which our caste system has been built.

> Jensen subsequently stated, in an interview at the Center for the Study of Democratic Institutions, published in the Center magazine for September, 1969, that "I think that the degree of probability with which racial genetic differences can be stated today is not

adequate as a basis for policies to deal with racial issues." For years this [statement] will be vainly chasing the assertion in his paper that there are sufficient grounds for entertaining the hypothesis of substantial genetic group differences in intelligence between whites and blacks (Hyman, 1969, p. 31).

It is thus important to indicate something about the general characteristics of the present conception, both as introduction to what follows and also to begin to indicate that the conception, although founded in a basic science, is humanistic and provides the basis of a benign social philosophy. It is in part for this reason that some of the preceding discussions have been made. It is nevertheless important to indicate that while the present approach does challenge some strongly held organic-mental conceptions of human abilities, the approach at basic points is congruent with biological principles.

Behavioral Inheritance and Adaptability

The preceding section indicated that it is conceivable there could be variations in biological characteristics of the brain that would play a role in individual differences in the rapidity of learning, the quantity of complex learning that could be made and retained, and the like. Research to isolate any such biological mechanisms involved in learning is of course of central importance, as is research to isolate any possible individual differences that could contribute to differences in learning. (At the present time, however, we do not know the biological mechanisms by which learning and retention take place.)

In addition, however, biological concepts are involved in the present conception in other ways—and it may be stated in general that a learning conception of human behavior should be in agreement at major points with basic facts and principles of the biological sciences. Thus, one of the points underlying rejection of the present notion of the inheritance of specific behaviors or behavior potentialities is that the notion is not a good biological concept. While there is ample evidence to indicate that the biological structure is the mechanism by which the individual learns and retains complex responses to complex environmental (stimulus) configurations, it is quite a contrary thing to suggest that the fantastically complex stimulus-response coordinations man displays are predetermined biologically in any way. That would be a poor biological conception, as a matter of fact.

An important evolutionary finding is that specialization *hinders* adaptation to a changing environment. Extinction of species may occur when the species has biologically evolved in a manner specialized for one type of environment, and then the environment changes. Specialization of biological structure and function can also limit the species to a narrow environmental circumstance and prevent widespread proliferation of the species.

Thus, the conception that is rejected—which conflicts with basic biological concepts—is that specific *complex* behaviors (not simple reflexes) are laid down in the biological structure of man, as they are in lower animals. It is suggested that man does not inherit in his biological structure *any* complex human behavior. To inherit specific behavioral skills as a member of the human species would have been maladaptive. A Stone Age man who had a repertoire of higher mathematics, or chemistry, or courtly manners, perfect pitch, ethical behaviors, a pacifist conception of human interaction, or what have you, would have had a useless set of skills. Fortunately, such men had no such skills, because training that would have produced these skills was absent. Rather, such men *learned* to shape rocks, fight savagely, throw spears, club prey, make fire, plan group hunts, stitch furs, carve fishhooks, find and eat insects, discriminate subtle cues in tracking prey, communicate, and so on. The intelligent cave dweller was the man who had the advantages of learning in these areas of skill and profited from them. It is also fortunate that we do not inherit most such skills as he displayed, for they would be largely useless and interfering today.

These points are important in the context of a conception of man. *It may be suggested that the marvelous adaptive powers of man are due to his nonspecialization—to his generalized adjustmental (learning) capabilities.* His hand, for example, is not a special tool as is a hoof for running, a set of claws for predatory purposes, or a nonopposable thumb for swinging in trees. His hand is a *general* tool, capable of many different skills, if not so good for certain special tasks.

It is suggested that *behaviorally* specialization refers to a specific stimulus configuration that calls out specific responses, built into the organism by the biological structure. Thus, to illustrate, the blue crab responds in a specialized manner, a stereotyped dance, to the stimulus provided by another blue crab which is a potential mate. The stimulus complex is specific, as is the response. Generality, on the other hand, is given by having no, or few, stereotyped behaviors to stimuli—but, rather, in having the structure by which a stupendous number of responses can be learned to a stupendous number of stimuli. If man were specific like the blue crab in his sexual behavior, he would respond specifically to specific stimuli. This is hardly the case, however. Historical, anthropological, sociological, and psychological data reveal the differences that occur in man's sex behaviors as a function of experience. Man's variations in sexual responses are of course multitudinous. They are not preformed via biological structure.

This is but one example. The fact that man does not have specific preformed behavior mechanisms wired in can be seen extensively. Man has learned to adjust to all the extremes of environment, circumstances requiring vastly different response skills. Man's behavior is fantastically complex and varied—and it all occurs within the same species. It has been said that there is no customary behavior in one culture that does not have an opposite in some other culture. The evidence that man can acquire new behaviors readily is so ubiquitous that it hardly commands notice, but it is quite certain that no other organism has this capacity in any proximate quantity.

Evolution of the species has been heavily documented; better biological specimens are selected by better adjustment to environmental conditions—including competition with members of the same species as well as members of other species. It is also quite evident that as one moves up the animal scale there is a progressive increase in the complexity of species' sensory input mechanisms and response mechanisms, and the integrating neural mechanisms that connect the two.

It is suggested that an improved biological conception is that as a species the evolution of generality reaches its zenith in man with the development of a central nervous system—the human brain—which is the *least specialized* of all the species. The generality of the human brain occurs in its prodigious capacity for the reception of stimuli and the instigation of responses, and for the *acquired* integration of these two realms of events. The human brain has such vast generalized complexity that it is capable of "handling" input that for all intents and purposes is infinite in complexity.

With his biological structure, man inherits organs for responding in a fixed manner to certain stimuli in a sensory and emotional fashion, as well as a number of fixed reflex muscular connections of a simple sort. He inherits also neural pathways connected to muscle groups—and sources of sensation internal to the body in muscles, tendons, internal organs, and glands. In addition, he inherits vastly complex mechanisms for "associating" the stimulus and response processes according to learning laws (whatever the mechanism involved, as is not now well known). But again the suggestion should be stressed that he likely does not inherit *any* specific complex human behavior or skill. Such behaviors are ordinarily composed of very complex sequences and combinations of responses under very complex and subtle sensory (stimulus) control involving sensory responses, muscle responses, emotional response, and so on—grouped together through learning in exceedingly complex ways. Moreover, these complex skill constellations must vary widely for the individual and across individuals and groups.

Man's biological structure and biological nature may be considered that of a marvelous mechanism by which behaviors can be acquired through experiential conditions. The child, for example, does not inherit a fantastically complex behavior like language (as Chomsky has erroneously suggested, Staats, in press b) consisting of many different kinds of responses under various types of stimulus controls. Nor does he inherit the skills we loosely call intelligence—again consisting of variegated responses under variegated stimulus controls. The child is a superb mechanism who can "receive" complex and subtle environmental stimuli, who can learn and retain marvelously coordinated responses, and in whom the stimuli and responses can come to be related by means of the intricate associations provided by the brain and central nervous system. It is the writer's conviction that the individual becomes what he is largely through learning. He would not be the magnificent biological organism that he is were this not the case. It is in large part because of his stupendous ability to learn, to acquire different complex repertoires, that man is set apart from lower organisms.

To continue, it is quite reasonable to speculate—within the context of biological concepts—that the conditions which, in an evolutionary sense, selected for man's biological superiority in brain structure occurred long ago. "[W]hile the psychobiological characteristics of the hominids would seem to be relevant to an explanation of the emergence of cultural traditions from their infrahuman background as well as the early development of these traditions, *there does not appear to have been any significant change in the neural structure of the human species since the Upper Pleistocene, perhaps as much as 50,000 years ago*" (Kaplan, 1968, italics added). This means that man's biological structure has remained unchanged during a period when his intelligence—his skills of various kinds—has changed fantastically.

It is reasonable also to speculate that all intact men inherit as a member of the species a brain of the highest class, capable of all the learning necessary to become accomplished human beings. In the writer's opinion, a child who has learned a normal language for his language community has shown the highest level of learning ability—for this learning is of the greatest complexity—and under suitable learning conditions, carried on over the years necessary to produce accomplishment, should be able to acquire intellectual, emotional, or social skill of high order. But the years of good learning would be required.

The statements of this last section, of course, are the notions of a social philosophy, not explicitly buttressed by systematic and detailed evidence. But the statements are as well or better buttressed as other social philosophies on the general topic, it is suggested. The current conceptions of intelligence, human abilities, and other personality traits—and this includes the several varieties of organic-mental conception—may be considered to be general philosophies. That is, they involve naturalistic observations of various kinds. The conceptions involve analogies—for example, from the animal laboratory to the human level. Many broad extrapolations are central. This is not an unjustified extension of scientific evidence, for sometimes the extrapolations serve as bases for experimental hypotheses. However, it is necessary to remain cognizant of what one's conception consists of, as well as the social significance of the conception, in the present case as in the others. In this respect it may be suggested that the present conception is humanistic, gives impetus to important research concerns that presently are not well supported, and constitutes a useful counterweight to the more commonly held conceptions.

The following sections of the book will be devoted to more specific principles, procedures, and concepts. While it is useful for the reader to relate the specifics to the more general philosophical points, the following material may be utilized productively even in those cases when one's general philosophy is of a different order than just described. Moreover, it should be stressed that it is in dealing with the actual behaviors involved that a conception of intelligence and other aspects of personality comes to grips with its central subject matter.

part II
BASIC BEHAVIORAL REPERTOIRES: CONSTITUENTS OF INTELLIGENCE AND OTHER ASPECTS OF PERSONALITY

chapter 3 / Infant Learning

Various types of important behavioral skills acquired by children will be discussed in the present book. Many of these learnings take place at the same time—they do not take place in discrete periods or stages. However, the task of describing the various learning circumstances and outcomes is not manageable unless discrete presentations are made. In addition to the practicality of separate discussions, different learning principles are sometimes involved that make separate discussions necessary.

The strategy of separately discussing the different types of basic behavioral repertoires will be followed generally. The present chapter, however, will generally describe several of the very first types of learning that occur with the infant, without specifically stating or distinguishing the learning principles involved. This will be done to introduce the conception of the child as a learning organism. In addition, the description of some of the types of skills learned by the infant will serve as a foundation for later extensions. The types of learning to be discussed in this chapter are considered at their beginnings. The more advanced stages of the learning will be added in later specialized sections in which the learning laws or principles will be made explicit.

Before going into specific types of learning in the infant, it may be generally said that most people do not realize how early in the child's life his experiences begin to produce important, basic types of learning that are the foundations for later progress. Many parents, impressed by maturational or other conceptions of child development, believe that good physical care and a generally loving atmosphere are all the child needs. Some parents because of prevailing disbelief in the natural role of learning even feel that to systematically attempt to train the child is undesirable and potentially dangerous. That is, it is widely assumed that the child should develop from within, at his own rate of maturation.

For many parents the conception they hold of child development is not so crucial. They have received good training themselves or have seen good training practices; they enjoy interacting with their children in a natural way that produces the necessary learning. In not so fortunate cases the maturational conception may lead the parent to be unduly passive in his relationships with his child, to be unconcerned with presenting appropriate learning experiences, to neglect many positive opportunities for productive training, and to be unaware of much undesirable learning. In some extreme cases the parent may treat the child as a vegetative organism, simply waiting for the child to blossom biologically.

There have also been literary conceptions of the infant, stemming from Freud's theories of child development, which have been very influential. These are also essentially maturational, suggesting that the child goes through maturational stages of development. Some of these conceptions make interpretations of what the infant feels and knows about the world, and wants from the world. These interpretations give to the child various intellectual functions and emotional desires that we have no way of verifying or demonstrating.

A conception more in line with what we know of learning, following from what has already been outlined, would suggest that the child is essentially a fantastically capable learning mechanism as yet empty of input. The infant's biological structure provides sources of input (stimulation of the senses) and avenues of response. However, there are no connections between the two. Moreover, the responses the child makes have not been combined into skilled sequences, so they appear to occur randomly or haphazardly.

We can thus consider the infant to have stimulus (sensory) and response capabilities, but no skills. However, the environment ordinarily begins immediately to occur in ways that make systematic co-occurrences of the sensory and response events, and the randomness of the child's behavior gradually begins to change to reflect that systematization. Certain stimuli come to control certain responses; this begins to give the behavior of the child the appearance of meaningful responsivity. Moreover, the random responses that first occurred begin through learning to occur in ordered sequences (as in reaching or crawling), and this contributes to the "systematic" appearance of the infant's behavior. This type of development, however, occurs only if the appropriate training circumstances (not necessarily formal) occur to the child. Several types of early learning will be briefly described in the following sections. It may be noted here, however, that there are various laboratory studies that support the fact that the child is capable of learning when newly born (see, for example, Rheingold, Gewirtz, and Ross, 1959), and that behaviors commonly considered to be inborn are subject to learning (see, for example, Lipsitt, Kaye, and Bosack, 1966).

STIMULATING ACTIVITY AND THE DEVELOPMENT OF SENSORY-MUSCULAR COORDINATIONS

At one time, to be a child psychologist in a university meant in most cases to be largely concerned with observations of what children generally do at different ages. Investigators such as Arnold Gesell, for example, systematically observed children "longitudinally"—over extended periods of time—and noted the development of behavioral skills in the child. These observations of infant behavioral development actually constitute standards against which children can be compared. It can then be ascertained whether the child demonstrates behavioral skills in advance of or behind typical children. Used in this manner such developmental scales have proved useful to parents and the advisers of parents (pediatricians, child psychologists, and so on)

However, the conception employed by the early child developmentalists, as has been suggested, was that the behavioral development was a function of internal biological maturation. As a consequence, while the developmental scales were very useful in spotting children who were retarded, for example, the approach had little to offer the parent in terms of prescribing remedial actions to take. The approach offered little with which to understand or deal with the child's learning. This situation still exists largely today.

It is common for parents to consult a pediatrician and ask whether their child is developing as he should. Many times the question is whether or not the child is retarded. The following was taken as an example from a newspaper column offering pediatric advice to parents. "Question—I have seen a number of newspaper and magazine articles on mental retardation. One of the things emphasized is the importance of recognizing signs of retardation early. . . . What I want to know is, what signs should a parent look for in a child to make sure he is or is not developing normally?— Mrs. M. W." (Crook and Harrison, 1967). The advice given was to summarize some of the behavioral skills that children typically demonstrate at particular ages. The statement also implied that the development of such skills occurs on the basis of the healthy child's biological development. Thus, if the particular child does not show the behaviors, this is thought to indicate a defect in the biological processes. As examples of this advice, it was suggested that an infant eight to ten weeks old *should* follow with his eyes an object moving through an arc of 90 degrees; the twenty-week-old infant *should* reach for objects; the six- to eight-week-old infant *should* notice parents and smile briefly when smiled at.

As is usual in such cases, the behavioral skills are *taken to be diagnostic* concerning whether or not the child's biological processes are healthy. Nothing is ordinarily said about the possibility that the child *learns* the skills described. Neither is anything said of how to produce the desirable learning. From a learning approach, on the other hand, one must ask whether the child would follow a moving object with his eyes if he had had no contact with such events? Moreover, have such learning trials been the same for the particular child as for the typical child? Can there be individual differences in learning opportunities? If so, what are these differences?

As another example, would the child smile at parents who had never fed and physically cared for him, whom he had never seen? If these are pertinent questions, and it is suggested they are, then what parents need to know is *what experiences* will produce normal behaviors in their child.

With this in mind, several of the skills described will be analyzed to indicate how the parent can ensure that his child develops normally, and in the process the parent can begin to (1) realize that his baby is a learning organism and (2) be an effective instigator of adjustive learning in the child.

First, let us examine the experience that will lead to an infant visually following faces or objects through a 90-degree arc at or before eight to ten weeks of age. It should be noted that the movements of the head, neck, shoulders, and eyes are muscular responses and are subject to the same laws of learning as other muscular skills. If a parent will ensure that his face and especially his smile and his voice are rewarding stimuli, because these "stimuli" are paired with such rewards as being fed, then he can easily train his child to follow him when he moves. All he has to do is to present himself after an absence, so the child looks at him, and then move to one side. At first the movement should be relatively small. When the child falteringly moves his eyes to focus on the parent's face again, the parent can smile and say some pleasant words.

With repeated trials, when the parent increases the arc of the movement he can soon have the child following him with his eyes through 90 degrees. The parent may play a game with his child in this manner, a primitive "hide and seek," and many parents do this. The parent may use other objects than his face as the moving stimulus. Thus, the parent may hold a set of keys in front of the child and jingle them slightly. Then he may move them and jingle them as the reward when the child moves his eyes appropriately in "tracking" the keys. Again, it is by gradually increasing the difficulty of the task (the amount of movement necessary) that the most effective learning trials can be conducted.

This type of experience is usual for most children, whether or not it is done systematically by the parents. Thus, most children acquire the basic skill of directing the head and eyes toward objects that are rewarding to see. It is edifying for the parent to systematically produce the behavior, however, to convince himself that the child learns, rather than develops, and that the process begins very early.

The range of the child's visual "tracking" of moving objects can then be extended by the parent through the same type of "game." It is thus suggested that the child *learns* such visual skill. Without apropriate learning circumstances—which usually take place without the parent being aware of the process— the child could not be expected to develop the skills listed on the developmental scales.

Taking another example, at twenty weeks the scales indicate that the infant "should" reach for objects with both hands. Again this is a learned sensory-motor skill. A child acquires this skill because such "reaching responses" are rewarded by obtaining the object. The parent may systematically produce this skill by holding some attractive object close to the child, getting him to look at and reach for the object, and then waiting until he fumblingly reaches the object. Reaching the object is the reward, the response that achieves this will be learned, and the next time an object is presented in that position the child will reach for it more unerringly.

If the parent varies the position of the object he uses, and thereby makes the task gradually more difficult, the child will acquire a general repertoire of reaching skills under the control of appropriate stimulus objects. A child who has no such experience will not acquire the repertoire. Inadequate learning experience could result from the child being left alone for the most part, or conversely because the parents give the child everything immediately without letting him "work" to reach objects—both cases preventing adequate learning trials.

Most of the sensory-motor skills that develop in the child are taken for granted by parents, believing the skills to be natural skills that develop from within. We customarily feel that we "naturally" reach toward objects . when we want them, that we naturally follow moving objects, and so on. In each case, however, these are learned skills. Moreover, they are skills that can be developed to a very high level of ability through appropriate experience. For example, focusing on a moving object, a ball, is an essential part of an expert athlete's skill in any ball-playing sport. The tennis player has to learn the highly developed skill of following a speeding ball until it strikes his racket, as does the baseball batter, and so on. The less trained person cannot do this with the same skill. One can demonstrate easily the need for learning in the development of this skill by telling a two-year-old child to "watch the ball as I throw it to you." The child will not be able to watch the ball. He will look toward the person throwing the ball, but will not track the ball as it approaches him. Only with continued learning trials will this skill be developed.

This learning analysis may be extended to other sensory-motor skills the child must acquire, skills that do not develop simply from biological growth. Crawling and walking are thought to come about through maturation, but consideration of these acts shows that they are complex learned skills, as the author has indicated (Staats, 1963, 1968a). If you want a child to crawl—a skill that developmental scales also list as defining normality versus retardation—you can produce this repertoire. Simply place an attractive object in front of the precrawling infant lying on his stomach. The object should at first be placed just out of reach. If he has already been trained to reach for things, he will do so and will stretch himself toward the object. When this is repeated, an object may be placed slightly farther away and the child will laboriously wriggle toward it. If this is done gradually, the child will gradually acquire wriggling, creeping, and crawling skills. The length of time (the number of learning trials involved) will depend upon the skills the child has already developed at the start of the training.

Walking may also be produced in an accelerated manner through gradually providing the child with experiences that give him the constellation of skills involved. A child of only six months of age (or less) may be held so that most of his weight is supported, but he supports the rest of his weight by standing. If he is moved along as this is done, the friction of the floor will result in alternate leg movements. The parent may have to manipulate the child a little from side to side to ensure alternate leg movements. With such learning trials the child will begin to acquire the leg movement coordinations involved in walking. The leg musculature may also be gradually strengthened from this experience, as well as through gradually introduced standing experience. Later the child, when able to stand by himself, can be further trained to perform the walking movements when holding onto the parent's hands or, better, to the back of a stroller or some such device. When the child has learned to walk readily holding onto something, the experience can be extended where supports are gradually removed for short distances, and then longer distances. The attention and approval of the parents, which acts as a reward for the child, can be effectively employed throughout such training.

Why be concerned about the development of such behaviors, especially if they really are not reflections of some internally developing "intelligence" process? The answer is that these are basic skills which, when acquired, will allow the child to learn other things equally important to later adjustment and later learning. The child who walks early, for example, can be introduced to other experiences that will produce valuable learning, social as well as intellectual, sensory-motor, and so on. Furthermore, as will be elaborated later, it is important to establish a good teaching-learning situation between the parent and child. The parent in this early training can discover that his child is a learning organism and can begin to find out how to help the child acquire desirable behavior.

It is also true that it is good to give the child attention when he is learning positive things, rather than to wait until he has done something undesirable before attending to the child—since the latter practice will simply train the child to behave undesirably. The training circumstances that have been described, as well as those to follow, are examples of ways in which the parent can give the child attention for learning behaviors that will contribute to the child's welfare and to his social desirability. Moreover, the parent will find a great deal of reward himself in contributing to the child's behavior development, and this will have positive effects on later parent-child interactions.

INCREASING THE CHILD'S SENSITIVITY TO IMPORTANT STIMULI

The world is made up of events to which the child is sensitive because he has special sense organs. The child is sensitive to different sounds, light stimuli, chemical stimuli (taste and smell), mechanical stimuli (touch), internal stimuli in his muscles and tendons which provide "information" concerning the position of his limbs and body, and so in. While the child is sensitive to such stimuli on the basis of his biological structure, the behaviors of orienting toward stimuli—looking especially at a visual stimulus, listening especially to a type of sound, and so on—are acquired.

Furthermore, the child learns to respond selectively to certain stimuli because of his experience. If he responded equally to all sounds, for example, he would not adjust as well—that is, obtain as positive consequences—as if he responded selectively. This topic of selective attention will be discussed more fully later. It is edifying for the parent to realize, however, as will be briefly mentioned here, that the child can learn such attentional responses at a very early age, that the parent can intentionally produce such learning, and that the learning contributes to making the child a responsive, alert baby.

One of the indices of the child's responsivity (and appropriate development) is whether the parent's voice is a highly effective controlling stimulus. Does the child look around when the parent enters the room and says something? While this type of responsivity in the infant is ordinarily thought to grow from within, any parent may produce the behavior in the following way. Let us say the infant has been put down for a nap and after a suitable period the parent hears the child stirring as he awakens. The parent may then simply stand at the door to the room and say, "Daddy, Daddy," for example. After hesitating a second or two the parent may then enter the room and have a warm interaction with the child—lifting and hugging the child, or playing with the child in some way. This will act as a reward, especially after the parent has been away from the child for a time. If this is done before the child has had any experience with the parent's voice, he will not at first respond. After a few trials, however, he will begin to make a joyful response, perhaps smiling and cooing. He will also in this manner learn to orient toward and attend to the parent's voice in this situation. He will turn around and look for the parent after the parent has said "Daddy," or "Mommy," looking toward the source of the sound. These are types of skills referred to on the developmental scales as being "socially responsive."

Moreover, these relatively simple ways of responding to the parent's voice will ordinarily be elaborated into a most important type of language and social learning of the child, as will be described. Thus, this early training may be considered to be basic to later development of significant behavioral skills. At this point it will suffice to say that the manner in which the child learns to respond appropriately to verbal instructions of various kinds involves this type of learning, which can profitably commence when the child is just an infant. The manner in which the child becomes sensitive to social stimuli of various kinds involves similar experience.

INFANT-PARENT LOVE

It is frequently thought by parents in our culture that there is some sort of bond between natural parents and child, especially between the mother and child. Our folklore instructs us that there is a natural (biological) affinity involved. It is this conception that leads us, for example, to expect different relationships between adopted children and their adoptive parents, relationships which are lacking in some essential ingredient.

Again, however, there is no evidence of any kind of a bond between natural parent and child which is of a biological sort. It may be suggested that there is absolutely no bond or relationship that makes the natural parent more attractive to the infant. The parent may be considered to be a complex stimulus object for the newborn infant which is quite neutral. The parent is a complex visual stimulus, a complex auditory stimulus; the parent stimulates the child through touch, warmth, and so on. But there is nothing special about this type of compound stimulus object.

Through the child's experience, however, and the learning it produces, the parent becomes a very significant stimulus source. Although the child is not at first responsive to the parent any more than he is to any stimulus, the developmental scales show that by the age of six to eight weeks the "Baby should notice parents and smile briefly when smiled at." Translated, we would say that by this time the child has learned many responses to the parent, including those described.

One of the important types of learning is of an emotional kind. Simply put, the principle is that if a new neutral stimulus is presented to the child at the same time as something is presented that is rewarding, and which elicits a pleasant emotional response in the child, then the new stimulus will come also to elicit the pleasant emotional response and be rewarding also. It is suggested that this is how the parent comes to be rewarding and elicit pleasant emotional responses in the child. It is also suggested that this is the beginning of the child's "love" for the parent.

Thus, each time the parent pairs himself as a visual stimulus, as an auditory stimulus (his voice), and so on, with pleasant, rewarding stimuli, he is conditioning the child to "love" him. For example, when the parent feeds the child and at the same time talks to him, the child will be conditioned to a positive emotional response to the parent's voice. When the parent plays with the child and at the same time smiles and talks, these stimuli and others of the parent (such as his sight and touch) will become pleasant and rewarding. The same is true for removing painful or unpleasant stimuli. When the parent makes a cold child warm, removes chaffing diapers, and so on, he is conditioning the child to emotionally respond positively to himself as a complex stimulus.

Ordinarily, this learning will be elaborated to become a very important part of the child's social and emotional system. It should be understood, however, that the learning begins early in infancy, and its results may also be seen very early. It should also be understood in this case, as with all the others discussed, that there is also room for infinite variation in the way that different parents' behaviors produce different types of learning.

It may also be mentioned here that the parent also *learns* to love his child—again contrary to common conception. There is ambiguity in this area because many parents would report loving the child from birth, although frank parents with modern conceptions will frequently admit their love for their child increased as they had experience with the child. It is quite reasonable that some unlearned maternal caretaking behavior would occur in humans, as occurs with lower organisms. If that were not the case it would be difficult to understand how prehistoric man, with no language or training, could have successfully reared children. As with other things, however, by the time a contemporary woman becomes a mother her response to children must predominantly be a function of learning. Only in this manner can we understand the wide variations in maternal behaviors—ranging from killing, mistreating, and abandoning newborns, through a not uncommon immediate indifference, to the mother who reports deep and immediate love.

In the latter case the learning to love the baby may be considered to have taken place prior to the birth of the child. That is, little girls frequently have a multitude of experience that leads them to emotionally respond positively to infants. When this experience has been of a certain type, the young woman will "long" for a child—another way of stating that she has been conditioned to have strong positive emotional responses to babies. In the same manner, a person in our culture could long for a car of one's own or any other rewarding object.

Ordinarily, family members have many positive conditioning experiences together—for example, taking meals together represents quite extensive positive conditioning for each member toward the others present. The parent ordinarily also has many, many emotionally positive experiences with the young child which condition him to positive emotional responses to the child. We can see the effect that experience has upon parental love, however, in negative cases where the parent has learned to dislike the child. This may be influenced by the child's behavior. The child who cries a great deal, who continues to display many irritating behaviors, who is selfish, uncaring, unruly, mean, obstinate, does not learn well, and so on, other things equal, will not be responded to by others—including the parent—as positively as a child who learns more desirable behaviors.

In short, it may be suggested that parental love is to a large extent learned and will thus be influenced by the child. If the child's actions are loveable, that is elicit positive emotional responses in the parent, as is usually the case, the parent will grow to love him more and more. When the child's undesirable behaviors outweigh the positive ones, however, the parent will be affected in the opposite way. It is in part for this reason that the parent should be concerned with providing conditions for the child that will produce behavior that the parent and other people in the culture—including the child's peers—will find desirable and emotionally positive. The way that others feel about the child will help determine how they treat him. It is because many parents cannot train their children to desirable behaviors that unsatisfactory parent-child relationships come about, as well as generally unsatisfactory social relationships for the child.

This is an area of importance that could involve an extensive discussion. It is briefly mentioned here, however, simply to indicate that an objective understanding of parent-child relationships can be developed. Moreover, the usual common-sense views do not help solve parent-child problems. When there is lack of "love" between parent and child, we need more information than is given by the statement that there is ordinarily a biological emotional affinity between natural parent and child. When you ask what you can do with that statement to treat problems of parent-child love, you find that there is nothing productive that can be derived. Actually, the statement suggests some emotional handicap, for example, in the parent who does not feel as strongly emotionally about his child as most parents do. This interpretation only directs attention away from the primary problem in such cases—frequently the parent's inability to train his child to behave desirably.

EARLY LEARNING
OF MEANING TO WORDS

It has already been suggested that the child learns to respond emotionally to the stimuli of the parent. One of the important types of learning in this process consists of the fact that the parent's voice, as word stimuli, comes to elicit positive emotional responses because these words are paired with pleasant, rewarding conditions. This is an extremely important type of learning, and through elaboration it becomes an important aspect of the child's response to language and to his own learning of language. Again, the parent may systematically accelerate, broaden, and deepen this learning in ways that will benefit the child's "development."

That is, whenever the child is eating—in fact just before he is presented with food—the parent should say "food," "eat," and so on. If he does so he will observe that the child will come to respond positively to the word "food," and this type of language learning will have commenced. The parent may also usefully say "good" when the child eats, especially when desired foods are presented. The same training should be administered with the delivery of other rewarding objects and events.

Conversely, similar language training given with the opposite types of stimuli will produce a very important type of word meaning. That is, whenever the parent has to restrain the child from doing something undesirable or harmful, which perhaps involves mild aversive stimulation, he should at the same time say, "No." Through this experience the word will come to "stand for" the direct experience of the aversive stimuli themselves. That is, the word will come to elicit an unpleasant emotional response and will serve to restrain the child later in place of the direct experience.

As will be discussed later, both of these types of learning are crucial to the child's later adjustment. In addition, the parent should say the appropriate word for stimulus objects or events the child experiences—even when the stimulus is not either positive or negative emotionally. That is, the child will also begin to learn other word meanings by having a word paired with an object. Thus, when the child handles a set of keys the parent should say "keys keys"; when the child looks at or pets a dog the parent should say "dog, dog," and so on. The responses elicited by the objects will be conditioned to the words—and the words will begin to be meaningful. This systematic treatment will not be evident in the child's own speech for some time, but it can become important in the child's response to speech at an early age.

ENCOURAGING
INFANT SPEECH

The most central human repertoire, that which gives him his enormous advantage over lower animals, that which is requisite in every human personal or interpersonal activity, is that of language. This will become even more clear in later discussions. At this point, however, it is important to indicate that the child's acquisition of his own speech begins at an early age. Some aspects of this learning, as already indicated, involve the speech of the parents. In addition, the way in which the parents respond to the child's own speech responses will have an effect upon his language development.

The child will make vocal responses. Like other responses of the child, if these responses are rewarded they will occur more frequently. The child who vocalizes more frequently will learn skilled vocal responses (actual words) earlier. The parent may systematically reward the child's desirable vocal responses, and thus train him to respond vocally in various ways, several of which may be summarized.

If the child has been alone for some time (either napping or alone in his crib) the sight of the parent, and so on, will be an effective reward. If the parent waits until the child has stirred and made a pleasant (noncrying) vocal response before he goes to the child, then the vocal response will be rewarded and occur more often. (This training can thus be combined with the one previously described where the parent uses his presence as a reward.) The parent may also present other desired objects to the child when he vocalizes. The parent, for example, may give the child a bite of food when he has made a vocal response during feeding, or a toy may be presented at other times, a caress given, or a game played.

This treatment will increase the desirable vocal responsivity of the child. As the next section will briefly outline, the parent should largely attempt not to reward the child when he has made undesirable vocal responses.

HAPPINESS
AND CRYING

Ordinaritly we think of happiness or unhappiness as an internal state that "causes" appropriate external behaviors—not the reverse. Paradoxically, however, we judge a child's state of happiness by the overt behavior. A child who cries a lot is judged as an unhappy child, and we would consider this undesirable for the child.

Actually, there are many concomitants that go along with excessive crying as with many other undesirable behaviors. Crying is an aversive stimulus for the child. A child who cries also produces an unpleasant (aversive) stimulus for others within earshot. He thus is conditioning those people to negative emotional responses to him. If he conditions them preponderantly in this negative direction they will "dislike" him, which is to say they will find his presence unrewarding or punishing. They will thus avoid him, drive him away in various ways, and so on. The excessively crying child thus may make his own adjustment difficult.

For these reasons—because crying is personally unpleasant and because it is unpleasant for others—the less the child cries when it is not appropriate to do so (when a real hurt has not been sustained), the better off he is. That being the case, the parent wants to reward this undesirable behavior as little as possible, thus avoiding unnecessarily increasing the frequency of crying. It is thus suggested, as one example, that the parent should not use the cry of his child alone as a sign for giving him the bottle, for giving affection, and so on. The parent will want to go to the infant when he cries to see if there is something wrong. However, if he can discover nothing wrong, if he knows the child is not hungry, cold, irritated by wet diapers, or the like, if there are no signs of illness, and so on, then he should not reward the child. The parent's presence or affection may be considered a reward.

Infants cry for no detectable reason. Crying may well be a form of exercise. My own experience is that one can expect infants to cry a certain amount each day, even very healthy specimens who are receiving superlative care. Moreover, there is no evidence to indicate that this is injurious or otherwise undesirable.

As will be discussed later, one of the principles of learning indicates how behaviors can be reduced in frequency as well as increased in frequency. For example, an undesirable behavior that is not rewarded will weaken and occur less and less. It is quite possible that this process must take place with crying if the behavior is ever to be reduced to a desirable level. It is important to indicate this, because if one considers that crying in an infant is bad for the child, it leads to actions on the part of the parent which in terms of learning principles may be undesirable. That is, a parent who tries always to prevent the child from crying will give the child a bottle, walk the floor with him, give him attention and affection, and so on whenever the child crys. These events are rewards, however, and will have the effect of *training* the child to cry frequently.

It is also the case that nothing can be done for the crying infant when all possibilities mentioned above have been checked. If he is not hungry (and this should not be measured by the crying or whether he will take the bottle for a brief period), cold, wet, ill, and so on, then the attempt to reduce the crying by presenting rewarding events may be considered useless and in learning terms undesirable. To pick up the child in this circumstance and pace with him will only reward the behavior. Many a parent with a so-called colicky baby simply has a baby who has been rewarded for crying when the parent puts him down. So the child cries, stops when he is picked up, but resumes crying when put down again—repeated conditioning trials. It must be expected that the child will cry when put down, if to be held by the parent has become rewarding, which is usually the case by an early age. For his own sake, as well as that of the parent, the child has to learn to spend time in the crib, rewarded by the consistent sleep he gains in that circumstance.

This is not to say that the child will or should never be rewarded when he is crying. Such occasions are bound to take place, as when the child is actually hungry, when he wakes up crying because of wet diapers, when he becomes cold, and the like. It should be recognized, nevertheless, that each such occasion results in the child learning to cry generally. When the child does cry for no reasonable, detectable condition it will help the child not to be rewarded. If the parent attempts to not reward unreasonable crying, giving the child plenty of social reward (affection, attention, playing) when he is behaving nicely, the parent will produce a "happier," generally noncrying, and thus desirable baby. It should be remembered that being rocked, cuddled, walked with, and so on will not cure any organic conditions. The child is as well lying in his crib as in his parent's arms. Nothing is being withheld from the child when he cries in his crib, except that which under the conditions discussed should be withheld—that is, reward for undesirable, maladjustive behavior.

The parent who gives his attention, affection, and care to the child when the child is crying will fall into the habit of doing his other chores, resting, and so on when the child is not crying. It makes more sense to get into a pattern of giving attention, affection, and care as much as possible when the baby has been behaving desirably. Both the parent and the child will benefit from this pattern.

The preceding discussions have been employed as an introduction to the general conception as well as to some of the ways that the parent can utilize learning principles and the general conception in raising and training his infant. The chapters to follow will deal in greater depth with additional aspects of the crucial learning that takes place in childhood. Furthermore, the parents' role in this learning will be indicated, as well as methods the parent can employ to ensure that his child learns adequately the important skills involved.

chapter 4 / Responding to Speech and the Development of Comprehension

The preceding chapter introduced the concept of the infant as a learning organism. In that brief summary it was possible to describe informally the two types of major learning principles by which the child develops behaviorally. Moreover, the examples were intended to indicate that the child begins learning from birth. Even of greater importance is the fact that the parent may begin to systematically produce basic adjustive behaviors in the child when the child is but a few months old.

However, in each of the examples the child's learning was dealt with only in its first stages of acquisition. It should be indicated that in each case the child actually has a lengthy and complicated repertoire to learn. Much of the acquisition of these repertoires will depend upon the conditions of learning provided by the parent. Although these conditions are not vastly complicated when understood, the parent has the power to provide wide differences in the learning conditions for his child—and thus in the acceleration or retardation his child will evidence.

The parent, or the practitioner who advises the parent, needs information in some detail about how to provide benificient learning conditions for children in the various skills to be acquired. The author has been systematically testing learning principles in formal as well as naturalistic research, some with his own children, for a number of years, and this observational work has produced a good deal of information of this type. The following chapters will attempt to provide that information in a number of important areas of child learning, beginning with the way the child learns to respond to words—perhaps one of the most important aspects of his intellectual, social, emotional, and sensory-motor learning.

INTELLIGENCE AND LEARNING
TO RESPOND TO SPEECH

One of the basic skills that a child begins to develop in early childhood is that of responding appropriately to a number of different verbal (speech) stimuli. When one considers this basic behavioral repertoire in depth, the central importance of this repertoire of skills can readily be seen. To begin to indicate this importance, let us consider the intelligence test. Actually, every item on an intelligence test, or any intellective test, involves following instructions—in each case the child's behaviors must be under the explicit control of verbal instructions. As one example, the first item on the Revised Stanford-Binet (Terman and Merrill, 1937) for children includes a board with insets for a circle, square, and triangle. The examiner presents the following verbal stimuli to the young child: "Watch what I do." The examiner then removes the blocks and places each before the appropriate recess in front of the child. Then the examiner presents the verbal stimuli: "Now put them back into their holes" (p. 75).

When this intelligence item is considered specifically, the essential stimulus and response components can be seen. The first verbal stimulus, "Watch what I do," must control the child looking at the board and the pieces, and the examiner taking the pieces out of the holes in the board. The second stimulus complex must control the child's motor behaviors of attempting to place the pieces back in the holes in the board. The verb "put" must then control a putting type of response. The pronoun "them" must control a response to the pieces involved. The word "holes" must control a response to the holes in the board. What this means is that the child must have acquired some quite complex verbal-motor units in his basic behavioral repertoire if he is to succeed in the task. Moreover, it should be remembered that the child who does not have these verbal-motor skills will not be able to respond appropriately. He will be considered in this task to be unintelligent—his IQ score will be correspondingly lower.

Another item at the two-year-old level of this intelligence test involves the same thing. In this case the child must build a tower of blocks after the examiner has demonstrated the task. The child must follow the verbal stimuli (instructions) to observe the tower and make a product like that of the examiner.

Also at the two-year level is an item on which the child is instructed to point to various objects (such as a button, cup, engine, spoon) and is scored for the appropriate response. The child is presented the miniature objects and the examiner provides the verbal stimuli: "Show me the kitty," "Put your finger on the kitty," and so on (p. 75). The verb in the sentence must control the pointing response, and the noun and the object the specific place of pointing. Another item at this level involves the same type of basic behavioral skill. In this case the child must point to the parts of a doll's body which the examiner indicates by his verbal instructions.

The verbal control of different, specific behaviors continues to be important throughout the items employed upon the intelligence test for various age levels. It is noteworthy, however, to see that the items for the very young child so heavily consist of testing samples of these verbal-motor skills. This supports the suggestion that this basic behavioral repertoire is one of the child's early intellectual skills whose development is of great importance. The basic behavioral repertoire, since it is involved in so many items, is one that contributes heavily to general performance.

In general, intelligence tests are predictive of the child's success in school. That is, the child who receives a high score on an intelligence test is likely to do well in school, better than a child with a lower intelligence score. This is commonly thought to indicate that what the intelligence test measures is the child's inner quality, which also determines how well the child will do in school. The alternate conception proposed herein is that the intelligence test measures very important basic behavioral repertoires of skill of the child. These skills are basic to the child's further learning, including his school learning. Thus, a child who demonstrates on a test that he has the basic verbal-motor skills—where a wide number of complex verbal stimuli will control appropriate motor responses—will also in this respect do well in school. This occurs because the same basic behavioral repertoire is important to the success of the child in school. Other things being equal, the success of the child in school will vary importantly depending upon whether the teacher's words appropriately control what the child does, for what the child does in the classroom actually determines what he experiences and learns; that is, the quantity and quality of the learning trials the child will experience in the classroom. The teacher's words must control the appropriate attentional behaviors in the child to ensure that he *sees* the appropriate things presented to him, hears the appropriate sounds, and so on. Without this, learning cannot occur. Thus, two children with different development of their verbal-motor basic behavioral repertoire will receive a distinctly different quality of education in the very same classroom.

We can see this process clearly in the child who does not respond appropriately to verbal stimuli. The deficit in skill is severely incapacitating, even for a four-year-old in nursery school. The teacher will issue many instructions to the children concerning what they are to do and what they are not to do. The child who does not respond to language will continue to respond inappropriately in such a circumstance—not because of meanness, intransigence, or what have you, but because the words simply do not control the behaviors that are required. When the teacher requests attention and the verbal stimuli do not control the necessary behaviors, the child with this language deficit will miss out on the experiences other children receive.

Moreover, for the child with this language deficit, most of his interactions with other children will also be impossible or severely restricted. The interactions with other children constitute an important source of social learning, which the language deficit will rule out or disturb. That is, most of even the four-year-old's peer interactions are based upon following verbal instructions. For example, when the child with the deficit verbal-motor repertoire is told by another child that they are going to play house and he is to be the daddy, the verbal stimuli do not elicit appropriate behavior. The potential playmate under such circumstances will seek out a more responsive and rewarding companion. The author has seen a child be an almost complete isolate in a nursery school group because of the child's inability to respond appropriately to verbal stimuli. Even by this early age much social interaction is of a verbal sort where the verbal stimuli of one child must control the behavior of the other if a mutually rewarding relationship is to be maintained.

The child's interactions with his parents will also be difficult if this aspect of the child's language learning does not take place normally. That is, the child who does not respond appropriately to language will require the more effort-ful care usually only necessary for a much younger, preverbal child. The effortfulness of the parent's child-rearing responsibilities will be heavily ex-tended for a longer period, to an extent far outweighing the effort that would have gone into the original training of the language repertoire. In addition, the failure of the child to adjust to various aspects of his life, including school, the necessity for special treatment of the child, and the expenditure in time and money will also affect the parent-child relationship. These negative cir-cumstances can be expected to affect the emotional feeling between parent and child. A child who appears stupid or intransigent, in the manner de-scribed, past a time when other children are well controlled by verbal stimuli, will be responded to in and out of the home in many ways that are different from the treatment of a normally behaving child.

The importance of this repertoire for one's social adjustment does not diminish as the child grows older. Mutual responsivity to language continues as an important aspect of adjustment throughout life. Many examples are so common we do not think of their importance: for example, appropriate re-sponse to verbal stimuli such as "Close the door, please," "Can you bring me back a quart of milk," and so on. In addition, however, it may be suggested that the success of any social relationship will depend in part upon the ability of each party in the relationship to produce the verbal stimuli that will control behaviors in the other that are rewarding, the vice versa. In each case this ability will depend upon the extent to which the two have also learned to re-spond to complex verbal utterances.

Thus, we can see that the skills involved are crucial to child adjustment and further learning. The skeptic may say, however, that after all this is a most ubiquitous type of human skill. He may add that we all have this "skilled repertoire" in great measure—or nearly all of us. Furthermore, none of us recall any specific difficulty involved in acquiring our ability to respond to verbal stimuli. We thus generally have the feeling that all human beings just naturally inherit such behavioral skills. The other side of this interpretation, however, is to add that the small proportion of the children who do not de-velop this type of human skill must indeed be abnormal in some way. Certaintly if we all inherit this skill, then one who does not develop it must have some abnormal biological condition. Moreover, with classic circular reasoning, the argument may be bolstered by pointing to the general poor adjustment of children who do not respond to verbal stimuli appropriately with the suggestion that this shows the child's general abnormality. That is, the child not only does not respond to language, but in addition he shows general signs of deficient adjustment—"the child does not do anything that is normal for his age, he acts just like a baby."

The answer is, of course, that this central skill of responding to verbal stimuli is learned. Extensive training actually goes into producing a child who is developed in this basic behavioral repertoire. Without training the repertoire will not be acquired. If the training is poor, the repertoire will be poorly acquired. If the training is unusual—different from that which is received by other children—the behaviors elicited by the verbal stimuli will be unusual, or abnormal. This basic behavioral repertoire is so crucial that the child who has defective learning will be incapacitated. He will appear, no, *he will be,* stupid, intransigent, defective, immature, retarded, and the like.

Thus, it may be suggested that creating this type of language skill in the child is one of the most important aspects of child rearing. While most parents even without special information provide the types of experience that will produce this type of language skill, there are infinitely varied training conditions within different families and thus great variation in the level of the skill attained by the child. Variations may include extreme cases where practically no learning experience has been available to the child, and the child as a consequence develops no skill of this type. Variations more within the usual range occur when the child does not follow directions well (up to the complexity of other children his age), when it is difficult to get the child to stop what he is doing by verbal means, when it is difficult to get the child to start an activity by verbal means, when it is difficult to hold and direct the child's attention for any length of time by verbal means.

THE BASIC PRINCIPLES
OF LEARNING INVOLVED

In describing in more detail the way in which learning this basic behavioral repertoire takes place, and the role of the parent in this learning, it will be helpful to first state in more explicit form the learning principles involved. It has already been said that when a behavior (response) is rewarded it will be made by the individual more frequently. Or, it will be maintained as a frequent behavior as long as it continues to be rewarded at least a portion of times the response occurs. If the behavior is *consistently* not rewarded it will be made less and less frequently by the individual. The term "reward" is a common-sense usage. The more technical term is a "reinforcer" or "reinforcing stimulus" or "reinforcement." Reward and reinforcer or reinforcement will be used synonymously herein.

It is important to realize that in life reward for a response is ordinarily correlated with a certain situation or set of conditions (stimuli). That is, the consequences of reward and nonreward are usually correlated with specific cues (stimuli). The young boy is reinforced for roughhousing in the presence of other boys, not in the presence of girls. In such a case the behavior will come to occur in accordance with that correlation. That is, when the stimuli occur where the behavior has customarily been rewarded, then the individual will make that behavior—or make it more frequently. When those stimuli are absent, that is, when the stimulus situation occurs where the behavior has not in the past been rewarded, then the individual will not make the behavior. This principle has been shown to lawfully occur with various organisms from men on down, with various behaviors, and with various types of controlling stimuli, and with various types of rewarding (or reinforcing) stimuli. It may be accepted as a general law of human behavior: *When a response or complex act is rewarded in the presence of a particular stimulus, that stimulus will come to elicit or control that response or act.*

Thus, when the individual is subjected to this type of experience, such stimuli will actually come to control his behavior. We may speak of control because there are lawful principles involved, even though our subjective feelings are always that we do things spontaneously because we want to— not because an external stimulus brings on our behavior. One might say, however, that we "want" to do things because of our past conditioning history. (It should be noted, however, that more than one stimulus may exert control over our behavior, and sometimes the control is conflicting. That is, one stimulus may tend to control our behavior in one way and another stimulus control an opposite behavior. What we do in such a circumstance will depend upon which stimulus exerts the stronger control, and we will experience less "decisiveness" in that situation.)

The control of the child's behavior, exerted by stimuli in the presence of which he has been rewarded for the behavior, can be seen readily in many examples. We frequently see, as one example, that a child will behave with one person much differently than he will with another. Let us say that the child demands things of the mother and gets them, that is, the child is rewarded at least sometimes for this behavior with the mother. However, when this child demands things of the father the child is not rewarded; only when the child wheedles and begs does the father sometimes give him what he wants. With this experience we would see that the two parents would "control" two different types of behavior, demanding in the presence of the mother and wheedling with the father. (It is interesting to note that this type of learning will *generalize*. That is, in this case women in general would come to control demanding behavior in the child and men would control the wheedling, begging behavior.)

As was indicated in the preceding example, learning will occur even when the reward is not given every time a response occurs. As a matter of fact, studies with animals and with humans indicate that intermittent reward— where the response is sometimes reinforced and sometimes not—will produce more frequent responding. Moreover, if the response is no longer rewarded, the individual will nevertheless continue to make the response for many more times if the response has been intermittently rewarded rather than continuously rewarded. In any case where one wishes to produce a strongly learned behavior that will persist in the face of nonreward, the best possibility is to reward the behavior each time at the beginning and then to gradually reward fewer and fewer of the responses.

Early Examples of Learning
Speech Comprehension

These principles have been stated in this explicit manner here because they are general and apply to various types of learning important to the intellectual development of the child. One of these is the type of language repertoire that is under discussion in this chapter. That is, the child comes to respond to verbal instructions (stimuli) because the responses are reinforced in the presence of the instructions but not in the absence of the instructions. In an earlier section an example was described where the parent before entering the child's room first said "Daddy" or "Mommy." Then the parent went in and rewarded the child by hugging, playing, and so on. Under such circumstances the child, after such learning trials, would begin to make characteristic responses when the word was pronounced. The child would on hearing the word begin to turn toward the place where the parent entered the room. This constitutes a case where in the presence of a verbal stimulus, the "Daddy" or "Mommy," the response of looking toward the door is learned because it is followed by the reward of seeing the parent. That is, the word comes to control the infant's response because the response is rewarded in the presence of the word.

This type of learning must be elaborated to great complexity in the ordinary parent-child interaction. At a somewhat later stage, as another example, the parent may bring the child's approach response under the control of an appropriate verbal stimulus. The author, as an illustration of a later form of this learning, conducted the following training with his six-month-old daughter. He kneeled a few feet away from her and said, "Come to Daddy." He also held in his hand a key ring which was visible to the child and which previous experience had shown was reinforcing to the child. He said again, "Come to Daddy," and jingled the keys slightly, which controlled her approach (crawling) behavior. When she came to the author she was given the key ring to play with.

Later variations of this training involved other rewarding objects. Later the reward was not a visible object but a rewarding interaction, such as a toss in the air, a hug, or a romp of some kind. In each case, however, the essentials of the learning were involved; the presentation of the verbal stimulus, the approach response of the child, and the rewarding object or event. After a time the verbal stimulus reliably controlled the behavior—a most important aspect of the beginning learning of the child.

Ordinarily, the parent conducts many such training trials, of which he is unaware. That is, the parent sees the young child playing with a toy car that is "stuck." The parent says to the child, "Bring the car to me." This is the verbal stimulus. The child who has had the appropriate training already will respond by taking the object to the parent. When the training is not yet complete, the parent may accompany the verbal directions by other stimuli that will get the child to perform the response; for example, gesticulating, reaching for the toy, repeating the words, and so on. At any rate, the parent provides the reinforcement for the appropriate response of the child in this example by freeing the mechanism of the toy. This will constitute a learning trial bringing the child's response under the control of the word stimuli.

Or, as another example, the mother in dressing the boy says, "Lift your arms so I can pull down the sweater." Let us say that the child has not yet learned to respond to the words. The mother, however, will then raise the child's arms (thus the arm-raising response occurs) and this is followed by the sweater being pulled down, which removes the restrictiveness of the incompletely fitted sweater and also uncovers the child's face. These events constitute the reinforcement. In the same repeated act of dressing the child, the mother gives many verbal instructions and the child is made to make the response. The response in each case comes under the control of the verbal stimuli. Examples are "Turn around," "Put your foot in here," "Put your hand in the sleeve," "Put your fingers together so I can get the mitten on," and so on.

The father presents the same type of training to the child in numerous interactions. He says, "Give me your hand when we cross the street," and guides the appropriate response or waits for it to occur. The child is told, "Look both ways before crossing the street," and is restrained until he does so. The child is told, "Kick your feet" when his father holds him in the swimming pool, and the parent does not begin to pull the child forward until the response is made.

These and innumerable other training trials occur in the ordinary interaction of parent and child. The parent is totally unaware of having purposely trained his child to respond to words, but that is what he has done—extensively so in the advantaged home. Because of this training the verbal stimuli presented by the parent, or by other children and adults, become capable of appropriately controlling the child's behavior.

Without this type of training the child will not acquire this very important aspect of his intellectual repertoire. To illustrate a simple case of how this deficit in training can occur, let us take the case of the nonverbal, laconic parent. Let us say that the parent bends down and jingles a ring of keys for his baby and gives the keys to the baby when the approach response has been made—*but he does not say, "Come to Daddy."* The child will then not have the advantage of the language training trial. Let us say that the parent sees the child with a jammed toy car and goes to the child and fixes it. Let us say that the mother in various cases of dressing the child raises the child's arms, turns him around, spreads his fingers, and so on, but remains silent throughout. Let us say the parent in crossing the street takes the child's hand when he wants it, and so on, but says nothing. Each of these cases is a lost opportunity to increase the child's language learning and the development of what constitutes a most central intellectual repertoire for the child. It should be pointed out that the parent may be just as good a parent in terms of loving the child and taking care of the child's health and physical needs—and yet be a very inadequate trainer of this aspect of the child's basic intellectual repertoire. The same is true of the other aspects of the child's learning yet to be discussed.

Needless to say, the child requires training that commences with the types of elementary learning experiences already summarized. The child has to be trained to respond to the human voice with attention (as will be discussed more fully later), to begin to perform simple actions under the control of verbal stimuli, and to *gradually receive training in responding appropriately to more and more complicated verbal stimuli.* This will also include training in making those more complicated responses. It is this type of training that will determine in part whether he *comprehends* well in many different situations. The child's power of comprehension, a central aspect of the common-sense notion of intelligence, may actually be seen to heavily involve the extent to which the child has learned an extensive repertoire of responses that are under precise verbal stimulus control.

Although it is not possible to go through each and every type of verbal stimulus to which the child must receive training in responding, or even a very small sample of such stimuli, the general principles involved have been outlined. Moreover, it is also suggested that the parent should be alerted to this learning on the part of his child and the importance of this learning. The parent should be alerted also to the numerous opportunities he has for producing such learning. As a general rule, it will be suggested here, as well as in respect to the other types of language learning to be discussed, that the parent has to get into the habit of verbalizing as he interacts with the child. He must use the principles of learning involved to provide the child with the innumerable learning trials necessary to acquire the large number of responses to specific verbal stimuli. With such training the child will come to respond appropriately to a wide number of verbal stimuli and to stimuli of increasing complexity, and thus behave more intelligently in many situations. However, as will be discussed later, this is not a suggestion that the parent sit the child down and attempt to formally train the child to this basic behavioral repertoire. The training must involve reinforcement for the responses, and the most appropriate reinforcers are those of the natural life situation, as in the examples given.

THE SOCIAL CONTROL OF DESIRABLE
BEHAVIORS THROUGH LANGUAGE LEARNING

The examples have been restricted to cases where rewards were used in the training and where the verbal stimuli came to control a positive (approach) response. It is equally necessary that some verbal stimuli come to control not making a positive response but rather the cessation of making an undesirable response. That is, some verbal stimuli must come to have a repressive effect upon particular motor behaviors. To illustrate, there are many situations in which a particular stimulus would control the child making a response because the response is rewarded in some way. Nevertheless, although the response may be adequately reinforcing to the child, the response may be undesirable for other reasons—it may have aversive features (like whining), or it may be damaging or injurious in some way. The parent can physically prevent or stop such responses by restriction or punishment. But, although necessary in some circumstances, these means are undesirable and should be minimized. A much higher level, more benign mode of interaction is possible when in such cases the parent or other person may simply present verbal stimuli requesting cessation of the response, and the verbal stimuli control terminating the response or making another desirable response. In this case, the control of the verbal stimuli must be strong enough to counteract the control of the stimulus that gets the child to perform the unwanted behavior. When this type of verbal stimulus control has been established in the child, the need for physical restraint and punishment is markedly decreased—a very important by-product of this basic behavioral repertoire.

The examples are straightforward. The word "no" must gain control over the child's behavior so that he stops what he is doing. The same is true for "don't do such and such," "please stop that," "I'm sorry, I'm using this now," "You will have to be quiet now," "you have to stop playing and go to sleep," "don't touch that," "leave that alone," "that belongs to me," "that is annoying," "you are making me angry," "that is dangerous," and so on. Unless the child is appropriately under the control of such verbal stimuli, he will perform many responses that are undesirable to other children, adults, and to himself.

It is also the case that the child must receive specific training in this aspect of his language repertoire. If he does not he will not develop the appropriate behaviors. It will then be seen that the child's behavior will be called uncontrollable, unmanageable, undisciplined, destructive, unsocialized, mean, and so on. The training in principle is of the same type as that just discussed. However, in this case it is not a reward that is used but some mild aversive stimulus, many times just the restraint of the child's behavior. Sometimes, also, the training involves ensuring only that the child is not rewarded for the undesirable behavior. A few examples are in order here.

Let us say that a child requests a piece of candy before dinner or at a time when the parent does not feel the candy is appropriate. If the parent says, "No, you can't have candy before dinner," this constitutes the presentation of a verbal stimulus. Let us say that the child, as would be expected if the child has not been trained not to do so, continues to ask for the candy, to wheedle, to whine, and finally to cry. If the parent does not reward this behavior this will consist of a learning trial in which the behavior of "trying to get something" is not rewarded in the presence of the negative verbal stimulus. This experience will weaken the striving behavior in the presence of the verbal stimulus (crucially the word "no"), and the child will be less likely to persist in this behavior after a number of such training trials. Ultimately, such verbal stimuli will readily control "desisting" behavor.

It should be noted, on the other hand, that if the behavior is rewarded the parent will have trained the child to respond in a very inappropriate way to a verbal stimulus that *should* come to have a very important power in the social control of the child. That is, the child will have received training to continue to strive for things in the face of verbal instructions to desist. The parent who does reward the behavior is not doing the child any favors, quite the reverse.

It should also be noted that there are various ways by which this behavior could be rewarded. The parent could give the candy. In addition, the parent may reward the undesirable behavior by attempting to soothe the child's disappointment. That is, the parent might, after the child begins to cry, promise the child that he can have the candy later, by sympathizing with him, and so on. The best advice is that after the parent has uttered a verbal negative, with good justification, he should ensure that the undesirable, importunate behaviors of the child not be rewarded. Learning appropriate behavior to *no* and other negatives constitutes an important aspect of the basic behavioral repertoire under discussion. The learning involved will serve the interests of both the parent and the child.

As another example, the child may begin to take a toy away from another child. The behaviors of taking things away from others are not desirable for a number of reasons. An important aspect of such behaviors is that they are aversive to others, and the child who displays inappropriate behaviors of this type will not have good interactions with other children. If the parent says, "You can't have that because so and so is playing with it," and restrains the child from taking the toy, this will constitute a training trial that will bring the appropriate behavior under the control of the verbal stimuli. Again, if the words are uttered but the child gets the toy anyway, then the controlling value of the words will be weakened, and the child will *learn* to be "uncontrolled."

Although, as will be discussed later, the author suggests that punishment be used with great restraint in training a child, it does have its place. When punishment is employed in appropriate situations it should be done so with a major concern of developing the child's language learning. Thus, there may be times when a child has been told to stop an action and will not do so. If the action is very undesirable for the child to display—because of possible danger, to avoid the damage to property, and so on—the parent may wish to provide an appropriate verbal stimulus and, if the behavior persists, to apply the designated consequence. Let us say that the child has been told not to pull on a lamp cord because the lamp might fall off the table. Let us say that the child continues to play in the undesirable way. The parent might say, "If you don't stop that I will give you a smack," and proceed to carry out the stated contingencies if the behavior continues. Such training will weaken the behavior of continuing an action when the child has been told that if he continues an undesirable consequence will occur. It is suggested at times it is necessary to apply such aversive consequences in raising a socialized child, and that this should be done with the presentation of the relevant verbal stimulus. This will shift the power of the punishment to the words, and later it will no longer be necessary to actually punish the child—his behavior will be controlled solely by the verbal stimuli.

As another example, there are also various times when a child is told to do some necessary action and will not respond. At such times the parent may wish to maintain the controlling power of his words by ensuring that the action occurs. The child because of some undesirable behavior, for example, may be told to go to his room. This is a mild aversive circumstance, ordinarily, because it removes the child from the company he finds rewarding. Being able to instruct the child to go to his room may be thus used to discourage many undesirable behaviors, ranging from crying when it is inappropriate to do so through various kinds of disturbing behaviors. Banishment to the child's room may be employed instead of corporal punishment. However, it may be necessary to have a few training trials to bring the child's going to his room under the control of the instructions to do so. In such a case, after saying, for example, "If you are going to cry you will have to go to your room," the parent may have to take the child there. If this is done with some mild aversive qualities involved, the verbal stimuli will come to control the behavior.

The same type of procedure may be conducted to produce other behaviors in the child, under the control of verbal instructions—behaviors that in themselves involve the loss of reward for the child. Thus, as another example, sharing some rewarding object or event with another involves the partial loss of the reward to the child. The child will not perform acts that lose reinforcers, unless he is trained to do so. As with the just preceding example, the child may be trained to share, to be unselfish, through the type of training where sharing behavior is required in the presence of the verbal instruction "to share." It is also possible, as with some of the other cases to employ positive reinforcement here also, that is, although the sharing behavior may be required by the parent, after it has occurred the child may be given social approval which will act as a reward.

It may be noted that the principle of behavior involved in each of these examples is a variation of the principle already recounted. That is, a response reinforced in the presence of a stimulus will come to be controlled by that stimulus. In addition, as one variation, if a response is not reinforced in the presence of a stimulus, that stimulus will come to control not making that response. The case where the parent does not reward "importunate behavior" after once having said "no" produces this type of control. As a second variation, if a response is restrained in the presence of a particular stimulus, the stimulus will come to control not making that response. Not allowing the child to take another child's toy when told not to is such a case. As a third variation of the principle, if a response is punished in the presence of a particular stimulus, that stimulus will come to control not making that response. The parent who says, "If you don't stop pulling that cord you will get a smack," presents training that will yield that type of stimulus control. Lastly, a response that is required (to remove restraint or punishment) in the presence of a stimulus will come to be made to that stimulus.

Many times it will be seen that a parent will not "spare the rod" with his young child and yet the child's behavior will be very poorly controlled. Sometimes the parent may use punishment frequently and heavily with the same result. One of the reasons that this may occur is that the parent has failed to utilize the episodes when he administers punishment to produce appropriate language training in the child. As with the positive learning of the verbal-motor basic behavioral repertoire, it is not only necessary that the child have the appropriate experience, but also that this experience is paired with the presentation of the verbal stimulus that is to come to control the behavior. To illustrate, many parents physically prevent their child from doing annoying undesirable, destructive, asocial things—but they fail to label the acts and to provide the other appropriate verbal stimuli at such times. The child is thus not provided with the language training that would make the experience have general portent. The child is punished, but he does not learn to respond to words. Each transgression is thus a new one—calling for more physical punishment. This deficit in the training situation makes it necessary that the parent continue to use punishment. With proper language training, however, and the establishment of the necessary basic behavioral repertoire, the parent may simply instruct the child and thereby secure the appropriate behavior. At this time, direct punishment is no longer necessary—an essential development if the parent-child relationship is to continue to progress in a productive and positive manner for both parties. As a general principle, one wishes to minimize the use of punishment in child training, and the child's verbal-motor language learning is a primary means of attaining this goal.

The general point here is that certain verbal stimuli have to come to control the behavior of the child through the use of (1) nonreinforcement for persistent behavior in the presence of the verbal stimulus, (2) measures that require the child to perform a behavior in the presence of the verbal stimulus that he would otherwise not perform, and (3) a mild punishing condition for continued undesirable behavior after having been told not to continue the behavior and what the consequence would be. In conducting the training the parent has to be reasonable in his requirements, not expecting better behavior in the child than he has been trained to give. He must also be humane, if sometimes firm, in his treatment. Above all, as will be discussed later, the use of aversive circumstances should be relatively rare, much outnumbered by the use of positive rewards in the training of the child and in other parent-child interactions.

INCREASING INTELLIGENCE BY EXPANDING THE VERBAL-MOTOR REPERTOIRE

It has been suggested that the child has to learn a very large repertoire of types of motor responses under the control of word stimuli. The resulting verbal repertoire is very important to the child's adjustment as well as to his further learning. The principle of learning involved is straightforward—that of instrumental conditioning. A response reinforced in the presence of a stimulus will come to be elicited by that stimulus. The principle has been demonstrated with a variety of organisms with simple, explicit, behaviors (Simmons and Lipsitt, 1961). The principle is also well verified and easily demonstrable in the context of language and intellectual learning (Staats, 1968a, in preparation).

The most important class of words involved in this basic behavioral repertoire is that of verbs. That is, there are many, many verbs that ordinarily come in the child's training to control specific motor responses. Examples are *push, pull, walk, run, hop, give, take, hand, pass, climb, reach, lift, close, go, look, see, examine, listen, feel, smell, follow, watch*. At first these words will only come to control the appropriate response in a long-term and slowly conducted type of training—as was exemplified in the case where the infant was trained to respond to "come to Daddy." The training involved was basically like that which occurs with a lower animal. One has to arrange, sometimes laboriously so, for the response to occur in the presence of the stimulus, and then provide reinforcement.

It should be noted that child learning does not remain on this level. After the child has learned a basic repertoire in this area, the learning becomes much easier and progresses much more rapidly, and thus consists of a good example of the concept of the basic behavioral repertoire. That is, when the child has learned to follow in motor action what the parent has done, or what the parent has indicated by example the child should do, the verbal-motor learning of the child may progress more rapidly. For example, when the parent can demonstrate an action and motion to the child to repeat the action, then the parent no longer has to go through the extensive task of originally training the child to make the response—as was the case with the infant learning to crawl to his daddy. At this later time, the parent simply has to get the child to perform the response and to say the word that he wishes to become the controlling stimulus for the response. Thus, as an example, the parent may say, "Push, push," at the same time as he pushes something and thereby gets the child to push it also. He may say, "Stick out your tongue," and stick his out, and in so doing get the child to perform the action also. He may take the child's hand and run and say the word to get the child to repeat it. The learning then only requires that the parent give the child some social reward, approval, to ensure the response is reinforced. In many cases the activity itself may be the reward. (These various training sequences involve imitation behavior on the part of the child. The manner in which imitation behavior is learned may be assumed at this point. This learning will be described in a later chapter.)

After the child has learned a partial verbal-motor repertoire, the further learning of the child may progress even more rapidly—which is another important function of this basic behavioral repertoire. An example may be employed that the author has conducted to demonstrate the principles involved. The principle is that when one word has come to elicit a motor response, if the new word is paired with the already learned one, the new word will also come to control the response. (The principle of learning involved here is that of higher-order instrumental learning. See Staats, 1968a). In demonstrating this principle of learning, the author told his three-year-old daughter, "Wug means close. . . . Wug means close." Then, a few moments later, he told her, "Wug the door." At this time she closed the door. This may be seen as the creation of a new verbal-motor element through pairing the new word with a word that already elicits the motor response. After this process has occurred a number of times—which ordinarily happens fairly early in the child's life— it is not even necessary that the child make the response at the particular time of the training. An individual might be told (or read in a dictionary), "Osculate is to kiss." At some much later time, let us say, he is told by an appropriate partner, "Osculate me," and the verbal stimuli immediately control the appropriate motor response involved. Naturally, a person who has missed this particular training also misses out on the reinforcement that follows the response.

Under propitious circumstances the parent will provide training that will provide the child with a very rich language facility in the verbal-motor repertoire. Ordinarily, most of the training will be conducted on the purely verbal level outlined above. The child customarily learns synonyms in this way, for example, whose synonymity consists in part of controlling the same motor response. Thus, the child will learn to respond appropriately to the word *push*. And later, through paired presentation of the words, he will learn the same response to *shove*. The same is true of *hit* and *strike; lift* and *pick up; start, begin, commence,* and *initiate; stop, cease, terminate; look at, explore, investigate;* and so on.

The greater the parent's speech complexity, the more complex is the training he is prepared to offer his child in this central language skill (and in others to be discussed). Ordinarily, the parent does not purposely attempt to train his child. However, the parent who is aware of the possibilities of increasing the training his child receives may systematically introduce new words into his speech interactions with his child. Thus, understanding of this type of learning would enable the parent to improve the informal training he offers, in many cases.

The training must be done appropriately, however. That is, the parent should not introduce too many new words or the training will be too difficult. Moreover, he should be sensitive to his child's level of language training so that he introduces new training based upon already learned words. Thus, he must know that the instruction, "Look around your room for the toy," will control appropriate responses in the child before he introduces the instruction, "Explore your room." If the first skill has been learned, when the child says, "What do you mean?" the parent may simply say, "Explore means look around," or, "Exploring is the same thing as looking around." Many parents systematically attempt to increase the extensiveness and sophistication of their children's language in this area as in others—and the result to be expected is a child with a richer language repertoire (that is, a higher level of intelligence). Other parents do the same without being aware of what they are doing. Still other parents could benefit from the suggestion that they attempt to provide such training.

It should be noted that higher-level units of this aspect of the child's language-intellectual skills may be composed of lower-level units. This is one of the ways that the child's language progresses in terms of becoming more abstract. Take, for example, the action of shaking hands. Let us say that a young child has been instructed by someone to shake hands and he has never learned the response, under the control of the verbal stimuli, and hence the words are meaningless. The young child then asks the parents what "shaking hands" means. The parent may then say, "Shaking hands means to reach out and take someone's hand and move it up and down." The verbal stimuli *shaking hands* would then come to elicit the complete act composed of the several responses—provided the child had already learned the responses under the control of the words *reach, take,* and *move up and down.* It is easy to see in this example that in order for the child to profit from such experiences, he must first have the necessary basic behavioral repertoire of verbal-motor units. The words *reach, take,* and *move up and down* must be already learned as elicitors of his behavior if he is to learn the newer, higher-level word. This is generally the case, where new units are only learned if a basic repertoire has already been formed.

Many higher-level motor skills and coordinations may be learned through this means. This can be seen very extensively in coaching. That is, the coach provides verbal stimuli, instructions, which control certain sequences of behaviors. The student may learn the verbal instructions and then give himself self-instruction that better controls his motor responses. After he has done this a number of times, the new sequence of motor responses will itself be well learned. However, this learning could only have taken place if the verbal instructions were effective in controlling the appropriate behaviors.

One further point may be made at this point. The examples given of this basic behavioral repertoire have primarily involved everyday commonalities. It should be indicated, however, that verbal-motor learning, based upon more basic elements, is also involved in special intellectual skills and artistic talents. Let us take an example that will illustrate the role of the verbal-motor repertoire in dancing. One of the basic repertoires of the dancer is that skilled motor responses are learned under the control of specific words. This repertoire constitutes one of the prominent aspects of being a trained dancer. When this training is complete, the choreographer in creating a new dance routine simply gives his dancer a sequence of verbal stimuli (instructions). Each verbal stimulus then elicits its appropriate dance response. At first, the dancer's new sequence is elicited under the control of the verbal stimuli, later the sequence is combined into a higher-level unit through practice.

For the musician, as another example, the names of notes must come to control the motor responses involved in making the appropriate sound on the instrument involved. The "verbal" stimuli of the score must control sequences of musical responses in very complex arrangements. The composer is in principle doing the same thing that the choreographer does—that is, he puts the controlling stimuli together into new combinations which, when they elicit the combined and sequenced responses of the performer, produce a form that is pleasing.

The same is true for the mechanic who receives instructions concerning the sequence of disassembling, repairing, and assembling a part of a new car. Because of his previous training, the verbal stimuli control a sequence of skilled responses. After performance of the sequence a number of times, the instructions are no longer needed.

Any science also ordinarily involves special verbs that control motor responses important to the field. As in the arts, the responses themselves may be of such a level of skill that they require long training programs in and of themselves. However, these motor responses must also be under the control of the appropriate verbal stimuli. The verb form *titrate,* as one example, must control the necessary complex motor-response acts in the chemist, and the verbal-motor element constitutes part of the special skill involved in being a chemist. The same is true in physics, physiology, psychology, and so on. All of the technical skills that are under verbal control enable appropriate behaviors to be elicited by one scientist or engineer from another trained individual. This is frequently the heart of a science or craft. The development of these types of skills may be considered to begin formation in very early childhood, as has been described.

In each case these complex verbal-motor skills are only acquired on the basis of a previously acquired basic behavioral repertoire that the child should begin to acquire as an infant. The child's intelligence, in part, depends upon —or, rather, consists of—such a learned repertoire of a vast number of elements that are capable of infinitely varied combinations.

chapter 5 / Beginning Speech Learning

As has already been implied, there are a number of aspects to the child's language learning. The important one just described concerned the manner in which speech stimuli come to control the behavior of the child. This is a central aspect of the child's intellectual development, which unfortunately is not recognized many times. This controlling function of verbal stimuli is frequently spoken of as "passive" or "receptive" language, and the contrast with "active" language seems to make it less significant, which would certainly be in error.

It is quite evident, of course, that what is called "expressive," "productive," or "active" language is also of central importance. Several aspects of this type of learning will be described here, along with indications of how the parent contributes to these important learning processes.

In Chapter 3 it was very briefly suggested that it was possible to "encourage" the development of speech in the infant according to the principles of reward learning. This suggestion requires considerable elaboration to provide understanding of the child's learning of speech and to describe methods by which the child's speech development can be accelerated. The child does not begin saying his first words ordinarily until after ten to twelve months of age, and the age may be considerably extended (eighteen to twenty-four months) even in children who later turn out to acquire normal language-intellectual skills. Frequently, this interval from birth to the first spoken words is considered to be the period required for the child's biological *maturation* to occur, and little consideration is given to learning processes. The maturational conception, however, has nothing to offer in terms of aiding or understanding the child's behavioral development. A knowledge of learning conditions, on the other hand, provides the parent with opportunities for understanding and producing desirable development in his child and also for treating problems of development.

Two types of learning involved in the first acquisition of speech will be described in beginning consideration of this vital aspect of child development. One learning process involves experiences that make the parent's voice a rewarding sound, and thus imitation of the parent's voice also rewarding. On this basis the child's speech that sounds like the parent is learned because it is rewarding to reproduce the parent's voice. The other type of learning is that briefly described in Chapter 3. That is, if the parent responds to and thus rewards the child's speech responses, the child will learn those speech responses. These principles require further elaboration in describing the child's first acquisition of speech.

To begin let us go back to the principle already discussed. When the parent's voice occurs in contiguity with some rewarding condition (such as feeding, playing, and so on), learning takes place that makes the parent's voice a reinforcing stimulus itself. Several results of this learning have already been described. In the present context, however, when the parent's speech becomes rewarding this sets the stage for the beginning development of the child's vocal imitation of the parent. That is, the child ordinarily makes a number of vocal responses that produce sound stimuli. Responses that produce sounds that are rewarding like those of the parents will now be reinforced. The more the sound is like that made by the parent, the more the reinforcement value. As a consequence of this, it would be expected that those responses would become more frequent—the child would be expected to learn those responses that sounded like those of the parent.

Observations of infants' vocalizations support the expectations of the analysis. Long before the child has uttered his first recognizable word, his speech goes through a gradual development in which he begins to utter sounds more and more like those made by his parents, and to do so with greater frequency. If one were to plot a graph throughout infancy and childhood of the relative frequency of speech of the child like that of his "speech community," in contrast to speech unlike that to which the child is exposed, the emergence of the former and the decline of the latter would be seen. Moreover, we can see readily that two children raised by sets of parents who speak different languages will gradually learn different responses, that is, those in the language of their parents. There are no biological differences in children that correlate with such differences in language development.

To recapitulate, the sounds that the child makes that are like those made by the parents are rewarding. Because of this reward, the *vocal responses* that produce those imitational sounds are strengthened. Thus, the child gradually learns through this "self-reinforcement" to make syllabic and word sounds like those made by the parents. This being the case, the parent who speaks a good deal, especially while he is taking care of (rewarding) the child, will produce a child who begins to talk at an early age. In this process the parent's vocal sounds will become rewarding, and thus the child will learn to imitate the sounds. Because the effects of the parent's speech while attending to the child are so indirect, they are not commonly understood. Therefore, ordinarily people do not understand the parent's "training" role in this respect, as with others, and are apt to think of the child's development in terms of physical maturation.

In addition to this source of reward for learning speech sounds, the parent, as has been indicated, ordinarily will also directly reward the child for responding vocally. In this way the parent also trains the child to make speech responses. One of the earliest rewards of vocal responding occurs with crying, as has been indicated. That is, when the child cries the parents attend to the child, and this acts like a reinforcement so that the child learns to cry (see Etzel and Gewirtz, 1967).

As a means of generally strengthening the class of vocal responses, this type of learning may have some functional quality at the beginning. Since crying is later not adjustive for the child, its reinforcement should be minimized. However, many parents ordinarily also reward other types of vocal responses that lead the child to more desirable vocal skills. The mother goes to the infant when he awakens from his nap and coos and burbles. As another example, when the infant happens to make a sound that is even remotely like a recognizable word or syllable, the parent is likely to socially reward the child. Let us say, for example, that the infant happens to say something like "Maa." The alert mother is likely to say in return, "Ma . . . ma, yes you know your Mama, don't you?" and hug and kiss the child or in some manner administer a rewarding type of affection. This process may be considered to be a learning trial where the child has been reinforced for making the vocal response.

With many parents this type of interaction occurs a great number of times during the child's preverbal infancy. Any sound the child makes that is in some way like an English word will be responded to by such a parent, and in the process the child is trained to make such sounds. It may be added that this type of "training" program would be recommended for all infants to ensure a normal language development. Such training is effective even before the child has come to respond with recognizable words. Research has shown that three-month-old children socially reinforced for (noncrying) vocal responses will begin making such responses more frequently (Weisberg, 1963). It may be concluded that speech behavior is developed through learning, beginning at a very early age. This learning should be maximized through the two types of procedures described.

SINGLE-WORD
RESPONSES

After a time, where both of these learning circumstances are taking place, the child will begin more frequently to make vocal responses that resemble English syllables. And he will begin to join syllables together in a manner that is even more like a word.

At the point where the child makes sounds like words he may be ready for more advanced language training. The child may be at this level by eight to nine months of age or less if his language training has been sufficiently rich. At any rate, the parent who is alert to the child's vocalizations may notice at this time that the child is making a vocal response that is similar to the word for some object, for example. The parent may then begin to arrange circumstances so that the child's vocalizing comes under the appropriate control of the stimulus of the object. That is, it is not only important that the child learn vocal responses. Speech does not become functional until it occurs under the proper circumstances. For example, we would not say that a child had speech if he said "da-da" under various conditions. However, if the child said "da-da" when his father entered the room, and so on, and he did not make the response at other times (even though the discrimination might not be perfect), we would consider this more like meaningful speech. The fact is, our language is adjustive because it occurs in the appropriate circumstances, because it is stimulus-controlled. This aspect of language, a very important development, is also learned.

Using the principle of learning already explicated, a procedure for producing this type of controlled speech in the child may be elaborated. Let us say, for example, that the parent has heard the child saying "bee-bee" every once in a while. The parent might then plan a training trial in which after the child had made the vocal response the parent would produce a favorite doll of the child and say, "Bay-bee," and reward the child by smiling, attention, and so on. The author, as a matter of fact, did this with his baby daughter when she was eight months of age, and the child then repeated the word.

Later, the author hid the doll behind him for a moment and said, "Bay-bee." When the child repeated the word, the toy was shown to her again. After this training situation had occurred a very few times, the child came to say, "Bay-bee," when the doll was presented. (There are several types of learning involved here, including imitation, as will be described further on.) In this process one of the child's first words (under stimulus control) was learned. This learning process was complete when the child was nine months old.

In this manner (at an earlier time) the child was also trained to say "eat" when she was seated in her high chair and there was food before her. The first part of the training involved saying the word while she was eating. Later, when she could say "eeh," she would be fed several spoonfuls and then the author would pause until she said, "Eeh," sometimes saying it first himself, and then rewarding the speech response by giving the next spoonful. Each act consisted of a learning trial. (Actually this training had a fairly long history, since at first simply making a vocal response was rewarded. Later, responses more like the response "eeh" and then "eat" were selected for reward.) The child in a similar manner came to say "mama," "dada" (for father), "doh" (for a toy dog), "bah" (for ball), and so on, by the time she was nine months of age.

Each of these word responses was a response that would produce immediate reward for the child, and at this point the learning of new words accelerated in rate. Under this type of training the child's word-naming vocabulary grew in number as well as in the precision with which the word responses were under strict control of the appropriate stimulus object or event. The expansion of this rudimentary speech repertoire may proceed naturally in the following way. Whenever the parent sees the child trying to get a common object that is out of reach, whenever the child indicates that he wants something, the parent may first say the word of the object or event and ask the child to try to say it too. The parent may thus see the child reaching for a piece of bread and say simply, "Bread," or, "Bread, can you say bread?" When the child has attempted an imitation of the word, however poor, perhaps saying something like "dud," the bread may then be given. This constitutes a reinforced training trial. The many, many opportunities for such trials provide the potential training program in the child's early learning of the basic behavioral repertoire of verbal labeling.

Moreover, this type of training may also be used in increasing the quality of speech responses, as will be described. In any event, systematic training procedures of this type can quickly produce a small stimulus-controlled speech repertoire in the child before he is a year old and prepare him for a rapid increase in his language learning. These procedures, as well as those involved in training the child to his other basic behavioral repertoires, can also be employed in treating problem children who have failed to develop the repertoires at the normal times.

IMPROVING THE QUALITY
OF SINGLE WORD RESPONSES

To recapitulate, although at first the parent will want to reward the child for making a vocal response of any kind that is well modulated, later, in a gradual manner, the parent will want to respond more to vocalizations that are more and more like the words and syllables that occur in the parents' language. By the time the parent begins to reward speech responses in the presence of particular objects and events, the speech responses will have progressed to the point where they are approximations of the appropriate English word.

Even then the process of perfecting the speech response in each case is far from complete. The child will require training in which better and better examples of the word response are rewarded. The perceptive parent, for example, will want at first to reward the child with a drink of water when the child in the process already described comes to say, "Wah-wah." This should be done to strengthen the response and maintain it in good frequency, as well as to bring it under the control of the appropriate stimulus conditions.

Later, when this training has been accomplished to some extent, the parent may begin to reward better responses more heavily (actually, more quickly) than less good responses. That is, when the child says, "Wah-wah," the parent may respond, "Wah-dah, can you say wah-dah," and then wait until the child has made another response. If the child makes a better response a good deal of approval may be given him, so the response is more heavily rewarded. When the child makes the better response on first request, the water may be given immediately, which will strengthen this response more than the response that leads to the necessity of repetition and delay. The parent in this manner may advance the child to say, "Watah," "Wata," and finally "Water." Ordinarily, much of this training will also be self-conducted by the child. That is, saying words more and more like the parent will be rewarding, in the process already described. Thus, the child will many times be heard "practicing" words when he is alone—playing, just before a nap, and so on.

It should be noted again that many times the correct type of training described is to some extent given by some parents even though they do not realize how they are influencing the child's learning, or indeed, what the principles of learning are that are involved. That is, as one example, the parent whose child says a word but with poor pronunciation is less likely to attend to the child than if the word is said precisely. After all, the parent behaves according to lawful principles also. Thus, most parents do not withhold the drink of water on purpose when the child's word response is unclear, and only give water for the better pronunciation. However, the same effect is achieved when, because of his own training, the parent can respond more quickly to the better speech responses of his child. It may be suggested here, nevertheless, that although this training may be given naturally by many parents, systematic use of the principles can hasten the development of the child's speech and improve its quality. Where the parent himself has had problems in training, the knowledge becomes indispensable.

At any rate, through this type of training and self-practice—and through the imitation learning yet to be discussed more fully—the child will come to acquire a basic behavioral repertoire of speech sounds. In linguistics these speech sounds are referred to as phonemes. The basic behavioral repertoire of phonemes will differ for various languages. The child, of course, ordinarily receives training in the phonemes of the language of his parents.

Once this phoneme repertoire has been acquired, the child is prepared to pronounce any word in his language. This is a complex repertoire to acquire. When it has been acquired, however, it sets the child up for much further learning, and the repertoire is significant to the child's adjustment in countless ways. The rapidity and quality of the development of this basic behavioral repertoire will depend upon the extent and quality of the learning experiences the child has. The next section will describe how the early language repertoire may be considered to be a constituent of the child's intelligence and affect his later intellectual learning.

In summary, it may be concluded that the child begins learning his speech repertoire at a very early age. When he has acquired a few word responses, or approximations, it is time for the child to begin learning the appropriate naming of various stimulus objects and events. The first few words learned will ordinarily be those of familiar objects and events in the child's environment. Many times the first naming responses are those made to the mother and father and other family members. Familiar toys may also be the controlling stimulus, as may be food, culinary implements, and so on. A later section will elaborate upon how the child's naming speech repertoire is expanded and how this important basic behavioral repertoire is involved in the complex intellectual performances involved in thinking and reasoning.

THE RUDIMENTARY NAMING REPERTOIRE AND EARLY INTELLIGENCE

This chapter has primarily indicated the learning process involved in early learning and the rudimentary speech repertoire that is acquired on the basis of this process. However, it is significant to indicate how even at this early level this basic behavioral repertoire is important to the child's adjustment. Furthermore, as we might expect, the repertoire is also one of those that is measured on intelligence tests for young children.

From the standpoint of the child, when he has acquired even a rudimentary single-word speech repertoire he is able to obtain objects and events that he wants (reinforcing objects and events) very readily. As examples, the child who can say "milk," "doll," "water," "look," "give," "take," "eat," "play," and so on may obtain these objects or events, or may obtain them more quickly, with less effort, than can a child who must employ gestures and nonspecific vocalizations such as whining and grunting. This word repertoire constitutes a general skill that involves a considerable amount of generalization. A child who has learned a number of word responses and who has learned also that such word responses are very effective (result in immediate reinforcement with little effort expenditure) is set up to learn new word responses to objects and events. It will be seen that such a child will now be much more amenable to training than is a child whose learning has not taken him to this level of behavioral advancement.

Thus, other things being equal, a child who has acquired this basic behavioral repertoire in comparison to another child who has not been subjected to the necessary training will have a more advanced adjustment and be a better language learner. It should thus be expected that intelligence tests would include items measuring the presence of this basic behavioral repertoire—and such is the case. The Stanford-Binet (Terman and Merrill, 1937) includes various items that measure the "naming" speech repertoire. At the two-year-level on this test, for example, the items that ask the child to point at various objects such as a button, a cup, a spoon, and so on actually involve this naming repertoire. This type of item has already been discussed as involving the verbal-motor repertoire (following instructions), but these items equally involve having learned to name the objects. It is only through such learning that the child can point to the correct object from among the several presented.

In addition, however, the young child is shown pictures of common objects and asked in each case, "What's this?" or "What do you call it?" (p. 77). The child must then name the picture correctly to make points toward his intelligence score. (Actually, naming pictures involves additional training to that of naming the actual objects, as discussed in Staats, 1968a. However, the manner and principle of learning these naming responses is the same as for naming objects and events.)

It is interesting to note that the central feature of the Peabody Intelligence Test is measuring the extent of the child's verbal naming repertiore. It is apparently possible to assess the general extent of the child's behavioral development by measuring this one basic behavioral repertoire. The fact that this can be done suggests that the quality of the parents' training of the child on this central language-intellectual skill is generally representative of the quality of the parents' training on the other aspects of the basic behavioral repertoires that are involved in what we call intelligence.

LEARNING TO LEARN: SIDE BENEFITS OF SPEECH TRAINING

It has already been suggested that the child becomes a better language learner after he has acquired a rudimentary speech repertoire. This type of acceleration in learning through learning has been well documented by the author with young children engaged in intellectual learning tasks (Staats, 1968a). This topic will thus be expanded in a later chapter. At this point, however, it is relevant to anticipate this discussion a bit in indicating some of the side benefits that accrue from the early conduct of speech training.

It should be pointed out that in this instance (and the other types of training situations discussed herein), in addition to the specific response being learned, the child is learning very important general responses to learning situations. That is, in this learning process he is faced with a problem situation, reward is delayed, a response of some effort is called for, the child makes the response, and he is rewarded. This type of training, as a consequence of the reward and the acquisition of a functional skill that enables later reward, produces in the child a positive orientation toward learning situations—a positive learning-work attitude—at a very beginning level. A child who has had this type of learning experience with gradually increased demands will not balk later at other learning situations—even training that is further extended in delay, effort, and complexity. On the other hand, the child who later avoids learning situations is the child who is abruptly introduced to learning situations that are beyond his skills and attentional repertoires, and who thus receives aversive stimulation in the learning situations rather than reward.

LANGUAGE PROBLEMS AND PERSONALITY
DISORDERS AND DEFICITS

Later discussions in the present book will deal more specifically with experiences that yield a child who does not learn to profit from learning circumstances, including not approaching learning situations with general behaviors that will result in learning. This topic will not be dealt with in any detail here. A few words will be said, however, in the context of the specific behaviors of concern to the present chapter. The brief discussion has an additional purpose of alerting the reader to the manner in which training in each of the basic behavioral repertoires being dealt with can be awry and can lead to deficits in the child's adjustive behaviors, or the acquisition of behaviors that are inappropriate and maladjustive.

The processes whereby the parent ordinarily provides experiences for the child which begin the child's speech learning have been introduced. The learning circumstances, however, are not always so benign. Sometimes, for example, with the best motives and intentions, the parent may not gradually reinforce better and better speech in his child. Sometimes the parent may become familiar with the child's idiosyncratic speech and continue to respond to it in the same manner as to appropriate speech, with no systematic endeavor to train the child to gradual improvement. Such an example is given by the parent who indiscriminately, let us say, continues to reward the child for saying "wah-wah" with no training trials where the reward is delayed until the child repeats the word. The parent may also continue to model his speech after the child's. If the parent thinks the child's response is cute and gives it special social reinforcement, the speech response will be well learned. When this type of training is widespread, the child may generally acquire baby talk as a strongly learned type of behavior, and the baby talk may persist far past the usual time for children.

A more severe form of defective training may take place with the parent who is oversolicitous and who attempts to meet every need of the child as quickly as it arises, and who believes that the biological development of the child takes care of his behavioral advancement—as long as the child's needs are met. To begin this example, it will help to realize that the parent can learn to "anticipate" the child's needs a great deal. That is, the parent knows when the child should be hungry, thirsty, when he needs to sleep and so on. Moreover, the parent can see what the child wants (that is, what objects and events are reinforcing for him). It is thus possible to provide these reinforcing objects and events to the child on the basis of the knowledge of the child's condition as well the indications provided by the child's motor behavior of trying to get such objects or events. The parent may also be oriented toward finding out what it is the child wants and immediately giving it to the child, without any attempt to use the situation as a learning experience.

It has been said that important language learning can take place when the parent sees the child trying to get something. The parent then says, "Can you say . . . ?" and then names the object and waits for the child to try to repeat the word. When the child has made an approximation, the child is reinforced for the attempt by receiving the object. Let us say, however, that the parent behaves quite differently. Let us say that he systematically gives the child what he is striving for, without the language training. Let us say, moreover, that the parent attempts to improve his own ability to sense what it is the child wants. The parent may then begin to respond to the child's grunts, whines, tugs, gesticulations, and so on.

If the child is given reinforcing objects and events when he has pointed to an object, tried to reach it, tugged at the parent, whined, grunted, and so on, then that is what he will learn. Actually, a child can learn such a repertoire to a high level of skill. And he can learn this repertoire of skills in great persistence and generality.

Moreover, at the beginning it is less of an effort to the parent and to the child for the parent to generally sense the child's "wants" and to provide the child immediately with the reinforcing events involved—without first providing a speech-learning trial. To conduct a speech-learning trial requires more time and effort than simply handing an object to the child, especially in the beginning. However, this is a case of being penny wise and pound foolish. The child who does not develop speech and instead develops non-language behaviors for obtaining things will shortly become a much greater responsibility to the parent—and the child himself will eventually have to expend more effort to obtain his wants, in a less effective manner.

Even worse, the child who acquires the nonverbal repertoires mentioned will have strongly learned "skills" that interfere with his further language-intellectual learning. That is, once the grunting-gesticulating repertoire has been developed, it is more effective than the child's undeveloped speech. Training must then require that he abandon a more effective response for one that is at first less effective because it requires more effort. Many children have serious problems of language development because their parents have not introduced training at an early level—training by which the child will advance in speech precision and in the control of speech by the necessary stimulus objects, events, and people.

To continue, once the child has acquired the maladjustive nonverbal repertoire described, the situation is set for acquiring additional behaviors that interfere with learning. That is, after the child has developed the "tugging-gesticulating-grunting" behaviors, the parent may try to train him to a better repertoire. For example, the parent may see the child is trying to obtain a piece of fruit. Let us say that at this time he says, "Banana, say banana." If the child does not attempt the vocal response but continues his other more primitive responses with greater insistence and intensity, and the parent is forced to reward the child, the child will have learned how to actively avoid the learning situation. On repeated learning experiences of this sort the child may acquire a new repertoire of skills that gets him what he wants through more extreme types of behavior. If a great deal of this experience occurs, the child will indeed become a very difficult learning problem and have some behaviors that in their undesirability and extreme quality will be considered abnormal.

Moreover, when the grunting and gesticulating continue past a certain age, the child will come to be considered "abnormal" by the parents and others. Once this occurs it is more likely that the child will not receive appropriate training, but instead will continue to be treated in a manner that will enhance the "abnormal" behavior. It is suggested this type of history is involved in such disorders as childhood autism where the child has no speech.

Perhaps the foregoing indicates that the parent has an important role to play in the child's development of speech through training. In most cases this training takes place informally and the parent is not even aware of the fact that he is providing the training. Even in these cases, however, an understanding of the principles involved and systematic application of the principles and training possibilities could increase the child's rate and quality of speech development, in what is an important aspect of intelligence. With the parent who would not ordinarily present the necessary training, or who might even present the "tugging-gesticulating-grunting" training, knowledge of these aspects of child learning is essential. Any practicing pediatrician, child psychologist, and so on will encounter these and other difficulties of child training frequently and should be prepared to provide the parent with the necessary information and specific direction on how to conduct the child's learning of speech.

A CASE OF RETARDED
SPEECH DEVELOPMENT

As will be described later, it is the author's contention that problems of behavior development should be prevented by providing appropriate child training. The preceding section, however, indicated that the present principles and procedures, and methods of analysis, do apply to cases of speech pathology and problems of language-intelligence development. From time to time in the book there will be examples of how the learning conception may be employed to understand and deal with behavior problems. This may be enhanced in the present context by referral to a problem of language development and to the type of pediatric advice usually given to the parent.

Question: My 2½-year-old son doesn't talk much. He says only a few words like "mama," "dada," "bye bye," yet he understands everything I tell him.

I took him to the doctor who said, "There's nothing wrong with him as long as he understands and hears. He's just a little slow."

Since my two older boys were saying more words when they were his age, I'm worried. I would appreciate any help you can give me.—A worried mother

Answer: Have your child checked by an ear, nose and throat specialist and/or your local speech and hearing center.

Although many children with normal hearing may not talk as soon as the average child, I feel it's important to have a slow-talking child's hearing carefully checked.

Evaluating the hearing of a young child isn't easy, but it can be done by people experienced in this field (Crook, 1970, p. D-2).

This example was taken not only for the problem involved, but also to indicate the very general deficiency in medical information concerning learning principles, the conditions of learning required for normal child development, and the parents' needs for taking an active training role in dealing with either normal or problem child development. This deficiency resides as well in the other professions consulted by parents for help. As a consequence, the parent with a special problem is left ordinarily in a state of ignorance. To add to the problem, it is usually felt that there must be organic-mental reasons underlying the child's failure to develop normally. In the present case the first suggestion in this direction is that the child may have a sensory (hearing) deficit—even though he responds very well to speech stimuli. The next suggestion, already implicit in the mother's fears and explicit in the first physician's response, is that the child is slow— a euphemism for the terms *retarded,* or *abnormal.*

Acceptance of the conclusion that the child suffers from some organic-mental deficiency may have the effect of heightening the difficulty. For the "sick" child is given special treatment. The same things are not expected of him as of normal children. This can mean that deficient training methods will be provided, such as those already described, and that greater demands will not be made upon him. Frequently, the parent will avoid putting the child in learning situations because in the past, due to the child's lack of preparation, the child has failed to learn, which has been painful to parent and child. The parent who has been told (or suspects) the child is "retarded" may also avoid doing anything that gives evidence of poor learning ability, which again means the parent does not put the child in learning situations.

The present case illustrates clearly a situation where the parents need to know of the various aspects of language: how these aspects of language are learned, and of the good learning conditions that can be provided that will result in the child learning those basic behavioral repertoires. In many cases a child with very slow language development who does not receive the type of treatment he needs will continue to be slow. Later, he will be diagnosed as mentally retarded or as having a learning disability. The information that is important in such a case is that which will prevent the child's continued retardation because of deficits in learning.

The present case is probably one where the training opportunities for the child have not been totally absent, but have not been sufficient. The child has acquired some speech responses, and he also has acquired behaviors under the control of speech stimuli (speech comprehension). In the realm of the child's slow development of speech, the parents and the other members of the family are probably not providing the training opportunities discussed in the previous sections. For very innocuous reasons, this can easily happen in a family. In the case of a youngest child among several siblings, as in the present case, the child may receive deficient speech training since the parent, who now has two other children, does not spend as much time with the youngest child as she did with the others. Fewer training opportunities are thus provided. Also, the older siblings may, to a large extent, take care of the child and they may not provide the speech training experiences necessary to normal development, as most adults would. Or, the child may have had some type of illness so that members of the family try to treat him tenderly, which means they anticipate his needs and never provide training trials for him. Or, as already described, the child may have been inadvertently trained to the grunting, gesticulating repertoire which enables him to get what he wants without speaking. Treatment of the case of retarded speech development would require information from the parent concerning these various possibilities. And treatment would require providing information to the parent concerning the learning involved as well as the procedures by which the training could be conducted.

CONCLUSIONS

Language is common in all of our lives. Anyone reading this book will have well-acquired language skills. The acquisition process will ordinarily have occurred in the informal interactions of parent and child—not in a formal learning situation that calls for long-sustained attention and participation. Language training is distributed throughout the day in the usual parent-child relationship. It is thus not experienced as work, or as a learning task that was of any difficulty.

It may be suggested here, however, that the commonness of language and its seeming automatic appearance should not delude us. Language, both "active" and "receptive," is of central importance to human behavior. Language is involved in every action that we make, in our values, interests, all personality traits. Additionally, language is central to what we call intelligence or the individual's intellectual quality. Lay people interested in human behaviors ordinarily focus upon "glamorous" types of behavior that intrigue them because of their uncommonness. Thus, popular accounts tend to be concerned with abnormal and bizarre behaviors, hypnosis, supposed extrasensory perceptions and other "wondrous" workings of the "mind," extraordinary talents, and so on.

On the contrary, our interest should be the study of behaviors that are crucially significant to human adjustment. Language is such an area of human behavior. It is thus wise to indicate how important language repertoires are to human behavior—how the child's later adjustment and success in life will be importantly affected by his early and continued language learning. The preceding sections have shown that what we call intelligence is actually composed of such language skills as are being described. Succeeding discussions will continue to demonstrate that various aspects of "common" language learning are basic constituents of our intellectuality as well as other aspects of personality.

chapter 6 / Imitation Learning and Learning Through Imitation

The processes of speech learning that have been described so far are relatively long and drawn out, involving many learning trials for each response that is learned. If the child had to acquire his total speech vocabulary by these processes, it would require an enormous amount of time and an immense amount of training. Fortunately, there are learning mechanisms that short-circuit these processes. An important one in the area of language learning, as in other aspects of behavior development, is that of imitation. The child acquires much of his speech skill as well as other social and sensory-motor skills on the basis of imitational learning.

It should be noted that while learning through imitation produces much of the child's behavioral advancement, the skills of imitation are themselves learned, as has already been briefly described. Furthermore, the plural "skills" is used because imitation involves more than one type of learning and one repertoire. This point requires emphasis because of current conceptions of learning through imitation that are erroneous. That is, it is frequently thought that the child has an innate tendency to imitate. However, many children do not imitate and do not learn the behavioral skills other children acquire through imitation. As with other complex human behaviors, moreover, there is no indication that imitation skills are biologically determined. Some investigators (such as Bandura, 1962), although nominally employing learning approaches, have actually treated imitation skills as givens—or basic—in the child. However, the skills that constitute imitation must be made explicit, as is also necessary for the manner in which these skills are learned. Only in this way can one devise methods for producing desirable imitation skills in children, as well as methods for using the child's imitation skills in producing learning of other types in the child.

Imitation consists of several types of learning. And imitation skills play various roles in the child's general behavior development. For example, the child's imitation is selective; that is, through learning children come to imitate certain things and not others. Moreover, they will learn imitation to varying degrees of skill. The manner in which imitation is learned and some of the ways imitation functions in further learning are thus important topics for understanding the behavioral development of children. This chapter will describe several aspects of the imitational skill acquisition, beginning with elaboration of the imitation learning already briefly mentioned in first speech development.

REWARD VALUE
OF IMITATION

Basic to the action of imitation of the adult by the child is the acquisition of reward value of the adult for the child. Simply stated, if the adult as a complex stimulus acquires reward value for the child, then it will be reinforcing if the child does something like the adult—if he imitates the adult. Thus, the learning of imitational skills first depends upon the stimuli of the adult becoming rewarding. As has been indicated already, the stimuli of the parent become rewarding because they are paired with other rewarding circumstances that occur when the parent is present.

It has been stated that because of the fact that the parent's voice becomes rewarding to the child, he gradually learns to make sounds like that of the parent. These are imitative behaviors. In addition to the speech sounds of the parent, it would be expected that his other stimuli would also become rewarding. Thus, at a later age we see that the child finds it rewarding to dress like the parent. There is no special reason that clothes the parent wears should be rewarding for the child except through the process described. We will also see that the child will find it rewarding to mimic the parent's mannerisms in various ways and to do various things like the parent.

It would be expected that the child would learn many imitational behaviors in this manner. However, the present section is concerned with the motivational (reward) properties of imitation, and it is important to indicate that there are additional ways that imitational stimuli become reinforcing. That is, the child ordinarily receives specific (if informal) training experiences that also contribute to making imitation of the parent rewarding. In describing this it is relevant to indicate that the imitation response in any case results in the production of a stimulus circumstance by the child that is like the stimulus produced by the parent. This may be taken as a definition of an imitation or matching response. It is when the child's stimulus matches that of the parent (or other child or adult) that we say the child has imitated.

The child will have many experiences when he is reinforced after producing such matching, or imitational, behavior. To illustrate, the child will be told by the parent, "Do it like I do," and so on, and be rewarded to the extent that he produces a good match of the parent's behavior. The child will be told, "Sit up at the table like so and so does," and he will be rewarded if his behavior is like that of an older brother or sister. The child will be told to comb his hair like . . . , brush his teeth like . . . , not cry like . . . , and to perform many other imitative acts. Each time the child is reinforced when his behavior or other attributes match those of another person, this will have the effect of making such matching or imitational events (stimuli) into rewards. (See Baer and Sherman, 1967; Staats, 1963, 1968a.)

It would be expected that the extent to which the child is rewarded when he has produced such imitational stimuli will determine in part the extent to which the child will find imitation reinforcing. The parent may in his interactions with the child arrange (usually informally) many such training experiences or, conversely, relatively few. The extent to which the child will learn through imitation will in part be determined by how much reward value imitational stimuli have for the child. Other things being equal, the more reward value imitational events have for the child, the more he will learn through imitation.

The foregoing thus suggests the manner in which it becomes rewarding for the child to learn to imitate. A child who has a deficit in this type of training, and thus a deficit in imitation motivation, will not learn as developed an imitation repertoire as the child who has had more such experience.

Actually, the child may in certain cases even learn to do the *opposite* of what someone else does. Then, in many situations that call for imitation, rather than learning appropriate behaviors he may learn the opposite. A moment may be spent in describing a learning situation that could produce such a "negativistic" child. Let us take the case where the child has sparse experience in which he is rewarded for doing something like the parent. Rather, it is when the child *refuses* to do something like the parent that he receives much social reward in the form of the parent coaxing and wheedling the child to perform the action. Such training conditions, inadvertently conducted, can lead in many circumstances to a deficit in imitation reward for the child as well as the learning of obstinate, or negative imitation repertoires.

One other general problem of imitation motivation may be mentioned here. Ordinarily, although at first imitation of both parents will be equally rewarding (depending of course upon the child's experience), after a certain age it is our custom to discourage the child from imitating to the same degree the parent of the opposite sex—at least in certain areas of behavior. The child will continue to be rewarded for imitating the same-sex parent in a wider number of behaviors than in the opposite-sex parent, and conversely punishment in the form of social disproval will follow "incorrect" imitation of the opposite-sex parent. This can be expected to ordinarily affect the imitational motivation of the child along sex lines. Where such differential training does not occur in some form, the child may not demonstrate the desirable differentiation in motivation.

In summary, it has been the purpose of this section to indicate more fully that the child learns the skills of imitation at the beginning to a large extent because the behaviors of the parent become reinforcing. Behaviors of the child that imitate the parent are thereby also reinforcing, and are thus learned. In addition, the child also comes to find imitating—attempting to match the stimuli of his behavior to the stimuli of someone else's behavior—to also be reinforcing through direct experience. This occurs when the child has been reinforced many times for imitating. We will then see that the child will strive to imitate others simply for the reward value involved in making the imitation.

It may be added that the parent thus affects his child's imitation learning in these two ways. That is, if the parent has many interactions where he as a complex stimulus (his voice, appearance, and so on) is paired with rewarding stimuli, he will become a rewarding stimulus himself. The child will thus find imitating him rewarding. Moreover, if the parent rewards the child for imitating him and others, the child will learn that matching his behavior to that of someone else is rewarding. Ordinarily, these things occur in the informal parent-child interaction. However, this is not universal, and it is important to understand the principles involved in the child's first learning of basic imitational motivation. The actual skills of imitation that are learned must also be explicated, for many of these require direct training. The next section will deal with this topic.

ATTENTION AND IMITATION

In addition to the learning of imitational motivation, the child also must learn specific skills of imitation—as has been implied in some of the fore-going discussions. There are several items important to consider concerning the actual motor skills of imitation as well as the circumstances that control imitation responses in the child.

The usual conception of imitation is that it is due to a basic propensity of "human nature," not that imitation is learned. One of the errors that derives from the "human-nature" conception of imitation is the expectation that imitation should occur automatically. Actually, in order for imitation to take place, the child at a very basic level must have attentional skills that result in the child seeing (or hearing, and so on) the stimulus to be imitated. These observational skills are themselves acquired through learning, and constitute a topic with which to begin the discussion.

An important aspect of the imitation repertoire is that the child look at the actions of other people and the stimulus events that are controlling those actions. Some children when in a situation where their own behavior is not controlled by the situation—for example, problem situations where the child has no learned responses that produce a satisfactory result—will look at the ways that others behave. These attentional responses are basic to learning through imitation, for in such a situation if there is someone else who has learned a response the child will then observe (see, hear, touch, or what have you) the response.

Thus, basic to the imitational repertoire are the attentional behaviors that allow the child to sense the actions of another individual, as well as the relevant stimuli that are controlling the individual's behavior. Two children can be in the same situation where someone else performs a desirable response. Yet the two may profit differently, because one has closely observed the action and the controlling stimuli for the action while the other child has not.

The fact is that we learn to observe other people's behaviors when we have had the training to do so. This may occur in many, many parent-child interactions, as well as in interactions the child has with others. A child may be instructed, for example, to "watch how I do it." This can be done in great detail, with the trainer drawing the attention of the child to the relevant stimuli, as well as to the stimulus events of his own behavior. A child who has had a rich experience of this kind—where he observes and imitates and is then reinforced when he behaves in kind—will acquire a rich attentional repertoire for observing other people's behavior, as well as a rich imitational repertoire.

For example the child in class who watches the teacher closely as she performs actions which the children in class are later to perform, and also pays attention to the stimulus objects she manipulates, and so on, will learn rapidly. The child who does not have this repertoire of attentional behaviors will not even observe what has occurred, let alone be able to imitate the action. Other things being equal, the second child will not learn as rapidly. In addition, of course, as will be discussed, the child must have learned the actual imitational repertoire that is involved. That is, in this example the child must to some extent be able to repeat what the teacher has written, said, or done, for the learning to be complete.

It should be noted that in many cases the first step in imitating a behavior that is different from one that we have in our own repertoire may be to first discriminate the difference. As one example, before we can imitate a spoken dialect that is slightly different from our own, we must be able to discriminate the dialect—be able to respond to it differentially. This again involves close attentional behaviors, of the type described in Chapter 9. The extent to which the child can discriminate stimuli that are similar will depend upon the extent to which he has been presented with the different stimuli and has learned to respond differently to them. Once an individual has discriminated two types of dialects, for example, or other sets of like responses, he can practice the speech that is different from his own and learn to make imitational responses that match the new dialect. The reinforcement for this learning is provided when a sound is produced that matches or imitates the new dialect.

It may be added here, however, that we can *overlearn* the imitation repertoire. Or we may not learn other skills that should later replace the imitational repertoire in many situations. To illustrate, in addition to learning to imitate, the child must also learn to work things out by himself so that he does not have to depend to too great an extent upon the cues provided by other people's behavior. And he must also be trained to imitate selectively.

For example, he should imitate some people, but other people should not control his imitation behavior. Moreover, some situations should control his imitational repertoire—but not others. Thus, during an examination, imitational (copying) behavior in a child is not ordinarily rewarded. Examples will be given later of ways in which the child learns appropriate nonimitational behaviors. This point is added as a qualifier to indicate that the child cannot be trained only to imitate, to the exclusion of learning the other basic behavioral repertoires essential to the child's adjustment and further learning.

THE SENSORY-MOTOR
SKILLS OF IMITATION

It should be apparent that there are motor skills involved in an imitation repertoire. When we say that a child has imitated someone or something, we mean he has done something that produces a stimulus that matches a stimulus made by someone else. This is true whether the child dresses like someone, copies a letter like someone, makes a construction of blocks like someone, sings like someone, says a word like someone, or whatever. The next chapter will deal specifically with the manner in which the child learns language through imitation. The present section will describe several examples of learning imitation skills that do not involve speech on the part of the child. Learning of imitation repertoires has not been generally studied.

It is interesting to demonstrate how a child develops any set of skills, and this is also the case with imitation skills. For example, it can easily be seen that a three-year-old child simply has not learned the motor skills required to imitate many actions, even when his attention can be directed to the relevant stimuli and he attempts the imitational response. As an illustration, the parent may ask such a child to "look to the side" while keeping his head pointed straight ahead. The parent may act as the model and demonstrate the response. The child can look at the parent, and attempt to make the response, but he will ordinarily fail to perform the imitation. Although the response is in the child's repertoire, the response is ordinarily only under the control of an object that moves across his visual field—not under the control of the verbal instructions to imitate and the sight of the parent as the imitation stimulus. Later on, children ordinarily learn to make such responses quite readily under the control of these stimuli.

Another example can be given where the thing that prevents the child's imitation is the lack of the response itself, not the absence of the control of the response by the imitation stimulus. That is, the parent may ask the three-year-old child to imitate him in closing one eye, but one eye only. The instructions and the parent-model will ordinarily control the child's behavior of attempting the response. But a young child of that age is unlikely to have learned the response involved in the imitation. He cannot close one eye without closing the other—or he will only be able to imitate the response very grossly (ordinarily in a very amusing way).

Again, the first example was given to illustrate the point that imitation skills involve learning the stimulus control of the behavior as well as the particular behavioral skill involved. The child may have learned the imitation behavior, without the behavior having been learned as a response to an imitation stimulus (the instructions to imitate as well as the stimulus of the model). Or, as the second example shows, the child may simply not have learned the necessary imitation response. If the response is a complex skill, extended training may be involved in its acquisition, as will be shown in the next example. The example will also show the extended training that may be necessary to bring the imitation response under the control of the imitation stimulus.

A good illustration of the learning of the sensory-motor skills of imitation may be taken from some of the research the author has done on the intellectual learning of preschool children. The particular imitation skill in this example is that of copying letters. The training involved procedures for producing the individual motor skills of writing each individual letter. Moreover, the training involved bringing the imitation letter-writing skills under the control of varying stimuli. The child first began by learning to imitate (copy) lines by tracing upon the lines. He then learned in each case the motor response of writing the letters under the control of the tracing (imitational) stimulus. Then the child had training in imitating the letter stimulus—not in tracing on top of it, but rather below it. This began with a largely drawn letter as the imitation stimulus. The size of the letter imitation stimulus was then reduced gradually in three stages to primary-size type. When the child had learned to make such imitation (copying) responses, this skill was employed in further training in which the child learned to write letters under the control of orally given instructions—and finally under the control of his own self-instructional stimuli. (In this latter part of the training the child was learning the types of verbal-motor units discussed in Chapter 3. It may be briefly noted here, as a subject for later discussion, that the imitation letter-writing responses the child learned in this training were thus basic to the learning of a more advanced repertoire—that of writing letters on command, self-given or otherwise.)

This type of learning will be illustrated by showing the results of the training for two children. The first child was a four-year-old, culturally deprived boy with an IQ of 89. His results are shown in Figure 1. The actual time of training involved in the learning of the complex imitational skills was a total of seventeen hours and eighteen minutes, during which time the child had 929 learning trials, most of them involving writing multiple letter sequences. In this training the child learned to imitate (copy) the letters from a through u, as well as to write them under the control of the trainer's or his own instructions. The training sessions averaged five to eight minutes in length. In this training a system of rewards was employed in which each response the child made was reinforced with a token. The child could then exchange the tokens for things that he wanted. Under ordinary circumstances the attention and participation of a four-year-old child in arduous, repetitive, and massed learning trials would not be possible. In the present procedures, with adequate reinforcement for learning, the training progressed smoothly. The present results also demonstrate the importance of reward in learning.

Figure 1 shows samples of the child's copying of a model letter (or letters), as the child produced them over the period of training. The samples are numbered in the order of occurrence. The first response was obtained by asking the child to write his name, or any letters that he knew. Then the child was introduced to tracing and copying experience with lines and circles as the models. After 185 of these training trials he was tracing as shown in response number 2. The child's first copying of a large a is shown in number 4 (response number 216), and the first copying of a primary-size a is shown in number 5 (response number 370). (These two responses, and others, are starred to indicate they were reduced in size by one-half in comparison to the others.) Number 6 in Figure 1 shows the child's first attempt to write a letter with no imitation stimulus—solely under the control of the trainer's oral instructions to "write an a." In the procedure, when the child had learned to copy and to write one letter, a new one was added and he received training on the new letter itself for a few trials. Then he would receive training on copying and writing all the letters in sequence. Increase in the child's imitational and letter-writing skills can be seen by selecting for presentation a sample of his writing trials where a new letter has just been added to the sequence of letters he has already learned to copy and write in series. Imitational trials where the child is copying the sequence with one new letter added are shown in samples 7, 9, 11, 13, and 15. At these points the child had received respectively 407, 527, 595, 631, and 788 training trials.

Thus, each sample shown which involves a letter model to be copied represents an imitational learning trial. Moreover, the record illustrates the development of these complex sensory-motor imitational skills. When the child began the training program, his imitational skills or copying were very primitive. Even after 216 training trials, as shown in sample 4, his copying of a medium-size a was poor. When the stimulus model was then reduced in size it did not elicit a skilled imitation writing response from the child. In fact, under the condition where the model stimulus was small and additional letters were introduced, the child's imitational writing behavior deteriorated. Further training, however, yielded improvement. By sample number 11, response 595, the child's imitational writing showed great improvement in skill, and this was increased in later learning. At the end of the training, which actually involved a short period of time but many learning trials, this culturally deprived child who would ordinarily be considered as retarded—and a very difficult educational problem—had acquired the cognitive skills of writing imitation and the ability to read and write the letters in advance of normal middle-class children of his age.

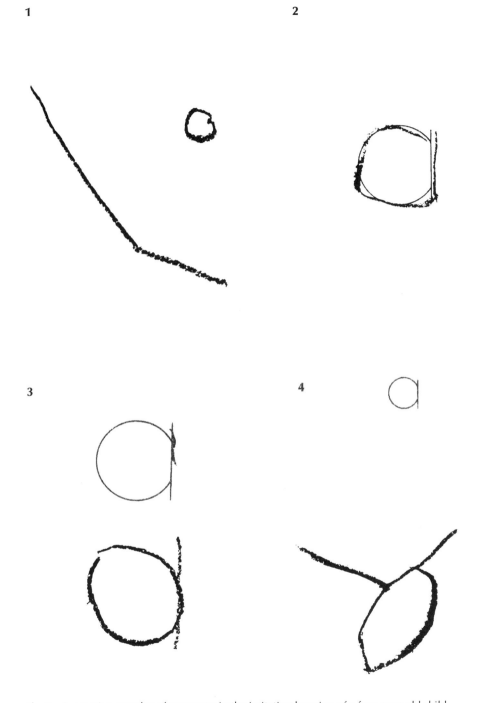

Fig. 1 Successive samples of responses in the imitation learning of a four-year-old child, IQ 89. In the training process the child learned to copy letters of the alphabet and to write them on verbal request.

*5

*6

*7

*8

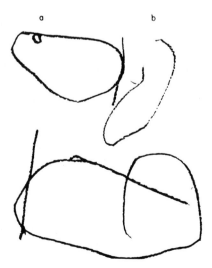

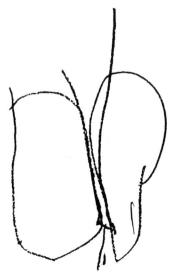

9

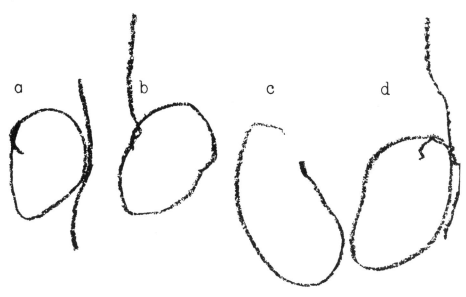

10

11

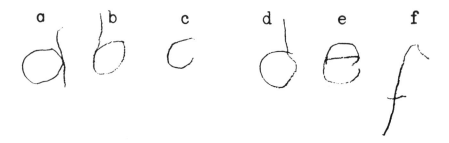

a   b   c   d   e   f

*12

13

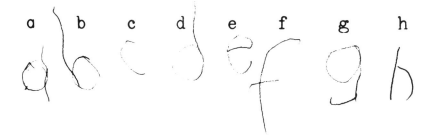

14

15

16

17

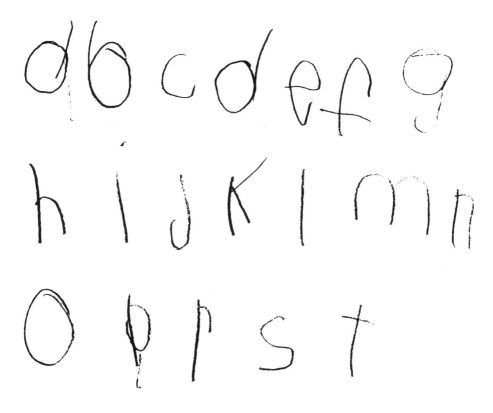

This training was conducted on the basis of the learning principles that have been described herein, as will be presented in detail in a later work.

It should be noted that the training in the imitational writing skills also produced advances in free writing where there was no model to copy. Illustration of the child's growing ability to write leters under this condition, controlled at first by the trainer's letter-naming instructions and later by the child's self-instructions, is given in samples 8, 10, 12, and 16. These represented trials 419, 533, 599, 640, and 792. These samples were taken in each case within a few training trials of the just preceding copying trial. It may be added that the child was also trained to read the letters in the process of learning (see Staats, 1968a).

The results for another child—with an IQ of 130—are shown in Figure 2. As can be seen, the process of learning is very much the same for these children, in the same training procedures. This occurred even though these children would ordinarily be considered as markedly different in terms of learning ability. The time of training for the latter child was sixteen hours and forty-three minutes, during which time this child learned to imitate in writing and to write under verbal instructions the letters a through w. The child with the IQ of 89—a difference of forty-one intelligence points— learned a through u in seventeen hours and eighteen minutes. These and other results that will be treated later indicate that under appropriate learning conditions, children generally appear to learn rapidly, without the large differences we generally attribute to some inner personal quality that we term intelligence. It may be noted also that the training was conducted by a person not previously experienced in training young children in intellectual skills.

The major point in the present context, however, is to suggest that imitation skills are sensory-motor skills learned according to the same principles as other sensory-motor skills. Although the child has at first little skill in producing a particular motor behavior under the control of some imitational stimulus, if he receives training in doing this, where the responses are rewarded and thus maintained, he will acquire the sensory-motor imitational skill. As these two children's learning results illustrate, many learning trials must be involved in learning an imitational repertoire that includes complex sensory-motor skills. If we wish the child to display the imitation repertoire, we must ensure that the child has the necessary training. Actually, the child must have training in many different areas of imitational skills if he is to learn readily and rapidly in various situations.

LEARNING TO LEARN
TO IMITATE

The results of the research with the imitation learning of preschool children has a good deal of additional significance that should be stipulated. One of the important considerations in the present context is that the child in

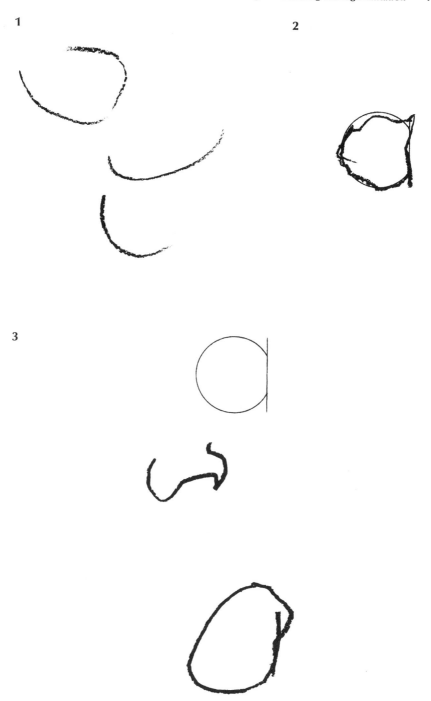

Fig. 2   Successive samples of responses in the imitation learning of a four-year-old child, IQ 130. In the training process the child learned to copy letters of the alphabet and to write them on verbal request.

4

5

6

7

a   b

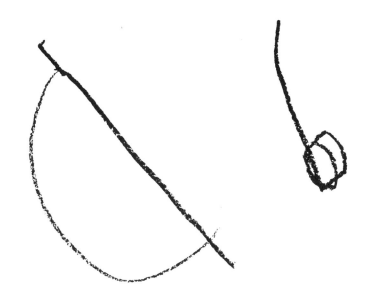

8

*9   *10

11

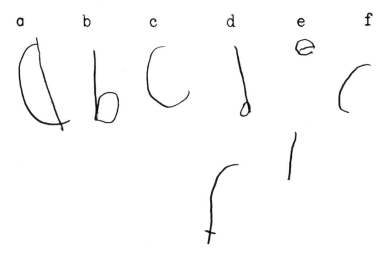

12

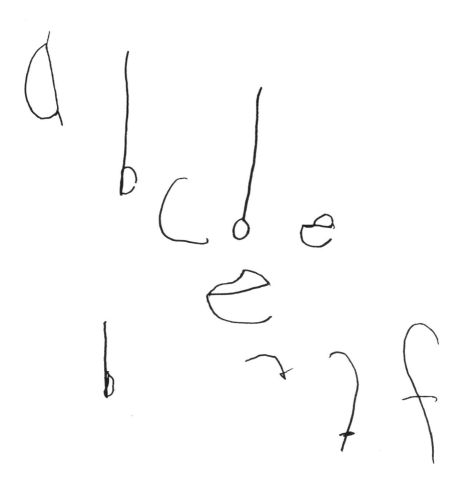

13

a   b   c   d   e   f   g   h

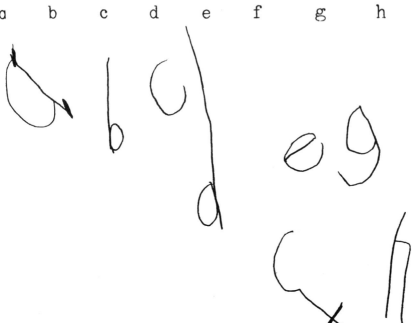

14

15

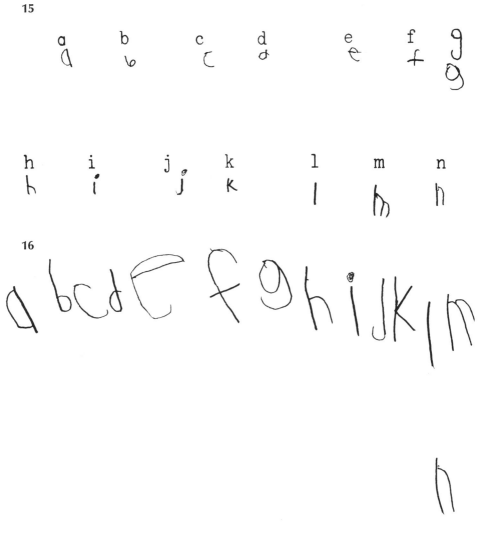

each case was learning things that had a great deal of generality. He was not only learning to imitate things for which he received specific training, but he was also learning something that allowed him to perform better when presented with new imitational learning tasks.

Thus, as has been described thus far, the acquisition of an imitational behavior requires a good deal of training and consequently a long period for its development. Later on, however, we see that the child will be able to imitate new things on one presentation, or at most a few—in tasks where the child has never been asked to imitate before. This fact can erroneously give the impression that surely some internal, general imitation capacity must be involved. However, there are several learned mechanisms involved in this process of acquiring general imitation skills.

First, in the process of learning to imitate a model, as well as in other types of training, the child learns skilled behavioral *units*. Thus, at first it was difficult for the children in the writing training merely to hold a pencil properly. (For this reason the training actually began with crayons.) Moreover, there are general skills in being able to make under verbal demand straight and curved lines, and so on. Once these skills have been acquired, however, they can easily be brought under the control of new stimuli. Thus, the child in being trained to copy single letters is also learning general motor skills that will be available when he is presented with the task of copying a new letter, or imitating any visual stimulus through copying.

In addition, of course, in the process the child was acquiring a number of attentional skills. The child had many training trials in which he had to look at the model stimulus and then at the stimulus he had produced. In the procedures when he was trained to compare two stimuli, the model and the one he had written, he was developing attentional and discrimination skills that would generalize to many new instances.

Furthermore, the child was receiving training in having his behavior controlled by a model. He was being trained in general to attempt in appropriate situations to match his behavior to someone else's. When he was reinforced for this, the imitation (matching) would also become rewarding as has been described, and in addition the model stimuli would come to acquire the ability to elicit imitation attempts on the part of the child. An important part of this process also involved the child's learning to respond to the verbal instructions to imitate. That is, the child was told to "make an a like this one," and so on, and was reinforced for doing so. This had the effect of bringing the child's imitational behaviors under the control of the appropriate verbal instructions to do something like so and so. The children's increase of skill in this respect, through their training, was very evident.

It is because of these general imitation repertoires that the child who is properly trained will come to be able to imitate in new circumstances, with new responses on which he has had no training. One of the reasons the findings with the training of preschool children to copy letters was introduced was because the research showed clearly how imitation training produces such general imitation skills that transfer to new tasks. This characteristic was shown by the fact that there was a strong acceleration in the rate of learning the imitation skills of copying. That is, the author tabulated the results for twelve culturally deprived four-year-olds subjected to the writing imitation training and found that it took an average of 288 training trials for the child to learn the first four letters with which he was presented. The last four letters he learned, however, required only 76 training trials. The children were learning four times as rapidly after the training as they had at the beginning. This occurred within the brief training process described, which lasted an average of fifteen hours and forty-two minutes for twelve children. Actually, the children's performance indicated they could copy newly introduced letters much better as the training progressed—as may be seen by scrutinizing the last letter in each sequence, which was a first trial on that particular letter. It would be expected that if this type of training had continued, the children's imitation skills would have approached the point where a new letter, or some other stimulus of that type, could have been imitated precisely on the very first trial. If one compared the child who had had that training with one of the same age who had not, one would get the strong impression that there must be something truly different about the children's internal "imitational abilities."

It would seem that if a child was trained in some complex imitational skills over an extended period of time that unusually fine imitation skills would result. Thus, imitation—whether in writing, artistry, mimicry, or the general imitation skills necessary in various aspects of child learning—is not a given, a proclivity inborn in the child. Rather, imitation consists of skills that must be developed in long-term learning processes. These ordinarily take place in informal circumstances, which have not been generally observed and of which most people, including most specialists, have been ignorant. When the learning process is made explicit, however, the tuition that must be involved becomes clear.

It may help to indicate a few other examples of high-level human sensory-motor skills that appear to depend upon the prior acquisition of advanced imitation repertoires. For example, a trained dancer can quickly learn a new dance step by watching a model—in a manner the ordinary person cannot even approach. This is because the trained dancer has the skilled imitative motor responses in her repertoire. In addition, she has learned attentional and discrimination skills so that she may more closely observe what the model has done. Furthermore, she has verbal responses that she can use in describing the model and later use the same verbal responses to help direct her own imitation. It may be noted that this later ability depends upon two of the basic behavioral repertoires already described. That is, the skill of describing (naming or labeling) complex stimuli is involved in this type of imitation, and the dancer must have learned complex verbal-motor units if her own verbal description is to control her imitative dancing responses.

Another type of complex human skill (or talent) dependent upon the type of imitation described herein is that shown by the artist who duplicates with drawing implements some complex visual stimulus. It is suggested that the artist's copying skills are acquired in the same learning process demonstrated by the preschool children—only carried to a much finer point of skill. It should be noted, also, that once the artist has acquired his basic skills, he can reproduce (copy) stimuli that he sees for the first time. For him the imitational learning has "accelerated" to the point where little or no additional training is even necessary. The child, similarly, who has learned special imitation skills can learn new things in a better manner than a child who has not been so fortunate.

At any rate, it is suggested that the child ordinarily learns imitation units that will transfer to new instances. These units are the skills that enable the child to learn in many new situations in which his behavior has to imitate that of a model. Previous acquisiton of imitation skills is assumed in the schools. The teacher herself is the model in many training situations. For example, the teacher will write things on the board, and so on, and the child's task is to respond in kind. In addition, the child through his imitation repertoire will learn many things from other children. In each case, however, the child must have the necessary imitation repertoire.

ATTITUDES TOWARD (REWARD VALUE OF) MODELS AND IMITATION

As has been suggested, it is frequently thought that the child imitates because of his nature rather than through his learning. According to such a view the children would be expected to imitate other persons equally, without distinction. The fact is, of course, that our imitation of other people is quite selective. This is the case because there are learned mechanisms that determine when, whom, and in what circumstances we will imitate. One of the important mechanisms that is involved concerns the reward (attitudinal or emotional) value of the person who serves as the model to be imitated.

Actually the mechanism is quite complicated when it is described in detail, as are the learning principles involved (see Staats, 1968a). This can be simplified for the present purposes, however. Thus, let us say, that the child will ordinarily be rewarded many times when he imitates people who have high reward (attitude) value for him. As a consequence, his attitude toward (the reward value of) people will come to control imitational responses.

It is also the case that imitation behavior is apt to be rewarded more frequently and heavily when the model is a skilled person than one who is unskilled. This will have the effect of making evidence of skill have a positive attitudinal (reward) value for the child, as well as further emphasize the mechanism where positive reward value will control imitational behavior. For example, it would not be hard to see how, in primitive societies, the individual who was skilled in observation and swift of limb, who acquired the skills necessary in hunting, might become a "leader." If this individual continually returned from the hunt with game, whereas others failed, it might be expected that "imitation" of his behavior would soon be acquired. That is, in traveling with this person and using the same hunting techniques, the others in the group would also gain their ecological rewards and the pattern of following (imitating) this man would thus be rewarded. The behavior of the leader would in this process become a stimulus for further imitation.

We can see in everyday life the same process operating. When an adult or an older child makes a response of a certain type which is more skilled than that of the younger child, the younger child receives more reinforcement when he matches the behavior of the more skilled person than he would on his own. The little preschool boy, for example, who imitates and follows another boy who is more skilled in athletic prowess will be more highly rewarded than when he imitates the less skilled child. This is a general circumstance for imitation behavior. The circumstance is not restricted to imitation in children, but is also important for understanding social behavior in general.

The same type of development of leader-follower interaction also occurs in realms of intellectual skill. Again, imitation behavior is more strongly rewarded with highly valued people. That is, there are "status" or high-valued people whose intellectual conceptions when imitated result in more reward than when the statements of low-valued people are imitated. As a result, for example, we see that the child soon comes to repeat (imitate) the statements of more valued people to a greater extent. This continues throughout life; we are more likely to mold our statements after some high-valued person.

Negative Imitation

In general, through this and various other experiences, the attitude or reward value of social stimuli come to control the imitative and following behavior of the child. The stronger the reward value, the stronger the positive control over such behavior. It would also appear that the child learns, conversely, *not* to imitate some people and some types of actions, and so on. It may be suggested that one of the important mechanisms involved here is analogous to that just described, except rather than learning to imitate people with positive reward value, the mechanism involved is learning not to imitate when the person has negative attitude value. Nonimitating behavior may also involve negative imitation—that is, doing the opposite of what someone else has done. Thus, it is suggested that the child ordinarily receives training in which in the presence of nonrewarding models he is reinforced for nonimitating or negative imitating behavior.

For example, a young boy who as is customary has been admonished or teased (both punishing) for imitating girls will have less reward value for girls. In this process the boy will also have learned not to imitate girls, and more generally not to imitate people who elicit in him negative attitudes. The learning processes involved in this may be considered to be the same as those in the positive rewarding case—except the opposite in reward valued is involved, and the opposite type of imitation behavior is learned.

Thus, the negative reward value of a person ordinarily comes to strongly control negative imitation, or nonimitation, in the child. This type of basic behavoral repertoire is also important in what the individual will learn. For example, we depend upon this mechanism when we attempt to lower the reward value of a political candidate or movement by invective. By lowering the reward value we decrease the extent to which the candidate will be followed (imitated).

Manipulating Imitation
by Manipulating Social Attitudes

This analysis indicates that the reward value of other people (that is, the type and intensity of attitudes we have toward them) is an important variable that helps determine the extent to which the child will imitate people, and thus the extent and content of what the child will learn in many situations. For example, in the schoolroom if the teacher has a good deal of positive reward value for the child, the teacher's behavior will control imitational behavior in the child. The same is true for other children in the class. If for a particular child other able, hardworking, children have high reward value, then their behavior will be more highly imitated by the child. Anything that lessens the reward value of these able children will lessen the controlling effect they have in producing like behaviors in the child. On the other hand, if a group of rebellious, negligent students have a good deal of reward value for the child, he will imitate their behavior instead.

Once the mechanism has been learned by the child so that people who have positive reward value tend more to control his imitation, and those having negative reward value control negative imitation, then the extent of the child's imitation behavior is affected by the manipulation of the reward value of people. It is then not necessary that the imitator previously have had any direct experience with the particular model. The analysis thus indicates why celebrities, leaders, and so on are imitated even though the imitator has had no direct contact with the model. It may also be noted here that these effects of reward value on imitation can be manipulated by increasing or decreasing the reward value of the model—and this can be done in various ways. Reward value may be increased or decreased by words, for example, through communication procedures that will be described more fully later on.

An illustration is pertinent at this point, however, in the context of imitation. Let us say that the parent associates negative emotional words with able, hardworking students. He does this, let us say, because the child is having a difficult time in school and the parent, who has little value for education himself, attempts to provide solace for the child by saying such things as, "Those bookworms spend all their time studying, and they don't know how to do anything worthwhile." This experience would have the effect of lessening for the child the reward value of other children in the class who were diligent, college-bound students. Moreover, lowering the reward value of these successful students would lessen the extent to which the child would imitate them in school. By the same token, the parent who gives relatively high verbal praise to baseball players, football players, fighters, and so on will be ensuring that these types of individuals are rewarding for his child and consequently that his child will emulate the behaviors of these types of individuals.

Thus, different children, exposed to different reward-conditioning experiences, will acquire different reward (or attitude) systems—that is, different types of people, among other things, will become rewarding to them. The reward the children will get from imitating these people will vary, as will the extent to which these people will control imitative behavior. Thus, the way that people come to be rewarding for the child is very important. Later sections will deal with the manner in which the child's reward system is affected heavily by his language experience, as well as with the basic language repertoires that are involved.

IMITATION
AND INTELLIGENCE

In a gross way it has been realized for a long time that imitation is important to human adjustment and to human learning. The traditional conception, as has been indicated, has been that imitation skills are an innate given of the individual. The conception presented herein is that imitation consists of types of skill that are acquired directly through learning, beginning in the child's early experience. It is suggested also that these imitation skills constitute a basic behavioral repertoire which, also according to the same learning principles, enable the child to adjust positively in many situations and to learn profitably in many situations. These suggestions have already been illustrated by the examples in the preceding discussions. This should be elaborated briefly to show the general importance of imitation skills in the child's learning and adjustment. A central purpose of the present section, specifically, is to illustrate that the types of imitation that have been shown to be learned constitute important constituents of what we call intelligence, as measured by intelligence tests.

The manner in which the child's first learning of imitation comes about has been described—largely in terms of how the imitational stimuli become reinforcing. In addition, it was stated that basic skills of imitation—such as attentional responses—had to be acquired by the child. The two types of the further imitation learning dealt with were the acquisition of the actual sensory-motor skills of the imitation acts and the manner in which the imitation acts come under the control of the attitudinal or reward value of people. Children can vary in either of these two types of learning. Thus, two children could have learned the same repertoire of the sensory-motor skills of imitation. However, different types of people could have reward value for them because of differences in learning histories. Let us say that for one child teachers had high regard value and for the other child teachers had low reward value. In such a case we would see that the first child would imitate the teacher's actions in a very desirable way. The second child would not pay attention to the teacher's behaviors and would not imitate them.

On the other hand, the children's learning with respect to the reward value of people could be the same, while their learning of repertoires of the sensory motor skills of imitation might have been quite different. Let us take an example where for both children teachers have high reward value. Let us say that with one child, however, the imitation skills have been learned to a high skill, while in the other child this learning has been very defective. In such a case the first child will imitate the teacher very well. The second child will display deficient imitation skills, and his school learning will suffer as a result.

The child's imitation behavior is thus a function of these several types of learning processes. Thus, what is usually spoken of grossly as imitation depends upon various types of learned repertoires, not just one. It is important to the conception of intelligence and child development being developed here to indicate that these aspects of imitation are important to the child's adjustment and to his further learning. These aspects of imitation are to be considered to be basic behavioral repertoires.

In indicating the importance of imitation to the common conception of intelligence, it is edifying to consult again the items of intelligence tests for young children. It becomes clear when this is done that many items measure the extent of the child's learning of the two aspects of imitation that have been discussed. Take, for example, an item already mentioned on the revised Stanford-Binet Intelligence Test (Terman and Merrill, 1937). The child is instructed to watch the test administrator construct a tower of blocks and, with the blocks left standing as a model, to build one just like it. The child must have learned the attentional responses involved in watching the administrator and scrutinizing the block model, under the control of the verbal stimuli. And he must have the sensory-motor skills in imitating the tower.

This item is at the two-year level of the test. At the three-year level the child has to imitate a more complex block design. As other examples will also suggest, the same task of imitation, as well as other basic behavioral repertoires, appears in somewhat more complex form as the level of the test items advances. Thus, as in the present case, the level of skill in the particular basic behavioral repertoire is tested a number of times. In the present case, this demonstrates that imitation is not only important for the very young child but continues to be an item of his measured intelligence as he grows older and meets more complex learning tasks.

On another item at the 2½-year level the child is told, "Watch what I do," a classic instruction that will establish control of an imitation act in the child who has had the necessary training. The examiner then takes three geometric forms out of the corresponding holes in a board and says, "Now put them back into their holes" (Terman and Merrill, p. 75). This may be considered to call for a type of imitation behavior that is the model's behavior run back wards. Ordinarily, the child receives training in this backward imitation skill when the parent plays various kinds of "replacement" games with the child— as well as in the child's own experience in doing and undoing things. Another imitation item of this type occurs at the three-year level.

There are a number of intelligence test items of the copying variety. The extent to which the child will succeed upon these items and thus be judged to be more intelligent will, it is suggested, depend quite straightforwardly upon the extent to which he has received the type of imitation training given to the two children whose results are summarized in Figures 1 and 2 on pages 105 and 113. For example, at the three-year level an item involves giving the child a pencil, pointing to a circle in a booklet, and saying, "Make one just like this" (p. 82). At the 3½-year level an item involves the examiner drawing a cross and then requesting of the child, "You make one just like this" (p. 85). More complex items of the same type occur at the five-year level and the seven-year level.

At the three-year level the child is told again to watch while the examiner strings wooden beads on a shoestring. The child is then instructed to string beads himself like the examiner. By the six-year level the imitation behavior required by this type of item is considerably more difficult. The child is told, "Watch what I do." The examiner then makes a chain of seven beads using alternately square and round beads. Then the examiner says, "When I'm through, I'm going to take this one away and see if you can make one just like it" (p. 95). At the nine-year level the child has a similar item where he has to imitate the examiner in folding and cutting paper. The instructions must control very assiduous attending behavior.

There are also a number of items that involve the child imitating what the test administrator has said, upon command. For example, at the three-year level there is an item in which the child is instructed to repeat two numbers pronounced by the examiner. The examiner says, "Listen! Say two." "Now, four . . . seven." (p. 79), and so on. These are straightforward speech imitation items. At the five-year level, also, one item consists of the examiner asking the child to imitate a sentence ten words in length, which is another type of speech imitation item.

As with the other items illustrated in this and the other chapters, these are but examples. Many more of the skills of the basic behavioral repertoire of imitation could be illustrated by the use of intelligence test items.

In the present case, each of the imitation items requires that the child have the two types of repertoires that have been described. That is, it is important that the examiner have reward value for the child and thus control his attentional and imitational behaviors. If the child has learned negative attitudes toward adults, the examiner may elicit negative imitation behaviors, or general nonresponding. Furthermore, the stimuli presented by the examiner must control the sensory-motor responses of the actual imitation acts. If the child has had the necessary learning history, and thus has the necessary behaviors, he will respond appropriately to these items and receive points toward his intelligence rating. Thus, the basic behavioral repertoires of imitation that have been described also contribute toward the child's measured intelligence; in fact, the repertoires are constituents of intelligence, one part of personality.

The next chapter will demonstrate at length how the child's basic behavioral repertoire of imitation is the foundation upon which one of the child's central intellectual skills is built. Other discussions will add to this also. However, it will contribute toward indicating the general importance of the imitation repertoire in the child's adjustment and further learning to give a few additional examples here. The present book emphasizes intellectual types of learning, and it may serve to indicate the generality of the learning principles being dealt with by showing that other types of learning are also involved.

A study by Bandura, Ross, and Ross (1963) may be used as an illustration. In this study children had a brief experience with two adults, one of whom was associated with rewarding objects. The children were then shown how each of the two adults could perform a complex sequence of responses, each in two distinctly different, characteristic ways. The children were then allowed to perform the same actions, and the extent to which they imitated either adult was tabulated. The children imitated the adult who had been associated with the rewards more than the other adult. This experiment can be reinterpreted as demonstrating how the reward or attitudinal value of an adult will determine how much the adult is imitated in a naturalistic type of situation.

The types of new learning acquired through imitation acts controlled by individuals with reward value are quite numerous. Thus, for example, it has been shown that a child who has observed other persons perform aggressive behaviors will later display (imitate) those behaviors more than a child who has not seen such aggressive actions. It can be expected, thus, that a child will acquire many of the parent's social behaviors, prosocial as well as aggressive, as well as skill behaviors of various kinds. The family behaviors and the behaviors of the associates of the child may be considered to be very potent sources of "training," for in imitating the behaviors of others the child will be acquiring his own general behavior patterns.

It is not even necessary that the child observe the model directly. The same results will take place when the child has seen someone else's behavior on film. A recent study by O'Connor (in press) has shown, for example, that the behavior of nonsociable, isolated children became more sociable after watching a particular film. The film showed various sequences where an isolated child joined a group of other children and was socially rewarded. It may be noted that negative behaviors can be learned through imitation as well as desirable behaviors. As an example, the author's son began imitating a lisp of a playmate in a manner that was so general that remedial treatment, of the type to be discussed in a later section, was employed.

Such demonstrations as these are important in providing evidence of the importance of imitation in determining what the child learns. However, it is also necessary to indicate what imitation is—the skills of which imitation is composed—as well as how imitation skills are learned and how they function in the child's adjustment and further learning. Studies of imitation in psychology, as in the just preceding examples, have ordinarily been of how *already acquired* imitation skills function for the child in producing further learning. We need also studies of what the basic behavioral skills of imitation are as well as specification of how these skills are acquired. The author's investigation of the imitation skills of copying exemplify the knowledge we need of imitation learning. Additional specifications of learning will be given in later chapters. This will help elaborate the present learning conception of imitation. Moreover, additional basic behavioral repertoires that are important to what we term intelligence will also be treated, and the means by which such basic skills can be produced by the parent will be discussed.

chapter 7 / Speech Elaboration

Chapter 5 described the manner in which the child learns his first speech responses under the control of appropriate environmental objects and events. Chapter 6 dealt with imitation, because it is part of personality central to adjustment and because the basic skills of imitation are also involved in much language-intellectual learning, including the speech elaboration treated in the present chapter. It will help to summarize several of the principles already described in the context of speech learning, including imitative speech learning, as a means of introducing the manner in which the speech learning of the child is elaborated to produce more advanced functional language-personality skills.

SPEECH IMITATION
AND THE IMITATION REPERTOIRE

The process described in the first acquisition of speech was extended in time and involved several types of learning. As the speech sounds of the parent became rewarding to the child, it was said that the child would learn to make such sounds himself, since the responses that produced such rewarding sounds would be learned. In addition, however, the parent can also directly reward the speech responses of the child, selecting certain wordlike vocalizations of the child for special attention.

Furthermore, it was suggested that the child also comes to learn imitational speech responses. The actual vocal responses themselves are those the child has learned to make which are like those of the parent. For the child to have an imitational response, however, the response must additionally be elicited by the parent's identical vocal stimulus. That is, as an example, the child may say "ma-ma, ma-ma." The sound produced by the child's response may be very much like that of the mother saying, "Ma-ma," but the child's response is not an imitative act until the mother (or someone else) can make the response and then the sound stimulus elicits the child's repeating the word. It will serve in returning to the topic of the child's speech learning to illustrate a procedure for producing the child's imitative speech learning.

The example is intended to illustrate a way in which the child may be straightforwardly trained to imitative speech—a topic that has not been made explicit. As one example, the parent may play a sound-imitating game with the child. In this game the parent may observe that the preverbal child who already babbles has quite good control for making a sound, let us say "ah." However, the child does not make the sound under any particular stimulus control, although he makes the sound frequently. The parent may use such a vocal response to train the child to speech imitation. Let us say the parent, noting that the child can repeat the sound, waits for the child to make the vocal response and then himself repeats the sound after the child—while smiling and giving the child social reinforcement. The child is then likely to repeat the sound, and the parent can then repeat the sound again, through several cycles. The child is receiving the reward of the parent's attention, and he will in this way learn to imitate the speech sounds of the parent.

In this "game" the parent can take over the lead from the child and not wait until the child makes the first response. That is, after the game has been played a few different times—with the child learning to vocally imitate the parent on each occasion—the parent may be the one to initiate the game. Moreover, later the parent may introduce new responses after the game has commenced: After a few reciprocated sayings of "Ah," for example, the parent may switch to another vocal response he has heard the child make frequently. Furthermore, the parent may later introduce a wordlike sound that he wants the child to make in learning an actual stimulus-controlled word. One of the first examples of a controlled speech response of the child (Chapter 5) was "dah," which was learned to the stimulus of a doll. It may be noted here that the child had learned this speech response through the author's imitation training of the type just described. More recently, there have been studies conducted that support this analysis, albeit not with very young children learning their first imitation skills (Baer and Sherman, 1967). As with the other procedures described herein, however, systematic studies could be made of the principles and analyses involved.

(The parent can also employ this type of game to extend nonverbal imitation skills as well as speech imitation. Thus, the parent can introduce nonverbal responses of a simple nature into the game, such as nodding the head, turning the head, opening the mouth, raising an arm, and so on. This type of interaction can provide valuable imitation learning for the child at the very beginning stages and it also constitutes a primitive form of game that is fun for parent and child.)

One of the central basic behavioral repertoires that the child must acquire is an imitational speech repertoire that includes all of the unit vocal responses necessary to produce all of the sounds (phonemes) in the language the child must learn. Linguists indicate that in the various languages the number of different unit speech responses includes in any case between fifteen and fifty. The child has to learn to make these different vocal responses in the language community in which he is reared. Moreover, he must learn to make these vocal responses in sequences in which two or more phonemes are combined. Actually, in our language the child learns most of these sounds in combinations of at least a consonant and vowel. For example, the child learns to make the *d* sound followed (or preceded) by a vowel, not by itself.

At any rate, the important point is that when the child has learned to make a number of the different syllable sounds that make up the sounds of which the language is composed, *under the control of the imitation stimuli of the parent's voice*, then the speech learning of the child enters an accelerated stage. In this manner the parent can get the child to say new words that the child has never said before. Let us say, as an illustration, that the child can imitate the "chi," "co," and "ry" sounds but has never said "chicory." The parent in training the child to such a new word response simply has to provide the syllable stimuli in sequence. Each syllable stimulus controls the appropriate syllable response in the child, and after a few learning trials the child will have acquired a new, smoothly uttered word response.

The author has designed an exercise to demonstrate this type of learning in preschool children. This is one of a set of exercises to be used in teaching graduate students how to employ learning principles in training young children and in studying the learning processes involved (Staats, in preparation). In the exercise the young children are trained to say the words *drosophilus melanogaster*. The words are presented to the children syllable by syllable, and a new syllable is not introduced until the preceding ones are well learned as an integrated combination. It is edifying to see the several principles of learning involved as the child acquires a new and complex word response. The demonstration shows clearly how the child's learning of new language is built upon the previous acquisition of a basic behavioral repertoire of speech imitation. The demonstration also shows how new words can be formed from novel sequences of already learned syllable responses. The importance of the elaboration of speech through imitative speech learning will be described in the following section.

THE LABELING OR NAMING SPEECH REPERTOIRE

The child actually has to acquire a vast repertoire of speech responses that are elicited by the appropriate stimulus objects and events of his life. This is such an essential repertoire that it deserves separate description. First, as has been noted, when a child has acquired even a small repertoire of such speech responses, he progresses to a more advanced level of social interaction. Prior to being able to name objects, for example, he must physically get the adult to look at the object he wants through physically pulling the adult, gesticulating, grunting, crying, and so on, in order to get the adult to obtain the object for him. This is analogous to the sequences we see in animal movies, where the animal tugs at the master, barks, or what have you in order to get the master to follow him. At the preverbal period the child is functioning at this level. After he has learned the speech response "bread" under the control of the object bread, and also has learned appropriate speech responses for doll, ball, milk, shoe, scissors, pencil, spoon, glass, and so on, he simply has to say the appropriate word to the parent to obtain what he wants. This labeling speech repertoire, even at this level, is thus very, very adjustive to the child, and to the parent as well.

Linguists have traditionally not been concerned with language until the point where complex combinations of words are spoken. They are concerned with describing the rules by which different classes of words are combined in grammatical speech. It is thus important to indicate that the single-word speech repertoire that the child first learns is very important in language development. The single-word repertoire has a great deal of adjustmental (reinforcing) value for the child, which helps maintain the child's general learning of language. Furthermore, it is out of the single-word speech repertoire that more complex speech forms will grow, as will be described further on. Actually, one of the primary characteristics of language, which gives language the features of a system, is that it is formed of combinations. One of the constituents of those combinations consists of the vast repertoire of labeling responses.

It is thus important to understand the way that this speech learning takes place and the manner in which the parent employs the imitation repertoire in producing the speech learning. The learning process for the first few of the child's word responses is laborious and requires a long time. However, once the child has acquired an imitational repertoire, this repertoire is the foundation upon which the child more easily and more rapidly learns an extensive labeling speech repertoire.

Early Noun
Learning

The process is quite simple and has already been stated. The parent merely has to say the name of the stimulus object which the child is attending to, and then reward the child when he has imitated the word. This learning trial will serve to strengthen the child's saying of the word when he again attends to the stimulus object.

This type of training may take place in many different situations. Let us say the parent takes the child for a ride and observes the child looking at a cow. If the parent says, "Cow, that's a cow. Can you say cow?" the child who has an imitative repertoire and has been rewarded in the past for repeating words in similar situations will in this situation say, "Cow." The parent who then rewards the child with approval, saying, "Yes, that's right, that's a cow" with enthusiasm, will be training his child to a new labeling response. In addition, he will be training his child to respond appropriately in later instances of such training. That is, the child will be learning a general skill so that when he is instructed to perform responses by which he learns, he will do so. He is also learning, because of the reward, to have a positive attitude toward such situations. These by-products will be discussed more fully later.

It should be emphasized that a child who has this type of training from his parents will be set up to learn also from other adults. That is, the same type of training trial could be conducted by another relative as well as by friends of the family. Seeing a child reaching for a book, an uncle may say, "Book, do you want the book?" The child is rewarded for saying "book" by receiving the book. When the child has come to respond with the appropriate imitational speech response to these various situations and requests for a vocal response, he is also prepared to learn from interaction with other children who may have in their repertoires a labeling response that he does not yet have.

It should be noted that the instructions given the child will vary widely in this training. Sometimes the instruction will be part of an act that is not explicitly a language-training situation. Let us say an adult says, "Hand me the scissors . . . scissors," and points to the object. The child, because of his past training, will imitate the word (overtly, in the beginning) as he also picks up the scissors. In doing so he will be learning to label the object. The child will ultimately come to learn new labeling responses also just by hearing another individual name an object. For this type of learning to take place, however, the child must have learned well the imitational speech repertoire in the ways described. And he also has to have acquired attentional responses of looking at objects that another person is looking at as the other person names the object, and the like.

At any rate, after the child has acquired the basic attentional responses and the imitational skills, he will learn to label new objects simply by seeing them and hearing someone else name them. This learning is then highly informal, and the parent will ordinarily be unaware of its occurrence. It would be expected, however, that great individual differences in parents' language habits would be reflected in the rate and quality of the child's language development. That is, a parent who is verbal and speaks a great deal as he does things —sometimes especially for the benefit of the child—who labels many of the different objects with which he comes in contact, and so on, will be providing many training trials for his child. The parent who has a poor language development himself and who employs speech sparsely, who does not systematically verbalize purposely for the child's benefit, will not provide training for his child to the same extent.

Thus, wide variations in the quality of parental training exist. For example, the parent with botanical interests who shows a flower to a child will point to and name the pistil and stamens—not just the whole flower. This will enable the child to discriminate these parts of the flower, and through this experience the parts as stimuli will come to elicit the correct word responses. The parent who has a well-developed anatomical vocabulary will name different parts of the body—the cornea, pupil, tear ducts, cuticle—as well as describe internal organs in greater detail than is usual. In this manner his child will acquire a more elaborate labeling vocabulary than is usual. However, the objects of the labeling speech need not be technical in nature, and usually are not. There are great differences in the extent to which parents train their children to label the objects and events of everyday life, social as well as physical. It may be noted, nevertheless, as these examples suggest, that any special-interest area generally involves special acquisition of speech responses under the control of stimulus objects. At any rate, a good part of the child's vocabulary will depend upon the richness of the experience he has had in verbal labeling.

Early Verb Learning

To this point the discussion has involved the learning of speech responses to stimulus objects. Much of the child's speaking repertoire of nouns will be acquired in the ways described. This is not to say, however, that the types of training described pertain only to nouns. Thus, the same analysis is relevant to the child's learning of many verb speech responses to stimulus events—to actions and happenings. However, actions and happenings are not such straightforward stimuli as are stimulus objects. Thus, training on words labeling such events ordinarily commences at a somewhat later period— after the child has already developed good attentional and imitational repertoires and a small repertoire of noun responses. Training to verb labeling will nevertheless be of the kind already described—the parent may see a barking dog, for example, and say, "Barking, dog barking. Can you say dog barking?" In this type of training, as depicted in this example, it is often advantageous to get the child to say the already learned noun-labeling response with the new verb response that labels the action. Other examples could be "boy runs," "Daddy sits," "baby sleeps," and so on.

Many of the stimuli that come to control verb speech responses, it should be noted, are evanescent and more difficult to point to as a specific stimulus. As the child acquires the necessary noun repertoire and the attentional and imitational behaviors, however, he can readily and informally learn labeling responses to such events. As another example, when the child comes to the mother and says, "What are you doing, Mommy?" and she replies, "Sewing," the suitably prepared child will learn a label for the action. Through this type of experience the child will learn a repertoire of verb speech responses as labels of events (in addition to learning to make motor responses himself to verbs spoken by someone else, as described previously). The richness of the child's language repertoire in this area will depend upon the extent and quality of the training and experience that he receives. Over the years of the child's language development there are also ample opportunities for infinite variation in the rapidity, quality, and quantity of the training different children receive in this aspect of language.

Early Adjective Learning

In the same manner as for the other labeling repertoires, the child will ordinarily also receive training and experience in the acquisition of repertoires of adjectives. Again, types of stimuli are involved that through the same type of learning must come to elicit adjective speech responses. However, as with the verbs, adjective speech responses must come under the control of stimuli that in many cases are not as straightforward as those involved in the learning of the first noun-labeling responses. A doll is an easily point-at-able stimulus object. The child learns to say "doll" to the whole stimulus constellation of the object—not to one aspect of the stimulus that is singled out as the only relevant stimulus. That is not as true of the color blue, for example. Colors are only a quality or aspect of stimulus objects. Furthermore, colors will be part of many stimulus objects—there are blue cars, blue dresses, blue balls, blue houses, and so on. After the child has been trained to label several objects, if a red ball is presented to him and he is told to name it "red"and he does so, it will be seen that he will call another ball of a different color by the name *red*. The labeling response will be under the control of the stimulus object itself, not its color aspect. To some extent this probably occurs because the child's first speech training is to objects themselves, not their part characteristics.

At any rate, it will take many learning trials, where the child is rewarded for saying the color to many different objects, before he learns the color-labeling response. This will ordinarily take place only after the child has acquired a repertoire of speech responses labeling objects and events. Then the adjective can be combined with the name of the object in the training of the child. He may be shown a blue car, blue ball, blue book, and so on and be trained to name the color in the manner already discussed. That is, the child can be told, "This is a *red* car. Can you say *red* car?" (It is frequently seen that a child just beginning to learn colors in this way will, because of this training, use the adjective and noun together in circumstances where the adult might use the color alone.) The child will also have to learn to respond to the questions concerning color. This requires training in answering such questions, and can be commenced by the parent saying, "What color is this? This car is blue. Can you say blue car?"

A child who has a well-developed language repertoire can profit from these types of training when he is not yet two years old. In the process the child will begin to acquire language responses that are commonly called concepts. In summary, the child will ordinarily receive many training trials of the labeling type where an adjective is paired with a noun and he is trained to call the object by two words. The child will in this manner learn to say "pretty" with a number of other words, as well as adjectives like "big," "happy," "tired," and so on.

Early Number-Concept Learning

Number concepts constitute a class that are important also in the child's early language learning. This topic cannot be discussed fully here. However, it may be noted that the first aspects of number concepts are acquired in the same manner as has been described for other adjectives. That is, numerosity is not a stimulus property that stands alone; it is an aspect of various objects and events. If the child in the process of first number learning is prompted to say "two" in the presence of two oranges, for example, the speech response would come to be elicited by the stimulus of an orange, or oranges—not by the stimulus of numerosity. Thus, for the response to come to be elicited by *twoness,* it is necessary that the child have many of these learning trials where the speech response "two" is rewarded as the child looks at two apples, two fingers, two pennies, two rocks, and so on. Through this extended training the stimuli of twoness, irrespective of the objects or events involved, will come to elicit the response of saying "two." The same process of learning is necessary with the number concepts one, three, four, and perhaps five.

Above five the learning task involves discriminations that are difficult. Types of training (see Staats, 1968a) are thus required that involve additional principles and procedures. It is important to indicate here, however, that the child's first number learning takes place in the manner indicated, and this learning is basic to later elaborations of the number repertoire. Discussion of the elaborations will be more germane to a later book dealing with the child's early academic learning. The present type of limited number-concept learning can begin very early, however. The author, for example, began training his daughter to this repertoire when she was eighteen months of age—nine months after she began talking. At any rate, after the child has a repertoire of labeling objects, training on number responses can begin. If the child has learned to name oranges, for example, training can be commenced where the child is taught to label "two oranges" and "one orange." The same training can be conducted with one and two fingers, one and two apples, spoons, rocks, and so on. (Pictures can also be used if the child has been trained to respond to pictures.) Various little games can be played in this type of learning—for example, the parent can hold one or two objects out of sight and play a guessing game. Or, as in the other examples, the child may be *given* the object or objects (such as two raisins) after he imitates the number response and thus can constitute the reinforcement.

After this learning is sufficiently strong so that the child can respond appropriately according to the number (one or two) of objects, then training should be conducted where the name of the objects is omitted. The child should also be given training in responding to the question, "How many are there?" and the like by giving the appropriate number response. In addition, with the same type of training procedures the number of the objects should be extended to three and four, along with two and one.

It should be emphasized that many parents present this type of training to their children without even being aware of it. Furthermore, if a child associates with other children who have learned a number repertoire, he will usually also receive some training in the repertoire in informal interaction with the other children. Thus, a child will ordinarily learn this minimal number-speech repertoire by the age of three or four. However, many parents do not present this training—or not as soon as other parents—and thus their children will not develop the skills as rapidly. Therefore these children will not be prepared to learn additional number skills as rapidly. At any rate, when the training procedure is described explicitly, the information enables the parent who might not otherwise do so to provide his child with these beginning and basic skills of number.

Early Adverb Learning

An analysis of the learning of adverbs could be made which is similar to that made for adjectives. That is, after the child has learned to label actions and events appropriately, as in learning a basic repertoire of nouns and verbs, the training may be expanded to include adverbs. For example, the word *slowly* may be combined with verbs, and the child may receive training in this type of labeling response. The same is true of *loudly, rapidly,* and so on. As an example, the child may be told, "The dog is barking loudly. Can you say barking loudly?" When the child repeats the words, the stimulus event involved—the intensity of the sound—will begin to come to elicit the appropriate adverb speech response. In this example the training would ordinarily have to include response to many different situations and stimuli that had this quality. The parent, for example, might say, "Listen, now I speak loudly . . . . And now I speak softly." Then the parent may get the child to do the same. Such a "game" will provide the child with training in several aspects of his language-learning repertoire—including his adverb speech repertoire.

Again, as with the various types of learning involved, parents many times conduct this type of training without realizing the valuable learning their child gains. However, it is important to understand the processes systematically so they may be instituted more effectively, and so they may be instituted in cases where they have not occurred or would not occur without special advice—as in the clinical treatment of developmental deficits.

LABELING INTERNAL STIMULI

The child also receives training from his parents in naming stimuli that arise internal to his body. Although we do not customarily consider this aspect of language, a child has to learn to make speech responses to various internal stimuli as well as to his own behavior of various kinds. This is also a type of learning that can be conducted to varying levels of richness, with varying degrees of speed—and this variation will have important effects upon the child's adjustment.

Consider the following example. Let us say that the child has skinned his knee and comes to the parent in tears. If the parent in consoling the child says the word "hurt," perhaps saying, "That must hurt," the child will through the type of imitation learning already described learn to respond to the internal painful stimulus by saying "hurt." This learning will be elaborated later on in further experience. That is, the child may come to the parent and say, "Hurt," with no visible source of pain. The parent may then see the child rubbing his head, or ask the child, "Where?" If the child points to his head, or rubs it, the parent will say, "You have a headache," and the child will acquire a new speech response under the control of the appropriate internal stimulus.

Each child must normally receive this type of training with many internal stimuli. Let us say that the child has not had anything to drink for some time. This will produce aversive internal stimuli also. As a consequence the child will behave in an irritable and restless manner, but not be able to appropriately name the circumstances involved. The parent who has observed both the behavior and the deprivation circumstances may say, "You are thirsty . . . thirsty." The child may then repeat the word. Giving the child water will constitute reinforcement for the response and for participation in the training interaction.

Through this type of training the child will acquire a basic repertoire of speech responses elicited by internal, deprivation-caused stimuli. As another example, in the presence of the stimuli produced by a distended bladder or rectum, the child may be prompted to say "potty," and then be rewarded by being helped to reduce the aversive stimulation. Through this type of training the internal stimuli will come to elicit the speech response. When these internal stimuli have come to control the child's verbal and overt behavior, then the child is toilet-trained. The author has presented a more complete analysis of the toilet-training procedures involved (Staats, 1963), which has been verified in experimentation (Marshall, 1966). Further elaboration is not germane to the present discourse, however.

Until the child has learned in this manner to "label various internal stimuli," he is not able to indicate what is wrong with him or what he needs, feels, and so on. The source of stimulation must be inferred from the child's actions and from the parent's knowledge of previous conditions. It is interesting to note that a great deal of medical diagnosis rests upon the patient having acquired a repertoire of labeling responses under the reliable control of internal stimuli. Young children are more difficult to treat than adults because they have not yet learned to name internal stimuli. When the child's labeling responses have come under the control of internal stimuli, it is often possible to reduce or remove the aversive stimuli—which serves to maintain this type of speech through the principle of reward. Thus, this speech repertoire also aids the child's adjustment. Ordinarily, the parent and others will train the child to fine discriminations to internal stimuli, such as, "It burns," "It throbs," "It is a dull ache," "It is a sharp pain," and so on.

There are many internal stimuli besides those from injury, illness, or deprivation, and the child must also learn to respond to many of them with speech responses. The child will ordinarily be trained to say "I am happy" in the presence of happy circumstances and the internal emotional responses elicited. He will learn later to say "I am frustrated" in circumstances where he has been deprived of a rewarding object and prevented from getting it. He will learn to say "I love you," "I am jealous," "That is unpleasant," "I am impatient," and so on under the control of the appropriate internal and external stimuli.

LABELING BEHAVIORAL STIMULI

The child must also learn to label the stimuli produced by his own movements. Some of these stimuli are internal to the body. Thus, each movement made by an individual will produce internal stimuli by activating sensory nerves in the muscles and tendons. It is through these stimuli that we "know" where our limbs are at any time without looking at them. It is also true, however, that our actions produce external sources of stimulation. Thus, we can see our body move, the environmental stimuli change as we move; we see the physical products of our actions (as in chopping down a tree) and we see social stimuli that stem from our actions (as in winning a race, or doing something that makes another person laugh or be angry). The child has to learn a repertoire of speech responses to these stimuli also, and this training begins early in life.

To begin, it may be said that in the same manner that a child learns to label an object or event he learns to label his own behavior on the basis of the stimuli his behavior produces. For example, the child may be prompted to imitate the word "running" while looking at a boy running and be rewarded for doing this. The stimulus of a running boy will later tend to elicit this speech response. In the same manner the child can be prompted to label his own behavior of running in the same way. The parent may simply say, "Running," when he and the child are running, and reward the child's saying of the word. The stimuli that would come to elicit the response would include the internal stimuli of the rapid muscular movements as well as the external visual stimuli produced.

The child will normally learn speech responses to many of his movements and actions. For example, any individual with a normal learning history will be able to report that he has lifted his arm, crooked his finger, shaken hands, winked his eye, squatted, is standing, sitting, and so on. This constitutes a repertoire of learned speech responses. These aspects of the speech repertoire may be learned to fine and detailed motor skills—where unusual training programs are involved which are conducted by the parent, coach, or teacher. We would find, for example, that an expert diver, ballet dancer, boxer, singer, football player, or violinist would have a repertoire of speech responses to different movements that are much more finely discriminated than the speech responses of people in general. Moreover, these speech responses will play an important role in the further learning of the individual in his special field and in the verbal interactions by which individuals in the field affect each other's behavior (that is, communicate). As with the other repertoires dealt with, this type of specially trained labeling repertoire can be a part of an advanced intellectual skill.

SOCIAL SELF-LABELING
AND THE SELF-CONCEPT

The developing child will learn such speech repertoires not only to the stimuli produced by specific movements but also to the complex stimuli of various kinds produced by the social response to his acts. For example, let us say that a child strikes another, who then cries. An adult may say to the aggressing child, "That was mean. Do you know what you did?" The child may also be prompted to say, "I was mean, I am sorry," and be rewarded by forgiveness. This experience would train the child to one example of a specific self-labeling response. With wide variations in training circumstances, the child must learn a host of such self-labeling responses. In various situations, as a consequence of the self-labeling repertoire he has learned, the child will thus come to say, "I was mean," "I was kind," "I was amusing," "I worked hard," "I was successful," "I was sociable," "I behaved like an idiot," "I like apples," "I dislike conventional people," "I did it better than he did," "I enjoy a challenge," and so on.

The verbal responses the child learns to his own stimuli—internal, external, and behavior produced—are heavily involved in what has been called the self-concept. The self-concept will also ordinarily include the individual's labeling of other people's responses to him, such as, "People like me," and so on. The individual's "self-concept" will also include verbal labels the individual has learned to make to his performance in many evaluative situations involving social, sensory-motor, and intellectual skills; for example, "I am a hard worker," "I usually accomplish what I attempt," "I don't learn as easily as others do," and so on.

Since these are learned verbal responses, the labeling of one's behavior can vary even though the actual stimuli are the same. As one example, a child may have training that produces very skilled behavior on his part, and yet also be trained to label his behavior as less than complimentary. Another child, who has learned the same level of skill, may be trained to label his behavior more positively. Everyone has had experience with people who label their own behavior erroneously—sometimes in a positive direction, sometimes in a negative direction. In common-sense terms we say in such cases that an individual thinks too highly, or poorly, of himself.

It is important to indicate that these "self-concept" behaviors are learned, because the way an individual describes himself will have widespread effects. That is, the child's labeling repertoire is an important part of his problem-solving and reasoning equipment, as will be noted later. In the present case, the individual's labeling of his own behavior will figure into his social reasoning and the solution of various problems of life. The individual who describes himself as brilliant, resourceful, enterprising, productive, and so on, when confronted with an opportunity that demands these types of behaviors, is likely to reason that he should accept the offer. The individual who describes himself in negative terms in these respects will not accept the opportunity. It is true that, ordinarily, the individual's self-concept is dependent upon the behavior he has displayed in the past and the response to him—that is, upon reality. The present discussion stresses, however, that the individual's self-concept will also be a function of his language training as well, and if this training has been unrealistic, so will be his self-labeling. Since self-labeling that is really unrealistic will result in social problems, it behooves the parent to train the child to label events, including those involving himself, as they really are—or perhaps leaning a little toward the positive.

It is also important to indicate that the person's self-labeling will not only affect his own reasoning but will also affect other people as well. The individual who describes himself in deprecatory terms, other things being equal, will not be responded to as positively as the individual who describes himself in more positive terms. However, if to a large extent the individual's self-labeling does not agree with the quality of his behavior, people will tend to discount what the individual says about himself. It is the case that the parent who trains a child to a rich self-labeling repertoire that allows him realistically to describe (1) his own emotional responses to various situations, (2) his own behaviors of various kinds, including essential sensory-motor skills, and so on, and (3) other people's responses to his behavior, will be providing the child with a repertoire important to his intellectual, social, sensory-motor, and emotional adjustment.

These sections cannot deal specifically with all of the types of labeling responses the child must begin to learn in his early years. However, the discussions are meant to indicate that this is an essential type of learning important in the child's later development and adjustment.

PICTURE LABELING
AND SPEECH ELABORATION

As was briefly noted earlier, training on pictures themselves is necessary if the child is to label them correctly. Pictures are different as stimuli from the stimulus objects themselves. Thus, having learned to label a stimulus object or event will not guarantee that the young child will be able to label a picture of the object. However, it is important that the child learn to respond to pictures of objects as he would to the object itself. When he has learned to respond similarly to pictures as he would to objects, and vice versa, then learning that occurs in the one medium will transfer to the other. It is because of the transfer that the learning of verbal labels to pictures is so important.

Thus, although this is in part a digression here, it will be instructive to suggest that the parent should train his young child in labeling pictures. After the child has a rudimentary labeling repertoire, the parent may present a picture of an object that the child can already name. (The picture should be lifelike so that the discrepancy between picture and actual object is minimized.) The parent may then display the picture, and point to the pictured object if that is necessary. When the child attends to the pictured object, the parent can say the object's name. Let us say that the child can already say *dog* in some form and can also imitate the parent when he says the word. When the child says the word while looking at the pictured object, he will begin to learn to make the labeling response to the picture.

The parent may profitably do this with pictures of all of the objects that the child can label. More than one picture for every object will also help the child to learn to respond to different but similar picture stimuli with the same labeling response. In this training the child will be learning to respond to two-dimensional depictions of an object as he would to the object.

Moreover, once the child has learned to respond to pictures in this way, it will be possible to expand his speech-labeling repertoire on the basis of pictures, without waiting for the child to have first-hand experience with the object itself. The parent may later show the child a picture of a zebra, for example, and prompt the child to say the name while looking at a picture. After the child has learned the picture-labeling response, it will be seen that he will on first seeing a zebra make the appropriate verbal response. It is this potentiality, of course, that enables the child to learn on the basis of picture presentation. Moreover, the ability to respond to pictures is a useful skill in later learning of other kinds—as will be elaborated in later discussions in this chapter.

PRINTED WORD LABELING:
READING

The manner in which the child's language training by the parent is essential in the child's later reading learning will not be developed in this text (see Staats, 1968a). It suffices to say that all the types of learning discussed herein are important in the child's reading learning. Specifically, here it is germane to indicate as an example that the imitation repertoire is the mechanism by which the teacher produces reading learning in her pupils—that is, the labeling of printed word stimuli.

When stripped down to principles, we can see that the child learns to read by attending to a word (or letter, or syllable) stimulus that the teacher (or other trainer) presents visually, and by repeating (imitating) the word that the teacher says. Let us say that the teacher holds up a card upon which the word cat is printed. Let us say that she also says to her class, "This is the word cat. Can you say cat?" The child who attends to the card and to the teacher's voice, and who imitates the word she has pronounced, will have received one training trial in learning to read the word cat. The child who is not controlled by the teacher's verbal stimuli, who does not attend to the card, and who does not imitate the word the teacher presents, will not have received that learning trial. When this is multiplied by thousands and thousands of learning trials, we can see that two children in the same classroom situation will learn to read in a markedly different manner—and will learn differently other aspects of intellectual development as well.

THE LABELING SPEECH REPERTOIRE AND INTELLIGENCE

It has already been shown in Chapter 5 how the first units of the child's labeling repertoire that he learns will contribute toward his adjustment, toward his further intellectual learning, and thus toward the estimates of intelligence made of the child. This was shown to be true on the instruments that have been devised to measure the child's intelligence. That is, it was indicated that some of the items on intelligence tests actually measure the extent to which the child has acquired a simple labeling repertoire of word responses.

The examples used from intelligence tests were rather simple, however; actually those that occur at the lower age levels. The labeling repertoire is also important to measurement of "intelligence" at somewhat later ages, and it also involves additional types of responses. Moreover, some of the more complex aspects of intelligence—aspects of behavior we would commonly refer to as concepts—actually consist of some of the forms of labeling learning that have been described.

To begin, it will help to indicate another item on the Revised Stanford-Binet Intelligence Test (Terman and Merrill, 1937) that involves labeling pictures instead of stimulus objects. For example, at the 3½-year level the child is shown pictures of common objects and asked, "What's this? What do you call it?" (p. 83). Thus, the type of picture-labeling training that has already been described yields a language-intellectual skill that will be important to the child's performance on intelligence and aptitude tests. It is also useful to indicate that there are additional items on intelligence tests that measure more complex picture-labeling responses. Thus, as one example, the child may be asked to look at a picture and to tell the examiner all about it (see item number 4, Terman and Merrill, p. 84). This calls for sequences of observing responses and sequences of labeling responses—as well as other learned language skills of the types already described or to be discussed.

To continue, however, even at the 3½-year level of the intelligence test there are items that measure more complex forms of the verbal labeling repertoires. Thus, one item involves presenting the child with two sticks and saying, "Which stick is longer? Put your finger on the long one" (Terman and Merrill, p. 84). Certainly, it is important for the child's adjustment and further learning that he can respond to differences between objects in terms of their length, weight, shape, and so on. This particular item tests for one of these skills. It is important to indicate that the child learns such skills according to the same principles already described, in the same type of learning process.

That is, the response the child must have to answer the item correctly is but a more complex labeling response. He must have learned to respond to the "relationship stimulus" of the two objects involved, not just to the object itself. The training is somewhat more complex, but is in principle the same as for any labeling learning. The parent may produce this type of concept learning in the following manner. In the first example, let us deal with number. After the child has learned to correctly label one, two, or three objects according to the number present, the parent may present the following training: Let us say that he holds two raisins (or any reinforcing objects) in one hand and only one raisin in his other hand. Let us also say that the parent says, "What do you want, one or two raisins? You tell me—one or two?" If the child says "two" he is given the two raisins, which will reinforce the response of saying the larger number in similar situations. If the child says "one" and is given the one raisin, he will ordinarily express disappointment. At this time the parent can say that they will play it over and repeat the questions. This time the child will say "two."

In any event, after a few such training trials the child will begin to make the larger number response when such situations are posed. It should be noted that this is a response to the relationship between the two number stimuli shown to the child, as well as a response to the one number stimulus chosen. In essence, the child is being trained to respond to the more or less relationship between two numbered stimuli.

The training of the child to respond to the longer of two sticks as "long" or "longer" and the shorter of two sticks as "short" or "shorter" is very similar to this. The parent can in the same manner very easily present two licorice sticks to the child of obviously unequal length and say, "Which one do you want? This one is the long one." When the child has pointed to the long one, the parent can then say, "That's the longer one. Can you say longer?" After the child has imitated the word he can be given the appropriate stick.

Similar types of training can be conducted so that the child comes to respond to the short stick with the appropriate verbal response. It is not necessary in conducting this training to use only objects that the child wants to consume, it should be noted. However, it is necessary to have some form of reward for the child on a percentage of his training trials. If this rule is not followed, it will be found that the child will not attend when such repeated training trials are conducted. The topic of the general principles of reward involved in child training will be described in greater detail in Chapter 12.

At the five-year level of the intelligence test there is an item measuring another form of the labeling speech repertoire—this time the item tests number-labeling skills. The child is presented with four blocks and is asked, "How many?" If the child has received the number-labeling training that was described in the earlier section, he will be able to respond, "Four," and thus score points toward his intelligence rating.

There are a number of other items that consist of or involve the basic behavioral repertoire of labeling. The preceding items, however, will serve to illustrate how this repertoire is an important constituent of what we consider to make up human intelligence throughout childhood. The next chapter will indicate how the labeling repertoire is involved in more complex adjustments of the individual, and will thus further illustrate the importance of the repertoire to intellectual skill and other "personality repertoires."

SPEECH PROBLEMS

In Chapter 5 the manner in which the parent trains the child to increasingly better pronunciation of words was outlined. It may be briefly noted here that one type of speech pathology involves idiosyncracies in speech, where no organic difficulty is involved, that are either unusual enough or persistent enough to be recognized as problems.

When the child is just beginning to speak he will have many speech characteristics that deviate from adult speech. There may be certain sounds that he cannot yet make. He may substitute other sounds for them, or he may leave the sound out of the word completely. He may also make sounds not quite like those an accomplished speaker makes.

These sounds generally occur in the young child who is just learning to speak and as the learning progresses will ordinarily disappear. There are some speech responses, however, that can persist and become problems. One type of problem may be dealt with briefly, demonstrating the extension of the principles and procedures into this area of speech pathology.

A speech response that frequently gives children trouble is that of vocalizing sibilants. It is not unusual that children will first make the s sound by putting the tongue under the upper front teeth, slightly forward of the teeth, or by thrusting the tongue against and under the front teeth. (In the latter case this response creates an orthodontal problem as well as a speech problem. The tongue thrusting may result in forward displacement of the upper front teeth, commonly called "buck teeth," with problems of malocclusion.) In any case, the sibilant response is in such ways made incorrectly—since the tongue should lie behind the front teeth in making the response. Incorrect placement of the tongue produces an incorrect, lisping, sibilant sound.

For a child who is just learning to speak, who has been unable to make a sibilant sound, it will be an improvement when he comes to make the lisping sibilant response. He will be able to pronounce words more clearly than he could before and will be more immediately reinforced, and so on. The child will generally go through such approximations to his final speech with other sounds also—where he goes from no response to an incorrect response to the final correct response. In the general development the incorrect lisping sibilant will not be different than other incorrect responses the child makes and will receive—and need not receive—any more attention than the others. The parent's training procedures for generally improving the child's speech responses will be quite appropriate.

In many cases where the parent does not use procedures to improve the child's speech responses, however, the sibilant response of lisping may become habituated and difficult to change. The response is very similar to the usual sibilant, both in the tongue response employed as well as in the sound produced. The parent may thus fully accept the response when the child is young. If nothing is changed the child may not discriminate a difference between the two sounds and he may continue to speak the incorrect and potentially harmful, sibilant. In addition to the physical problems that may result, he will, as a consequence of the lisp, be considered by others to have immature speech. If the problem continues for a boy he will also be considered feminine by virtue of his speech.

In the context of the present discussion of the treatment of speech pathologies, however, it is important to note that it is quite easy to remediate the incorrect sibilant response. Two considerations are especially important here. First, the response is quite easy to change if remedial training is conducted when the child is only a few years old, before the response has become strongly integrated with and linked to other skills of speech. Second, the response is quite easy to change if the parent has already established the learning situation as a positive circumstance into which the child enters willingly, a topic that will be discussed at greater length further on.

At any rate, when the parent has noticed that his child makes the incorrect sibilant he may employ the techniques of the imitation game that have already been described to correct the response. If he has already employed the procedures in the early speech learning of the child, its use in remediating the incorrect sibilant will be so natural it will not be noticed. In any event, the parent may introduce the procedure by asking the child if he can make the s sound as the parent is doing, with a long drawn out hissing sound. The parent can make the sibilant with the lips drawn back so the child can see that the teeth are fully, or almost, closed (preventing incorrect tongue placement). When the child tries the response he should be given approval. If he has made it incorrectly the parent may then indicate how he can do it with his teeth together. Not much instruction will be necessary to get the child to make the correct response, provided he already has an imitation repertoire and has the verbal-motor (following instructions) repertoire.

The parent may then have a few such, well-distributed practice sessions. The training must be maintained with adequate reinforcement—employing either social approval or some other means. Following this, the parent may then introduce training in the context of saying a whole word. After the child has made an appropriate sibilant response by itself, the parent can then ask the child to imitate him in a simple word that begins with the sibilant, for example, *see*. It helps, first, to draw out the sibilant before pronouncing the rest of the word. Training trials under adequate reinforcement may be conducted here until the child can make the word response. Other words can then be introduced, including words in which the sibilant occupies the terminal and medial positions in the word.

If the training is conducted early in the child's development of the problem response it will not be necessary to include all of the training steps. Just the practice on the *s* sound by itself may be enough. The better learned the incorrect response is, the more extensive the remedial training will have to be. If the training sessions are short, well rewarded, and widely enough distributed, and if the training is begun early enough, remediation will progress easily. Because properly conducted training proceeds so easily, as with each case of training the child to normal repertoires of skill described in the present book, it is difficult to realize that the parent thereby is preventing the later development of serious and intractible problems of behavior development. As long as the training is made rewarding—with no suggestion that the child is at fault (or use of any other aversiveness)—there is no problem of conducting such remedial training.

The present learning approach, unlike traditional maturational approaches, does not recommend passively waiting for the speech problem to disappear through the child's physiological development. Speech problems, as with other problems of human behavior, are considered to be learned, and must be removed through appropriate learning procedures. In this, early detection and treatment of the speech deviance is important.

chapter 8 / Language Sequences and Language Development

Recent trends in the field of linguistics have focused upon the grammatical aspects of language. For example, there have been linguists who have insisted that language may only be considered to be such when it involves grammar—that is, when complex sequences of words are uttered that involve relationships between the words that can be described and codified in grammatical rules. Such an approach inappropriately belittles the importance of the first stages of language learning—and in fact encourages one to remain ignorant of the early development of language. If one is interested only in describing and comparing the grammatical aspects of languages, ignoring early acquisition may be justified. If one is interested in understanding the causes of language, if one is interested in procedures by which to affect language development, then early learning cannot be ignored.

It has been stressed that the processes of learning that lead up to the child's acquisition of a single-word repertoire are crucial indeed. The basic behavioral repertoires the child is acquiring up to the period where he still says only single words are the foundations of his later learning of more complex language-intellectual repertoires. Nevertheless, even when we restrict our attention to child learning, it is important to also understand something about the manner in which more complex sequences of language are learned. It is also important to understand some of the functions that more advanced language development has in the adjustment, learning, and personality of the child. The present chapter provides some of this understanding, but without going into great technical detail.

LEARNING WORD SEQUENCES

It has also been said by some linguists (for example, Chomsky, 1968) that the child does not learn his language, but that he has an innate, biological structure that allows him to develop language with but minimal exposure. One of the facts that is thought to support this conjecture is that the speech of adults is quite different from that of children. Therefore, it is erroneously concluded that the child could not have learned his language from the adult by imitative learning. The assumption that language and intellectual development are biologically given has been refuted at some length herein. The author has also refuted the idea that the child could not learn language partly through imitation because adult speech is different from child speech (Staats, in press *b*). However, there is a point involved in this linguistic misunderstanding of speech development that should be made explicit.

The parent ordinarily does not, and should not, speak to the young child as he does to other adults. The child learns his early speech to a great extent from the parent, largely based upon the imitation repertoire as described. However, the speech from which the child learns by imitation is not that of the parent speaking to another adult—at least at an early period in language development. As an appropriate training stimulus, such speech is far too complex—analogous to the stimulus of hearing a fluent person speak in a foreign language. The language training of the child has to begin on the simplest level, and only gradually can the training stimuli presented to the child be increased in complexity. First the child has to learn single-word responses, then two-word utterances, and so on.

As a matter of fact, it is the sensitivity to cues indicating how rapidly to advance the training that in part distinguishes the good trainer. In this task the parent may err in either direction. That is, we have all seen or heard of cases where the parent, for example, continues to use "baby" talk long after the child has learned a better pronunciation. On the other hand, there are parents who will frequently present their child with sentences that are more complex than the child can respond to. A child who is at the level where he has just learned to appropriately label a few breakfast foods, as single-word speech responses, will not be able to appropriately profit from the sentence, "Do you want scrambled eggs with bacon or sausage or would you rather have pancakes and syrup?" On the other hand, the child might very well respond appropriately when asked, "Eggs or pancakes?" Moreover, in the latter case the child would be learning skills that would bring him closer to the point where more complex verbal stimuli could be presented to him for both training and interaction purposes.

The next section will continue to discuss the *gradual* increase in the complexity of the training given to the child, which is necessary in developing his language repertoire.

EXTENDING LANGUAGE
SEQUENCE DEVELOPMENT

The preceding section has described some of the extensions of the child's language development that should take place in the ordinary interactions of the child with the verbal parent. Additional aspects of the parental training task are involved, however. The parent plays an important role not only in bringing about the child's development of single word and double word utterances, but also in developing the complexity of the child's language-intellectual repertoires.

Let us say that the parent has trained the child to name objects, and in suitable circumstances the child will make appropriate speech responses—to the extent of his single-word repertoire. At one stage the parent is content with prompting the child to name objects and events with single words. Later, however, when a single-word response has been well learned, the parent may provide the child with training to expand the utterance to the two-word level. This has been described in discussing the learning of adjectives and adverbs. The parent may say, "Pretty doll," instead of just "doll," for example. Moreover, the parent may elaborate the child's utterances by use of verbs and nouns together in primitive sentences.

For example, the parent may be satisfied with the child first saying only "bread" when having first learned to request this item. After the response is well learned, however, the training should be extended. When the child has said only the one word, the parent may say, "Say, *want* bread," and wait for the child to repeat the two-word utterance before giving the rewarding stimulus. (Of course, the child's imitational speech repertoire must also be up to the difficulty of this task as well. Moreover, the child's imitational repertoire will be gradually advanced in the process of the training being described.)

When the child has been trained to say, "Want bread," "Want spoon," "Want water," and perhaps a few other "wants," it will be observed that the child will say the two words to situations on which he has never been trained. The repertoire will appear to elaborate on its own, giving the impression that the child must have internal, spontaneous sources of development or originality. The latter conclusion is gratuitous, however. It is in the nature of the learning that generality (that is, originality) will derive from the learning of specifics. There are various mechanisms involved, as will be described later. In the present case the child is learning to say "want" in the circumstance where he sees something of which he has been deprived for a period and which would be rewarding to him. This may be considered to be the stimulus event that comes to elicit the "want" speech response. If the child has also learned to name specifically the object involved, the object will also elicit the specific name, be it a wagon, a dog, a banana, or what have you. Thus, at this point the child may just have learned to name a new object, let us say a rabbit, and then immediately say, "Want rabbit," or whatever. In this case, and in others, when the stimuli of deprivation of a rewarding object and the stimuli of the object are brought together, the two stimuli may both elicit a new, original, compound response. The uttering of the two-word response would occur with no training on the two words together.

To explain how such originality derives from past learning, seemingly making it a less extraordinary feat of the child, by no means decreases the importance of such learned "originality" as a source of behavioral development.

It is well to stress this, for the parent should not get the idea that he is going to train the child in each and every utterance that his child will be able to make. In the first place, language is a system. When the component parts have been acquired by the child, they will be put together in many different combinations—under the control of the stimulus situations in which the child finds himself. The child will continue to learn language skills on the basis of his own experience. Having learned to say, "Want," and to name objects, the child then has a repertoire of combinations that will be called out by the appropriate stimulus combinations—whether or not he has ever had training upon the specific combination. This is true in each of the types of language combinations the child learns. When the child has learned to say, "Pretty doll," "Pretty dog," "Pretty dress," and so on, the child will make appropriate two-word utterances employing "pretty" in various novel ways, under the control of new stimulus combinations. Sometimes the novel productions may not follow the rules of the language and will be considered errors by adults—albeit cute ones. Many of them, however, will be correct and will extend his language repertoire.

(One may nevertheless see that each word response has been learned individually to stimuli. That is, if the child is shown an object that he wants but has not learned to name, he may simply say, "Want," and point. Usually the child will also soon learn the catchall word *that,* which can be combined with *want* in such a situation. In further indicating the separate learning of object and request, however, it may be noted that the child can also name objects that would not be rewarding without also saying, "Want.")

When the child has started saying two-word utterances, the parent can then begin to provide training that produces three-word utterances. Using the previous example, when the child says, "Want ball," the parent may respond, "Can you say, *I* want ball?" When the child has repeated this it will constitute a training trial. When the child has had a sufficient number of training trials with various requested objects, he will generally expand his utterances to include the personal pronoun. Later, the child can be given training on articles, and so on.

GRADUALLY INTRODUCED COMPLEXITY: A TRAINING SKILL

Thus, the alert, sensitive, verbal parent will ordinarily (and should) elaborate the child's speech repertoires by this process of "expansion" training. That is, the parent should gradually train the child to include more and more of the speech responses that must occur in finished language in sequential utterances. As will be described later, the young child's utterances will consist of what has been called "telegraphic speech." The child will learn at first only the most crucial words needed to obtain the desired response in the listener. He needs, however, to learn the other complexities of language. This cannot be done in one fell swoop. The parent has to be sensitive to the firmness with which the child has learned the speech skills he already displays before introducing new learning. Moreover, the parent cannot successfully introduce too many new points at one time. He should employ the method of expansion training, where one new point is added to the sentence the child has already said. Introduction of several new words at one time would only be confusing.

This is true in every aspect of the child's training. To be a good trainer in this respect the parent must know something about the learning the child must acquire, and be observant about the child's behavior and what he has already learned. Many parents do not become aware of how the child is progressing until they notice a large deficit in the child's skills. Then they attempt to make up for the deficit by concentrated training. Ordinarily, this means that the training will be massed and thus aversive. Moreover, in such a case the parent will frequently attempt immediately to advance to a level of training appropriate to the age of the child rather than to his level of skill—which means that complexity is not gradually introduced. When this occurs the child will fail to learn. The parent, realizing the negative consequences of failing to learn, may resort to punishing methods such as admonition. However, if the training is aversive the child will simply learn to generally avoid such learning situations. Then child training may become very difficult and unpleasant for parent and child—which will have further unfortunate by-products, as will be described later. It should be borne in mind, therefore, that the efficacy of one's training methods will depend upon the continuing introduction of new material into the child's learning at a pace that can be learned without aversiveness. A parent who understands the principles of learning given herein, who tests them in producing the first simple behaviors in the infant, and who has been sensitive to the child's language learning, should have no trouble in the child's expansion training. The parent who is taking an active role of this type should observe what the child is capable of, and should be ready to simplify the training when it does not meet with success.

These are not large or demanding tasks for the parent—he need only put in the usual amount of observation of and interaction with his child. Understanding the principles, however, can sharpen his observations and increase the training efficacy of his interactions. It may also be added that as the child's language skills advance, the parent will be able to converse more and more with the child as with an adult. The principle of presenting language stimuli to the child just in advance of the child's level of skill will remain an important one for some time, however.

It should also be noted that the parent is not the sole source of training for the child. Even at an early age the preschool child will begin having perhaps an even greater number of language interactions with siblings, playmates, other adults, and so on, than with the parents. These will all provide learning experiences that will mold the child's language and personality development. For example, the author set up a remedial training program for a four-year-old emotionally disturbed child who had no functional language. It was interesting to observe the manner in which the training in relatively few speech responses resulted later in great elaboration through the child's inter-action with other children. Whereas the child could not interact with other children until he had a primitive speech repertoire, when this had been given him through specific training (which included the parent), the child's interac-tions with his playmates increased the speech repertoire a great deal. This is again given as an illustration that the parent provides the child with basic be-havioral repertoires, but not with the child's full language-intellectual skills. On the foundation of the basic behavioral repertoires, the child will learn extensively from his varied experiences with others. The parent continues to play a role in adding to and maintaining the child's learning, but his role be-comes more and more that of contributing to and maintaining the child's learning rather than being the sole determiner.

VERBAL SEQUENCES AND ECHOLALIA

At any rate, it is important that the parent gradually introduce more com-plex sequences into the training of the child. Moreover, it is also important to train the child to *functional* speech that will enable him to adjust better in his social interactions and in obtaining the things that he finds reinforcing. This is said because the author has seen cases where a mother who wants to help the child develop language—usually in cases where the development is retarded —will read to the child who has not yet developed a single-word repertoire. In one case involving a child with very retarded language development, the mother had attempted to produce language development in the child by hav-ing the child imitate in reciting nursery rhymes. Under these circumstances it was not unexpected that the child did not have functional speech—he would only display what is called echolalia. Echolalia is the name applied when a child only displays imitational speech, which is in most instances inappropri-ate. Thus, if this child was asked, "What is it?" on an intelligence test, instead of labeling the object he would repeat what the examiner had said. This child's mother, not understanding the types of language repertoires the child had to learn, or what is involved in language development, had restricted her efforts to imitation. When the mother had been given information on more appropriate language training procedures, the child's language development improved rapidly.

Speech imitation by itself does not constitute a functional language reper-toire. Neither are word responses alone functional. The child must have the appropriate speech responses, *but they must be under the appropriate control of stimuli*. This involves the type of labeling training that has been described. It is suggested that speech disturbances such as echolalia (which disturbed or artistic children display) arise because the child has received only part of the necessary speech training, not all that is necessary. Thus, it may serve to indicate that reciting poems, singing songs, or saying prayers may be desirable verbal sequences at a later stage of language development. Nevertheless, they are in the nature of interesting tricks for the young child and should not play a central role in early language training until the child has functional repertoires of the sort described in the present book.

LANGUAGE SEQUENCES
AND INTELLIGENCE

The importance to the child of his developing ability to utter sequences of speech responses is quite evident and needs little exemplification. However, following the pattern that has been employed already, it is interesting to note that there are items on intelligence tests that consist entirely of measuring the extent to which the child can spontaneously emit verbal sequences—as well as the extent to which he can imitate word sequences.

As one example, one item at the two-year level of the Revised Stanford-Binet Intelligence Test involves noting the child's spontaneous word combinations that occur at any time during the testing session. If the child says two words in sequence, such as "Bye-bye Mama," "Pretty cat," "Want car," or some such, he is considered to be more intelligent. It is quite easy to see that a child who has received the type of training in sequences of words that has been described herein will have the ability to suceed on the item. Other things being equal, the richer the child's speech repertoire in multiple-word utterances, the greater his likelihood of being rated as more intelligent.

As another example, at the four-year level there is an item in which the examiner asks, "Why do we have houses?" An important aspect of the child's success in answering the item will depend upon the sequences of word responses he has learned with respect to houses. The child is also asked why we have books.

At the eight-year level the child is told a story (which he can also read if he wishes). Following this he is asked questions concerning the story, such as "What is the name of this story?" "What did the pony do?" and so on. The test actually measures the extent to which the presentation of the story to the child results in the learning of the language sequences necessary to answer the questions. The extent of the learning, however, will depend upon the extent to which he has already learned a rich repertoire of word sequences. If he has to learn basics at the point where he is given this test item, he will not suceed in the task. To succeed he has to have learned already the component sequences in the passage, and thus has only to learn the new combinations the story presents.

Many other items on intelligence tests depend upon the child's word sequences or word associations. Examples will be given in following sections that more specifically discuss additional types of word associations that are part of the child's developing language-intellectual repertoire.

WORD ASSOCIATIONS, GRAMMAR, AND CONCEPTS

As the preceding discussion has indicated, the child must not only learn single words, he must also be trained to acquire words in sequence. Each time the child says words in sequence he will tend to learn them that way. That is, having said the first word, he will tend to also say the second word. The stimulus of the first word, said by himself or even someone else, will tend to elicit the second word response. This is usually spoken of as a word association—to characterize the "associational" nature of the relationship of the two word responses.

As will be referred to again, the child in normal circumstances actually will learn a system of word associations that is fantastically complex, and these multitudinous associations will be involved in much of his intellectual functions. The establishment of such word associations, as has already been described, begins very early and can be expected to depend upon the richness of the child's language experience. Several points should be made on the topic of this type of learning to indicate its role in personality development and also to indicate the significance of this development.

Grammatical Word Associations

It should be noted that many word associations are learned in the process of the child being prompted to extend his language sequences. Many of these word associations may be considered to be the basis of the "grammatical rules" that characterize the child's speech. That is, if the child hears words presented in grammatical sequences, if he receives training in saying grammatical sequences, he will learn word associations that result in the child speaking grammatically.

As an example, let us take the correct grammatical use of adverbial word endings. Thus, a child may say either, "The car was moving slowly," or "The car was moving slow," of which the former is the correct form. A child will learn the association between "moving" and "slowly" if he is exposed to the correct usage in the speech of his parents.

Moreover, this grammatical association will be formed in the child if he receives training in making the correct sequence of word responses himself. If the child utters the less desirable sequence, the parent may simply correct the child and request a repetition in the correct form. For a child who has had the types of language training already described, such a training trial will be responded to readily and quickly. Social approval will be sufficient reward for maintaining such learning at the point that it is introduced.

It should be noted, however, that the child will not need training on every combination of verb and adverb. Thus, after he has experience on "moving slowly," "climbing rapidly," "walking clumsily," "talking loudly," a word association structure will emerge that will ensure that the child speaks grammatically in this area even in new instances. That is, the child will learn an association between "ing" and "ly." Whenever a word ends in "ing" and the child is to say a qualifying word following it, he will tend to add "ly" to the second word. For example, let us say an individual with this learning is asked on a grammar test, "Which is correct—The boy was scrudging slowly or The boy was scrudging slow?" The *ing-ly* word association, once acquired, would ensure that the first sentence would be uttered or selected rather than the second. The person would thus answer the novel grammatical question correctly. Moreover, the person would tend to speak correctly. In the same manner, let us say the question involved the choice of "The boy was walking leply" versus "The boy was walking lep." The individual who had acquired the *ing-ly* association would select the first sentence. The "word" association would result in grammatical speech—even with words presented for the first time.

It is interesting to note that the same word association mechanism may produce errors in the child's speech as well as correct forms—although word associations ordinarily have a positive function. To illustrate, the first verb word responses the child learns are ordinarily irregular verbs—verbs such as *eat, sit, drink,* and so on, which in the past tense do not add an *ed* as regular verbs do. The past tense of the above examples are *ate, sat,* and *drank,* the regular forms would be *eated, sitted,* and *drinked.* As it happens, the most commonly used verb words, and thus the first ones the child learns, are irregular. The past tense of these verbs will also be learned as individual words by the child.

The finding that has seemed paradoxical to some people is that later on, after the child has already been using the correct *irregular* forms—*ate, sat, drank,* and so on—the child will begin to make errors. He will regularize these words incorrectly. That is, the child will say, "I ated," "I sitted," "I dranked," and so on. This observation has been employed by linguists as "evidence" that the child could not possibly *learn* his grammar. Otherwise, how could it happen that something once learned would then be lost? How would the irregular forms once learned then be turned into incorrect speech?

The learning mechanism involved is the type of word association just discussed. The child first learns the past tense of irregular verbs as single words. However, as the child has more experience with language, he learns also a number of regular verbs. What this means is that many, many times he will receive experience where he hears, or is trained to say, a verb with an *ed* ending. He will say, "I walked," "I talked," "I teased," "I pushed," and the like. This means that as the child has experience with regular verbs, he will learn a strong word association between the verb root and the *ed* ending. This occurs because *every* regular ending is the *same; all* the irregular verbs are *different* and provide no systematic word associations. Thus, whenever he utters a verb, even an irregular verb, the *ed* ending will now be elicited. He will continue to make these mistakes for a time, until the nature of his language experience strengthens the irregular verb forms against the regularized endings. (The author has discussed this more fully in Staats, in press *b.*)

For the parent, this means that there should be no exasperation when the child seemingly grows less adept in his grammatical usage. He is not retrogressing. He is simply learning the regular forms. And because this regular-form word association is repeated, it will interfere for a time with the correct irregular-form usage. The parent will accelerate the child's language development at this point, however, by providing training of the already described. That is, when the utterance is incorrect the parent may simply repeat it correctly, at least a portion of the times, and ask that the child then repeat the correct sequence. Errors of grammar when corrected will provide training in correct speech. When this training is conducted in a rewarding manner, it will also train the child to a positive attitude toward learning situations in general—including the parent-child training situation.

This discussion is not meant to be a complete analysis of grammatical learning of children. It is meant to suggest, however, that the grammatical aspects of the child's language are learned in the same manner as are other aspects of the language-intellectual repertoire. This may be elaborated a bit by referring to another aspect of the child's speech development, that is, the natural speech habits of children between the ages of twenty-four and thirty-six months. These have been systematically observed (Brown and Fraser, 1961). It has been noted that the number of word responses included in each separate sentence increases as the child grow older. The speech of young children is systematically abbreviated in comparison to more accomplished speakers. The fewer the words included in the child's sentences in his general speech, moreover, the greater the abbreviation of the speech. Children who produce a low average number of word responses will be more likely to say, as examples, "Going home," rather than "I am going home."

In having the children repeat sentences, these investigators furthermore found that certain types of words were left out in the younger children's abbreviations. When words were excluded they tended to be the less essential words.

> Words that occur in intermediate positions in the sentence, words that are not reference-making [labeling or naming] forms, words that belong to such small-sized grammatical categories as the articles, modal auxiliaries, and inflections; words that are relatively predictable from context and so carry little information, and words that receive the weaker stresses in ordinary English pronunciation (Brown and Fraser, 1961, pp 37–38).

It is suggested that this development from abbreviated to full speech takes place on the basis of the child's learning. He is first trained in single words, the "reference-making" or labeling variety. Then he receives the gradually expanding training in longer and longer sequences or words. As this occurs he learns to include in his utterances the more advanced grammatical forms.

This type of training may be considered as the establishment in the child of the more advanced word-association structures that allow him to utter longer and longer grammatical sequences. This learning will be reflected in the grammaticality of the child's speech, in his ability to repeat longer and longer sentences, in his ability to remember such sentences, and so on. The child's grammatical speech associations are thus of great importance in the child's developing language-intellectual skills.

Perhaps this helps to illustrate that the child's grammatical speech, and the general complexity of the child's speech, will depend upon the nature of his learning. If the child is presented with learning experiences that are advantageous, he will acquire a vast repertoire of word-association sequences that will be of a grammatical sort. When he utters sequences of words in this case they will be grammatical utterances. The more extensive his learning, the longer and more complex speech will he be capable of uttering or comprehending. Whether or not the child acquires these advantageous grammatical and sequential word associations will depend in large part upon the quality of the parent's speech, the extent to which the parent provides explicit training to the child, the extent to which the parent and child interact in gradually increasing language complexity—and upon these same factors between the child and the other people with whom he associates. Later, his reading will constitute a primary source of continued advancement.

It should be noted that the child's word-association learning will have functions other than his speech. When the child is faced with tests that measure the extent of the child's "grammatical knowledge," his ability will depend in part upon the grammatical word-association structure that he has learned. That is, ordinarily, many of the questions will present the correct usage and an example of incorrect usage and ask the child to select one. If he has learned the correct word association it will sound more familiar to him and he will select that alternative. His English grammar achievement will then be judged to be higher as a consequence. Additional functions of the child's word-association learning will be presented in the next section.

Concepts and Word
Associations

Ordinarily, the parent will provide much additional language training in the natural circumstances of his interaction with the child. This will produce what are commonly called concepts in the child. Some of these "concepts" involve the establishment of complex word associations.

As one example, when the parent tells the child, "An organge is a fruit," "An apple is a fruit," "A banana is a fruit," and so on, word associations are established between each of the specific words and class word *fruit*. This does not have to be conducted in formal training sessions. The interactions may occur just in the general conduct of living. Let us say the child has already learned the labeling responses *orange, apple,* and *banana.* Let us also say the parent then says, "Do you want a piece of fruit . . . an orange, apple, or banana?" This informal language interaction would result in the child having training in the new word *fruit* as well as in establishing associations between this word and the other three words.

It should be realized that parents will vary in the amount and complexity of their own language usage, and in the extent to which they interact verbally with the child. Ordinarily, a parent who considers that the child develops mostly through biological maturation will be less systematically concerned with ensuring that the child has extensive informal training circumstances—at least in comparison to the parent who accepts that a *child is what he learns.* Moreover, the other children and adults who interact verbally with the child will affect his language learning—and there is great variation in these factors also. Thus, children will receive different degrees of learning experience in these areas as well as in all the other areas of learning.

It should be noted that words such as *fruit* are considered to be (superordinate) concept words. (The individual fruit words may be called subordinates.) There are many, many superordinate-subordinate concepts that the child must acquire. The extent to which this occurs will help determine the fluency and flexibility of the child's language.

Thus, the extent of the child's language experience will determine the extent of his word associational conceptual development. Of course, language interactions in addition to that had with the parent will also determine the child's conceptual development. The child's social environment will therefore be very important. In addition, the type and amount of the child's reading will have an important effect. It is especially through reading that more abstract and complex word associational concept structures are later learned, since everyday language interactions usually are restricted to common topics.

SYNONYM WORD ASSOCIATIONS

In addition to learning associations of the type just described, the child will also extend his vocabulary through learning based upon imitation and his other labeling responses. For instance, the child's vocabulary will be extended by learning synonyms, which in part involve learning word associations. As an example, the child may ask the parent, "What is an automobile?" When the parent says, "An automobile is a car," the child who has already acquired the speech response "car" and has the appropriate imitational repertoire will acquire an *automobile-car* word association. The child may also learn to repeat the two words in succession, and through this method strengthen his learning of such word associations. (Repeating newly presented words in this fashion is a mnemonic device the child can learn informally or through instruction.) After the experience, if you ask the child for another word for car he will say "automobile." Moreover, other stimulus situations that would elicit the speech response "car" will now elicit the speech response "automobile." Actually, in this process of learning, other word associations would have been learned that were also of a grammatical sort. These are too complex to go into here, however. It may only be added that the associations established in the process would ensure that the new word introduced in that manner, automobile, would be used in a grammatically appropriate manner.

At any rate, part of the child's vocabulary will be learned on the basis of word associations. Some of these will be synonyms. Others will be introduced in similiar training, but not be considered synonyms. For example, if the child heard the statement, "A vacation is for fun and rest," he could learn the word associations between vacation, fun, and rest. This would help introduce a new word into his vocabulary provided he had already learned fun and rest. Again, the fluency and flexibility of his language-intellectual skills will in part depend upon the richness of such associations, and this will depend upon the richness and quality of his language experience.

NUMBER WORD ASSOCIATIONS

The very beginning number discriminations the child must learn have already been described. It is not intended in this volume to describe in any completeness the child's number-concept learning. It may be briefly mentioned , nevertheless, that the establishment of word associations is very heavily involved in the acquisition of number skills. Take the addition tables, for example. Although more is involved than just the establishment of number word associations, the associations play a very prominent role. The child has to acquire such word-association sequences as "One and one are two," "One and two are three," "Two and two are four," and so on. These are acquired by straight word-associational learning.

Although in the very beginning there will be additional aspects of the training, much of this takes place simply through the type of learning already described. That is, the parent or teacher (or book) provides the word stimuli, and the child imitates or reads the numbers in sequence. In so doing he learns a word association chain. As anyone will see in observing the child learn the various word association chains in the addition or multiplication tables, each table is no mean learning task. Mastering either table requires learning trials in which each word association chain is uttered correctly a number of times.

It should be understood that the number associations depend upon other word association chains—and other basic behavioral repertoires—

which have been previously established. Without the previously established skills, the later word associations are meaningless. This is what we descry about "rote learning." What is popularly called rote learning occurs when the child is trained to word association chains without the addition of the other types of learning involved to make the word association chains functional. This would be analogous to the mother who taught her child words and sequences of words by imitating rhymes. Without the words being under the control of actual objects and events—as in labeling—the child's speech would have no function. Thus, although the word association chains are necessary and important to number skills, they are not the only skills involved—and by themselves number associations are useless, as is the case with any one aspect of language (see Staats, Brewer, and Gross, 1969).

WORD ASSOCIATIONS
AND MEMORY

Memory or memory span is a term frequently used in a manner that suggests the individual has an internal quality that determines how much he can repeat material with which he has been presented. The suggestion is that it is not the acquired skills that are important, but rather the personal (biological) structure of the individual that determines the performance. However, it may be suggested again that the common biological conception has made us ignore the actual variables involved—that is, the nature of the individual's learning and the state of his basic behavioral repertoires. Specifically, it may be suggested that word association repertoires are very important to memory.

As an illustration, if we were to ask a child or adult to repeat the numbers 5, 5, 5, 2, 2, 7, 2, 0, 1, many would not be able to repeat this or other nine-digit numbers. This would be accepted as an indication that they had a lesser biologically determined memory span than required by the task. For the author this would be a very easy memory feat, however, because the digits constitute his social security number—long ago learned securely as a word association chain.

We could all repeat easily the sentence, "Now is the time for all good men to come to the aid of the party." We would have more difficulty in doing this with most sixteen-word sentences. The reason the above sentence is easy to repeat and remember is because it is already well learned as a word association sequence. The person who hears the sentence presented for the first time, on the other hand, faces the task of acquiring the word association sequence—which requires more training trials.

The important point here is that children, because of different language experience, will acquire different basic behavioral repertoires of word associations. With very rich language experience, the word association structures they acquire will be rich and complex. The lesser the experience, the less rich the associational repertoire. The child in the latter case will face many more situations in which he must *learn* new word association sequences entirely, rather than simply being required to repeat in new combinations sequences he already has largely learned.

It may be noted here that the ease with which a child will read will depend in part upon how many of the word associations he covers are already well learned. Thus, in reading, "A stitch in time . . . ," it is not necessary for most of us to look at each word in the complete sentence. After the first few words have been responded to, the whole word association sequence is elicited. A person without the appropriate word associations must read all the words, which requires much more time and effort. This is also true in listening to speech. Other things being equal, if the listener has a rich repertoire of word associations that are like those of the speaker, he will follow the speech more easily and retain more of what is said. The richness of the listener's word association sequences is important in any communication act—and is central in profiting from educational lectures and lessons.

Thus, the richness of the individual's word association repertoire will help determine his ease of learning verbal material in general, the extent to which he retains verbal material that has been presented to him, and the like. It is also true that the *type* of word associations he has learned will be an important factor. If his associations are like those of the source of the verbal material he confronts, he will find the material relatively easy. If his word associations are atypical, the converse will pertain. Similarly, if the material is atypical or unsuited for the particular child, the learning task will also be more difficult.

WORD ASSOCIATIONS
AND INTELLIGENCE

The preceding sections have already indicated some of the ways in which the word associations the child learns are important to his adjustment and further learning. It should thus be expected that there would be items on intelligence tests that would measure the types of word associations that have been described in this last section. Several examples will be given to indicate the manner in which these types of word association skills will affect the estimate of the child's intelligence made on the basis of tests.

For example, at the six-year level of the Revised Stanford-Binet Intelligence Test (Terman and Merrill, 1937), the child is tested on his vocabulary. This involves the oral presentation of a word, with the child asked to say what it means. One of the items asks, "What does *envelope* mean?" The child will gain an intelligence point if he answers, "An envelope is for a letter." This sequence could have been acquired as word associational sequence simply from having heard someone say, "An envelope is for a letter." Vocabulary items continue to occur at various levels of the intelligence test. And in many cases correct response can occur if the child has learned the necessary word associations. As another example, at age twelve the child is asked what *constant* means. If he has learned a synonym association—"Constant is to stay the same," or "constant-steady," or some such—he will be scored as being more intelligent.

At the seven-year level of the test there is an item that shows rather clearly the function of the types of word associations involved in what were called concept word associations. Thus the child is asked, for example, "In what way are apple and peach alike?" (p. 97). If the child has learned the type of concept word association between *apple* and *fruit* and between *peach* and *fruit*, the two stimuli *apple* and *peach* will both elicit the verbal response "fruit." The child will be considered more intelligent as a consequence.

These word association mechanisms function in other items also. Thus, at the ten-year level the child is asked to say as many different words as he can in one minute. The child's rapidity of saying words, his verbal fluency in this task, will depend in part upon the richness of his word association structures. A child who has learned a large number of superordinate concept words, for example, each with a number of individual word members, will have a larger number of word responses available in this task. For example, he might say "apple," and this word would elicit its associate, "fruit." Now the word *fruit* for this child, let us say, is associated with *orange, banana, cherry, fig, date, pear, persimmon, watermelon, cantaloupe,* and so on as subordinates. A rich word association repertoire such as in this example will provide the child with the responses to be fluent and to succeed on this intelligence item. A child who does not have such a rich vocabulary, bound together in concept associations, will not be as fluent in general and will not be considered as intelligent.

Many other items either consist of, or involve, the measurement of samples of the child's word associational repertoire—including his number associational skills. The present items, however, are intended to illustrate the importance of the child's word associations in judgments of the quality of his intelligence. A later chapter will describe how language sequences, learned in complex word association combinations, function in thinking and reasoning, and in the child's self-direction through speech.

STUTTERING

The stress in the present approach has been on describing the learning conditions for producing normal language development in the child. This has been done, as will be indicated more fully, because it is the production of normal behavioral skills that prevents the development of abnormal or undesirable behaviors. Moreover, even when a child has developed an abnormal behavior instead of a normal repertoire of skill—or in cases when the child has a deficit of the normal repertoire—it is necessary that the child be given training in the acquisition of the normal repertoire.

There is, however, a type of difficulty with speech development that is one of the most general and most troublesome and about which there is insufficient general understanding either by professionals, researchers, or parents. The general conditions of learning involved will thus be outlined herein, since the problem is so germane to the purview of this book. This problem of speech development involves repetitions of syllables and words, and hesitancies in speaking that may be prolonged and accompanied by facial and vocal contortions. These speech characteristics are referred to in their more extreme manifestations as stuttering and stammering. Actually, hesitancies and repetitions of words may not be unusual in young children and are not ordinarily considered to be abnormal, as the following quotation indicates.

> **Question:** My 2½-year-old grandson, who has been talking distinctly for some months, has developed a stuttering problem. Is there a reason for this? Is it just a phase he's going through, or because he tries to talk too fast? I would appreciate any help you can give on this.—Worried Grandma F.
>
> **Answer:** Children normally repeat words during the first year or so after learning to talk. (Just as they stumble and fall down a lot a year after they first learn to walk.) So it is a phase he's going through —a normal, developmental phase.
>
> The important thing is to ignore the speech repetition. Do not say to the child, "Slow down." Do not show anxiety and concern. I repeat—ignore this temporary speech pattern. By so doing, as the child's nervous and speech mechanisms mature, he will overcome the tendency to hesitate or repeat syllables and words (Crook, 1969, p. C-3).

This case has been cited for several reasons, in addition to showing that verbal disfluencies in young children may not be unusual or indicative of a problem. First, the response of the pediatrician is another example of how internal physiological processes—in this case the immaturity of "nervous and speech mechanisms"—are inferred incorrectly to supposedly explain the behavioral problem. The case also illustrates how the organic conception of behavioral difficulty leads to a prescription of passivity which in the face of a real problem would be very incomplete. Although the pediatrician's advice to the grandmother had some merit, as will be indicated, the organic conception of stuttering is generally inadequate to deal with the appearance of disfluencies in the speech development of children. It is important for the professional, the parent, as well as the psychological researcher, to have a better conception of some of the learning conditions involved in stuttering.

To begin, as has been suggested, the child learns his speech skills. In a lengthy, if usually informal, process he learns his first words. There is usually positive reinforcement involved in this learning in good abundance, and the general behavioral repertoire will be acquired in good strength. As has been indicated, however, the learning is quite complex. The child has to acquire very complex repertoires of various kinds. The child learns to label different types of objects and events, and he learns a complex imitational speech repertoire. There are many, and subtle, stimulus circumstances that must come to control the speech.

In addition, since there are many response members involved in the speech repertoire and many stimuli—many of them similar—it can be expected that there will be cases of error or competition. For example, a stimulus condition may tend to elicit two different speech responses and the result will be behavioral competition, which will be seen as a delay in any response, or perhaps a mixing of responses. As another example, the situation may involve "conflicting" stimuli. To illustrate, the child's father may ask him how he liked a new dish mother has served for dinner. The dish may have been disagreeable to him and tend to control some negative statement. On the other hand, if the child has had a history of being rewarded for saying positive things about his mother's food, and being punished (admonition) for saying negative things, the combination of the disliked food and the presence of the mother will produce conflicting elicitation of speech. Again, the conflicting stimulus control of the speech will produce behavioral manifestations in delayed, hesitant, stumbling, and perhaps conflicting speech. The more skilled speaker, having faced such conflicting situations before, will have learned "diplomatic" speech, which allows the resolution of the conflicts.

In addition to various types of conflicting controls over speech, there are other types of complexities that in a normal way produce speech disfluencies. Everyone has had the experience of making a statement that leads to the next emission of a word, only to have the word unavailable. At this time the person hesitates, strives to "get" the word, and may then resort to an alternative, or use a whole phrase to complete the statement in lieu of the more apt single word. There are also disfluencies from having to make very complex responses to very complex stimulus situations. Other things being equal, the person who has the richest language repertoire, the richest word associations, and so on will display the most fluent speech when presented with complex circumstances to which he must respond verbally.

Thus, the young child, who has only begun to acquire the complex repertoires, would be expected to show disfluencies of various kinds. In many cases he will not have the words to respond to the complex events. If he tries his speech will be poor and disfluent. In other cases the word associations he has will be in conflict. For example, because he has a strong "table and chair" word association, in the act of saying, "I am going to leave the table and go to my room," he may hesitate before saying "go" because of the partial intrusion of the word "chair." When the child's responses are not yet well learned, there will be more disfluency than will occur when he has better acquired the very, very complex repertoires he must learn.

It is suggested, however, that if the child displays less fluency than other children, this may be the result of a less propitious training history. The circumstances here would be expected to be the same as with any other aspects of language that have been discussed herein. Fluency in making complex sequences of speech depends upon past learning conditions. It is inappropriate to instruct a parent merely to await maturation of nervous mechanisms in his child. A deficiency in any aspect of his language development calls for increased quality of learning. For example, a child who has the opportunity of making extended speaking performances, with good social reinforcement for this type of behavior, will learn the various skills that go into this skill. A child who has had little occasion for making extended, complex utterances will be less fluent in a situation that calls for such behavior.

This suggestion brings this discussion to what will be the major suggestion of this analysis: Whereas learning experiences in the various aspects of language—including reinforcement for fluency in more extended speech sequences in the child—are very important to the development of speech fluency, when the child experiences aversiveness (punishment) contingent upon his speech, the opposite effect is produced. According to a principle that will later be described in greater detail, when a behavior is followed by an aversive circumstance of any kind, that behavior will be weaker on future occasions; the behavior will be less likely to occur. This may be seen in the behavior not occurring at all, or in some partial form of weakening. In the latter case, the behavior may be hesitant and only partially occur, it may have a long delay before it occurs, it may occur in lessened form as in a whisper, and so on.

Strong speech (fluency) may be considered to be a type of behavior that operates according to learning principles. When the child is rewarded for speaking in extended sequences, he will learn such speech responses in good strength. If, on the other hand, he receives any type of punishment (aversiveness) contingent upon his speech, his speech will evidence the signs of weaker behavior. Thus, the point that the pediatrician made to the grandmother in terms of not being anxious about the child's stuttering was correct as far as it went. It would help in keeping the grandmother from treating the child's speech aversively. The general statement should be, however, that *stuttering frequently (and perhaps always, at least in the older child) arises because the child is experiencing aversive circumstances contingent upon his speech.*

As concerned as parents usually are about their child's advancement, it is necessary to indicate how parents may actually punish their child's speech, in a manner severe enough to produce stuttering, even though they do not intend to have such a severe effect. To begin, it is important to realize that the punishment involved does not have to be of the type traditionally recognized as punishment. The punishment may be minor: admonishment, social disapproval, a curt cutting off of what the child is saying, a loud and definite, "No you cannot do that," or "Don't interrupt," or a sarcastic, "Can't you see that father and I are talking," and so on.

Actually, these examples indicate ways in which the parent can punish his child for speaking. It is important also to realize that the child's speech itself has aversive qualities for the parent, even in cases where a very benign development is taking place. Much of the child's speech consists of demands upon the parent that are effortful and nonrewarding for the parent. The child asks for things, requests the parent's attention just for the attention, needs care of various kinds, and so on. Even when the various verbal requests are reasonable, they occur on many occasions where the parent has to discontinue a rewarding activity to engage in one that is less rewarding, or aversive. This means that much of the child's reasonable speech behavior is actually aversive to the parent and sets conditions for the parent making an irritable response to the child's speech.

But many of the requests are not reasonable, and the parent does not want to provide the object or service or attention requested. He will at this time respond in the negative. The child, however, may persist in his requests until the parent responds in a manner that is aversive enough to suppress the child's continued speech. This is a stronger punishment. Moreover, this is not an infrequent occurrence even in the most benign of circumstances. The parent is frequently irritated by the unreasonable verbal demands of the child and will respond in a way that suppresses the child's speech through aversiveness. In all likelihood it would be impossible to raise a child without a goodly number of such occurrences.

When the experience of punishment for speaking occurs frequently enough in the child's history, or intensely enough, it can be expected that certain general characteristics of weak behavior will become evident. This can occur through various circumstances in addition to those mentioned above. As other examples, the parent may have in the past reinforced aversive speech characteristics in the child, which when the child gets older the parent will no longer tolerate—which means that he will punish them when they occur. This may mean the child at this time experiences too high a percentage of punished speech and his speech may become hesitant. When a child is overly demanding he sets the stage for the parent to respond aversively to his requests. Another circumstance the author has seen in operation is the case where the parent will want the child to develop speech fluency and will try to force the child to do so. Thus, the parent may ask the child what he did at school that day. The child, for whom the task of remembering his day's activities is effortful, may simply reply, "Nothing." The parent may be offended by the child's lack of concern and may attempt to gain a more adequate reply by reprimand. This is aversive, however, and will not set the stage for a good response on the part of the child. If the child experiences enough occasions where he makes a poor performance in the face of social requests for speech, such occasions will come to control anxiety on the one hand (which will elicit avoidance behaviors on the part of the child) as well as weak and nonfluent speech. It may then be seen that the child displays the incipient signs of stuttering.

Thus, it is suggested that there are various ways that a child may experience aversive events (punishment) contingent upon his speech. The aversiveness may not be intense upon any one occurrence. Therefore the parent will ordinarily be unaware that he is being aversive to the extent that the child is learning speech habits that may be a serious problem. Nevertheless, the author has had an opportunity of observing how such aversive actions presented contingent upon the child's behavior in the family situation can begin to produce the speech hesitancies of incipient stuttering, and as will be indicated, how this process can be reversed to take a more benign direction.

To continue, once the child displays incipient stuttering this sets the stage for the development of more severe forms of nonfluency. Other social events may occur that result in additional punishment of the child's already hesitant speaking behavior. For example, the family members may respond to the child's stuttering with anxiety and attempt to get the child to stop his stuttering. This may take the form of admonitions to try to speak more clearly, or more slowly, or think out what he wants to say before saying it. Parents whose own training has inclined them to attempt to guide their child's behavior by aversive methods are likely to treat this problem in this way. Of course, this will exacerbate the behavioral problem. The problem arising from social punishment of speech will be intensified by additional punishment for hesitant speech. Moreover, rather than allowing the child to concentrate upon speaking, such experiences are conflicting in that they train the child to attend also to *how* he is speaking. This divided attention will interfere with the elicitation of fluent speech.

The child may also meet punishment for his speech behavior in the form of derision from his peers. The child who displays incipient stuttering may happen to have playmates who will mock him, tease him, and in other ways present social punishment contingent upon his speech. These types of conditions will further weaken his fluent speech behavior and increase the speech hesitancy. It has been noted widely that boys display stuttering to a far greater extent than do girls. It is suggested that this is due in part to the fact that boys more frequently than girls will meet conditions where incipient stuttering is socially punished.

This short section cannot be considered to be a complete analysis of speech hesitancies and repetitions. However, there is sufficient detail to provide some indications for understanding this development and for treating early cases of such speech problems. To begin, it may be suggested that parents who are aware of the learning conditions involved in the child's language development will be less likely to produce conditions that will lead to speech hesitancies. It is even more clear in the case of the child who has already developed incipient stuttering that the parents need information concerning the principles involved in the child's learning of hesitant speech and the conditions that can produce such speech.

The parent will ordinarily not realize that he is providing conditions that are creating the problem speech. He thus needs to become aware of the possible circumstances. The professional who, in dealing with such a parent, understands the principles and conditions involved may explore the possible parent-child speech interactions that may consist of punishing the child's speech. In addition, parents may need information concerning how to change their behavior and yet deal adequately with the child.

Thus, for example, a usual situation in which the parent punishes the child's speech is when the child continues to request something that the parent does not wish to give or to allow. The parent may be in the habit, when he does not want a drawn-out haggle, of giving an intense negative— perhaps with some display of anger—before the child has finished his opening request. This may be the parent's defense against a child who otherwise would mount an exceedingly good or persistent argument. In such a case the parent needs information by which to be able to respond in the negative without making it a punishment for the child's speech. In this example, it may be suggested that the parent can say, "No," when he wants to, but the negative should be given in a different manner. That is, the parent does not want to suppress the speech by the negative, only to disallow the child's proposed actions. The speech of the child is to be encouraged. The parent may do this simply by allowing the child to state his case, fully and fluently, without cutting it off in the middle with some form of social punishment. Even when what the parent says is going to have an aversive quality, if there is a delay between the child's speech and the parent's response, there will be little general suppressing effect on the child's speech. The parent may even reward the speech, as part of the treatment of incipient stuttering, even though disallowing the proposed action. That is, the parent can say something like, "Yes, you have stated your case very well and I understand why you want to stay overnight at your friend's house. But tonight is a school night and it is not possible." It will be found that the child will persist longer in his arguments than if he is cut off quickly, and thus the interaction may be more effortful for the parent. The parent, however, may also further train the child that when he makes statements such as, "I see why you want to do such and such, but you definitely cannot," the definitive statement, while not being punishing, indicates further argumentation is unavailing. This process will be discussed further on.

In addition to searching out and removing the speech interactions with the child that have been punishing, the parent may also conduct "therapy" for the child's speech hesitancy in other ways. While it would be aversive to put the child on the spot and demand extended speech from the child, the parent can begin to reward the child for fluent speech occasions if he will systematically attempt to do so. The parent's attention and approval for the child's accounts of happenings and so on will strengthen fluent speech in the converse of the process in which the speech hesitancy is acquired.

There is one last point to be made with reference to the case of the grandmother concerned about the 2½-year-old's stuttering. The advice to the grandmother was to ignore the child's speech and to wait for "neural and speech mechanism" maturation. Although the advice not to attempt to get the child to speak more slowly was good, it is suggested that this type of advice is not adequate, although characteristic of the passiveness engendered by the maturational approach. That is, the child's stuttering may have been due to incomplete, but essentially normal, learning. On the other hand, the child may have begun to show the signs of speech hesitancy resulting from inadvertent social punishment of the child's speech. The time to pick up cases of incipient stuttering development is early in the process—before the secondary processes of punishment for the stuttering itself begin. At the early point the parent may still have the power of reversing the problem speech development. At the later point where individuals outside of the family begin responding to the child's speech in nonbenign ways (when the child will become overtly anxious about his speech) the process is not so easily reversible. It would seem necessary for the professional to give parents the information by which they can appropriately consider their child's speech development in any case, especially if there is a possibility that they are unknowingly producing a problem.

In conclusion, it is suggested that many children develop speech disfluencies because of social punishment for speech experienced in interactions with parents in the home. This process can be reversed when the parents are made aware of the circumstances and systematically attempt not to be aversive to the child's speech, on the one hand, while also attempting to provide conditions of positive reinforcement for the speech. Full procedures for dealing with early stuttering problems could be implemented and researched in the home on the basis of this analysis—a suggestion that also applies to other disorders in the basic behavioral repertoires.

chapter 9 / Learning to Attend

Many learning situations involve the learning of a response, which is already made to one stimulus, to a new stimulus. It should be noted that the innumerable cases of this learning could not take place without the individual making "contact" with the stimuli involved. Moreover, whether or not contact is made ordinarily depends upon the individual first making certain responses that enable him to see, hear, touch—"sense"—the relevant stimuli in some way. Thus, any learning that involves making a new response to a new stimulus also involves "attending responses" that establish sensory contact with the old and the new stimulus. It may be concluded that one category of behavior that enters into all formal and informal learning of the child—which is a given in the functioning of the other basic behavioral repertoires—involves what is called attention in common-sense terms. (The discussion that is to be presented follows a previously presented analysis of the author's; see Staats, 1968a.)

The discussion will attempt to show how learning principles underlie the development of the basic behavioral repertoire of attentional skills. This type of analysis is basic to an understanding of much cognitive learning. Moreover, until the analysis of the development of attentional behavior is made, many *problems* of cognitive learning cannot be dealt with. Thus, the learning analysis of attention, as with the other learning analyses made herein, is intended to yield applications as well as understanding.

ATTENTION
AS RECEPTOR-ORIENTING BEHAVIOR

The sense organs of the human body are placed in anatomical structures whose "movement," in many cases, results in variation in what stimuli will affect the organism. These movements are important determinants of what is commonly called attention. Thus, as an example, the organs sensitive to light stimuli are concentrated in the eyes. The position of these organs is varied by the movements of the eyes, eyelids, neck, and back, as well as the general movements and position of the body. It should be noted that these movements are responses, and thus are learned according to the principles already discussed. Any independent condition that controls these various sense-placing, or receptor-orienting, responses affects the stimulus input to the eye. Thus, two individuals may be in the same general environmental situation, but different past histories of conditioning with respect to attentional behaviors, or indeed different present variations in variables such as motivation, may result in the two individuals receiving largely different stimulus conditions because of variations in their sense-placing, or attentional, behavior.

Attention may actually be considered to involve a kind of "competition" between stimuli in the extent to which receptor-orienting responses are elicited. Let us say that the individual is in a situation that involves a multitude of stimuli. Let us say that in the past he has been trained to respond to one of these stimuli much more strongly than he has been trained to respond to the others. In such a circumstance this one stimulus will control his response, and thus be described in everyday terms as having "gained his attention." It is suggested, then, that attention in the naturalistic situation is influenced by the relative strengths of the stimuli in the situation for eliciting a sense-placing response. Moreover, what the individual does, what he learns, and so on will depend upon the type of attentional response elicited.

An individual who has, for example, been reinforced in the past for looking at a particular color, in contrast to other colors, will "attend" to this color more than to the others. Ordinarily, this training would probably take place in the process of training the child to name colors, so that the stronger attentional response to the color would include a stronger verbal response to the color. It has been shown that children will better learn and remember colors presented to them for which they have previously learned a labeling response than they will colors they have not learned to respond to with names (Brown and Lenneberg, 1954).

Furthermore, in addition to the "competition among stimuli" of one particular sensory modality for the control of the individual's response, there is also competition between the senses in this respect. In a situation in which the individual is presented with both auditory and visual sources of stimulation, if he has been reinforced more for responding to the visual stimuli than to the auditory stimuli, his attentional responses to the visual stimuli will be elicited. Of course, there would ordinarily be considerable overlap in any case, since some members of the less-controlling class of stimuli would be stronger than some of the stimuli in the "stronger" sense.

(As will be described more fully further on, stimuli in one sense also come to control attentional responses important for a different sense. As an example, there are auditory stimuli that come to control auditory attentional responses. In addition, however, *auditory* stimuli also come to control attentional responses for better placing the visual sensory organs. To illustrate, the sound of an approaching car for the hiker along the road will control a head-turning response that brings the eyes into position where they can sense the approaching car.)

The important suggestion here is that what we call attention, a very fundamental form of behavior, is subject to influence by the individual's learning history. This suggestion may be exemplified in the context of discussing an important type of attentional learning that must take place in early child training. For further learning to be effected in many different training circumstances, it is important that certain stimuli come to more strongly control attentional responses than do other stimuli. The untrained child will not differentially respond in this way—and this may mean that no new learning occurs. For example, something that must occur for the child if he is to learn well in school situations is that certain auditory stimuli strongly control his attention behavior. At a very fundamental level the sound of the human voice must become a stimulus that strongly controls "stopping and listening." Vocally produced stimuli, in "competition" with other auditory stimuli as well as stimuli of other kinds, must in general come to have strong control over the behavior of the child.

A child for whom this is not the case will be considered abnormal—if the deficit is severe enough. For example, a child who continues to respond to *other* stimuli in a situation where an adult is speaking to the child will be considered dull, or autistic, or uncontrollable. Many autistic children suffer from this deficit in attentional learning. A child in a preschool or kindergarten group who does not respond with attention to the teacher's words as do the other children will be considered backward or abnormal. Furthermore, he will not receive the same training circumstances as the other children and will not learn as well. Anyone who works with young children has noted that there are large differences among children in the extent to which their attentional behaviors are controlled by the auditory stimuli of an adult's voice. Although attentional skills are usually taken for granted as something the child gets from physiological maturation, it is suggested such differences arise from the child's learning history. Moreover, lack of appropriately controlled attention is a frequent underlying reason for the label of mental retardation.

In the infant and young child, of course, the normal adjustive attentional behaviors must be learned for the first time. Long before the child can emit language himself, the auditory stimuli produced by others will, under usual circumstances, come to elicit responses. For example, the parent will usually talk when administering to (that is, reinforcing) the child. This means the various "positive" responses elicited by the reinforcing stimuli will be conditioned to the parent's voice. The parent's normal voice, as has been mentioned earlier, will thus become a rewarding stimulus.

Consequently, as the child lies awake in his crib and the parent is in another part of the house talking or singing, the child's head movements that result in a clearer auditory signal of the parent's voice will be reinforced and learned. If the child moves in one direction he hears the reinforcing sound more strongly; if he moves in the opposite direction he hears the sound less strongly. Such experiences would be expected to result in general auditory sense-orienting response skills being learned according to the principle of reinforcement. Weak auditory signals come to control the attentional behaviors of "cocking" the head in the way with which we are familiar, uncovering the ears, and so on. It may be suggested that this type of attentional learning may begin at very early ages. As soon as a sound becomes rewarding, any response that results in clearer reception will be learned.

A similar process of early learning is involved in the acquisition of attentional responses for vision; that is, responses that bring the eyes into appropriate position and function. For example, in addition to the parent's sound becoming a reward, the sight of the parent also becomes a reward. As a consequence, movements within the eye as well as movements of the eye that result in a better visual stimulus of the parent will be learned. It would be expected that some of the learning of the movements of the child's lenses, his eyes, his head, and so on, would occur through the action of this type of reinforcement.

When the parent is out of focus, for example, certain particular changes in the muscles controlling the curvature of the lens of the eyes will be strengthened by providing a better visual stimulus of the parent. These responses will thus be rewarded. Movements of the lens muscles in the wrong direction, however, will result in a less clear visual image and consequently would not be strengthened. Through this informal learning it would be expected that a blurred image would come to control movements of the lens muscles that clarified the image. As with other types of sensory-motor learning, after a sufficient number of learning trials it would be expected that these visual attentional responses would occur rapidly and surely. In general, it should become reinforcing to have sharp rather than blurred visual sensations, since these types of sensations allow successful (better reinforced) sensory-motor behaviors.

Similar circumstances would also involve movements of the muscles attached to the eyeball itself, as well as movements of the muscles of the neck and other parts of the body. It is thus suggested that the child *learns* his basic attentional behaviors of visual perception, which in themselves constitute a very complex type of repertoire. This is said in contrast to the customary assumption that these very basic attentional skills of the child come about because of biological maturation. It may be added that although the parent has been used as the stimulus in the example, as was also the case in discussing auditory attentional learning, it would be expected that many other stimuli would be involved with this type of learning, since clarifying a visual stimulus is functional in any case where other responses are to be made to the stimulus.

There are attentional responses learned under the control of stimuli of the other senses as well. Thus, when one turns his head in the presence of a faint odor, he may receive either a stronger or weaker contact with the molecules stimulating the sensory response. With such reinforced learning trials the individual learns olfactory attentional skills. A more dramatic response that has an even greater effect in increasing olfactory "contact" is the response of sniffing. This may be considered to be an attentional response that is learned under the control of faint olfactory stimuli, reinforced by receipt of a clarified olfactory sensation.

Faint, or incomplete, tactile stimuli also come to control tactile attentional responses. The process, it is suggested, is the same. The individual will acquire a repertoire of responses of "feeling" things; that is, skills by which to improve contact with objects. When a person has received a "partial" tactile stimulus, for example, he will respond by moving the hands in such a way as to receive additional stimulation. These responses have been acquired in situations in which it is rewarding to make such hand movements as well as in situations in which such tactile attentional responses have escaped or avoided aversive stimuli.

These various repertoires of skills may be considered to be very basic types of attentional responses under the control of stimuli in the same modality as the attentional responses being controlled. It would seem likely that everyone would acquire a repertoire of these types of attentional responses, except perhaps in exceptional cases. That is, the physical environment itself provides reward for responses clarifying sensory input, at least to some extent. On the other hand, it is not unlikely that it is possible to acquire these attentional repertoires in varying levels of skill. Thus, as one example, some athletic skills involve special development of such attentional skills, and these skills are an essential feature of the athletic ability. In baseball the visual stimulus of a rapidly moving ball as it approaches the batter must come to control appropriate eye movements that follow the ball. Moreover, movements of the muscles of the lenses of the eyes that maintain the ball in good focus must be learned. Keeping one's eye on the ball is an essential constituent of any sport involving a ball.

The development of the appropriate eye movements for such athletic skills can be readily observed in young children. In the beginning a child will not track a ball that is thrown to him, even when told, "Watch the ball." Only after many, many training trials will this attentional skill begin to emerge. In noting the importance of learning to the young child's development, it is edifying to observe the process and causes of development. By the time the player has become expert, however, these attentional responses are well acquired. An expert tennis player will keep his eye on the speeding ball until it strikes his racquet. Obviously, there will be great disparities in these attentional skills of adults, depending upon their histories of learning.

The manner in which the attentional basic behavioral repertoire is acquired has been described as it occurs under normal or advantaged circumstances. It should be remembered, however, in this as in other repertoires analyzed herein, that even at a very basic level there is opportunity for development to be retarded or distorted. The training circumstances, for example, may be absent or awry; the parents may not have, or may not employ properly, the necessary reinforcement system, and so on. The child's experience with the physical world of objects may be deficient in extreme cases. Deficits in this learning can be expected to result in serious, basic deficiencies.

CROSS-MODAL CONTROL
OF ATTENTIONAL BEHAVIOR

In addition to the case where the stimuli of a particular sense come to control attentional responses relevant to that sense organ, there are various mixtures where the stimuli of one sense come to control movements that orient a different sense organ. These attentional skills must also be learned. Thus, for example, the infant is reinforced for attentional responses that bring his mouth into contact with objects that he has *seen*. Through this learning, *visual* stimulus objects come to control *muscular* responses that bring the child's oral sense organs into contact with the objects, and which orient the tactile and gustatory senses of the mouth, lips, and tongue. This is but one example. Ordinarily, we also acquire a vast repertoire of movements that are attentional responses for our tactile sense, under the control of visual stimuli. Thus, for example, we acquire eye-hand motor coordinations of various kinds in which the movement results in better tactile stimulations, under the control of the visual stimulus. (See the author's discussion of the acquisition of sensory-motor coordinations in Staats, 1963.) Additional examples of cross-modal control of attentional responses will be given in the following discussions.

Verbal Stimulus Control
of Attentional Behavior

An even more important repertoire of attentional responses, at least for the later learning of the child, involves control by auditory verbal stimuli. Although attentional responses of the various sensory modalities are involved, perhaps it is the control of visual attentional responses that is most important. That is, children must receive extensive training (usually informally conducted in the home) for making varied visual attentional responses under the control of verbal stimuli (instructions).

Thus, the child needs to be trained to respond correctly to such stimuli as, "Look to your right," "Look up," "Look at the small one," "Look at the third one from the right," "Look at the red one," "Look at the triangle," "Notice that the letter *m* has two humps while *n* has only one, "Watch what I do," "See how I make the letter," and so on. In addition, of course, such verbal stimuli must also come to control types of attentional responses other than visual. The following are examples of the control of auditory attentional responses, gustatory attentional responses, and tactile attentional responses: "Listen for the high note," "Taste the bitter aftertaste," "Feel the rough spot in the middle," "Smell the gasoline," "Lift it and feel how heavy it is."

Verbal-Motor
Attentional Learning

Attentional responses controlled by instructions may be seen as variations of the verbal-motor repertoires previously described. However, the behaviors involved in the present case are sense-placing responses that are so basic to the later learning of the child that separate discussion is deserved. This is specially true since deficits in this basic repertoire seem frequently to be at the root of early learning problems of children (as in mental retardation and autism) and thus the later behavior problems of the adult.

The suggestion here is that this complex repertoire of attentional behaviors, like the others, is learned. For example, the child has to receive experiences that train him to the verbal-attentional repertoire. Since this training is ordinarily not done formally, we tend to think of this type of behavior as given through maturation. Closer observation and analysis shows, however, that the verbal control of the child's attentional repertoire develops through training, not through physiological maturation. In this context it is very illustrative to take an infant and say his name. Before the appropriate learning the child will not respond differentially to this verbal stimulus with attention. With a young child, as other examples, one can give attentional instructions such as calling the child's name or saying, "Close your eyes," "Move your eyes to the right," "Look up," "Look down," "Turn around," and so on. Depending upon the previous training of the child, he will respond appropriately or not. In addition, it is quite easy and informative to take a child who has not learned an attentional response under the control of the verbal stimulus and teach him this aspect of the necessary repertoire.

It is very amusing to give a child an attentional instruction when some learning has occurred but it is incomplete. The partial response usually produces a very cute result. An untrained child told, "Watch the ball as I throw it to you," will look at it intently as it is held but remain with fixed eyes (and hands) as the ball is thrown to him. Before an attentional skill of this type is perfectly acquired, the child will emit some very ludicrous behaviors.

A good repertoire of verbally controlled attentional behaviors is absolutely essential for later formal and informal learning situations. Nevertheless, even though it is easily seen that there are vast differences in this repertoire among preschool children, little attention has been directed toward investigation of the conditions that produce the necessary repertoires of attentional behaviors. One of the main reasons for this seeming disinterest in the manner in which such attentional skills are learned is to be found in the common conception that individual differences among children are a function of differences in physiological maturation. Following the present analysis, however, it may be suggested that learning variables account for very large differences in this essential repertoire.

It will be productive to sketch out the principles involved in the establishment of the auditory control of attentive behaviors for the visual apparatus, as well as some of the first types of training involved in elaborating this repertoire. To continue with the previous example, because the sight of the parent is frequently paired with rewards, the sight of the parent becomes a learned reward—especially when there has been a period of absence (deprivation) of the parent. Let us say that the child has been isolated from the parent for a time, and the parent has then entered the child's room and made some type of vocal response. If in the presence of the parent's auditory stimulus (voice) the child turns his head and eyes a certain way, he will see the parent, and these movements will thus be followed by the reward involved in seeing the parent. This experience would be expected to produce visual attentional learning under auditory control. The stimulus is the vocal sound. The responses are the "sense-placing responses" of turning the head and eyes. The reinforcement is the sight of the parent. With a wide variety of this type of experience, auditory (verbal) sounds will come to control attentional responses for the visual apparatus. This is thus an example of the way that certain sound stimuli come to control responses that move the visual apparatus so the source of the sound is seen.

Of course, a great deal of experience is necessary before the wide varieties of sounds, emanating from a wide variety of locations, will come to control the appropriate attentional responses. To continue with training examples involving parent-child relations, this type of learning when greatly elaborated will produce a complex skill repertoire in which verbal stimuli will elicit specific attentional responses. To illustrate an informal parental training trial, when the parent says the child's name, or, "Look here," or "Look at me," or some such thing, there will be many instances when the attentional responses of turning eyes and head will be reinforced by something more than just the sight of the parent. That is, many times the parent offers some object (reinforcer) to the child as he says the child's name or utters one of the other sounds that must come to control the visual attentional responses. When this training first begins, the control of the child's attentional behavior will be weak, and it may be a moment or more before the child makes the appropriate attentional responses. The parent (trainer) may also be forced to produce some other stimulus that already has strong control over the attentional responses—such as saying "Hey" loudly, or clapping hands. With additional training trials, however, the verbal control of the child's attention will become stronger, until eventually simply saying the child's name will immediately elicit the responses that result in the child looking toward the source of the auditory stimulus. The parent who does not realize the importance of the verbal-attentional learning may not conduct the training. Moreover, at the beginning it is easier to simply walk over and dangle the reinforcer in front of the child. But by so doing the parent will have lost an opportunity for enhancing this crucial verbal-attentional repertoire.

Further training is necessary to bring the child's attentional responses under the control of specific verbal stimuli, such as "Look here," "Look under the bed," "It is on the table," "You will find it in the hall," "See the difference between the one on the right and the one on the left," "Look at the little one, then the big one," and so on. A complex, if informal, history of learning involving many training trials would be expected to be necessary to produce the correct repertoire of visual attentional responses under the control of complex vocal stimuli. As already suggested, in the early stages of establishing this repertoire, the parent may also use other auditory or visual stimuli that already control attentional responses. For example, through the same type of conditioning already described, pointing will come as a stimulus to control attentional behaviors—the child having in the past been reinforced by seeing reinforcing objects when following with his eyes a pointing finger. The pointing finger, once it has come to elicit attentional responses, can be employed as a stimulus that gets the child to make an attentional response at the same time that the parent is providing a verbal stimulus such as "Look here." After this has happened a number of times, sometimes followed by reinforcement, the vocal stimulus "Look——" will thus acquire control over the visual attentional responses.

THE ATTENTIONAL REPERTOIRE
IS BASIC TO FURTHER LEARNING

As has been suggested, this repertoire of attentional behaviors under appropriate stimulus control is basic to early cognitive learning. For one thing, this repertoire is what the teacher's instructional procedures rely upon. Where children have this repertoire well developed, the teacher need only present the verbal stimuli (instructions) to control the correct attentional behaviors. The children will thus sense the appropriate stimuli in their necessary sequences, and will learn. Where the attentional repertoire has not yet been developed by the pupil, it must be trained or the child will not sense the stimuli and consequently will not learn.

Both types of behavior and both types of performance occur frequently. When the teacher has classes in which the pupils customarily do not have well-developed attentional repertoires, a primary aspect of training must involve training attentional behaviors. It is not infrequent, for example, to observe that many of the activities of the kindergarten teacher constitute attentional training. The teacher will say, for example, "Everyone look here," strike a chord on the piano (which controls attention), and wait for the appropriate attentional response before introducing a new and reinforcing activity.

When a child has a deficit in the verbal control of his attentional behaviors, many types of training are impossible, and it is not likely that the child will gain as much from learning experiences as do other children with better attentional repertoires. Specific examples from the classroom are informative, for in many cases it is necessary that a child look at (attend to) a specified stimulus and also make a response. This is certainly true in the acquisition of reading, writing, and number-concept learning—as well as many other social behaviors. If the child does not attend to the stimulus, if the adult's words do not control appropriate looking and listening responses, the child does not see or hear the stimulus and learning does not occur. After a period of this the child will not only appear to be but he will be "retarded" or "disturbed."

DEFICITS IN THE ATTENTIONAL REPERTOIRE

Since the acquisition of basic attentional responses requires extensive training, if mainly informally conducted, it must be expected that many children will not have an adequate repertoire. For one reason or another, many parents do not provide the learning experiences that will yield the necessary repertoire. This deficit would be expected to occur more generally in families subjected to suppressed circumstances in socioeconomic-cultural factors; in families whose members have special problems such as parental instability, maladjustment, or retardation; in families where the child through illness or injury presents special problems of training; and so on. Whatever the circumstances, before children can be expected to profit from many learning situations, including our traditional formal educational training circumstances, training in this attentional repertoire is essential.

The author's work has shown with various children, including retarded children, that there are large differences in the quality of these attentional repertoires. For example, with the normally developed children, verbal stimuli (instructions) control the appropriate visual attentional responses. The child can be told, "Look at this picture first, then look at the pictures below," and so on, and the appropriate attentional behaviors are elicited. With even four-year-old children some complex instructions that control sequences of attentional responses can be given. With some of the more retarded children it is necessary to physically guide the child to make the necessary looking responses, or to use other direct controls such as pointing to elicit attentional behaviors. When this is necessary the learning task is immensely more difficult for the child and for the trainer.

REINFORCEMENT AND ATTENTIONAL LEARNING

The importance of adequate reinforcement in the maintenance of attention in the young child who is involved in an arduous or repetitive learning task cannot be underestimated. This topic will be returned to later. At this point, however, it may only be noted that the strength and quality of the child's attention in any learning situation will depend upon the extent to which the continued attentional responses required are reinforced. Parents who have attempted to train a young child in a task that requires repeated responding and attention of the child will have found that after a few minutes the attention wanes and the responses do not occur, if the sources of reward are inadequate. In fact, irrelevant and interfering responding will soon occur, and the training will cease unless the parent institutes some forceful measure.

It should be indicated, however, that the attentional repertoire does not customarily remain dependent upon immediate reinforcement after it has been *strongly* learned. That is, the attentional behaviors of preschool children cannot be maintained for long when they are voluntarily participating in an arduous and unreinforcing task (Staats, Staats, Schutz, and Wolf, 1962). However, by the time children are in the first years of school, many of them will have such a strongly acquired attentional repertoire that immediate reinforcement is not necessary. That is, when the child has had a long history of being reinforced for attentional responses under verbal control, the verbal stimuli will maintain control for some time even when no reinforcement is forthcoming.

It is also true that the verbal control of attentional behaviors becomes differentiated in other ways, according to the person supplying the verbal instructions. Thus, verbal stimuli from some people will ordinarily gain control over the attention of the child to a greater extent than will the verbal stimuli from other people. For example, the same words from another child will not as strongly control the child's attentional responses as when the verbal stimuli are produced by a parent. Later in life, of course, complex and subtle social stimuli will differentially control one's attentional behaviors. The words of one's employer, wife, mother, children, the grocery-store man, an expert, and so on will have differential amounts of control over the individual's behavior, including his attentional behaviors. (An important determinant of the strength with which a social stimulus elicits attentional behavior, as the next chapter will indicate, is the amount of reward or attitudinal value of the social stimulus.) Some of these differences in the control of attention must be learned early if the child is to succeed in a school, as one example. Thus, it is important that instructions of an adult gain strong control over the child's attentional responses—stronger than the control of other children and various environmental stimuli. When this is not the case, as will be described more fully, the child may be seen as difficult to control.

In summary, it is true that once appropriate stimuli have come to control behavior, these stimuli can be presented and learning will occur, even without reinforcement. Much formal education, for example, depends upon the prior establishment of these sources of control for attentional and working behaviors. Actually, school training procedures rest upon the child having a well-developed attentional repertoire that the parents have hopefully developed in the child. If this type of control has not been previously established, little learning will take place in the usual educational situation. That is, continued attentional behavior is not directly rewarded in school. Unless the child has strongly learned attentional skills, the control of the teacher's instructions will weaken and become ineffective and the learning will be negatively affected. This is the case for many children in school.

DISCRIMINATION SKILLS

Attention has been discussed as the fairly general movements involved in placing the sense organs so they may be more effectively stimulated. In addition to these important aspects of attention, there are even finer skills involved in much discrimination learning that is important to the child's further learning. What is commonly called discrimination appears to involve attentonal responses that are more subtle than simply looking in the general direction of an object—as some of the previous discussion has implied. That is the case when the task involves acquiring a different response to a complex stimulus only slightly different from another complex stimulus to which the response should not be made. For example, the child must learn to make a response to *m* and a different response to *n*. However, these two stimuli are very much alike. The child will never learn this discrimination, along with learning different responses to the other letters, by gross attentional responses of generally looking at the letters. In learning different responses to two similar stimuli, it may be observed even on a naturalistic level that the individual will scan the two objects and move his eyes back and forth from one object to another.

It is suggested that the child, if properly trained, acquires general skills so that when he is faced with a problem of discrimination he makes scanning eye movements, and comparing eye movements looking from one to the other of the objects involved, and so on. Furthermore, many stimuli are of such a nature they require scrutiny in fine detail before the important aspect of the stimulus is seen that is to control the relevant behavior. It may be suggested that the detailed scrutiny of stimuli, the comparing of stimuli, and so on are attentional behaviors that must be learned.

This topic cannot be discussed in detail here. It will suffice to say at this point that there seem to be additional responses that sharpen the stimulus, or the differences between stimuli, or that involve sequences of attentional responses, and so on. It may be suggested that having a repertoire of such fine attentional responses is also of great importance in the child's further learning. Also, such attentional "comparing" responses may involve senses other than vision. The individual may sniff a cantaloupe while shopping, for example, and then quickly sniff another—in this way bringing the two stimuli together for comparison (for differential response). The individual may judge the smoothness of a surface by rubbing another surface for comparison. Obviously these discrimination skills can be developed to a high degree through training—as is the case for the professional wine taster, for example, or the pathologist who compares tissue samples.

Many of these discrimination skills can be produced through self-conscious training—even in the parent-child relationship. As an illustration, take the mother who demonstrates to her daughter how you can comparatively feel fruit and vegetables, comparatively smell them, comparatively notice their color, and so on. These skills can enhance the child's ability to select prime fruit and vegetables—a skill that will delight the child's own family at a later day. Moreover, the child then possesses the skill, which she can later pass on to her own daughter.

As another example, the businessman may train a son to discriminate the facial expressions of customers as negotiating is being conducted. Attention to such cues, and the discriminations learned, may enable alternative strategies to be selected that result in business success. This and the above training may involve imitation processes as well as instructions, postmortems on failures, and direct reinforcement.

These examples are intended to suggest that there are various types of discrimination skills that provide the stimuli that enable other behaviors to be more effective. Some of these discrimination skills are so important they have been systematically developed as areas of special human skill—such as the preceding examples of wine tasting, the visual discriminations of a pathologist in reading tissue section slides or X rays, and so on. On the other hand, some of the discrimination skills are acquired, or are not acquired, in the informal learning at home. Some of the repertoires of discriminative skills are rather specific, and others have wide generality, relevant to many life situations.

INTELLIGENCE AND ATTENTIONAL AND DISCRIMINATION SKILLS

Almost all of the items on intelligence tests include tests of the control of attentional responses for successful performance. For example, at the two-year level the various items begin, respectively, by the examiner saying, "Watch what I do," "See all these things?" "Show me the dolly's hair," "See what I'm making!" "What's this?" and "Give me the kitty." In each item, a verbal stimulus has to control the attentional responses of the child. A child who has not acquired such a basic behavioral repertoire, it will be seen, will continue to perform what are irrelevant behaviors in the face of the verbal stimuli. He will sit and look at the testing objects, attempt to reach them, attempt to leave the room, sit in his chair leadenly, and so on. Such a child will be judged to be retarded, disturbed, brain-damaged, autistic, or what have you—depending upon the character of the irrelevant behaviors he displays.

The common tendency is to consider that every "normal" child will simply by his biological growth come to *attend* under the control of verbal instructions. When the child does not, he is considered to suffer from some biological defect. However, when one takes one of these children who displays such defects and trains him to a rudimentary attentional repertoire under verbal control, the part that learning plays in the intellectual development of the child can be readily seen. Attentional skills under verbal control are very basic in any intellectual performance.

In addition to this fundamental attentional repertoire under verbal control —which is requisite to beginning to solve any intelligence item—there are finer discrimination skills that play a central role in succeeding on many items. Each imitation item, for example, will ordinarily involve the child comparing his production to that of the examiner and responding to any difference between the stimuli. Thus, discrimination skills are usually basic to imitation skills.

In addition, however, there are items that can be selected to very straightforwardly illustrate the role of learned discrimination skills. For example, at the 3½-year level two sticks are placed on the table before the child and he is asked, "Which stick is longer?" This item not only requires that he look at a single stimulus, it requires that he look at and compare two stimuli. If the difference is slight the child may have to scan back and forth between the two stimuli.

At the four-year level the child is presented with a circle. The child also has ten other forms, including another circle. When the single circle is presented, the child's task is to select the matching circle from among the ten forms presented. The child is first told, "See all these things." Again, this verbal stimulus must control the general attentional responses of looking at the forms. Then the verbal stimulus next presented must control a more precise attentional response when the examiner says, "Find me another one just like this" (Terman and Merrill, 1937, p. 88). These verbal stimuli and the various forms must then control close attentional and discrimination responses. The child has to examine the various stimulus forms and look back to the circle, and examine additional forms and compare them to the circle, until he sees the form that he cannot discriminate from the circle. For the four-year-old child this is an item that measures the skill of his discrimination responses under verbal stimulus control. These skills are also tested with a square and triangle.

It is interesting to note that if the first directions do not control appropriate behavior in the child on this item, the examiner will attempt to gain control of the attentional and discrimination behaviors by additional verbal instructions. He will say, "Do you see all of these things?" and indicate the other forms. Then he says, "And do you see this one?" and points at the circle. Then he adds, "Now find me another one just like this," and passes his finger around the outline of the figure. Thus, pointing stimuli may be used as well as verbal stimuli to control attentional responses on this item.

At the six-year level the child is presented a card with six pictures on it. He is told the following: "See these crosses that are just alike? Here's one (pointing) that is *not* like the others. Put your finger on the one that is *not* the same as the others" (Terman and Merrill, 1937, p. 96). The child has to have learned scanning and comparing discrimination responses in order to make a correct response on the following discrimination items of this type.

Perhaps this will illustrate the importance of the child's attentional and discrimination repertoires of skills in judgments of the child's intelligence. The skills involved, again, may be considered in very straightforward learning terms. If the child has had the advantage of the learning, he can succeed on such items and be judged to be intelligent. If he has not learned the complex skills involved, he will fail and he will be judged to be—and he will be—less intelligent. Again, the discussion is also intended to illustrate that the catchall term "intelligence" that is so grossly defined actually refers to repertoires of learned skill important to the child's adjustment and further learning. It is thus important to identify these repertoires of "intelligence" behaviors. The repertoires are important in the child's general intellectual development as well as in the development of other aspects of personality.

chapter 10 / Motivation Learning: The Motivation System as an Aspect of Personality

The learning that has been described in the child's personality development takes place on the basis of reward for the behavior involved. Some learning, it may be noted, involves another principle yet to be discussed. However, most of the skills that the child acquires in his informal learning in the home as well as in his educational learning depend upon reward—at least in the original acquisition of the behavior.

This is frequently not realized in general, and especially in the school and the home situation. It is frequently said, "Learning should be its own reward," and learning that takes place under some tangible system of reward is frowned upon. This view is entirely misplaced, and stems from an inadequate conception of what is rewarding, and how individual differences in what is considered rewarding are dependent upon the learning history of the children.

In educational circles some types of reward systems are quite popular; others, which in principle are just the same, are frowned upon or completely eschewed. Moreover, the rejection occurs on the basis of prejudgment, without bothering to consult fact—actually, experimentation that would demonstrate the importance of reward has even been ignored. Again, it is important to explore these ideas a bit because of the significance that our conception of child development has upon our approach to solving child-development, clinical, social, and educational problems.

It is necessary to note that differences in motivation account for wide variations in human beings. In every sphere of life we see that people who find different things rewarding (or punishing) behave differently. People strive to gain objects and events that are rewarding, and they strive to avoid objects and events that they find aversive. Thus, what it is that people find rewarding or punishing actually determines what they will do, how they will behave.

For example, let us take two children who both find learning new intellectual skills, and demonstrating their proficiency in those skills to each other, to be very rewarding. We will observe in such a case strong behavior that leads to the development of new skills. The two children will spend much time in studying and working to acquire new intellectual skills. As a contrast, let us take two other children who are not rewarded as highly by the acquisition and demonstration of intellectual skills. Rather, these two children find the acquisition of and demonstration of athletic skills and physical supremacy in competition to be very rewarding. We will in this case observe strong behavior that leads to the development of these skills. The behavior of the two sets of children will be quite different.

It is not a difficult extension to see how this principle will affect children's learning in various situations, especially the classroom situation. In the classroom the activity of learning new intellectual skills and the display of such products are the primary stimuli available as rewards. To illustrate, two children are placed in a classroom. Child A finds learning and its products rewarding, but child B does not. As a consequence, we will see the development of different behaviors in the two. Let us say that the children receive the same treatment in the class. Whenever they pay attention to materials the teacher presents and respond in the manner directed, they learn new skills and can produce new things (letters, words, and so on) which result from those skills. Under such a circumstance, child A's attentional and working behaviors will be rewarded and thus maintained in good strength. As a result he will continue to develop new skills. Child B's behavior, on the other hand, will not be maintained because evidence of learning is not rewarding. His attentional and working behaviors will wane, and other behaviors that are reinforced by effective rewards will increase in strength. The latter behaviors are frequently antithetical to intellectual learning and may generally be disruptive of class activities.

It may be added that child A will be seen as interested, motivated, hardworking, and *bright*. After a time this child will also measure that way on class, IQ, and achievement tests. That is, he will learn a great deal in the classroom. Child B will be seen as disinterested and dull, and he will ultimately measure that way after a few years of being present in school where he will develop skills only very slowly or not at all. This latter child is also likely to learn other things that are maladjustive—for example, negative emotional attitudes to the school, teachers, and successful students—as well as behaviors that disturb the classroom situation. That is, his experience in the classroom will be aversive, and the stimuli associated with the classroom will become aversive.

It is in just such circumstances that we can see the perniciousness of the biological conception of human behavior. When we see such differences in two children—whom we assume have been subjected to the same situation and thus the same opportunity for intellectual learning—we attribute the differences largely to personal (biological) characteristics of the children. As already indicated, when a child does not learn we assume he is less capable of learning. In general we also assume that people, including children, differ in their *inborn* needs for achievement. We feel that the strength of "ambition" is a personal characteristic that some people are lucky to have in good measure and others have in short supply. We tend to feel that groups of people differ in this way, and we tend also to consider that races can differ in this respect as a result of their biologies.

As has been suggested, the conception that one has of human behavior will determine what he does about problems of human behavior. In the present case a conception that some children have personal or constitutional weaknesses in their "motivation" for learning has different social implications than would a conception that the children's difficulty in learning is a consequence of the use of reinforcement systems in education that are inappropriate for some children because of their learning histories. The social implications can be seen readily when it is realized that it is groups such as lower-class children, racial minorities, or the culturally disadvantaged in general, as well as children with so-called "emotional problems," and so on, who are deficient in the display of "learning for learning's sake." Constitutional interpretations of these differences are highly derogatory and lead to social solutions of a negative nature to the problems involved.

From a learning conception, however, we can derive a much more humanistic interpretation. Not only is the learning conception supported by experimental evidence, but it also offers us an understanding with which to better raise children, to better approach clinical and social problems. *It is suggested that the child's motivational system is largely learned.* By this is meant that most of the stimulus objects and events which will be either rewarding or punishing (aversive) for the person come to be so on the basis of his learning experience. Moreover, the intensity of reward or punishment of an object or event is also a function of learning.

Not all rewarding objects or events are rewarding or punishing on the basis of learning, it should be noted. Thus, for example, food, water, air, tactile stimulation (especially of the sex organs), warmth of a certain level, and so on are all stimuli that have reward value for the suitably deprived infant. These stimuli are rewarding on the basis of the infant's biological structure—without learning being involved. These stimuli continue to be rewarding on this basis during one's lifetime. However, even in the case of biological rewards and punishments, the person's experience will also influence what objects and events are motivators, and to what extent. For example, through learning, some foods will become rewarding to one person and not to other persons, although to the suitably deprived individual almost all edible substances will have reward value.

The same is true of aversive stimuli. Cold, intense sounds, intense tactile stimulation (slaps, cuts, shocks, and so on), intense thermal stimulation (burns), and the like are aversive to the human organism on the basis of his biological structure. Even in these cases, however, considerable learning is possible, as we see in the case of the masochist, for whom some painful stimuli have come to have some reward value instead of just aversive characteristics.

Although there may be individual differences in the sensitivity of different infants to these rewarding and aversive stimuli, there is great homogeneity in the human species. Children for whom such stimuli were not rewards or punishments would be unlikely to survive. Unless the child learned behaviors that got him rewarding stimuli necessary for biological maintenance, as well as behaviors that avoid aversive stimuli that are biologically deleterious, the child would not be likely to survive, at least in primitive cultures.

The important point, however, is that many of the stimuli that become effective rewards and punishments for the individual are developed through learning—on the basis of the original stimuli that have reward or punishment value on a biological basis. Because learning is so heavily involved, and because it is complex and variegated, each individual will acquire a unique set of stimuli that are rewarding or punishing for him. The author has used the term "motivational (or reinforcement) system" to denote the set of stimuli that has reward value for the individual.

To varying degrees, individuals, and groups, will learn similarities in their motivational systems depending upon their learning experiences. It is also suggested that the immense individual and group differences that occur in the motivational systems of man are primarily learned. This includes what would ordinarily be referred to in common-sense terms as *interests, needs, attitudes, values, likes, dislikes, motivations, cathexes,* and so on.

Thus, once again, it is suggested that the common-sense organic-mental conception is erroneous in the context of human behavior. There is no evidence of biological differences that underlie the great multitudes of variations in the stimuli that *come* to be rewarding or punishing for various individuals and peoples. Although we customarily think to "explain" an individual's behavior by positing a host of internal *needs, wants, interests, attitudes, values,* and so on, as if they were biological givens, there is no evidence that is the case. As with the other aspects of human behavior already discussed, no biological differences have ever been found to account for the motivational differences we see in humans—and these differences are gigantic and multitudinous. There is thus no justification for associating personal excellence or righteousness with motivated behavior that we desire, or defect of a personal and moral sort with the lack of such motivation. These points will be elaborated in the discussions to follow.

THE PRINCIPLE
OF MOTIVATION LEARNING

The principle of learning involved in motivation learning is simple. *If a stimulus that is a reward is presented to the person at the same time as another stimulus that is neutral in reward value, the neutral stimulus will also become a rewarding stimulus.* The process of learning is not complete with one trial but increases with additional trials. Thus, although many stimuli are neutral to the child at first, if they are paired with rewarding stimuli they will become rewarding stimuli themselves and form part of the child's motivational system.

This type of learning has already been referred to herein, however, without stipulating what principle of learning was involved. For example, it was said at the very beginning that the parent comes to be a reward for the child because the parent in taking care of the child actually pairs himself as a stimulus with many rewarding objects and events. It is important to make a general statement of the principle, however, for it plays a widely important role in the child's learning. For *any* neutral stimulus that is paired with *any* rewarding stimulus will itself become a rewarding stimulus. When a stimulus has come through this conditioning process to have reward value, it is called a learned (conditioned) reward or a learned (conditioned) reinforcer. In the opposite case, where a neutral stimulus comes to be aversive, the same term applies. That is, the neutral stimulus becomes a learned reinforcer—but a learned *negative* reinforcer—when it is paired with an aversive stimulus.

The principle of learning involved is called classical conditioning. It was first discovered by Ivan Pavlov, although not in the context of learning rewards. However, this aspect of the principle is also well verified in controlled laboratory research. Moreover, as will be mentioned, a great deal of research may be cited in support of the present suggestion that the human motivation system is learned according to the principle of classical conditioning.

Thus, according to the principle of learning, new motivational stimuli are formed when a neutral stimulus is paired with a stimulus that is rewarding. An example may be employed from the basic laboratory to show clearly the principles involved. Let us say that we arrange a circumstance so that if a rat goes to the food bin in his cage when a buzzer rings (a neutral stimulus), he will find a pellet of food (a rewarding stimulus). Conditions are so arranged that he only finds a piece of food there just after the buzzer has rung, and this is done many times. It would be expected that the buzzer, which formerly would not have this effect, would under those circumstances of training become itself an effective reward. In a way it seems strange, but there is much evidence to support the expectation, and Zimmerman (1957) has clearly demonstrated the specific effect. That is, after the buzzer had been paired with food a number of times, it alone could be used as a reward to train the animal to other behavioral skills. The fact that the buzzer now had reward value could be demonstrated by presenting the buzzer after a response. If it is a reward the animal should learn the response—that is, make the response more frequently. Thus, if we put a lever in the animal's cage and whenever he pressed the lever down, the buzzer would be sounded for a short period (with no food given), we would find that the animal would learn the behavior of pressing the lever, *with the buzzer being the only reward.*

Furthermore, this situation can be used to illustrate the important effect of his learned system of reinforcers upon the individual's future learning. Let us say that we have two rats of the same biology. One of them, rat *A*, we subject to the training in which the buzzer is presented many times, each time paired with food. With the other, rat *B*, we alter our treatment. We could simply not present the buzzer at all, or we could even present the buzzer the same number of times but never paired with food. In either case, for the latter animal the buzzer would not become a rewarding (reinforcing) stimulus.

Now let us take these two animals and put them into the same learning situation, involving a lever which, when pressed, results in the short sound of the buzzer. We will see that rat A will be an enthusiastic learner. He will quickly acquire the new "skill" and he will perform it vigorously. If an observer were to typify this behavior, rat A would be called "hard-working," "interested," "motivated," "a good learner," and the like. Rat B, on the other hand, would press the lever a few times incidental to his other explorations, but would spend most of his time "fooling around." In this situation he would not learn the behavior, and would be a desultory worker. The *difference* between the animals, however, would rest solely upon the fact that for one organism the stimulus had become a reinforcer, a motivational stimulus, while for the other it had not.

This example is included not only to demonstrate the principle in precise form, but also to demonstrate the universal nature of the principles that are being discussed herein. That is, the principles of learning rewards, as well as learning through reward, are general throughout the animal kingdom. The lawfulness of the principles can be shown very easily with lower animals, in each case, and there are also many demonstrations with children in well-controlled laboratory circumstances. This is not to say that the complexity of the learning of lower animals is anywhere near that for man. But the principles of learning involved are the same. This should not be surprising, because the principles of learning under which all organisms operate are adaptive—they provide means of adjusting to environmental conditions. Unless they all adapt through learning, they do not survive.

SOCIAL ATTENTION
AS A LEARNED REWARD

The preceding discussions have presented the *principle* of learning involved in the child's development of his motivational system. It is also important for the behavioral scientist as well as the parent and practitioner to understand the specific conditions involved in learning important types of rewards and punishments. Not all of those important to human behavior can be described herein, nor even a major portion. However, examples important to the child's intellectual learning can be given. The description of these examples can yield suggestions for contributing to the child's development in this area.

As has been indicated, there is ample opportunity during human infancy and childhood for the systematic pairing of the parents and others with primary rewards. The infant is completely helpless for a long period of time during which the presentation of almost all positive rewards and the *removal* of all aversive stimuli is accompanied by social stimuli—the sight, sound, touch, and so on of others.

By attention, in the present context, is meant the stimulus properties of someone looking at, listening to, or touching, in some instances—that is, making attentional responses to—someone else. At first presentation, when the child is a neonate, the stimuli of the attention of a parent would not have reward value. It may be commonly observed, however, that most young children later develop very strong "attention-getting" behavior and may be observed on occasion to demand of their parents, "Look at me." Because this type of behavior has been so widely observed, it was suggested by early investigators that everyone has an "inborn need" for attention. When it is understood, however, that the stimuli of someone looking at us or listening to us become reinforcing through the operations of the principle of classical conditioning, the assumption of an "inborn need" becomes an unnecessary concept. Moreover, the learning conception again is advantageous. It tells one what to do to make the parent's attention into a reward. This would be valuable in cases where such a development had not taken place, for example, with some autistic children, or in cases where the parent would not arrange the necessary actions without instruction. Thus, for example, the learning conception indicates it would not be a good practice to prop up a bottle and allow the child to feed by himself. This practice does not allow for the parent to be paired with the food consumption and to thereby become a rewarding stimulus himself.

It may be said in general that being looked at and listened to is reinforcing because in our past histories these stimuli have been paired with primary rewards. It is ordinarily when the parent is "paying attention" to the child that he is fed, uncomfortable pins are removed, warmth is provided, and so on. Each situation pairs the parental "attention" with primary reinforcement. Thus, the "attention" of other people should become a very strong learned reward. It may then be observed that behavior which is followed by the attention of others (which "gets attention") is strengthened.

Let us take the case, on the other hand, of a child for whom attention was frequently accompanied by the presentation of aversive stimuli; where punishment was delivered customarily when other people attended to him. Later in life this child's behavior would not be strengthened by "attention." He would not be likely to say, "Look at me." Rather, any behavior that was followed by attention would be weakened. Actually, it would be unusual for a child to be raised in a situation where attention was not at least sometimes paired with reward. However, there are wide possibilities for having aversive stimuli also paired with attention, and thus children differ widely in this type of learning. For example, some parents are very "strict" and expect a child to behave perfectly at an early age. Such a parent my use various types of primary and social punishments whenever a behavior occurs that is considered undesirable. And, to further add to this, the parent may not train the child to positive behaviors that can be responded to with positive attention and reward. To continue with this example, the practical outcome of such a situation can be that when the child is quiet and is not disturbing the parent, the child does not receive aversive stimulation. It is when he does things actvely that the child is more likely to be punished. Under such a general circumstance, the attention of the parents, and thus other people, can come to be punishing rather than rewarding.

It is also true that a child who has learned few desirable behaviors and many undesirable ones will experience to a greater extent than usual more punishment later in life, paired with attention, relative to the reward that he receives that is paired with attention. Thus, for example, in school when a child with poor skills is called upon to recite he will more frequently experience teacher and group disapproval. Many times, also, as he does irrelevant or undesirable things in school it is when the attention of the teacher is directed upon him that he will be punished, and his undesirable but rewarding activities discontinued. For such a child attention will not come to be as rewarding as it will for a child who because of the excellence of his behavior has been rewarded when attended to.

On the other hand, sometimes children are raised in homes where the children are largely left to shift for themselves. The child may have ready access to the food that is kept in the house. To a far lesser extent in such cases is the attention of the parent requisite for rewards to occur. Attention will to a lesser extent become rewarding to the child with such a learning history. In contrast, most middle-class parents do various things for the child which the culturally deprived, the ill, the disturbed, the alcoholic, the incompetent parent may not do. Food from the beginning is systematically controlled by the middle-class parent, and is prepared by the parent and given to the child. The typical middle-class parent plays with the child (which is the presentation of rewarding events), he takes the child to interesting places, he gives the child treats, and so on. Innumerable times during the day, especially for the preschool child, conditions will be nonrewarding for the child until he gets the parent's attention. Because of this, attention comes to be a strong reinforcer—which within reasonable bounds will be an important part of the child's motivational system.

This can be carried to extremes, of course. There can be negative effects if sources of reward other than the parent's attention are not established and the child is "dependent" solely on reward administered by the parent. This of course leads to "dependent" behavior. As a result, such a child may not have social experiences by which he broadens his motivational system and acquires various social skills. The child needs many "learning trials" where the parent's attention is paired with rewards. But this is not all that the child needs in learning a social reward system. The attention of other individuals must also become rewarding. Thus, the parent will wish to formally or informally arrange it so that the child has reward in social interaction with other people, particularly with the child's peers and playmates. This experience will make the attention and company of others rewarding also—and thus free the child from dependence upon the parent.

In the usual case, since primary and learned rewards occur frequently when the child is in the presence of others, people in general become strong rewards. The so-called "gregarious instinct" in man may be accounted for in this way. Of course, as just mentioned for all the processes discussed in the present book, each person has a different learning history. For this reason, individual differences can be expected in the "trait of gregariousness," that is, in the extent to which the general presence of other people is reinforcing and, consequently, the extent to which the individual displays the behaviors that lead to socializing.

It may be added that there are many experimental studies that indicate the manner in which attention serves a rewarding function for children (as examples, see Rheingold, Gewirtz, and Ross, 1959; Harris, Johnston, Kelley, and Wolf, 1964). Moreover, attention as a rewarding stimulus has been dealt with herein because it is so important in various types of the child's learning. For example, the child learns many desirable behaviors because such behaviors are followed by attention. Thus, the young child may be vocalizing wordlike sounds without receiving attention from the busy parent. Let us say, however, that the child happens to say, "Daddy," or "Mama," and the parent gives the child attention. This reward would make it especially likely that the child would learn to say that particular word.

The child may also learn undesirable behaviors because such behaviors are followed by attention. Thus, most children learn undesirable speech behaviors because the behaviors are effective in getting the parent's attention. The busy parent, or the parent engrossed in conversation with another adult, will not attend to the well-modulated voice of a young child. If the child, however, suffering the deprivation of attention, happens to begin speaking in an unpleasant whining voice—or any unpleasant speech mannerism—he is likely to gain the attention of the parent because the speech is unpleasant. This occurrence, nevertheless, and in a manner contrary to the parent's intent, will train the child to whining, unpleasant speech characteristics. Staats (1957) indicated how the attention of doctors was involved in a schizophrenic patient learning abnormal behaviors, and research with hospitalized psychotics has supported this analysis (Ayllon and Michael, 1959). Hart, Allen, Buell, Harris, and Wolf (1964) have demonstrated the same principle in the context of early child learning. They showed that it was the attention of a nursery school teacher that maintained the child being a social "isolate," avoiding interaction with other children and seeking only interaction with the teacher. The manner in which disruptive behavior in the classroom is learned because it gets the teacher's attention has also been shown, along with procedures for reversing this process (Thomas, Becker, and Armstrong, 1968). The same principles have been demonstrated with retarded patients in a state hospital ward (Bostow and Bailey, 1969).

SOCIAL APPROVAL AND DISAPPROVAL AS REINFORCING STIMULI

It may be added that ordinarily a child will learn a discrimination between attention that is positive (rewarding) and attention that is negative (punishing). That is, when the parent is smiling, nodding, speaking softly, and so on, this type of attention tends to be paired with rewarding stimuli. On the other hand, when the parent attends to the child and frowns, shouts, and displays the other cues of anger, aversive stimuli are apt to be presented. Thus, although simply being looked at usually becomes a positive learned reward, social approval in the form of smiles, laughter, clapping, affectionate responses, and so on becomes even more of a reward. Social disapproval in the form of frowns, shouts, and so on becomes a strong punishment.

This type of learning, as with all others, is subject to infinite variation, of course, in accordance with the infinite variation among children's experiences. Thus, there are children who have not had an opportunity to learn the discrimination between attention that in our society should be rewarding and attention (disapproval) that should be negative. There are many children who learn behaviors even though those behaviors are followed by disapproval—because the disapproval has positive reward value rather than the punishing value it is intended to have. Some of the studies just cited are cases in point; for example, the case where children learn to misbehave in class because such behavior is followed by the attention of the teacher—even though the attention is of the disapproving type. A recent experiment has shown very clearly how disapproval can be a reward to some children (Tharp, Gallimore, and Kemp, 1969).

It is thus worth noting that it is important for the child to learn not only that approving attention is a positive reinforcer, but also that the various stimuli of disapproval—verbal as well as in tone and facial expressions—become aversive. When the child has had the necessary learning experiences, his behavior will be sensitive to approval and disapproval of others, and in this way he will be able to learn socialized behaviors. For the words of disapproval to become mild punishments the child requires training in which such words are paired with aversive consequences. This is a topic that will be dealt with in Chapter 12.

DEPRIVATION
AND REWARD VALUE

It should be noted briefly that the extent to which the individual has access to an event or object that is rewarding will effect the reward value of the stimulus. This is the case with the biological rewards such as food, sex, warmth, and so on. Food is a strong reinforcer and can promote a great deal of learning. However, food is not a strong reward just after the individual has eaten to satiation.

This principle should be noted in the general context of understanding the principles of human motivation. Thus, for example, the effects of deprivation-satiation upon the strength of reinforcing (motivating) stimuli such as attention would be expected to follow the general principle. Although the parent's attention will serve as an effective reward for the child, continued attention will satiate the child for this attention. Thus, as will be discussed later, it is not possible to employ attention and approval repeatedly as reinforcers in learning tasks that require many responses in massed presentations. Attention and approval work most effectively in training tasks in which learning trials are widely spaced.

Experimentally, Gerwitz and Baer (1958) have shown that children deprived of social interaction with an adult for twenty minutes learned a task under the action of attention and approval more readily than other children who had free access to (satiation on) the attention and approval of an adult. The mount of deprivation and satiation that children have for various types of re-inforcing stimuli can also be expected to effect the motivational properties of the stimuli. Several types of important motivational stimuli for the intellectual learning of the child will be described in the following sections.

THE SELF-REWARD SYSTEM

In beginning this chapter it was stated that the traditional view of the child's intellectual learning is that "Learning should be its own reward." It has been suggested, however, that it is through his learning history that the child comes to find objects and events rewarding which are not "naturally" (or originally) rewarding. Sometimes, nevertheless, we tend especially to feel that what is re-warding must be determined internally, by the quality of the individual, be-cause it is evident that there is no external (extrinsic or material) reward in-volved. Even in cases where the individual's behavior is active, persistent, and effortful, there may be no source of material reward or punishment. When we see no external reward maintaining the individual's effortful responses, it is common to consider this as supporting the conception that it is the personal quality of the individual that is responsible.

As has been suggested, however, this conclusion is unwarranted. Much learning does take place where the attentional and working behaviors of the individual are maintained by the products of the activity—by the learning itself or learning-related products. These may be called examples of "self-reward." Self-reward is used to define the case where the stimuli produced by the activity itself are the rewards that maintain the activity. When this state occurs it is not necessary to provide external reward, at least to the same ex-tent as it is when no intrinsic (self) reinforcement is available. There are various types of intrinsic reward important in the child's intellectual learning. Several of these will be described, as well as the types of training that pro-duce the reward system involved.

Imitation

The topic of the rewarding value of imitation has already been described. However, a brief mention in this more general context is pertinent as both a summary and as an introduction to the other types of self-reward to be de-scribed.

In terms of the specific acts involved, a primary aspect of imitation involves the fact that doing something that is like or matches that of something done by someone else is the source of reward. It has been said repeatedly herein that parents as stimulus objects become learned reinforcers. This occurs because they are paired with many other rewards. The principle involved is that of classical conditioning.

Furthermore, through the same experiences and the same principle, the *behaviors* of the parents become learned rewards. The behaviors of another person constitute stimuli—visual, auditory, and so on—and pairing them with rewards will make these stimuli learned rewards. The same holds true for the accoutrements associated with parents—for example, the clothes, jewelry, hair style, and so on—as well as for stylistic mannerisms of speech, walk, gestures, and the like.

Thus, imitational rewarding stimuli constitute a form of "self-reinforcement." There appears to be no extrinsic reward involved in many cases. The child imitates another child or adult, the behavior being acquired or maintained solely by the fact that his behavior is *like* that of the other person. The individual may dress like, speak like, obtain possessions like, go to the same places, engage in activities and recreations like some other individual or group. His behavior is reinforced by the fact that he is producing stimuli that match those of the other individual or group.

In this manner the source of motivation appears to be within the person himself. However, the analysis of the motivational stimuli reveals the learning principles involved in their creation. This is thus another case where human behavior appears to be self-initiated, because there is no clear external reward that is provided for the behavior. Furthermore, as in the other cases, people vary in the types (and intensities) of social stimuli that are reinforcing for them and that they will imitate. This again gives the appearance that individuals "select" the things they do. In general, in fact, it may be suggested that human behavior in this case appears to be spontaneous, or self-initiated, because different individuals have learned different reward systems and thus strive for different things.

It should be understood that the reward value that different people have for the child will determine to an important extent the degree to which the child will imitate different people. A parent who pairs himself with more rewarding conditions and employs aversive stimulation (punishment) less frequently and intensely will have a greater amount of reinforcement value. This will set the stage for the child to imitate the parent more, and to in general follow the instructions, advice, directives, and example of the parent.

The parent can affect also the extent to which the child will imitate others. That is, when the parent contributes to the child experiencing reward in the presence of other children and adults, the parent contributes to the reward value of those people and thus to the imitation value these people have for the child. Moreover, as will be more fully described later, reward value can be learned through language. A parent who, for example, makes positive statements about other pupils in his child's class who are diligent, hardworking, and able will increase the reinforcing value of these children. These children will then better control imitational behavior in the parent's child. On the other hand, as another example, the upper-class or intellectually snobbish parent who looks down on teachers may say to his child, "Teachers are not very bright, and Mrs. So-and-so is the dullest of the lot." This statement would lessen the reward value of teachers in general and also Mrs. So-and-so, according to explicit learning principles. As a consequence the child would imitate the teacher's behavior less and follow her instructions and so on to a lesser extent. The next section will describe several additional types of self-reward.

Standards, Achievements, and Rivalry as Self-Reinforcers

In the preceding section one type of self-reinforcement was described, the matching stimuli produced by imitative behaviors. It is because the matching stimuli, one of which is produced by the child's own behavior, "carry" the reward value that the term "self-reward" is used. In addition to imitation, however, there are other types of self-reward, at least for the child who has had the necessary past conditioning history. The rewarding stimulus in each case described will involve a matching or comparing of one's own behavioral product to that of another—the standard stimulus. The training that produces a motivational system that makes such matching stimuli reinforcing results in a basic behavioral repertoire fundamental to much of human learning.

To elaborate, a type of motivation that is commonly referred to in the context of intellectual learning is that of the so-called "achievement need." Again, individual differences in the reward value of achievement are usually considered as part of the person's personal makeup. For example, it has been suggested that people have to varying degrees a need "to accomplish something difficult." Murray (1938) made a definition of achievement need that may be paraphrased in the following manner:

> To accomplish something difficult. To master, manipulate, or organize physical objects, human beings, or ideas. To do this as rapidly and as independently as possible. To overcome obstacles and attain a high standard. To excel one-self. To rival and surpass others. To increase self-regard by the successful exercise of talent (p. 164).

This definition includes many of the facets of human behavior from which the common-sense notion of need for achievement, ambitiousness, and so on are inferred. The conception that each individual has to varying extents such inner needs has implications for our understanding of human behavior. That is, the view that the individual's personal (biologically determined) "need" system determines his achievement behavior places the responsibility for achievement upon the individual. If the individual achieves he is considered of high quality, and frequently this is coupled with a conception of moral righteousness. If he does not achieve he is denigrated and is considered morally weak. There is no justification for such interpretations in a learning conception of human behavior, as the following will show.

Consider the stimuli associated with attaining a high standard. Certainly in a naive organism, overcoming obstacles and doing something difficult are not activities that are originally rewarding. As a matter of fact, effortful behavior actually produces stimulation that is aversive (Hull, 1943). Without some change in these aversive features, it is to be expected that an organism would *escape* from hard work, that is, the *cessation* of work would act as a reward (Azrin, 1961). The same would be true of working as rapidly as possible. Rapid responding is not in itself rewarding; unless such behavior has been reinforced many times in the child, the behavior would not be expected to occur.

The same is true of accomplishment, attaining high standards, and achievement. Objectively these various terms refer to behavior that produces stimuli or stimulus objects that the social community responds to as achievements, accomplishments, and what have you. Ordinarily, these achievement products are positively reinforcing to the group, and the group rewards the child who produces such achievements.

These achievement stimuli, however, have no unlearned rewarding properties. Their reward value for the individual, if any, may be considered entirely learned. Thus, for example, the act of a child in reading letters may be very reinforcing to the parents, to the teacher who obtains her livelihood (reinforcers) from teaching children to read, and so on, but it would not be expected to have reward value in and of itself for the child. Actually, the acquisition of new skills of many types by the child is ordinarily rewarding to the middle-class parent. Thus, such a parent will consequently reward the child heavily for behavior that produces achievement stimuli of various kinds. Many, many times—when the child has learned to walk, to go to the toilet, to dress himself, to speak new words, to tell stories, to count, and so on—he will have been given many social rewards and perhaps material rewards of various kinds. Under such a circumstance the learning analysis would suggest that for such children the products (stimuli) of acquired skills would themselves become very rewarding. In common-sense terms, for children with such fortunate backgrounds, *learning* (or its products) would itself become rewarding, fulfilling our general expectations. Moreover, there are many observations that have been made in social psychology, sociology, anthropology, and education that support this analysis and the suggestion that practices that produce such reinforcers for children vary from family to family and from social class to social class (see Goldman, 1937; Rosen, 1956; Carter, 1964; Maccoby and Gibbs, 1954).

The process in which learning becomes its own reward should be examined in greater detail in terms of learning principles. It has already been suggested that one mechanism that appears to be involved is that of matching stimuli. That is, to a large extent the "proof" (and reward) of having learned something is when the product of the behavior (the stimulus produced by the behavior) matches the standard stimulus provided by an authority source. In these terms this reward value of learning may be seen as analogous to imitational reinforcement.

In addition, however, "improvement" in performance also becomes reinforcing in the child who has had the appropriate experience. Thus, a child may be reinforced for improvement even before his behavior *matches* a standard very well. In this way, improvement, which is actually the behavioral production of a stimulus that is closer to the standard stimulus than could be formerly produced, can come to have reinforcement value. When this has occurred we will see that *trying* to improve becomes rewarding. It is thus very important in training a child to any skill to reward the child for improving even though his level of skill has not begun to approach final performance. Not only will this maintain the child's participation in training, but it will additionally make improvement a more general reward.

Not all reward for acquiring new skills appears to be based upon matching a standard, however. In this brief exploration of "achievement motivation," it is necessary to include an example that does not involve reward in the presence of matching stimuli. Let us say that a child's parent has told the child that the world is round, and has also given the child a rather complete explanation of Earth as a planet. To continue, later on, when the child is in a group of young children, the question arises concerning where the "end of the Earth" really is. Let us say that at this time the informed child gives his account. Because it is more comprehensive, more reasonable, and more impressive in the terms in which it is stated, the account "wins" out over the accounts of the others and the child consequently receives social reinforcement. Having verbal skills that we call "knowledge," as in this case, becomes rewarding, because recitation of the verbal behavior is rewarded. Such sources of reward also maintain the learning behaviors involved in acquiring the verbal skills. In fact, it is suggested that the social approval of "knowledge" is a common source of reinforcement for successful students.

One additional point may be made in this context. It is commonly said that children differ a great deal in their "standards of performance." This is frequently thought to result from some "personal" selection by the child, as the following quotation indicates.

> Children differ dramatically in the standards of performance which
> they set for themselves. Some children decide that performance
> just a bit above average for their class is adequate to meet their
> standards; others demand of themselves the top position in the
> class. The child's commitment to work and persevere will be a
> function of the standard that satisfies him (Kagan, 1965 pp. 558–559).

The observation that for different children different standards are rewarding certainly appears to be the case. However, the present learning analysis suggests that such individual differences in children's standards, and the work and study habits that result, are produced through individual learning experiences according to the principles of classical conditioning.

Thus, it is suggested that the child does not set standards for himself spontaneously. Although he may carry them "within," they are learned. Moreover, it is important for a human learning theory to indicate the processes involved. As one example, we may observe a solitary boy practicing a certain "move" in football until he is satisfied, that is, until he has attained his own internal standard. The standard stimulus within may be an image (see Chapter 11) the boy has learned from observing an expert player. As another example, the novice actor may practice a walk or gesture in the mirror until he attains the standard of an internal image. The painter or musician acquires similar sensory standards through a long history of learning, and he continues working on a piece until an internally represented standard is reached. Sometimes attaining the standard depends upon a verbal expression of the individual that carries the reinforcement value. Thus, in a simple example, the child might continue to practice reciting a poem, after missing one word, because he says to himself, "Last time I recited and missed a word I got a B instead of an A." When at last he recites perfectly, he says to himself, "Now I will get an A, and he is reinforced. The subject of verbal rewards, a topic relevant to the present discussion of internal standards, will be treated in the next chapter.

Another important source of reward for child learning is to be found in "rivaling and surpassing others." In fact, the act of competing may itself be reinforcing. Again, this involves comparing one's behavioral product to that of someone else. In rivalry, however, exceeding the standard, not matching it, is rewarding. The stimulus consequences of surpassing standards by themselves, however, prior to learning, would not be expected to have reward value. Such events ordinarily gain this value because they have in the past been paired with other rewards. Actually, children have to be trained (formally or informally) to find "winning" rewarding, to find competition rewarding, and so on. The author remembers vividly as an undergraduate his experiences as a counselor in a day camp, attempting to teach four- and five-year-old children group games. The customary competitive events that were involved—strong rewards for adults—were quite neutral to these children. Winning a race, for example, is ordinarily a very neutral stimulus for a young child, and the verbal stimuli, "Run as fast as you can and try to win," may have no controlling value whatsoever. When your supposed rewards have no reward value, it is very frustrating to attempt to use the principles of reward in training a child. The same children after appropriate conditioning experiences, however, will later become very competitive. They will then have well-developed competitional reward systems, and will respond well to instructions "to try and win."

Again, there is much social and behavioral science evidence that familial, social, and cultural groups provide different training conditions for their children of the sort that produce different types and strengths of competitional reward. Some cultures produce intense competition reward systems; others do not. Moreover, in our society some children will learn well-developed reward systems in terms of competition—a central motivational constituent of the usual classroom situation—and others will not.

It is commonly assumed that these various types of self-rewards are present for all pupils, or should be, traditionally on the basis of genetic factors. However, in view of the preceding analysis, these rewards cannot be counted upon for every child, or in certain circumstances for even a large percentage of children. Many children do not have a past history that has established many achievement stimuli as reinforcing, or made reinforcing the stimuli of competition and winning or attaining high standards. When this is the case, it is ineffective simply to invoke the plea that learning should be reinforcing, and to expect such consequences to be effective. Although this is not the place for a full discussion, it should be noted that competition by definition includes losers (those punished) as well as winners (those rewarded). As a system of reward for training children, this method is justified only if one concludes that the able are the righteous and deserve the rewards. On the other hand, when one is concerned that the system of rewards is effective for all children, one begins to question the value of competition for producing intellectual learning.

ANOTHER PRINCIPLE BY WHICH THE REWARD SYSTEM DETERMINES BEHAVIOR

One further point should be made in the present context. It has been stated that the child has to learn that many types of stimulus events and objects have reward value. He does not gain an appropriate motivational system through biological development. The principle involved is classical conditioning. If certain objects or events are paired with other rewarding stimuli, these objects or events will also become rewarding themselves. This will mean that any behavior that is followed by such rewarding object or event will be learned. The behavior will occur with greater frequency in the future, or the behavior will be maintained at high strength if it is already frequently emitted. Reinforcing stimuli have their effect when they are presented after a behavior, and they strengthen future occurrences of the behavior.

The stimulus objects and events that become rewarding to the child have another important influence upon his behavior, however. That is, stimulus objects and events that are rewarding to the child will not only reinforce behaviors *after* they have occurred but will also "attract" him. The child will learn a wide variety of behaviors that allow him to obtain stimulus objects and events that are rewarding. This learning occurs because these stimulus objects and events reward the behaviors that obtain them.

Thus, through the child's experience, a wide variety of different stimuli that have reward value will come to elicit responses that result in obtaining those stimuli. These responses will be quite varied, including crawling toward, walking toward, running toward, climbing over and around obstacles for, reaching and grabbing for, fighting and struggling for, asking and crying for, and many other types of behavior. Later on, even more complex behaviors will come under the control of rewarding stimuli, such as working for, wheedling for, arguing for, flattering for, being ingratiating for, being respectful for, as well as competing for in various ways, attending to, imitating for, conforming for, and so on.

Thus, it should be understood that the stimuli that become rewarding for the child will be a strong determinant of how the child will behave. Moreover, a person for whom unusual stimuli have become rewarding will display unusual behavior in trying to obtain those stimuli. Many "abnormal" behaviors fall into this category. For example, if sexual contact with members of the same sex is rewarding for an individual, he will "strive for" such contact —that is, display behavior that results in that contact. In school, if the approval of a group of rebellious pupils is more reinforcing for the child than the approval of his teacher, then in striving for that approval he will display behaviors antithetical to the purposes of the class. In general it can be said that the nature of what is rewarding (the reinforcement system) helps determine our characteristics of behavior in this manner.

The converse principle is also true. The child will also learn a wide number of behaviors of escaping and avoiding stimuli that have aversive properties. These responses, both of a verbal and motor nature as in the preceding case, will include cruel behavior, derisive or insulting comments, obstructionistic behavior, antagonistic responses, oppositional voting, and the like. In addition, servile, cringing, fearful behavior and the like will also be acquired under the control of the aversive value of stimuli. Again, abnormal learning of aversive stimuli will produce abnormal behavior. Thus, for example, a person has an agoraphobia when the stimulus of being outside the house is aversive. The result is that the person with this disorder of his reinforcement system will not go out. The abnormal behavior is produced by the abnormal reinforcement system in this area.

After the child has learned "striving for" or "striving away from" responses to the reward or aversive value of stimuli, conditions that form or change this reward or aversive value will determine how the child behaves toward those stimuli. Stimuli that are made to have positive reinforcing (attitudinal) value will then *elicit* "striving for" behaviors. Stimuli that are made to have negative reinforcing (attitudinal) value will then *elicit* "striving away from" behaviors. This is also another reason why the child's motivational learning is so important—the nature of the stimuli that have reinforcing value for a child has a strong eliciting effect upon the way he will act.

It is suggested that these principles are true also in the context of the present discussion. For example, when achievement stimuli become reinforcers they also come to *control* the behavior of the child involved. When achievement stimuli reinforce the child's behavior, it may be observed that they will also bring on or elicit his working behaviors. When achievement stimuli are rewards the child, upon seeing someone else's achievement, will work harder himself. Seeing someone else ahead of him in some competition, the child will try even harder when winning is a strong reward. When a high standard is presented to him it will elicit diligent working behaviors in the child for whom high performance has become strongly rewarding.

The same principles apply to the other reinforcers yet to be discussed. That is, another major aspect of the human motivational system involves the language repertoire. This aspect of the system actually involves both self-reinforcement as well as externally given reinforcement. For many words may be considered to be stimuli that have reinforcing value. Words the individual says himself or the same word given by someone else can have the reinforcing value. Although the next chapter by no means can describe completely the importance of this source of human motivation, several points can be made. One of the points is that each of the aspects of the motivation system already discussed can be formed on the basis of language experience.

THE MOTIVATION SYSTEM
AND INTELLIGENCE

Whether or not imitation stimuli, and other social stimuli, are rewarding to the child will also have a direct effect upon the performance of the child in the intelligence-testing situation—as in many other learning and performance situations. The same is true also of achievement stimuli, high standards, and so on. That is, the extent to which these stimuli have reward value will affect the child's performance on an intelligence test in many ways, on many items, just as the child's success in school is affected.

Since the principles involved have already been stated in the context of imitation reward, and since examples were given in this context, it is not necessary to repeat these matters. It should be noted, however, that much of the effect of the motivational system upon the child's intelligence performance, as is generally the case, will not be in the motivational effects in the testing situation itself. That is, the motivational system will have *had* its primary effect in many cases upon what the child has *already* learned, since what is measured on intelligence tests consists largely of the intellectual repertoires of skill that the child has already acquired. And, as has been stressed in this chapter, the skills the child will have learned will depend to a large extent upon the nature of the child's motivational system. This will include school learning as well as the informal learning of the home.

Thus, especially at older age levels, we might expect to see many items that test the extent to which the child has learned the intellectual skills taught in the formal educational situation. These expectations are fulfilled abundantly, as perusal of any intelligence test will demonstrate. As one example, many intelligence tests are administered in a group situation and require reading. The child's results will thus strongly depend upon the quality and rapidity of his reading skills. In addition, many items will involve arithmetic and mathematical learning of various kinds.

To follow the practice of the earlier chapters, several such items that appear frequently on the individually administered intelligence test already referred to may be listed. To illustrate, the child has number tasks on the Revised Stanford-Binet Intelligence Test beginning at the 4½-year level. Items involving arithmetic skills also appear at the following age levels: five through ten, twelve, and fourteen. Above that point there are also arithmetical reasoning problems. Moreover, many of the language skills being tested will also depend upon the extent of school learning—which in turn will heavily depend upon the nature of the child's motivational system. The items that would fall in this category are too numerous to exemplify. The next chapter, however, will indicate how the child's motivational or emotional learning is also involved in his basic language repertoire of meaningful words. Additional intelligence items will be indicated in which successful solution depends upon the nature of the child's language motivational system.

THE MOTIVATION SYSTEM AS A BASIC BEHAVIORAL REPERTOIRE FOR VARIOUS ASPECTS OF PERSONALITY

In describing each of the basic behavioral repertoires, and in indicating the importance of the repertoires in individual and social adjustment, the repertoires have been focally related to intelligence and its measurement. This has been done to show clearly and in detail how the basic behavioral repertoires are constituents of personality. It is hoped that this concentration allows the conception to be more profoundly characterized.

It should be stressed, however, that the basic behavioral repertoires dealt with in the book, and the general concept, have significance for various aspects of personality and for personality measurement. The motivation system, for example, is measured by other personality tests—by attitude tests, interest inventories, and diagnostic personality inventories (see Staats, 1968b). Several demonstrational studies have already shown that the items of interest inventories are composed of words that have the rewarding and eliciting (and emotional) functions of motivational stimuli.

Thus, it is to be emphasized that in all cases the same basic behavioral repertoires are constituents of various aspects of personality. This has not been recognized because of the traditional assumption that each personality trait has some underlying, unitary process. Traditionally, the descriptions of personality traits have been seen to be basic. Inspection of the behaviors involved in each case, however, reveals the basic behavioral repertoires involved. Moreover, the same basic behavioral repertoires may be constituents of more than one of the traditionally identified aspects of personality.

The major point here is that while the emphasis in this limited treatment must be selective, dealing more heavily with the personality category of intelligence, the basic behavioral repertoires pertain to other aspects of personality. This will continue to be exemplified.

chapter 11 / Word Meaning, Motivation, and Vocabulary Growth

In the last chapter a new principle of learning was introduced and was shown to account for the manner in which previously neutral stimuli come to be learned rewards or learned punishments. The principle was that if a rewarding stimulus was paired with a new one that was not, the new stimulus would also become a reward. This may be elaborated a little so that the principle can be used to account for additional aspects of the child's personality learning.

It is central to understand that a stimulus is a reward because it elicits certain emotional responses in the individual. Take food as an example. When it is presented to the organism it elicits in the organism a number of emotional responses. In the laboratory it can be seen that the food stimulus elicits a salivary response. When food is placed in our mouths, we salivate. In addition, when the food is presented the rate of our heartbeat will change, the volume of blood to various internal organs will be changed, and so on. These are all responses effected by the organism's "emotional" nervous system.

The same is true of aversive stimuli. If a shock is applied to a laboratory animal, it can be observed that the animal's heartbeat rate will change, as will blood volume to various organs, perspiration level, respiration, internal secretions, and so on. Various indicators of emotional response will be affected by any aversive, painful stimulus; and such a stimulus will consequently serve as a punishment.

Many stimuli serve as rewards or punishments because they elicit positive or negative emotional (or attitudinal) responses in the individual. It should be noted in each case that the particular stimulus has three functions. One function may be to elicit a positive emotional response, to use the positive case. Such a stimulus has a second function; it will *also* function as a reward, and any response followed by the stimulus will be learned. In addition, the same stimulus will have another function. When it is present it will elicit "striving for" behaviors whose aim is to obtain the stimulus. These functions may be referred to respectively as the attitude function, the reward function, and the eliciting or discriminative function. (The author has called the system of stimuli that have these functions for the individual his A-R-D system, 1968*b*.) Each function has separate and important psychological (behavioral) effects. Whether or not a stimulus elicits an emotional response is important in and of itself to the individual's health and happiness. Whether the stimulus will serve as a reward or punishment in affecting the other behaviors the individual learns is equally important. And, the manner in which the stimulus will elicit striving for or striving against behaviors in the particular situation has the same import.

As has been described, when one of these attitudinal stimuli is paired with a new stimulus that is neutral in a rewarding-emotional sense, the new stimulus will acquire the three functions. The new stimulus will come to elicit the emotional response, and as a consequence the new stimulus will function as either a reward or punishment, and also elicit "striving for" or "striving away from," as the case may be. The ways in which different aspects of the child's motivational system are acquired under these principles have already been recounted. It will now be indicated how another aspect of the child's intellectual development involves the same type of learning.

THE EMOTIONAL (ATTITUDINAL) FUNCTION OF WORDS

An important function of many words in our language is that they have motivational properties—they will elicit an emotional response and thus serve as either rewards or punishments, and also control "striving for" or "striving away from" behavior. These words have acquired their rewarding or aversive qualities from being paired with other stimuli that have such qualities. That is, ordinarily many words are systematically paired with either rewarding or aversive stimuli in the life experience of the child. The words, *dirty, hurt,* and *bad,* for example, are customarily paired with aversive stimuli early in the life of the child, and thus they come to elicit mild conditioned negative emotional responses in the child. On the other hand, ordinary words such as *milk, mommy, play,* and so on will come to elicit a positive emotional response because these words are paired with stimuli that elicit such responses. (The author and associates, 1957, 1958, 1959, demonstrated in the laboratory that pairing a word either with a positive or negative emotional stimulus would result in the word coming to elicit the emotional response.)

As time passes, the individual will have innumerable learning experiences where a word is paired with another stimulus that elicits an emotional response. Many, many words are involved in this experience, and thus we ordinarily learn a vast number of such word meanings. It has been shown that difference in meaning among words is contributed by their positive or negative emotional meaning (Dysinger, 1931), and that this type of word meaning is one of the most prevalent types of meaning (Osgood and Suci, 1955). Examples of such positive emotional words for most of us in the English-language community include *cheerful, famous, fun, holiday, enjoy, brave, family, swim, laughter, surprise, Christmas, smile, honest, blossom, joy, favorite, dollar, happiness, sunshine, America, gift, home, hero, angel.* Examples of words that elicit negative emotional responses include *guilty, afraid, spoil, ugly, pain, bitter, die, sad, starving, foolish, hate, fat, blame, thief, sick, hunger, fell, harm, ashamed, lost, shock, hurt, worry, poison.* There are many others of each type.

The importance of emotional words is largely in their functions. As has been indicated there are three important functions, which will be further described. First, the words may stand for the actual objects and events—a symbolic function. Through words, humans can thus experience emotional responses similar to those that would be experienced by direct contact with the actual emotional stimulus objects and events. Reading pornography is a good example, or any emotion-eliciting passage in a novel—since the emotional responses are so apparent. In reading pornography, for example, the elicitation of sexual physiological responses of emotion can be directly experienced and observed. There is no reason words as stimuli could elicit such responses except through learning. As a negative case, the person who is told by a doctor that he has cancer experiences an intense emotional response to a message that consists of word stimuli.

Many of our emotional responses in life come about through language, according to the principles that have been described. In this respect it should be noted that the words a person says to himself will also elicit the same types of emotional responses as those said by someone else. Thus, other things being equal, a person who tends to "speak to and of himself" in positive emotional words will be in a more positive "emotional" state than a person who ruminates heavily with negative emotional words. It is not possible to discuss these individual differences here. It may only be said that such differences are affected by the language-learning experiences the individual has had as well as the conditions of the individual's life situation.

THE REINFORCING
FUNCTION OF WORDS

Important as is the function of these types of words as elicitors of emotional responses, perhaps even more important functions reside in the new learning that such words can produce. One of these functions is the capability of rewarding or punishing other behaviors of the individual. It will be remembered that if a rewarding stimulus (positive emotional stimulus) follows some behavior of a child, that behavior will become more frequent—the child learns behaviors that are rewarded. The converse is true of behaviors followed by negative emotional stimuli (punishment). The child learns not to make such responses.

The important point here is that words that elicit positive emotional responses will function as rewards, and words that elicit negative emotional responses will function as punishments. This process has been shown clearly by Finley and Staats (1967) in a controlled laboratory experiment with sixth-grade children. When a motor response of the child was followed on each occurrence by a positive-meaning word (such as *smile, joy, fun*), it was seen that the response was learned, in contrast to another response that was not followed by such words. With another group of children, when the response was followed by a negative-meaning word (such as *fat, sick, bitter)*, the response came to be made less and less frequently. These words served as punishments in the sense of making the response less strong. With another group of children, words of neutral meaning (such as *box, that, of)*, when administered following each response, had no effect upon the learning of the response.

Thus, one of the powerful functions of language is the motivational function where new learning of behavioral skills can occur through the use of rewarding or aversive word stimuli. Much human behavior can be understood in terms of these motivational aspects of language. It is suggested that words delivered by other people mold our behavior according to the principle of reinforcement. Much of the child's school learning, for example, is maintained by verbal reward. The same is true for his learning of social behaviors—much of the desirable behaviors are acquired because they are verbally rewarded. The parent also uses rewarding (and punishing) words to train the child. For example, if a child has performed a behavior that the parent does not like (does not find rewarding), the parent may say, "You should not do that because it is . . ." and then use "punishing" words such as *dangerous, unlucky, not wise, liable to hurt someone, disliked;* or in more extreme form may use *stupid, sinful, disgusting, dirty, unhealthy, sickening, disgraceful,* and so on. This process will lessen the frequency of the unwanted behavior in the child—provided he has had the necessary language learning experience (as will be discussed further on).

Many subtle forms of negative or positive rewarding words may be worked into conversation that is made contingent upon some undesired or desired behavior of someone else—and this can be expected to mold the behavior of the person so treated. The mother who sees the child studying and says to her child, "If you study hard and make good grades Daddy will be very happy," is making use of the principle of reward to strengthen the behavior of studying. Whether she realizes it or not, she is employing language as rewarding stimulus.

Moreover, not only do words of *other* people mold our behavior but our own speech responses perform the same function. Although our language repertoire is learned, it molds our own future behaviors. The individual may perform an action and then say out loud or to himself that what he has done is *dangerous, unworthy, silly, stupid, illegal, socially unacceptable,* and so on, thereby punishing himself and decreasing the strength of that behavior. This ability to affect his own behavior by his own words becomes an important aspect of the child's socialization. It should be remembered that this ability to "socially control one's own behavior" depends upon the previous language learning of the child. When the learning is deficient, social behavior will be deficient.

The individual may also say words following his behavior that positively reward the behavior and strengthen it in future occurrences. As an example, the child who says to himself, "I really worked hard on this lesson and I bet I do well on the exam," will have rewarded his study behaviors. His language training in this respect will be very important, for two children could have studied just as hard, but the child who rewards himself verbally will have his studying strengthened more than the child who does not. A significant aspect of human motivation may thus be found in the person's word responses to his own behavior.

It is also interesting to consider the implications of this process for explaining how the individual appears to be affected by future events such as goals or anything else he appears to strive for, or away from. The future event that has not yet happened cannot affect a preceding behavior, but what the individual *says* about the hypothetical future event can indeed alter his behavior by strengthening or weakening it. The person can talk to himself about future events and in this way reward or punish his own behavior relevant to that possible future occurrence. The student, as he returns home late on a study night, can say to himself, "If I keep staying out late every night I will not pass my final exam." This self-applied punishment would contribute to the decrease in strength of the behavior—*if* the words "not pass" elicit a strong negative emotional response and function as a punishment.

THE DISCRIMINATIVE (ELICITING) FUNCTION OF WORDS

It has also been said in preceding descriptions of the functions of rewarding and aversive stimuli that a rewarding stimulus elicits approach behaviors in the individual, whereas an aversive stimulus elicits escape and avoidance behaviors. This principle holds also in the realm of emotional words— constituting another important function of such words. As one example, the child is told, "Don't cross the street because it is dangerous." If the word *dangerous* as a stimulus *elicits* a negative emotional response (sometimes called anxiety) in the child, it will also elicit or control avoidance behavior. Here the emotional word is not acting like a punishment for a response that has already occurred, it is *eliciting* avoidance behavior. In the positive case, as another example, a girl may be described to a boy as *beautiful, shapely, affectionate, friendly, fun,* and so on. These words would elicit positive emotional responses in him and would tend to elicit such behaviors as calling her and asking her for a date. It is this eliciting or "controlling" function of emotional words that we see so frequently in social interactions where one person is trying to get the other person to do something—the parent with the child, a salesman with a prospective customer, the advertising copywriter, the propagandist, and so on. In general terms, by labeling people or events with emotional words we can make the person or event into a stimulus that will tend to elicit either "striving for" or "striving against" behaviors, as the case may be. (It should be understood that whether or not a person does something in any case is ordinarily influenced by factors other than someone else's words. The words will not be the only determinants of the action. Moreover, we also learn to some extent not to respond equally to everyone's words. The principles described herein do function lawfully, but there may be more than one determinant of the individual's behavior.)

In summary, it may be suggested than any stimulus event that comes to elicit an emotional word response in the individual will be responded to by the individual in a manner influenced by that emotional meaning. In common-sense terms, when any stimulus event (social, physical, or what have you) is "labeled" with a word that has rewarding or aversive value, the way people respond to the stimulus event will be influenced by the emotional value of its word label.

Finally, one other function of emotional words must be indicated to describe the importance of the learning that produces a large number of these words for the child. This function will be the topic of the next section.

EMOTIONAL MEANING LEARNED FROM OTHER WORDS: ANOTHER FUNCTION OF THE WORD-MEANING BASIC BEHAVIORAL REPERTOIRE

The discussion of emotional words so far has indicated how these words have their effects upon the behavior and skill-learning of the child. In addition, emotional words serve another crucial function in the development of the child's reward-punishment system. *What* events *come* to be rewarding for the child will depend in part upon learning that takes place on the basis of the child having learned a basic behavioral repertoire of emotional words. Without this the further learning of the child's motivational system will not take place.

To elaborate, once the child has learned to respond emotionally to words, experience with those words may then make additional words, objects, and events acquire emotional meaning. Once a word has come to elicit an emotional response, the word will "transfer" this emotional response to any new stimulus with which the word is paired. If the child has been spanked, let us say, at the same time that the parent has said, "Bad, what you did was bad," the word *bad* will come to elicit a negative emotional response. After the word *bad* comes to stably elicit the emotional response through learning, any new stimulus the word itself is paired with will also come to elicit the emotional response. Thus, for example, let us say the child who has learned a negative meaning to the word *bad* now reads the word *evil* for the first time. At this point the child asks the teacher what it means. She says, "Evil means bad," and the child goes back to his seat repeating the phrase. Each of the pairings of *evil* and *bad*, by the teacher or by the child himself, will result in the child learning to respond to the word *evil* with the same emotional response he has learned to *bad*.

The child, according to this principle of learning, will acquire much of his meaningful vocabulary of words in this and similar ways. This can only take place, however, if the child has already learned to respond in the appropriate way to the words involved. In the preceding illustration, for example, the child would not have learned the meaning of the word *evil* if he had not already been trained to respond to the word *bad*. In general, a child has to have learned a basic repertoire of emotional words before he is able to further profit from his language experience in further emotional learning.

Much of the establishment of what we call the child's system of values, interests, emotions, needs, ambitions, goals, and so on are acquired by virtue of his language experience. This occurs in a process where words that elicit emotional responses are paired with new stimuli (objects, events, and other words), and the new stimuli then gain those emotional-reinforcing qualities. For example, let us take the case of the child who has learned a positive emotional response to the word *good*. If this child is told, "Learning is good, working and studying are good, school is good, the teacher is good," and so on, these social objects, events, and actions will also become positive emotional-rewarding stimuli. The example is oversimplified, of course. Actually, the child will come to have a much larger repertoire of positive emotional-rewarding words than just the word good. Furthermore, these various words will be used in more subtle and complex ways in creating a positive set of values for education (in this example). However, the principle is correct. It is to a large extent through pairing already learned emotional words with new words that new values are formed. (Coleman, 1966, has supported this experimentally.) Thus, on the basis of the learned language repertoire, the child will in part acquire his value system.

The same is true of other aspects of the child's motivational system—his interests, needs, ambitions, goals, wants, desires, and so on. As one other example within the motivational system, take the manner in which language experience will influence heavily the development of the child's sexual interests. Long before a child has had any direct sex experience with another person, he will ordinarily experience a great deal of language conditioning from other children and through reading that will affect what will be sexually rewarding for him. As a consequence of this, for example, certain types of people will come to be seen as desirable to him. That these are learned desires can be seen by th fact that different cultures and groups hold different standards of sexual beauty. The child raised in each culture learns the cultural standards.

EARLY LEARNING
OF EMOTIONAL WORDS

Perhaps the foregoing indicates the extraordinary importance of the child's language learning in the area of acquiring a repertoire of emotionally meaningful words. The child who has learned to respond to those words is prepared to learn new emotions to important stimulus objects, events, and social circumstances—as well as to other words—simply on the basis of language. Moreover, the child can learn new adjustive behaviors guided by the reward or punishment value of the emotional words. His behavior will also be elicited or controlled appropriately by emotional words so that he avoids harmful situations, performs useful responses, and so on in a culturally desirable manner.

The child whose behaviors are not affected in the usual manner by words will be seen as undisciplined, uncontrollable, unmanageable, disturbed, retarded, dull, unmotivated, and so on—depending upon the nature of his intellectual-emotional language deficit. It is thus important that the parent realize the significance of this type of learning, so that if he would not ordinarily conduct the appropriate training he may do so. In this respect it is relevant to say a few additional words about training that the parent can introduce to the young child to begin the development of this important learned repertoire.

The primary principle is that the parent has to pair the appropriate word with the objects and events that constitute emotional stimuli for the child. By doing so the word in each case will come to also elicit the emotional response and thus acquire the important functions that have been described.

It has already been suggested that if the parent will say "food" when the child is eating, the sound of the word will come to elicit the positive emotional responses the food elicits in the child. The verbal parent who appropriately pairs additional words with many, many different emotional objects, events, and people will in this manner be training his child to a large repertoire of meaningful emotional words. For example, the child's repertoire of positive emotional words of the food variety may be extended by the parent saying *sweet, tasty, warm, sour, bitter,* and so on. As another example of emotional word-meaning training, the parent who plays a game with his child and says *game, play, fun,* and so on will be making these words appropriately meaningful. The parent who instructs his young child in swimming, as another example, should also capitalize on this happy interaction by pairing the appropriate words *swim* and *fun* with the experience. Only illustrations can be given, of course. The opportunities for producing such learning are potentially almost infinite in number and variety.

The preceding examples involved primarily the learning of positive emotional words. The same process ordinarily does, and should, take place with negative-meaning words. The word "should" is used advisedly, for part of the learning involved takes place when the parent "punishes" the child. Thus, the statement implies that punishment has a minimal, but justified, place in the training of the child. It is not possible to discuss this topic of the learning of a repertoire of negative emotional words without discussing the topic of the use of punishment in child training—and a separate section to deal with that topic will be part of a later chapter. In the present discussion, the manner in which such meaningful words can be established in the unplanned aversive experience of the child will be described. It should be noted that this pairing of words with aversive stimuli should also be a primary part of any punishment the child has to receive in his training.

To continue, it is inevitable that the child will receive aversive stimulation of various kinds in his interaction with physical objects in the environment and with other children. The parent may use such experiences to aid in producing a repertoire of negative emotional words in the child. Let us say, for example, that the parent sees the young child fall down and skin his knee. If the parent says, "Hurt," "It hurts," "When you do that you get hurt," and so on as he consoles the child, this represents a pairing of the word and the negative emotional stimulus. The word will then acquire the several functions of a negative emotional-reinforcing stimulus. As another example, if the child comes to the parent in tears and reports that he has been struck by another child, and the parent then establishes that his own child struck first, this experience can be used also to promote the necessary language learning. The parent might say, "It hurts when someone hits you," as well as, "If you hit someone they will hit you back," "You should not hit anyone first," and the like. When these words occur as the child is experiencing the aversive stimulation, the negative emotional responses will be conditioned to "hit," "should not," and "hurt." (Actually, the same conditioning would take place with the other words also, for example, "if," "you," and so on. However, this experience would not be systematic with respect to these words, and they would not come strongly to elicit negative emotional responses.)

The parent will also have an opportunity to pair the words *bitter, sour, pain, dirty, smelly, hot, loud, noisy, burn,* and so on with the actual stimuli that elicit negative emotional responses. This and experiences of this kind will create additional negative emotional words.

Once such words have been stably established, the child's word-meaning repertoire can be elaborated through the use of these words. When the parent says, "That is dangerous, you will get hurt," he will make the word *dangerous* into a negative emotional word, provided that the word *hurt* is already such a word. That is, pairing one word that already has emotional meaning with a new word will result in the new word also gaining the same emotional meaning. Even later, if the parent says, "Motorcycles are dangerous," or "Swimming out too far is dangerous," or "Driving too fast is dangerous," these words will also become negative emotional words. (As already indicated, this will also mean the child will avoid such objects or events.)

In this manner the individual's repertoire of meaningful words may be expanded almost infinitely. The same is true for the positive emotional words.

Once a basic set of positive emotional words has been learned by the child, the parent may employ these in combination with new words to make the latter emotionally meaningful also. After the word *pretty* has been paired with various positive emotional stimuli, it can be used to make words such as *lovely, beautiful,* and *handsome* emotionally meaningful. And these words in turn can be used to make other objects, people, and events elicit a positive emotional response.

At any rate, it is important that the child acquire a repertoire of negative emotional words as well as positive emotional words. The negative emotional words will be important in controlling the child's behavior without resort to physical punishment. Also, through this repertoire of negative emotional words the individual behaves in such a way as to anticipate on his own future aversive consequences and thus avoid them. More will be said of these topics further on.

SENSORY (IMAGE) WORD MEANING AND VOCABULARY GROWTH

The preceding discussion of word meaning has involved only emotional responses to words that are learned by the child. Emotional-word learning occurs when the child experiences a word paired with an object or word stimulus that already elicits the emotional response. In addition, however, words come to elicit other responses besides emotional responses. That is, there are many stimuli in the world that elicit responses in us, but not emotional responses. Words acquire meaning for the child—that is, come to elicit other types of response—through being paired with these types of stimuli also.

To elaborate, experimental research as well as naturalistic observation indicates that any stimulus we are sensitive to actually is eliciting a response in us. When we see a visual stimulus we are in essence making a "seeing" response to the stimulus. When we hear a sound stimulus we are making a "hearing" response to that stimulus. The same is true of stimuli that we touch, taste, smell, and so on. Furthermore, it appears that such sensory responses (or sensations) can be "transferred" to new stimuli, at least in part, through learning processes that follow the principle of classical conditioning.

It is suggested that many words come to be meaningful because they are systematically paired with some aspect of the environment (stimulus), and as a consequence come to elicit part of the sensory response elicited by the stimulus. For example, the word *squeak* is systematically paired with a type of sound stimulus and comes to have a different sensory meaning than the word *blue,* which is systematically paired with a visual stimulus. *Squeak, blue, white, rough* elicit different meaning responses in us, and this gives the words different meanings.

Thus, it is suggested that this principle of learning will account for what we call word imagery. That is, when an individual hears or reads a descriptive passage that presents an account of sensory objects and events, it is commonly said that he experiences in imaginal form the stimuli being described. The person in a reduced sense sees or hears, or whatever, something like that which the actual events would arouse.

This vicarious sensory experience may be regarded as one of the powerful functions of language. Besides the enjoyment of receiving experience not otherwise possible, we can have experiences through language that will provide us with learning similar to that which would have occurred if we had had first-hand contact with the actual events. Through words of this type we can vicariously experience social interactions not possible through direct experience; we can see lands and peoples; we can experience events that are in bygone times; we can experience combinations of objects and events that nature will not arrange; and we can learn how to respond to objects so that on first actual experience with them our behavior is adjustive.

The individual can thus acquire new sensory experience without ever having had contact with the objects themselves. To illustrate, many people have never seen what is commonly called a jellyfish on the coast of Southern California. However, if they were told that a jellyfish is "mottled purple, pink and white," is "gelatinous in substance," comes in "various sizes up to about eighteen inches across," and gives a "stinging sensation on contact," these words would elicit grossly appropriate sensory (image) responses. The individual presented with these words will acquire a *complex* of sensory responses that will approximate to some extent the direct experience he would have obtained from personal experience with the organism. Moreover, if the individual had also been told to avoid touching such an organism, he would make adjustive responses to the animal on seeing one for the very first time.

There are several points in this discussion that should be elaborated. First, it is suggested that individuals ordinarily acquire a repertoire of words that elicit general sensory responses. That is, white light is a stimulus that is part of many different objects. When the word *white* is paired with many different objects that reflect that type of light, the word comes to elicit a "white sensory response." That is, pairing the word with a white ball, a white dress, a white car, a white house, and so on will condition the sensory response elicited by white stimuli to the word. This word may then be used (as a "concept") in combination with many different words that elicit sensory responses to produce new combinations of sensory responses. The following statement will illustrate the process: "It was bright white, rotund, with short legs and hooves, and a very long neck, with bright black stripes around it. It had a thick, flat head with wide jaws, and long yellow teeth, and the animal growled loudly as it moved slowly forward." All of the sensory-meaning words in this example have acquired their meaning by being paired with various sensory stimuli, and they have come through this to elicit a particular learned sensory response in the manner described.

The above example also illustrates more clearly that when words are combined, each eliciting a sensory response, a larger, combined, or composite sensory image may result. It would then be expected that if a new word was paired with this combined sensory response, the new word would become capable of eliciting the total sensory image. That is, the individual would have acquired a new, complex image that would be elicited whenever that word occurred. Thus, if the word *glox* was paired with the sensory words in the above example—as in the statement, *A glox is bright white, rotund, with short legs,* and so on—*glox* would come to elicit the combined sensory response. The example illustrates that the child can learn a new labeling response for an object without having any training trials with the object itself. To learn in this manner, however, he must have the necessary basic behavioral repertoire, including the previously learned meaning responses to the relevant words (concepts).

The process is actually more important in terms of acquiring new vocabulary than the example shows. As another illustration, let us say that a child had never seen a zebra, had no word with which to label the animal, had no meaning response to the word *zebra.* If this child heard or read a story with the word *zebra* in it, he would not profit from the story as he would if he had the necessary repertoire. If he was told to select a zebra from among several other pictures of animals he also did not know, such as on an intelligence test item, let us say, he would not respond correctly. Or, if he was told to draw a zebra he would have no appropriate response.

Let us say, however, that this child has had conditioning experiences so that the words *animal, striped, horse, tiger, donkey, white,* and *black* have come to elicit appropriate conditioned sensory responses (images) in him. (Such words would usually be called concepts.) Upon the basis of this basic language repertoire the child would then be prepared to learn the word label *zebra,* as well as learn a composite meaning response (image) to the word just from his own language experience. That is, let us say that someone says to the child: "A zebra is a black and white animal that is striped like a tiger. The zebra has a head like a horse and is the size and shape of a donkey. Can you say zebra?" This language experience would have the following effect. The various words would elicit the learned sensory responses that would roughly form the composite sensory responses of an animal like a zebra. The child's vocal response of naming the animal would be learned to this composite sensory image. Later, when the child was shown a picture of a zebra, it would elicit the total sensory response to which the vocal response *zebra* had been learned, and the child would be able to say the appropriate name. (This labeling learning to a new object of the world could take place although the child had never before seen a zebra.) Furthermore, if the child now heard or read a story with the word *zebra* in it, the word would now elicit the appropriate image or meaning, and the child would comprehend the passage. He could also discriminate a zebra from pictures of other animals. All of these skills could give him a higher score on an intelligence test, reading test, vocabulary test, and so on.

It may thus be suggested that the child has to learn meanings to a basic set of words in order to profit from much of his language experience. In school, for example, if the teacher says, "A zebra has stripes . . .," and so on, and these words do not elicit the appropriate meaning responses in the child, then he will not be able to learn the new labeling response of saying *zebra* under the proper stimulus control, nor the meaning of the word *zebra*. Thus, having a large repertoire of words that elicit meaning responses is basic to much additional language learning.

It would also be expected that a child who begins by being retarded in the development of this basic language repertoire will fall even farther behind as he goes on. That is, he will be in a position to learn fewer new words from spoken and written context, in an ever-increasing process of retardation. The retardation will be relative to children who receive the very same educational experience but have the repertoire of meaningful words to profit more from the experience. It should be remembered that we especially get the impression that there are different personal qualities of intelligence when we see children who receive the "same" experience but learn to widely differing degrees. One reason lies in the basic behavioral repertoire of meaningful words.

Learning the Basic Sensory
Word Repertoire

The foregoing has shown how the learning of sensory meaning to words constitutes a basic behavioral repertoire important in much of the child's later learning. The basic word learning takes place in several ways. In the first instance it is through the systematic pairing of a word in the child's experience with some primary object, event, person, and so on that conditions the response elicited by the primary stimulus to the word. The parent, it may be noted, may add to the child's repertoire of sensory-meaning words by saying the relevant word as the child experiences any particular object or event. Actually, this type of training ties in with the child's word-labeling learning. Thus, for example, when the parent says "cat" when the child looks at a cat, and the child repeats the word, the child will learn to label the stimulus at the same time that he learns a cat-type image to the word. The child has to have a great deal of word-object experience, and in the process he will acquire a large repertoire of sensory-meaning words.

Once the child has learned a repertoire of sensory-meaning words he may learn the sensory response (image) to a new word by having the word paired with a word that already elicits the response. For example, when told, "Azure means blue," the child will learn to respond to the word *azure* as he has already learned to respond to *blue*. Later, of course, this type of learning will be extended greatly through the child's reading. For example, the child may read, "The dog was eager to go, he whined at the door, scratched, and pranced around until his master let him out." Let us say the child did not know the word *eager*. In reading this passage he would begin to acquire a meaning for the word. Thus, through reading the child would expand his vocabulary. (The manner in which reading contributes to the vocabulary growth of the child will be further described in a later section.)

The parent contributes to this aspect of vocabulary growth in several ways —as was the case with emotional words. In the beginning stages the parent is very important in terms of providing the primary experience for the child and in pairing the appropriate words with that experience. To differing degrees, children can receive greater or lesser experiences with various aspects of their world, even while they are still small. Some parents will introduce their children to and direct their attention toward various and detailed aspects of the environment. Other parents will not. Moreover, some parents will label the various aspects of the environment with the appropriate word. There are large differences in parents in this respect. The more "verbal" the parent is with the child in this respect, the greater will be the extension of the child's meaningful vocabulary.

This process of vocabulary growth in the child continues to be affected by the parent on the verbal level. The parent may also produce new meaningful words in the manner described, where a new word is paired with another word or words that already elicit sensory meaning and the new word in this manner acquires meaning also. This again will depend upon the extent and quality of the parent's use of language in general, and in the gradual introduction of new words in this process.

As will be described in Part III, the parent may also markedly enhance the growth of the child's vocabulary in this aspect as well as others by laying the foundation for his child to learn to read. Much of the child's later language development will occur through reading.

THE REWARD VALUE
OF IMAGES

It has been suggested that through the child's learning, words come to elicit images. When words of this type are presented in combinations, a composite image can then be elicited. Thus, words such as these can be brought together in different combinations and produce different composite conditioned images. Stories may be considered in part in terms of this analysis. In a story, series of words may be presented that elicit conditioned images in series. This may constitute what is analogous to a running sequence of actual experience of objects and events. If these actual objects and events would be rewarding upon direct experience, then the elicitation of the images will also be rewarding. Thus, if the child has the necessary repertoire of learned meaning responses to words, then the words when arranged in a suitable story form will elicit those meaning responses in a way that will be reinforcing. As an example, if the stimuli of a forest path leading to a grassy area by a brook elicit sensory responses that are reinforcing, then the words "forest path leading to a grassy area by a bubbling brook" will elicit a composite conditioned image that will also be reinforcing. The reinforcement value of the image elicited by words may not be large. But we frequently see that such reward value is large enough to sustain listening to and reading stories of various kinds. And it is clear that such language experiences will have important effects on the child's intellectual development.

Actually, storytelling may begin very early with young children, and it may be employed to hasten the child's language development. For example, the author's two-year-old son had a language repertoire that included such words as *car, driving, Daddy, Peter* (his name), *dog, lick,* and the like. *Driving* and *car* and *Peter* together elicited images that were rewarding because the author had let Peter sit on his lap and hold the wheel several times when driving along a deserted street, at which time the author (and then the boy) said such things as, "Peter is driving, "Peter drives the car," and so on. The word *dog* had also come to elicit its customary sensory meaning response because it had been paired with dogs Peter found to be very rewarding.

Based upon this type of language repertoire, the author told Peter a story consisting of "Peter and Daddy go driving, Peter drives the car. Brm-brm-brm-brm. Peter sees a dog. The dog licks Peter's face." The reinforcing nature of the image evoked by the words could be seen in the child's laughing and general enjoyment and in his continued requests for the story. Thus, it was possible to be a good storyteller with this young child because of information about the actual objects and events the child found to be reinforcing, as well as information about the language repertoire the child had.

The author has seen children in the early years of school who were considered to be behavior problems, to have an inadequate attention span, and so on, in part because they misbehaved when other children would sit quietly and listen to a story. Such behavior problems, however, may be a function of deficiencies in the child's basic language repertoire. When the words of a story do not elicit the appropriate images in the child, there will be no reinforcement for sitting and listening to the story. When that is the case the young child's behavior will not be maintained, which means he will do something else—which, of course, will be disruptive to the school group. This is thus an example of a case where learning of normal basic repertoires is the preventive treatment of a behavior problem.

In concluding, it may be noted that many words elicit two types of conditioned meaning responses—emotional meaning and sensory (or image) meaning. Sometimes the former depends upon the latter. To use an example already mentioned, pornographic writing involves words that, when presented together, will elicit both conditioned images as well as conditioned emotional-reinforcing responses that have observable physiological components. A child has to receive conditioning experiences that will provide him with a large repertoire of both general types of words.

WORD MEANING, VOCABULARY, AND INTELLIGENCE

It has been said that the "comprehension" of stories—the extent to which meaning responses are elicited by the relevant words in the story—depends upon the child having already learned a repertoire of words that elicit meaning responses in him. The child's comprehension will also determine his "pleasure" (reward value) in hearing or reading the story. Moreover, what he will learn from the story will depend upon his "comprehension." Thus, the child's repertoire of meaningful words is essential in various aspects of learning, including further language learning.

It should therefore not be surprising that many items on intelligence tests measure the child's repertoire of meaningful words in what we term comprehension. Vocabulary tests are prominent in many intelligence tests, including the test that has been used in illustrations in the present text. Many of the words on vocabulary tests will be meaningful to the individual because they elicit a conditioned sensory response or a conditioned emotional response, or both. For example, at the six-year level of the Revised Stanford-Binet Intelligence Test, the child is told, "I want to find out how many words you know. Listen, and when I say a word, you tell me what it means" (Terman and Merrill, p. 94). When the child is then asked what a *straw* is and responds, as one example, "Kind of round stick" (p. 304) and receives points toward his intelligence score, he may do so in part because he has a conditioned meaning response to the word. Many other words on the vocabulary test depend upon the extent of development of the child's word-meaning repertoire. It should be noted that this repertoire has its effects throughout the Intelligence Test, since vocabulary items appear again and again at the various age levels.

There are also items that measure other samples of the same basic behavioral repertoire. For example, at the nine-year level the child is read the statement, "Bill Jones's feet are so big that he has to pull his trousers on over his head." The child is then asked, "What is foolish about that?" (Terman and Merrill, p. 103). If the words elicit in the child a composite image of someone attempting to put on trousers over his head, the child who has the appropriate speech repertoires will be able to describe why this is foolish. It should be noted that the words *trousers, pull on,* and *head* each have to elicit a particular conditioned sensory response in order for the composite image to occur.

In addition, there are word comprehension items beginning at the 3½-year level. These comprehension items appear throughout the test at higher levels. It many be concluded that the basic behavioral repertoires described in this chapter are essential in the judgment that will be made of the child's intelligence upon tests. Moreover, these same basic behavioral repertoires will have important effects upon the child's adjustment to verbal stimuli, his enjoyment of verbal stimuli, and his ability to learn through language—all fundamental characteristics of the child's school adjustment and learning and his general life adjustment and learning, and all directly relevant to the learned skills he will demonstrate on an IQ test.

chapter 12 / Reward, Punishment, and the Learning-Work Attitude

It has been suggested herein that the conditions of reward and punishment are central features in all types of skill learning, including many language-emotional skills. This has been indicated also by the number of different learned behaviors that have been discussed in terms of these principles of reinforcement. At this point it will be productive to spend a moment in treating some of the general aspects of the child's learning as it involves the conditions of reward and punishment.

One of the things that should be understood is that both reward and punishment conditions have two variations that produce learning. Reward when it occurs following a response will increase the frequency with which the response will be made in the future; that is, the individual will learn responses that are rewarded. Many examples of this kind of learning have already been given. The converse is also true, however. The general principle is that taking away a rewarding stimulus following a response also has an effect upon what the individual will learn. The effect is opposite that of presenting the reward and is analogous to a punishment.

To elaborate, let us say that the individual has had possession of a reinforcing stimulus of some kind. The individual makes a response of some kind which is then immediately followed by having the reward taken away. This will have the effect of reducing the strength of the response; the individual will learn not to make that response. An example from everyday life is that of receiving a fine for some behavior that society considers undesirable. Specifically, a man who is fined for speeding—that is, has the reinforcing stimulus of money taken away following the undesirable behavior of fast driving—will demonstrate this behavior less frequently following the experience.

Thus, rewards, when presented following a behavior, will strengthen the behavior. Rewards taken away following a behavior will decrease the strength of the behavior. Rewards can affect learning in these two ways.

The same is true for punishing, or aversive, stimuli. If an individual makes a response and this is followed by an aversive stimulus, the behavior will be made less frequently in the future; the individual will learn not to make the response. This is the usual process we refer to as punishment.

However, aversive stimuli can also affect an increase in a behavior as well. Let us say that a punishing stimulus has been applied to the individual and it continues until he makes a particular response. Following the response the punishing stimulus is withdrawn—it terminates when the response has been made. Under this circumstance the individual will make the response more frequently; he will learn responses whose consequence is the removal of punishment. When someone takes aspirin his behavior is learned because it removes the aversive stimulation of the headache. If the aspirin intake was not followed by removal of the punishing stimulus, the behavior would not be strengthened and continue to occur on future occasions.

Thus, the child will learn new behaviors through the presentation or the removal of rewards. The child will also learn new behaviors through the presentation or removal of punishments. It appears that the more frequent occurrence is for a reward or punishment to be *presented* and in this way affect the individual's behavior. However, the *removal* of rewards or punishments may be equally effective in producing the learning of some response. Additional points concerning the general principles of reward and punishment in child learning will be discussed in the following sections.

REWARD PRINCIPLES

First, it may be repeated that *early skill learning of the child for all practical purposes requires some type of strengthening action provided by the use of reward or punishment consequences.* The role of reward in child learning will be treated before turning to punishment and its effects.

Partial Reinforcement
and the Richness of Reward

The above statement was not meant to suggest that each and every learning trial in which the child participates must be rewarded in some manner. Actually, it has been shown clearly that partial reinforcement—reward on only a proportion of the individual's learning trials—may maintain participation in the learning situation and yield good learning. As a matter of fact, it is sometimes more effective to reward only some of the child's responses instead of all of them. The results of controlled studies with animals exemplify the principle in its basic form. Let us say that we placed an animal in an apparatus where, if he pressed a lever, he would receive a bit of food. If we arranged the situation, however, so that only very rarely would a bit of food be delivered after he had made the response, the animal might never learn the response. Let us say that the situation was arranged so that the animal would have to make fifty responses before receiving a bit of food. Under these circumstances, if the animal pressed the lever several times in exploring the apparatus and there was no reward, it would make the response less and less frequently. The number and rapidity of the responses under this circumstance would not provide a sufficient number of occasions for reward to occur, and thus for any substantial learning to take place. The animal under these conditions would never learn to press the bar rapidly fifty times and thus secure the food that would be available for rapid and consistent responding.

On the other hand, we could place an animal in the same situation and by more judiciously employing our rewards produce a very rapid learner and a very hard-working animal—for a reward that still demanded fifty responses. To do this it would be necessary to first reward the animal for every response—or most of them. If we did the animal would soon begin to make the response more frequently, and we could say the response had been learned. At this point we could then begin to decrease the ratio of reward—the animal could be given a piece of food after every few responses. When we observed that the rapidity of response was maintained under this partial reinforcement schedule, we could then advance the ratio. We could require that several more responses be made before the reward was delivered. In this manner we could thus move gradually to the point where the animal would make fifty responses for every reward. If done in this manner we could see an increase in the rapidity of the animal's response.

The important point is that a richer ratio of reward to responding is necessary when an organism is first acquiring a response. This is true generally, and thus applies to children as well as adults. If you want someone to learn a behavior strongly so that the behavior will be maintained in the face of a lean ratio of reward to the number of responses required, the individual must first *learn* to work for the sparse reward.

The wise trainer, then, must be alert to the conditions of reward that he provides the trainee. Frequently, parents do not understand this principle and they do not provide sufficient reward initially to the child, so his behavior in the learning situation is not maintained. The parent may also err by too rapidly raising the ratio of responses required for the reward that is provided. When this occurs the child's behavior in the learning situation will become weaker and weaker. It will be noted then that the child participates with less and less eagerness, responding with less and less alacrity. Moreover, we will see that the child will begin to display other behaviors in the situation—behaviors that are not of the learning variety but are competitive with the learning. Ultimately, the child will refuse to participate in the learning situation.

Attention Span and Reward Conditions

The author has worked with many children and has seen the preceding process occur. If the child's responses are not rewarded with sufficient amount or frequency, the learning behavior will deteriorate. The length of time a child stays at a task with fixed reward properties is frequently spoken of as the child's attention span. That is, if we took children of various ages and placed them in the same learning task, we would see that the children would stay in the task for longer periods as the average age of the children increased. This type of observation has led to the conclusion that there must be some internal process involved that advances as the child matures physiologically. The concept of attention span, as commonly used, is thus that the child's attention span depends upon his physiological maturity.

As with the other biological conceptions of child development, however, there is no evidence that there is any physiological mechanism or process that advances with the child's age and that produces the child's increase in length of attention in a learning task. Moreover, there is much to suggest that the child *learns* to work for longer and longer periods as he learns to make more and more responses before he receives reinforcement. Ordinarily, this learning of more and more extended work habits takes time. Thus, on the average, children who are older will display better attention spans, or better work habits—whichever descriptive term one chooses to employ.

The author has shown the importance of reward principles on "attention span" time and again in controlled laboratory research with children as well as in work conducted in the naturalistic setting. For example, in one laboratory study four-year-old children were introduced to a reading-learning task. Social reinforcement was given to the children for each response. However, the task involved repeated presentations of word stimuli. The children had to attend to these stimuli and repeat the appropriate words supplied by the experimenter. The learning task was massed in that many learning trials were involved—and the length of each session was forty minutes.

The behavior of the four-year-olds was very instructive. The attention and working behaviors of the children were at first quite good. However, these behaviors quickly began to weaken and were replaced by "fidgeting and fooling around" behaviors. Most of the children requested to be allowed to discontinue the activity in fifteen minutes. One could say that the limit of their attention spans had been surpassed by this period of time.

It was very interesting to note, however, that when a source of reinforcement over and above the social rewards was introduced, the children's behavior changed. When the children were materially rewarded for each learning trial (with small trinkets and edibles, and tokens that could be exchanged for small toys) their attention and work behaviors again grew strong. It was found that preschool children could work and attend for long training periods. However, the rewards for this behavior had to be stronger than those of social reward (Staats, Staats, Schutz, and Wolf, 1962).

The author has also shown that preschool children's work and learning behaviors can be maintained by partial reinforcement schedules. After children have been introduced to a reading-learning task, the reward need not be presented after each learning trial. As a matter of fact, the work and learning behaviors of the child may be maintained in even greater strength if only a proportion of the responses are rewarded (Staats, Finley, Minke, and Wolf, 1964). For example, a four-year-old child who was free to complete as many learning trials as he wished made the learning responses more rapidly when he was rewarded variably on the average of once every sixth learning trial than he did when he was rewarded on every trial. In the arduous, repetitive task of learning to read letters, however, there was a limit to how "lean" the ratio of reward to learning trials could be made. Another child made more rapid reading learning responses as the ratio was increased, beginning with one reward to one response. He continued to attend better and work more rapidly as the ratio was increased from one to two, one to three, one to four, and one to five. When the ratio was raised to one to six, however, under the conditions of the learning provided, the child's work and attentional behaviors began to weaken. When the ratio was raised to one to seven there was clear evidence that the child would not continue to attend well and work consistently and well—and that his learning would thus not continue in maximal quality (Staats, Finley, Osborne, Quinn, and Minke, 1963).

The author has worked with mentally retarded children in the same type of learning task. Some retarded children, when provided with the types of material rewards already described, appeared to attend and work and learn very well. This finding supported the present approach substantially. The results suggested that if such children were provided with appropriate reinforcers, they would learn as well as other children. One of the first cases that was conducted within this context was with a culturally deprived, delinquent, backward child who was reading at the second-grade level at the time the program began (Staats and Butterfield, 1965). This fourteen-year-old child was an extreme conduct problem in school and had never passed a school course. When the appropriate reward system was introduced, it was found that this child who was intractable in the usual classroom situation attended well, worked hard, and learned well. This was not a short-term study, moreover. It was conducted over a period of 4½ months, during which time the child was presented with many words he did not know. He learned and retained these words very well, and his reading achievement scores increased markedly. In addition, he began to be less of a behavior problem in school, stating that he liked school better, and passed all of his courses at the end of the semester.

One finding is especially relevant to the present discussion. As the training continued, a progressively greater number of reading responses were necessary for the fourteen-year-old child to obtain a reinforcer. (The reinforcers were tokens that could be exchanged for material things the child wished to obtain.[1]) After about half the training was completed the child had to make

[1]The author devised this system, the token-reinforcer system, in 1959 in working with children with learning problems. He communicated the efficacy of the token reinforcement system to Jack Michael at the University of Houston, who with Lee Meyerson began to work with mentally retarded children employing a similar system. The possibilities for use of the token-reinforcer system were also discussed with Teodoro Ayllon who, with Nathan Azrin, developed its use in the psychiatric hospital (Ayllon and Azrin, 1969). Montrose Wolf, who as a graduate student had contributed to the present author's studies extending the token-reinforcement system to preschool children (already described herein), helped introduce the system to the child research program at the University of Washington. On the basis of such personal dissemination, along with publication of token-reinforcement studies, behavior modification work then began to employ the reinforcement system widely, as have a number of later education and special education studies.

about four times as many reading responses per reinforcer as he did when the training commenced. Nevertheless, the child's behavior was better maintained at this time than at the start of the training—although the reading material was more difficult. This finding, which has been duplicated with a number of other children, showed clearly that if the child is given adequate reinforcement at the beginning, it can be gradually decreased in amount and still maintain the learning-work behavior in as good or better strength.

On the basis of such findings it might be expected that the child's history with respect to work behaviors, and the manner and type of reinforcement made contingent upon such behavior, will greatly affect the extent to which he is capable of sustained and effective work behaviors. A history of gradually increasing work demands in the sense of the number of behaviors that must occur before reward occurs may be expected to produce greater work productivity than a history that is deficient in this respect. The author also has evidence of this in cases of retardates who had major differences from other children in their very deficient work and learning behaviors (Staats, 1968a). In the same period of time that other children will make many learning responses, these retardates would make very, very few learning responses. It is certainly clear that learning cannot take place without learning trials. After a long history of missed learning opportunities because of poor work and learning behaviors, the child is bound to be retarded.

EFFECTIVE TRAINING PRINCIPLES INVOLVING USE OF REWARDS

Actually, the preceding discussion has involved some very practical principles of reinforcement that the parent should know as he faces the many training tasks involved in producing an effectively behaving child. Thus, as one principle, it might be expected that a program of training that provides opportunity for increasingly longer and more effortful sequences of productive behavior, always providing adequate reinforcement to maintain the behavior in good strength, would be very desirable for producing a hard-working, productive individual. It is suggested that this type of experience should begin very early for the child. This is another reason that the biological conception of child development, which tells the parent to sit back and wait for the child to mature, is a very backward one. As has been outlined in the present book, the learning experiences of the child should begin very early. It is only in this way that the increase in the effortfulness of the learning tasks can be gradual. At the beginning the child is only asked to imitate a word, for example, before receiving the rewarding object that he is reaching for. The effortfulness of the behavior demanded before reinforcement is delivered is minimal, but a very real amount of effort is involved. Later, the learning task may involve saying two words in sequence, as another example. Even later, still more effortful and extended sequences may be required—if the child's work and learning skills have been provided by the earlier experience. A child who has received the various types of training that have been described herein will also have learned an effective learning-work repertoire, in addition to the specific skills acquired. This will prepare him for the even more effortful and extended preacademic learning he should face prior to entering school. Furthermore, in the desirable situation the preschool experience will prepare the child for the even more extended learning-work tasks he will meet in school.

Several aspects of child learning were stated in the preceding section. These will serve as the foundations upon which several rules may be derived by which to maximize the efficacy of child training. The important learning conditions to be considered are as follows. First, the schedule of reward is important in the learning task—that is, the number of responses that must occur prior to reward. The greater the number of responses, the more difficult the learning task. Second, the *massing* of learning trials per learning session is an important item in the difficulty of the training. The greater the number of learning trials per session, the greater the difficulty. Third, the effortfulness of the responses involved is important. A learning task that demands effortful attentional, searching, and discrimination responses will be more difficult than a task that requires less effortful behaviors. Fourth, the past experience of the child with respect to the difficulty of learning tasks will also affect the difficulty of the present learning task. A child who has had fewer past experiences with learning tasks will find a new learning task more difficult.

The general rule that must be followed in child training, if one is to employ positive reinforcement (versus punishment), is that *the amount of reward must be set according to the difficulty of the task*. This means that the task can be reduced in difficulty along any of the four dimensions in the preceding paragraph. Or the amount of reward can be increased to match the difficulty. Several points of illustration will be productive here.

When the rewards are very strong, more behavior can be required of the child. Although the child will gradually learn to be able to make more and more extended work behaviors as he receives training in these "skills," at any particular point in the child's development the parent should be sensitive to the fact that he cannot exceed the limits imposed by the present level of the work skill of the child. The less the previous work training of the child, the stronger the rewards must be; and the shorter and easier must be the learning task. When the child is quite young, when he has not been trained in long working sequences, less behavior may be demanded in the task than will be possible later on. This limitation can be counteracted in training situations by presenting rewards more profusely. In short-term training situations where one is desirous of rapid results, or in cases of special learning problems, a reward system may be used that is stronger than ordinarily employed. It will maintain attentive behavior in longer training sessions. One of the objects of the preferred course of child training, however, is to conduct the training so that a reward system of unusual strength is not necessary.

The extent of massing learning trials within a training session should also depend upon the level of the child's development of work skills. At first the child will be able only to have individual learning trials, relatively widely spaced. Later he will be able to have more learning trials massed within a learning session. The greater the massing the more effortful the task, the stronger the child's work-learning skills must be, as well as the stronger the rewards, and the stronger the reward payoff per response made.

In this respect the parent who conducts learning trials with the young child which are interspersed throughout the day will conduct the most effective skill training. When this is done the learning never becomes very effortful, and the usual rewards presented by natural circumstances are sufficient. One of the reasons that language training in the home has a higher percentage of success than reading training in school is because the language training is usually so well spaced. Thus, the parent who every now and then sees the child reaching for something, for example, and then conducts a learning trial in which the child says the name of the object, is utilizing several of the principals already stated. The intermittent learning trials keep down the effortfulness of the task. The giving of the object may also represent a rather strong reward. These features of sporadically spaced learning trials and strong reward are suited to the level of work-learning developed by the very young child. There are many possibilities for this type of training. The parent who utilizes them will be preparing his child for the more extended learning tasks he will later have to face. This preparation is certainly possible when the training begins early.

In summary, it may be added that when the reinforcers are lightweight, as frequently occurs, the training periods must be short and the amount and effortfulness of the behavior demanded must be low. In addition, when working with a very young child, the behavioral demands must be minimal and only very gradually increased. The trainer must also be very sensitive to signs that the participation and attentional behavior of the child are weakening. When weakening occurs it means that the limits in one of these variables is being exceeded. Then, either reinforcement must be increased (in quantity or through a richer ratio of reinforcement), the number of learning trials per session must be reduced, or the task must be made less effortful in other ways. Since the training that is being outlined in the present book need not be extended or arduous, and so on, further detail on these training principles will be left for a later volume dealing with more advanced learning in children.

Nature of Rewards

Again, in the primarily informal training that occurs with the language-personality development of the child, the nature of effective reinforcers need not be described in detail. A few words are pertinent here, however, concerning some of the reinforcers available to the parent.

One of the most important sources of reinforcement is the attention of the parent. For most children, as already described, the attention of the parent will have become a rewarding stimulus. Complex repertoires of skill can be acquired by the child, based upon the fact that the learning responses of the child are followed by the parent's attention. This is true also of the related reinforcers of social approval and affection. Words of praise and approval and the cues of affection will be effective for most children who have had an appropriate learning history with respect to such stimuli.

The latter statement, however, also sets the limits to the use of attention, affection, and social approval as reinforcers in training the young child. That is, these are learned reinforcers. It thus takes learning trials for attention, affection, and social approval to become strong rewards. In the very young child they will not be as strong as they will be later in life. Moreover, if these stimuli are presented again and again is massed learning trials, the reward value of attention, affection, and social approval will quickly be unlearned; the reward value will extinguish. Even when these social stimuli have been strongly learned, moreover, they do not serve well as reinforcers in a long-term, arduous task where they must be repeatedly presented. The child will satiate quickly on such social rewards.

Thus, attention, affection, and approval are very effective rewards, but they must be employed largely for single learning trials—not in massed training sessions, on effortful responses, or with long delays in reinforcement. When the parent, as is usual, conducts learning trials on language-personality skills interspersed throughout the day, he may work well within the limits of the rewards of attention, approval, and affection—and thus produce much important learning in the child.

The parent may also extend the strength and efficacy of his attention, affection, and approval by combining them with other reinforcers. Thus, when the parent has the child sit on his lap and shows the child pictures, the child has the reinforcement of the parent as well as that of the pictures themselves.

Actually, various activities, usually in combination with the parent's attention, may also be a source of reinforcement. The parent could say, for example, "Try to go pottie, and *then* I'll take you for a walk," after the child has requested the activity. In any event there are many reinforcing activities for the child that can be employed to reward learning trials that are of a somewhat more extended, more effortful type, as well as to reward less demanding learning trials. Games, trips, movies, and the like, are other examples.

As has already been referred to, there are many other natural reinforcers that will effectively reward learning trials. Thus, when the child requests by gesticulating that the parent hand him something, that something is a reinforcer and can be employed as such in a language-learning trial. There are many, many such objects and events. The parent who gives some thought to what these are for the child will also be noting for his information the objects and events he can use in training the child to various aspects of the basic behavioral repertoires dealt with herein, as well as other desirable behaviors.

One other type of reward may be mentioned at this time—material rewards that the parent introduces solely as a means of training the child. The author has suggested that material reinforcers can also be effectively employed even with the very young (Staats, 1968a), and has used them with his own children. These possibilities, however, are even more pertinent in discussing more drawn out learning tasks. These types of tasks can be introduced very profitably to two-year-old children, although it is more customary to begin them with children of three, four, or five years of age. The discussion of material rewards in preparing the child for academic success will be dealt with in a later book that will treat such types of learning.

USE OF PUNISHMENT
IN CHILD TRAINING

The use of punishment in training a child is a complex affair that should be understood by the parent. It is not possible to go into the full topic here, but several points will be made, and the relevance of such training for the language development of the child will be outlined.

First, whenever a child experiences a painful stimulus, the stimulus will elicit a negative emotional response. According to the principle of learning that has been outlined, any other stimulus present at the time will come through learning to elicit the emotional response. In fact, the new stimulus could have had no connection with the event that caused the painful stimulation to occur—but the conditioning will nevertheless take place.

In any event, whenever the parent applies a painful stimulus to the child, the negative emotional responses that are elicited will be conditioned to the cues of the parent. If this type of experience is frequent enough, the parent will come to elicit a negative emotional response in the child. The parent may administer the aversive stimulus to get the child to do something he should do, or not do something undesirable. The parent actually may be concerned with training the child in desirable behavior. But the effect is the same in terms of the negative emotional conditioning the child learns to the parent.

It should be noted, however, that each time the parent is present when the child receives a stimulus that elicits a positive emotional response, the parent will come through the same principle to elicit a positive emotional response. Thus, the two types of learning are in "competition." Whether the parent in sum elicits a positive emotional response in the child or a negative emotional response will result from the two types of experience the child has associated with the parent. Ordinarily, the child has more positive than negative conditioning—but there is room for infinite variation in this regard.

The important thing here is that much of the parent's ability to influence his child through learning principles will depend upon the extent to which the parent himself elicits positive emotional responses in the child, and thus constitutes a rewarding stimulus to the child, or has in his possession such rewarding stimuli. For example, it has been said that the more reward value the person has for another, the more the latter will imitate the person, follow him, respond to his instructions, and so on.

From this standpoint alone, in principle the parent should employ as little aversive stimulation as possible. In addition, it is apparently the case that the sensitivity of the organism to an aversive stimulus declines with the continued application of the stimulus. Thus, the parent who uses heavy and repeated application of aversive stimuli, such as in spankings or beatings, uses this avenue of training in a most ineffective way, for two reasons. He becomes a less rewarding stimulus to his child, thus curtailing his ability to train his child through positive means. Moreover, his repeated use of punishment will make the punishment less and less effective, and the parent's ability to influence his child's learning through this means will be progressively diminished.

The answers to these points are, first, that punishment should be used very sparingly by the parent. The use of punishment should in no way approach the intensity that it begins to counterbalance the positive emotional conditioning the parent extends to the child. Furthermore, spankings, where repeated aversive stimuli are delivered, are not necessary and in fact are deleterious both in terms of emotional conditioning as well as in making the child inured to punishment—not to mention the fact that the parent constitutes a model whom the child will later imitate.

Use of Punishment
and Language Training

To continue, it should be emphasized that when an aversive stimulus is going to be applied to an undesirable behavior of the child, a primary goal of the parent should be to use the experience to develop the child's language learning. In this way, through a word being paired with the punishing stimulus, the word will acquire the functions of the punishing stimulus. Later it will only be necessary to use the word—not the punishing stimulus—to control some undesirable behavior of the child.

Thus, if the child does something that should be stopped and the parent is going to punish the child—let us say by a smack on the bottom—the parent at the same time should say an appropriate word. A good word for use with a young child is *no*. After this has occurred several times, the parent will only have to say, "No," when the child begins a behavior that must be stopped. It should be understood, of course, that the power of the word at the early stages will depend upon the learning history of the child. If the parent says "no" frequently when the child is not given an aversive stimulus, or is not restrained from doing something (which is also an aversive stimulus), then the word will not come to control "stopping behavior." Even after the child comes to respond appropriately to the word, additional learning trials will still be required occasionally. However, the training may be conducted with decreasing use of punishment and increasing use of restraint, if it is done properly. In any case, the criterion is whether the word comes to control the appropriate behavior and whether this is maintained.

It has been said that aversive stimuli should be employed as infrequently as possible. This suggests that punishment is entirely undesirable in training the child. Actually, at least in our present state of social advancement, it is impossible to raise a socially controlled child without the use of some form of aversive stimulation. It is thus important to indicate how it should be used to minimize its adverse effects and maximize its productive effects.

In terms of positive effects, it is suggested that words which come to act as aversive stimuli for the child are very important to his adjustment—and one of the ways of creating such words is through use of the mild punishments that are administered ordinarily to the child. The fact is that social interactions of various sorts in society depend upon the individual having come to respond appropriately to words that elicit negative emotional responses and which act as punishments. In our society, for example, if the child's behavior is to be conventionally controlled, the words *don't, dangerous, bad, stop, forbidden, mean, unkind, unlawful, no,* and so on must come to elicit avoidance behavior and to suppress behaviors which they follow—that is, to function as an aversive stimulus. If this does not occur, the individual is likely to encounter harmful or socially aversive consequences of far greater severity than that involved in the aversive word stimulus. The child who does not respond conventionally when told by a teacher, "You are forbidden to do that again," by the policeman, "That is unlawful," by the older child or adult, "That is dangerous," by anyone, "That hurts," "Please stop," and so on, is likely to suffer later aversive stimulation of a physical or social nature. In short, it is important in the child's learning that words of social disapproval come to elicit negative emotional responses in him.

It is suggested that one's language training will thus be very important in the extent to which the individual is cautious in behavior, responsible, prudent, and so on. The importance of this language training may be seen even more clearly when the child begins to use his own language in his reasoning *to control his own behavior.* That is, when the child learns language reasoning sequences, as well as the repertoire of negative emotional meaning words, then he has a means of avoiding behaviors that would be followed by punishment without actually having to experience that punishment. In this way he becomes independent of the control of others to a much larger extent than he was without this language development. To illustrate, if the child says something to himself relevant to some later action and his logical sequence ends in an aversive word, then he will tend to avoid the action. For example, if the school child says, "If I do not study tonight I will fail the test," this sequence will lead him to avoid not studying, provided that the word *fail* elicits negative emotional responses. For students for whom the word *fail* does not elicit a negative emotional response, the reasoning sequence will not control desirable behavior.

As will be described in the next chapter, a future occurrence cannot determine behavior that precedes it, but language responses can occur before the future occurrence and affect behavior of the individual with respect to that future occurrence. An important part of this effect of language is the existence of words that function as aversive stimuli. The cautious man who "anticipates" in his verbal reasoning possible adverse conditions would seem to do so partly because of training from which he has learned effective negative emotional words. The same is true of the person who is "socially sensitive" and is careful to avoid actions that might affront someone. From this analysis it is suggested that the overcautious, timid person's behavior is so in part because of a superabundance of the training that goes into the learning of a repertoire of negative emotional words. The irresponsible, reckless, wild individual, on the other hand, suffers from a deficit in training that will make words aversive and capable of functioning as do aversive stimuli. This could occur because the individual has never received punishment in his training, *or because the punishment was never used to create negative emotional words* by which the individual could control his own behavior in a prudent manner. This is stated here to indicate the important learning that takes place when the parent presents some type of aversive stimulus to the child to suppress an undesirable behavior, and at the same time says an appropriate word or words.

This discussion does not justify the heavy use of punishment in training the child—whippings or extended spankings. It should be stated again that corporal punishment should be used sparingly. And with the types of training methods described here, spankings and beatings are entirely unnecessary. The most that is required in child training is one effective "smack" paired with a word. This means, however, that such learning must commence when the child is young enough for such a stimulus to have effective aversive qualities.

Furthermore, such mild punishments should be used in such a way that the child learns to respond to words, and then direct punishment is no longer necessary. Actually, the parent can use punishment to a great extent in controlling the child's behavior and yet not produce a child who is either well-controlled socially (by others) or by his own reasoning process. That is, the parent who attempts to control his child by spankings for specific behaviors, but who does not train the child to respond to the appropriate words, will affect only the specific behaviors. The child will not learn a basic behavioral repertoire that will generalize to many other situations. For example, a child who is punished for biting will not bite in the future. However, he may do something else that hurts another person. On the other hand, the child who through learning comes to respond appropriately to the words, "Don't do that, it hurts," will have acquired a basic socialization behavior that will generalize to many situations. Thus, the type of language learning being discussed here is frequently referred to under the terms *socialization* or *internalization of social values* as well as superego personality development.

By the time the child is four or five years of age, direct use of aversive stimulation of misbehaviors should be almost entirely unnecessary, if the child's language development has occurred as outlined. The child's behavior will be controllable largely by verbal instructions. If considerable punishment is required to control the behavior of a child at such ages and beyond, it is suggested that the training methods for the child have not been adequate.

Thus, it is suggested here that it is appropriate at times to use aversive stimuli in training the child. There are behaviors that the parent wishes to suppress quickly—usually for purposes of the child's own safety. Use of positive reinforcement in such training might take too long. In addition, there are behaviors of the child that are controlled by strong positive-rewarding stimuli—a cookie jar the child is supposed to stay away from, another child's toy, a delicate piece of furniture in a relative's house, or some such. In these circumstances it may be necessary to apply a smack to prevent the behavior, or to take away the toy, or to restrain the child. All of these are aversive stimuli and are justified both in terms of preventing the specific undesirable behaviors as well as in using the event to further the child's language learning. When punishment is employed, it is suggested that it be as infrequent as possible, as slight as is *necessary to be definitely aversive,* applied immediately but of short duration, *and be paired with words so the words will later on be capable of substituting for the direct punishment.* This type of training will help produce negative-meaning words that make social disapproval functional, and in this way may make the child socialized and capable of controlling aspects of his own behavior through his own reasoning (language) processes.

Withdrawal of Rewards
as Punishment

It has been stated that one of the ways of weakening a response is to remove a rewarding circumstance after the organism has made the particular response. If this is done the response will occur less and less. In this manner the removal of a rewarding stimulus performs the same function as the presentation of a punishing stimulus following a behavior.

The use of physical punishment can be lessened through the application of this principle of learning in very effective ways. As one example, which has time-honored acceptance as well as research validation, it will act as a punishment to the child to be removed from the presence of the family members by being restricted to his room. This procedure actually involves taking away the reward of the family presence and its activities. The author began applying this method to his own daughter for behavioral infractions in systematic procedures when she was less than two years of age, and there are now a number of studies that show that this can be employed to weaken undesirable behavior in a child. (Restricting the child to his room for a period has come to be called "time out," the term applied in animal studies; however, it is actually an example of withdrawing rewards to serve as a punishment.)

As an example of the application of this principle, let us say that the child has persisted in a behavior that is undesirable to the parent. The parent then may say to the child, "When you do that you have to go to your room," and carry out the consequence. After a number of such occurrences, the words "go to your room" will acquire an aversive quality themselves. Then it will be possible to simply tell the child, "If you do that you will have to go to your room." These words themselves will constitute a punishment and weaken the undesirable behavior. However, the strength of the words as punishing stimuli will depend upon the number of conditioning trials already conducted. Thus, the parent must ensure that the words are followed by the restriction to the room if the child does not cease his undesirable behavior.

Aversive verbal stimuli used in unreasonable ways may be described as threats. It is, of course, not desirable to threaten a child to control undesirable behavior. However, it is quite reasonable to state the consequences that will follow a certain behavior, if the consequence is reasonable. This has the function of training the child to come under the control of the verbal stimuli rather than the primary punishment itself. This is true of the presentation of punishing stimuli, or the removal of rewarding stimuli used as a punishment.

There are other types of rewarding stimuli that can be removed when the child does not behave desirably. Again, however, it is desirable to keep such punishment to the minimum, consistent with the child learning appropriately controlled behavior and learning the aversive meaning of words that must come to control his behavior.

Gradually Introduced Training Involving Punishment

It has been said that the conditions of reward have to be set to be appropriate for the child's level of behavioral development. Until the child has strongly learned social rewards, until he has learned extended work-learning behaviors, and so on, it is necessary to employ positive reinforcement in briefly conducted training situations. There are similar considerations in the use of aversive stimuli. If the standards of good behavior applied to the child are advanced too rapidly, then there will be too many occasions where the standards will not be met. If infraction of the standards determines the use of punishment, then when the standards are advanced too rapidly the child will be punished too frequently.

Again, the parent must consider the behavior of his child in terms of the learning conception. The child's ability to respond appropriately, to not perform behaviors that are undesirable, and so on, will be a function of the child's learning. The child has to *learn* not to misbehave. There are many stimuli in the child's life, for example, that have reward value and that attract the child—even though the behavior is undesirable. The young child will push over a lamp, put a screwdriver into an electric outlet, pull pots out of a cabinet, and the like. He will only *learn* not to perform such behaviors. He cannot be allowed free access to such behaviors and then punished for all of them. The situations in which he is allowed to behave freely should be appropriate for his level of behavioral control, with only a reasonable number of infractions occurring in which punishment can be delivered with good learning outcomes.

On the other hand, the parent can err in not raising standards rapidly enough. The child needs training in which he learns not to make certain behaviors. Even more importantly, he must learn to respond appropriately to the words that must come to elicit "stopping" responses. Some mothers who accept the biological conception of child development feel that the very young child is not yet "responsible" for his actions. Thus, they feel that the only thing that can be done with a young child is to follow him around in situations that might elicit an undesirable response and prevent the response from occurring. Or, they simply restrict the child in a playpen or some other enclosed area. The expectation in such a conception is that the child will later on mature and will be better controlled.

If this is done, if the child receives no training in not making certain responses, and especially if the child does not learn to respond appropriately to negative words, he will not advance in this respect. There are fully grown children and adults whose behavior is so poorly controlled by words and other social stimuli that they are considered uncontrollable and dangerous to society.

It is suggested that the training in socially controlled behavior should commence early so that it can be advanced gradually. In this way the parent can introduce into the child's learning the mild aversive consequences already described. If the training is delayed too long, it becomes necessary to employ more harsh punishment procedures, since uncontrolled behavior in an older child is ordinarily of a more serious nature than in a very young child, and the mild punishments effective for the young child are no longer effective. Thus, it is advisable to begin to introduce the mild but effective aversive consequences for undesirable behavior into the child's learning early, with the object of producing word stimuli that can be used as surrogates for direct punishment. This training will thus produce controlled behavior directly in the various situations dealt with, as well as the learning of the repertoire of negative emotional words that can be used later to control the child's misbehaviors.

THE LEARNING-WORK
ATTITUDE

Learning situations as complex stimuli have certain common features. There is an instructor, for example, or an instructional set of stimuli of some kind. The child is required to put forth attentional responses to the stimuli indicated in the learning situation. The child must also actively and effortfully perform responses to acquire new skills. Moreover, there is frequently some consequence attached to the child's performance, positive if he performs well and negative if he does not.

As these examples indicate, a learning situation can be considered to be a complex stimulus. Moreover, learning situations have certain distinctive characteristics in common. As such, it would be expected that the child could learn responses to learning situations in general. It is this type of learning—the acquisition of responses to learning situations as general stimuli—that is the concern of this section. One of the types of responses that a child can acquire to general learning situations involves his emotional or attitudinal learning. Whether a child responds to learning situations with a positive emotional response or a negative emotional response will be very important in what he does and in what he learns.

The Anti-Learning Attitude

It may be suggested that punishment should very rarely be used in a situation in which the adult is attempting to train the young child to some positive skill. This is contrasted with the situation where the task is to train the child *not* to make some response, in which case the use of punishment, as has been described, has a place. The rationale involved is as follows. It has been suggested that a punishing stimulus elicits negative emotional responses in the child. Each time an emotional response is elicited, it will be conditioned to all the stimuli present at that time. Thus, it must be expected that a child punished in a learning situation will learn a negative emotional response to the learning situation. If this happens in various learning situations, the conditioned emotional response will become very general—it will be elicited by all learning situations that share common features with the others.

This emotional conditioning will then have general effects inimical to the child's learning. It should be remembered that the child will have learned to escape and avoid in various ways any stimulus that elicits a negative emotional response and thus has punishing functions. That is, any behavior that escapes the aversive stimulus will be learned through the reinforcement of the removal of the punishment. Any behavior that avoids the stimulus will in the same way be learned. In general, then, when learning situations come to elicit negative emotional responses (anxiety) in the child, the child will learn behaviors that escape and avoid learning situations. The behavior skills of escaping and avoiding learning situations compose items of interest in themselves, as a later section will indicate. It is also of interest, however, to briefly consider the way in which the child can learn negative emotional responses to learning situations.

To begin, a simple animal experimental situation will help sketch out several principles of the role of punishment in training—as part of indicating why punishment when employed to produce positive skills has distinct drawbacks. Let us say that a rat is placed in an experimental chamber in which the floor is an electric grid that can be turned on to produce a punishing stimulus to the animal's feet. Let us say also that the animal is to learn a new response, the pressing of a lever that extends into the cage. The learning *could* take place by rewarding the animal with a piece of food whenever he happened to make the response. In contrast, however, the animal could be shocked through the grid, with the punishing stimulus remaining on until the animal made the response. After the animal had made the response, the punishing stimulus would be turned off for a stipulated time and then be resumed until the animal made another response. Under this type of training program the animal would soon learn to press the bar frequently. Having learned the response he would then rarely experience any punishment—since he would infrequently delay in responding sufficiently long for the shock to reoccur.

This would be an effective means of training the animal to the skill desired. If one noted only the performance of an animal trained through punishment versus one trained through reward, one might conclude that one method was quite as good as the other. It should be noted, however, that there would actually be a great deal of difference between the animals. If there were physiological recordings on both animals, it would be seen that the emotional responses elicited by the animal trained through relief from punishment would be quite different (and undesirably so) from those of the animal trained through reward. Moreover, if we looked beyond the performance of the animals in the specific situation, we would see large differences. For example, if we did not simply place the animals in the experimental chamber, but arranged a door into the chamber into which the animals could go if they "chose" to do so, we would find that one animal would enter the chamber and one animal would not. The animal that had been rewarded in the situation would approach the chamber without coercion and would enter and begin performing the skill. The animal that had learned through the relief from punishment would not approach the chamber, would not enter the chamber, and he would never perform the response. When this animal would be forcibly placed in the chamber he would perform very readily. But if there was an available exit this animal would quickly learn how to get out of the chamber; he would learn to escape the learning situation, or to avoid it if given the opportunity.

This would occur because there are actually several types of learning taking place in any skill learning. In the present example, not only does the animal learn the skill of the motor response of bar-pressing, he also learns an emotional response to the general situation. This latter type of learning has not been adequately considered in this basic laboratory situation. However, while the rewarded animal would have learned a positive emotional response to the situation, the punished animal would have learned a negative emotional response to the situation. Their emotional behavior with respect to the learning-work situation would be markedly different, and this would determine markedly different behaviors with respect to the situation.

This example has been given to indicate that the same situation exists with the learning of the child. It is true that a child can learn many skills if by so doing he will escape punishment (punishment as used here refers to any type of aversive stimulus, not just physical punishment). But when this has been the case, the child will also learn a negative emotional response to learning situations. He will escape them when possible, and he will avoid them also. We see evidence of this kind of training with individuals who have acquired complex skills through this "negative reinforcement," but who once they are free of restraint never engage in the skill. Many individuals show school histories of this sort—and they never engage in such learning situations when they are not forced to, and they do not practice the skills they have acquired.

Although it seems unreasonable, most people have never learned how to train a child in a complex skill that requires some massing of learning trials. Although the usual parent is adequate enough in his informal interactions with his child which produce many of the child's basic behavioral repertoires—at least to some extent—it is the unusual parent who can train the child to some complex skill. Thus, if he attempts to train the child in some skill such as playing tennis, reading the alphabet, playing piano, counting, and so on, he will not succeed. This type of failure is especially apparent when the parent has a child who has not learned the basic behavioral repertoires because the parent has been a poor trainer in his informal interactions with the child. Then the parent is forced to try formal, massed types of training, and with only common-sense knowledge of training methods he will usually fail in such things as toilet training, teaching the child language, and so on. Most often the usual parent does not know the principles of learning, does not have training materials to tell him how to proceed, and usually has no personal experience in individually training a child. (This description is not much different even for professionals such as psychologists, teachers, pediatricans, and so on.)

Thus, the usual parent when attempting a formal training task with his child, for whatever reason, will ordinarily have unreasonable expectations in view of the materials he has to work with and the skill that he has. The likely outcome is that the child will not make progress in learning the skill. When the parent meets this obstacle, his almost certain response is to begin to apply some aversive stimulus. This occurs because the child's difficulty in learning is aversive to the parent. This is almost invariably the case. The parent's learned response to aversiveness, moreover, is to be aversive in return. Thus, the parent will not ordinarily have learned the necessary principles and methods of reward learning, so he has nothing else to do but to try to *force* the child to attend, to try harder, to do better. So the parent resorts to forcing and remonstrating techniques; he will try to shame the child into learning—even without meaning to do so. He will usually do this with greater intensity as the child fails to progress, which will negatively affect the child's ability to learn, until the point is reached where the parent will give up.

The author has seen this happen many times, although the adult involved would be unaware of using punishment and of the effects this would have upon his child's behavior. For example, the author remembers clearly an incident that took place at a club pool a number of years ago. Before this time the author had conducted a long-term training program with his daughter on the skills of swimming. She was at that time less than three years of age, but the training program had been spread out over a period of two years. The training had commenced after the child had experienced the aversive stimulation of having soap in her eye when bathing and had come to refuse to bathe or have her hair washed. She would cry and try to escape such situations. At this time the author began rewarding the child in the bath until the "phobic" behavior disappeared. Later, in a gradual training program, water was splashed in the child's face gently in the act of playing a game in a small plastic pool. Then the game advanced to putting part of her face in the water, then the whole face. The level of the water was gradually raised and the skills of handling her body in the water were gradually acquired. Additional skills of being in a real swimming pool were later added in various ways.

This is summarized to describe the gradual nature of the training program which was conducted, always under the action of reward. This is not to say that there was not aversiveness involved for the child. Actually, each new step involved a certain amount of aversiveness—beginning with the first splash of water on the face. But the rewards outweighed the aversiveness by a good deal, and the original aversiveness of being splashed, and so on, decreased.

The incident important to the present discussion, however, occurred at the pool when another father was attempting to get his son to enter the water and to learn to swim. It was obvious that none of the preceding, more rudimentary skills had yet been acquired by the child—such as putting his face in the water, and so on. Yet the well-meaning father wanted the child to come into the pool and to attempt to learn to swim. When the child refused to do this the father remonstrated; he pointed out that the author's daughter was swimming and was younger than he was, and so on. This treatment, which constituted punishment for the child, is a typical parental reaction to such a situation.

The child absolutely avoided getting into the water with his father. He approached it several times and retreated. The only "accomplishment" that day was to condition the child's negative emotional responses to the swimming situation—and no doubt to his father and to other learning situations as well.

Another case in the context of intellectual learning that has the same implications occurred in a research project of the author. In this project children who had not learned to read by the time they were in the seventh and eighth grades were presented with the author's "motivated learning" treatment procedures (see Staats, Minke, Goodwin, and Landeen, 1967). The instructors were nonprofessionals who were administering the well-specified materials. The instructors were supposed to rely upon the material reward system to maintain the child's learning-work behaviors. One instructor, however, with the best of intentions, attempted to accelerate the learning of her subject (who was indeed slow). With very good intentions she would say to him, "You can do better than that," "You knew that word before," "If you try harder you can get it," and so on whenever he did not read something correctly. At the time the author observed the interaction, after several weeks of such training, the subject was becoming more and more upset and was initiating misbehaviors that would soon have culminated in his escaping the learning situation. Yet this behavior of the instructor was so natural that two of the author's assistants had missed seeing the occurrence of the punishment, and its negative effects. When the training situation was changed to use only reward, the misbehaviors of the child quickly subsided and his learning improved greatly.

These examples were given to indicate that poor training procedures involving punishment can be followed in various types of training—athletic, intellectual, artistic, and so on. Moreover, both examples show that punishment need not be physical. Verbal remonstrations will ordinarily function as punishments. When they are delivered they will also elicit negative emotional responses. The child will then come to respond to the learning situation with negative emotional responses on the basis of such remonstrations—as he will with any other type of punishment. Actually, it may be expected that the child is suffering punishment in any learning situation in which he fails to make the progress set by the task. It must be remembered that as we make achievement a reward for the child, we also set the conditions for nonachievement to elicit a negative emotional response. Each time the child fails he is being punished. He will learn to avoid situations in which he fails in the same way that he will avoid any situation in which he receives punishment.

In concluding, it may be suggested that punishment of any kind should be used advisedly in attempting to train the young child to some positive skill. One of the goals of child training should be to generally make learning situations elicit a positive emotional response in the child. This can only be done if in the child's experience in learning situations the rewarding stimuli presented outweigh the punishing stimuli presented—by a good deal. The parent should be concerned that this ratio is maintained in every learning situation for the young child.

It is not the intention of the present section to completely discuss the topic of punishment in child training. The discussion has indicated some of the principles involved and has raised the subject of the practical conditions involved. While use of some aversive stimulation has a function in child training, it must be employed sparingly in training positive skills, with the caution that the rewards be maintained in greater strength so that the child will approach the learning situation, not escape and avoid it. This information is essential for the adult who wishes to produce complex behaviors in the young child in any type of training situation involving repeated learning trials.

It may be noted finally that the emotional or attitudinal responses the child has acquired to learning situations will generalize to the intelligence-testing situation—which has many similarities to a learning situation conducted by an adult. Thus, the behavior of the child in the intelligence-testing situation will be determined in part by these learned attitudes. In general, positive attitudes will control behaviors that contribute to good performance. Negative attitudes will control behaviors that lessen the child's quality of performance. It is pertinent at this point, however, to briefly discuss the types of specific behaviors that the positive or negative attitudes toward learning situations will elicit in the child.

APPROACH OR AVOIDANCE
TO LEARNING SITUATIONS

The preceding section has dealt with the manner in which the young child learns positive or negative emotional responses to learning situations. It is important also to indicate something about the nature of the behavioral skills controlled by these two different types of emotional responses, as these behavioral skills are also important to the child's further learning.

Anti-Learning
Behavior "Skills"

Whenever a situation elicits negative emotional responses (anxiety) in an individual, any behavior that occurs that gets the individual out of the situation—or disrupts the situation—will be reinforced by the cessation of the emotional responses. As a general principle, it can be suggested that people learn responses that remove them from aversiveness. Children naturally follow the same principle.

Actually, it may be noted, any learning situation that demands repeated learning trials is aversive in and of itself—and this must be overcome with reward, as has been described. However, if in addition the parent has employed some form of punishment in learning situations so they have come additively to elicit negative emotional responses, the stage is set for the child to learn many behaviors that allow him to escape and avoid such situations. These behaviors will thus widely interfere with the child's learning and can be called "anti-learning behaviors."

For example, the child who daydreams in a class may perform the day-dreaming responses because they allow him to escape the unpleasant class-room situation. The same may be true of the child who cuts up in class, who talks to other children, who fools around in various ways, and so on.

With younger children the behaviors that are learned because they remove the child from anxiety-producing learning situations can vary widely. The child may "escape" the learning situation by insisting to the parent that he be allowed to perform the task himself, with the request, "Let me do it," even before the parent has finished the instructions. He may run to another activity, or begin another activity. The child may refuse to look at the relevant stimuli, or he may make other irrelevant responses.

The types of behaviors the child will learn will depend upon which of them are successful in getting him out of the situation. These can range from the mild behaviors just described to those that are bizarre enough to be considered "crazy." The author recently encountered a case where the child would become visibly upset whenever the situation took on the appearance of formal training. He would then become hyperactive and move about with increasing rapidity and frenzy as the parent attempted more strongly to bring him into the learning situation. He would not respond to verbal stimuli. He would not attend. This would continue until the attempted learning situation was abandoned. He thus had been learning hyperactive frenzies because through this behavior he avoided the learning situations in which he ordinarily received punishment, not reward.

It should be noted that, as in this case, a child with such a conditioning history will ordinarily learn a whole repertoire of such anti-learning behaviors. As with any skill, these will be acquired over a long period. Such behaviors will serve to escape and avoid various types of learning situations. When the anti-learning behaviors have been learned in wide measure, we will see a child who so successfully avoids situations that he suffers grievous deficits in the acquisition of his basic behavioral repertoires. These deficits will make learning even more trying for the child. Greater difficulty in learning will then make for further punishment in learning situations. It can be seen how a vicious cycle can be developed that hinders normal learning and on the other hand produces abnormal learning. As will be described later on, when such cycles are continued over a period of years they will result in a very abnormally behaving adult. Such anti-learning "skills," it may also be suggested, are frequently acquired by children we term emotionally disturbed, autistic, brain damaged, or retarded.

Ordinarily, a child who demonstrates such behaviors will have had a considerable history of negative experience in learning situations. The well-intentioned but unfortunate parent will not have been able to produce desirable learning in the child. The parent, seeing the child's backwardness, will then usually have attempted to force the child into more accelerated learning. Since the child will not have been prepared for the task with adequately developed basic behavioral repertoires, he will not learn at this time, either. When forcing and other punishing procedures are employed, the child will persist in attempted escape behaviors. If the parent lets the child go at this time, the child will learn the anti-learning behavior. After the development of many of these behaviors, the child will generally be considered to be intransigent, lacking in motivation, dull, retarded, and so on. He will be called mentally retarded.

Extreme anti-learning behaviors may also be learned by the child when subjected to unusual learning experiences. These may include (1) self-destructive responses such as knocking one's head against the wall, biting oneself, and so on, (2) hyperactivity, (3) crazy behaviors such as monotonous rocking, weird gestures and facial expressions, uttering crazy noises, and so on. These abnormal behaviors may also be learned because they lead to escape from the learning situation. Such behaviors will ordinarily lead to diagnoses of psychosis, autism, and brain damage, which will not help the parent or the child. The child, on the other hand, who learns escape behaviors of running away, uncontrollability, aggression, and the like, but who has acquired more usual basic behavioral repertoires, will be labeled as an "acting-out child." Many times this type of anti-learning behavior is acquired later when the child has begun to do poorly in school. That is, the child who does not succeed in school is actually being punished. He will receive social disproval (punishment) of various kinds in learning situations—rather than reward. In this way, learning situations can also come to elicit negative emotional responses and serve to further train the child to anti-learning behaviors.

The above discussion has illustrated more extreme cases of anti-learning behavioral "skills." This behavior is just as important to consider in the less extreme case, as has been indicated also. When the child learns attentional behaviors whose purpose is to get the child out of the situation, for example, these will interfere with the attentional behaviors necessary in the learning task itself. A child who approaches a learning situation with anxiety and with anti-learning skills will not present the picture of a confident learner—and this child will not profit maximally from the learning situation. It will be productive in concluding this chapter to indicate a few points about "pro-learning behavioral skills."

PRO-LEARNING ATTITUDES AND BEHAVIOR

Contrast the preceding types of developments with the child who has had many positive learning experiences of the kind that have been outlined in the present book. Let us say that the parent has been interested in the learning of the child from the very beginning. Let us say that he has observed the child and has found it enjoyable to conduct simple learning tasks with the child when yet an infant. The various types of learning suggested herein can be taken as examples. As the parent conducts the simple learning tasks for the infant, he will begin to discover how the child learns. This will be especially possible for the parent if he has the kind of information about child learning that has been presented. At any rate, as he learns about the child he will become capable of conducting more complex learning tasks with his child. He will thus be in a position to gradually advance the informal training largely through the use of reward. Many children have the advantages of having participated in many learning situations of the types discussed herein; where the child is rewarded for learning his first speech responses, for responding to speech, where he faces reward in the more or less formal learning situations of elaborating his speech sequences, speaking grammatically, and so on. A parent who successfully conducts these types of training will not have a child who has deficits in the basic behavioral repertoires. Nor will the child have developed anti-learning behaviors.

The procedures for the language-intellectual training that has been described herein should be extended also into other learning situations, such as those in toilet training, self-care activities (tieing shoes, dressing, cleaning, grooming), and so on. When the child has engaged in many learning situations and has been rewarded in these situations, he will not only develop specific skills and a positive attitude to learning situations, he will learn many pro-learning skills also. In comparison to the negatively treated child, he will *approach* learning situations, not avoid them. He will actively strive to spot the critical stimuli in the learning situation, he will strive to acquire the responses demanded, he will repeat the relevant stimuli, and so on. These various behaviors will be described as confident; the child will be confident in learning situations. And he will learn well.

It is thus important that the child be introduced to learning situations early and that he experience in the great majority of cases reward in those learning situations. This experience will also be one of the important determinants of how well he will learn in later learning situations—that is, how intelligent the child will be.

It should be added that the focus of these discussions has been on the young child. With the young child, learning should be conducted so the child will enter the situation without compulsion. It is reasonable within the situation at times to "demand" good attention—a demand that will be met if the child has previously been rewarded for such attention. The discussion, however, is not meant to suggest that mandatory attendance in learning activities is never desirable for older children. Mandatory attendance is the basis of the public school system, although if the present principles were followed (Staats, 1969) voluntary school attendance would probably be possible. The topic of later school training of children is not relevant for the present concerns, however.

part III
**PERSONALITY
INTERACTIONS:
BEHAVIOR-BEHAVIOR
AND BEHAVIOR-ENVIRONMENT
INTERPLAY**

chapter 13/ Thinking, Self-Direction, and Originality Through Learning: a Rapprochement of Personal Freedom Views with Scientific Determinism

It has been suggested throughout this book that people do not in general appreciate the central importance of learning in determining human behavior —both in the formation and the function of behavior. Some of the reasons for this oversight have been suggested; for example, that the development of an effective learning theory required much time—and is actually only now really possible. In addition, it has been indicated that the organic-mental conception of human behavior has preempted a more adequate learning conception.

One aspect of the contemporary common-sense conception of human behavior, which has militated against the acceptance of a traditional learning view, involves concepts of the "free" nature of human behavior and its self-direction as well as originality. We have a deeply ingrained cultural conception that human behavior is spontaneous—it comes from within. It is not bound, determined, or set—it is free. Moreover, in our own experience we have innumerable cases where our behavior occurs under our own direction. We decide what we are going to do and then we do it. Any conception that suggests that we do not have a hand in determining what we do fails at the very beginning. Furthermore, there is something wrong with a conception that is unable to account for the originality we see so frequently in human behavior. People, with varying degrees of social significance, make original behaviors—not just behaviors that they have been trained to make. Humans are not just automatons, and we resist a conception that suggests this, as traditional learning theories have.

Do not these demands upon a conception of human behavior pose challenges to any learning conception? It is true that the demands have been obstacles to general acceptance of a traditional learning approach. These topics cannot be elaborated upon at length in the present book. However, it will be productive to indicate how the types of learning that have been described herein will produce a child who thinks, who directs his own behavior, and who will make original behaviors. Although we learn our basic behavioral repertoires, these repertoires then enable us to influence our own behavior and to be original, thus providing us with the means to rise above our specific experiences. The learning conception being proposed by no means suggests that man is an automaton. We see how behavior can be learned, yet also be self-directive and innovative. Self-direction and innovation are foundations for a belief in personal freedom.

IMPLICIT SPEECH

To begin, as we all know through personal experience and through the reports of others, articulate adults not only speak overtly, they speak "to themselves." That is, it is possible for the skilled language user to make covert speech responses in the same manner that he makes overt speech responses. This activity of implicit or covert speech has been verified in laboratory experimentation (Miller, 1935) as well as in naturalistic observations and our own experience.

It is important to indicate, however, that the speech of the child is not originally learned in this manner. The parent could not reinforce the child with attention, for example, if the speech of the child were implicit and not capable of ordinary observational methods. It is thus clear that the child is trained by the parent to make overt speech responses, not implicit speech responses. For the child to learn to speak to himself he will require additional learning—learning not usually conducted by someone else.

Since there is no explicit training program for implicit speech, it will be seen that it emerges slowly. Thus, after the child has begun to learn to speak, and before he has learned implicit speech, he may frequently be heard to speak aloud when no one else is present. The child is thus speaking to himself, but not covertly as an adult would. The child, as a example, may lie in his crib and say words aloud that he has learned. Later, he may recount a few events of the day aloud—but speaking to himself.

There is a reason, however, for the child to learn to say words softly, imperceptively: It is less effortful to say them in this way rather than with more intensity. Thus, simply because in many situations it will be less effortful to speak implicitly, the child will learn to do so. Moreover, later on there will be situations in which overt speech will be punished. The child who says, "I hate you, Daddy," will usually be admonished. If he says it to himself, he is not. At any rate, the parent need not provide training in this type of speech skill. It will ordinarily take place over a period of time, largely through the further experience the child provides himself— on the basis of the original language training given him by the parent. In training the child in his overt speaking repertoire, the parent is providing the child with skills that will lead to the child acquiring implicit speech.

Implicit Speech
and Self-Direction

The important point to understand here, however, is that a good deal of the individual's self-direction will occur on the basis of covert speech as well as overt speech. Much of the apparent spontaneity of humans derives from the fact that they respond to their own covert speech. Frequently we see an individual in apparent repose. Following this the individual performs some action that appears to have been a spontaneous occurrence. If we had been able to follow the implicit speech of the individual, we could see clearly what the determinants of the action were. This is not to say that the determinants were not within the individual, since they were of the individual's own speech. But this qualification is no obstacle to consideration of the individual's behavior in this example as being learned—for he has learned his speech repertoire. These issues of behavior causation may be better treated through describing some of the ways that we can direct ourselves through our learned language repertoires.

SELF-DIRECTION

One of the controversies that divides psychology has been refusal of many cognitive psychologists to accept the suggestion that man does not contribute to his own behavior, but that his behavior is determined from external experience. Such psychologists insist, rather, that is the individual's *awareness* that determines what he does; it is how the individual perceives the situation, and so on. There have been many unresolved experimental and theoretical controversies between such cognitive psychologists and the traditional learning approaches. A rapprochement between these views is necessary, possible, and productive. A general conception of human behavior must thus show how human behavior is caused by the conditions the individual experiences, but at the same time also indicate how the "nature" of the individual contributes to his behavior. The manner in which self-determination or self-direction takes place is thus of central importance to a general conception of human behavior.

The elements by which to account for self-direction have already been suggested herein. It was generally said that behavior is both an effect (of learning conditions) *and a cause* as well. Each of the basic behavioral repertoires that have been discussed fits this description. This dual aspect of behavior is what traditional learning theorists have failed to see. Thus, the implications of the dual role of behavior for a conception of human nature have not been indicated. This failure is the major reason why people who have believed in personal freedom and those who see that human behavior is externally determined have remained at loggerheads. It may be said, however, that behavior is learned, but once learned it is a determinant of later behavior—it assumes the role of a cause, and thus it may be said that the individual causes his own behavior. For example, he does do things because he *decides* to do them. The way that he decides will be a function of past experience—but his past experience will also have been affected by his many past decisions. By the time an individual has become an adult, his own behaviors, primarily his language-emotional repertoires, will figure so largely in the determination of what the individual does that his behavior can be seen to that extent to be under his own direction. In that sense it is justifiable to term human behavior self-directed and spontaneous, if not in a sense which is antithetical to scientific determinism.

It is thus easy to see how two people can face for the first time the same situation and behave quite differently. This is because they bring to the situation different learned repertoires. It is pertinent here to briefly consider some of the mechanisms involved in the individual's self-direction.

Speech and Self-Direction

The manner in which the child acquires a speech repertoire has been described at length. The process was one in which the speech responses of the child were reinforced by the parents and others. It is important to emphasize this. Speech is acquired where someone else provides the reward by which the vocal responses are learned. For the child at this beginning stage, speech results in obtaining various rewards by affecting the behavior of other people.

Later, in addition, the child's speech repertoire becomes a component of the child's ability to direct his own behavior. At the level of the child's first speech development, however, it will not serve this function. At first it is largely restricted to single-word vocal responses, and then simple multiword sequences—always in response to immediately given stimuli, to secure rewards from someone else. But with further training, as has been described, the child's speaking repertoire will be elaborated. While at first trained to label simple objects with simple words, later he will be trained to more complex labeling sequences to more complex objects and events. He will be trained to describe social and physical interactions of various kinds. For example, he may learn to say, "If I make Daddy angry I will be sorry," or "If I have a dessert now I won't get one after dinner," or "If I clean up my room right away I can go out to play," and so on.

But learning the speech sequences, even under the appropriate control of stimulus objects and events, is not enough. The speech responses (or, rather, the stimuli of such responses) have to come to control appropriate behaviors in the child. The manner in which this verbal control of the child's behavior is learned has also been described. Chapter 4, *Responding to Speech*, described the learning process in detail. However, this description is of how the child learns a repertoire of behaviors to the speech of the parent, and this account must be elaborated. The speech of the parent is not greatly different from the speech of other individuals in the same language community. For instance, having learned to respond to "Come here" when uttered by the parent, the stimuli when uttered by someone else will also have control over the behavior. If the child is reinforced by others for his verbally controlled behavior, it will come under the control of speech stimuli in general.

When, through learning, the behaviors of the child have generally come under the control of language stimuli, this will include the stimuli of his own speech. That is, the child will also learn to behave in accord with what he says himself. Some of this learning will occur because he is trained to do what he says he will do. When the child says, "I'm going to wash my hands in a minute," he will be reinforced when he does so, and given aversive stimulation of some kind when he does not. The parent can in this way hasten the development of this learning.

In addition, however, there are other sources of reinforcement involved. The child learns to "follow" what he says because it is rewarding to do so. When the child has learned to say, "If I make Daddy angry I will be sorry," and also has learned to respond to these verbal stimuli as if they had been said by his mother, the behavior that is mediated may avoid a good deal of social aversiveness. When the child says, "If I clean up my room right away I can go out to play," and he performs the behaviors involved and is rewarded by the opportunity to play, the child is learning to respond to his own speech. In this way the child will learn that behavior that is mediated by his own sequences of verbal behavior will produce positive reinforcement and avoid negative reinforcement.

Thus, the child's speech behavior is first learned under the reinforcement provided by other people. However, once learned, the speech can improve the child's adjustment by mediating appropriate behavior to the nonsocial as well as the social world. At this point the child is not just the object of a training program administered by the parent. His overt and self-directing behavior "finds" its own reinforcement. This independence from the reinforcement of a parent or other person can be seen most clearly when the self-directing language is relevant to a nonsocial occurrence and mediates behavior that is reinforced by the nonsocial occurrence. For example, the child who sees the sky darkening and says, "It looks like it is going to rain, so I'd better get some books to read because I won't be able to play outside," will be self-directing his behavior. The boredom he avoids by adjusting to the impending physical events will provide reinforcement. Of course, we employ constantly our language repertoires for such self-direction, and as the child comes to do this there are sources of reinforcement for these aspects of language that are independent of other people.

In so doing the child has emerged as an organism that is directing his own behavior. This "freedom" in behavior ordinarily does not begin to emerge until after four years of age. Some observations of various kinds place the child's ability to direct his own behavior through his language between the ages of five to seven. It may be suggested, however, that the learning of the constituent basic behavioral repertoires commences from birth, as has been indicated. Closer observations than we now have would probably show that the child's direction of his own behaviors by his speech is a gradual process of the accretion of skills. As with other basic behavioral skills, it would be expected that great differences among children in the verbal direction of their own behavior would stem from differences in the children's language learning in general—and in their exposure to and training in making reasoning sequences of verbal responses.

Speech and Anticipating
Future Events

At the point where the child has acquired an extensive language repertoire of the various kinds, and where the child's own language functions to mediate his other behaviors, the child begins to function on a higher level. He makes a contribution to the determination of what he does—not only in the immediate situation, but with respect to things that have not yet happened. That is, events that have not yet happened cannot affect his behavior. However, through language he can bring future events into the present and behave in a manner appropriate to those events. For example, the opportunity of playing later is a future event that cannot be responded to until it has happened. But the child by saying that he will be able to play later if he cleans his room can bring the effects of the future event into the present control of his behavior.

As has been indicated, words will have this function whether they have been said by someone else or by the individual himself. This has a good deal of significance for understanding certain aspects of human reasoning, including social reasoning. For example, sequences of verbal behavior are many times elicited that are relevant to future events. The student is asked to accompany a friend to a show, and this and other stimulus circumstances elicit a long sequence of verbal responses. He says, let us say, "It is a very funny picture, but I have not studied for my exam tomorrow and if I do not I will fail the course." The word stimuli *very funny* ordinarily elicit positive emotional responses and would tend to control the "approach" behaviors of attending the movie. The word stimuli *fail the course*, on the other hand, ordinarily will elicit negative emotional responses in the individual, and these emotional responses will in turn control behaviors that avoid the proposed activity. What the individual does in this problem situation, as one of many examples, will be influenced by his sequence of verbal behaviors *and* the emotional value of the words, and thus their control over approach or avoidance behavior.

At any rate, with his various language repertoires, as they come to affect his behavior, the child can think, reason, decide, plan, and so on. These skills, of course, do not appear overnight. The learning is long-term, complex, and subject to great variation depending upon the nature of the child's vastly complex learning experiences and the basic behavioral repertoires that result. However, the child's own language is capable of serving all the functions for him that the language stimuli from someone else serve, including all those that have been described. Some of these functions will be illustrated in the remaining sections of this chapter.

REASONING

The whole topic of reasoning cannot be covered herein. The general conception can be elaborated in dealing briefly with the topic, however, and several points will be made with respect to the child's learning reasoning skills.

It may be said that much of the individual's thinking and reasoning involve the repertoires of language skills already described. Not all thinking involves speech responses. For example, the individual may make sequences of sensory responses (images) in imagining a sequence of experiences he has had. Frequently, part of such an act will involve implicit speech responses, but it would certainly be possible to have nonverbal sequences of learned sensory responses. The dog that whines and twitches in his sleep is probably experiencing such a sequence—albeit without the contribution of language. This is said to indicate that to say that much thinking and reasoning depends upon language is not to exclude that which can occur without language.

A primary characteristic of language is that it can parallel (or be isomorphic with) the events of the real world. This statement is apparently obvious, but it also has great significance. To illustrate by analogy, mathematics has been described as a formal system of signs with rules for relating the signs, whose significance lies in the fact that parts of the system are isomorphic with certain events of the world. That is, the signs and their relations parallel real events and their relationships. Not all of mathematics is isomorphic with the events of the world. However, when there is such isomorphism, manipulations of the mathematical signs will agree with what happens in the worldly events. As an example, when X is defined as rate (speed) and Y as time, $X \times Y = Z$, when Z is defined as distance. Since it is possible to make mathematical manipulations in many cases in advance of the worldly events, one may thereby obtain predictions or anticipations of the future. When one knows the car will travel 50 miles per hour, for eight hours, it is possible to predict a distance of 400 miles. The mathematical relations of the symbols parallel the worldly events—so manipulations of the symbols produce prediction of the actual events. When there is faulty isomorphism in the mathematical manipulations, however, faulty predictions will result. The goodness of the reasoning depends upon the extent to which the symbolic terms *parallel* the worldly events in their action.

The author has noted that language provides the same functions for the speaker that have just been described for mathematics. Languages may be considered to be formal theoretical systems developed in part because of their isomorphism with empirical events, and significant because of this isomorphism. To the extent of the isomorphism, one's language may also generate predictions through "manipulations" of its symbols (as in the overt or covert speech of the language user). The adjustive value of language for its user can thus be seen in this respect. That is, making predictions about important (reinforcing or punishing) events of the world can lead to gaining positive consequences and avoiding negative ones. As has been suggested, one's sequences of speech responses control or mediate one's behaviors. Complex sequences of language behavior may mediate complex adjustments of various kinds.

One of the expectations that could be drawn from this analysis is that when two individuals have quite different response sequences of language which control sequences of behavior, their behavior will be quite different. Using the situation of two children receiving change in a store, let us say that each expects change of thirty-nine cents. Both are given a quarter, a dime, and four pennies. One says, "Twenty-five plus ten plus four is thirty-four," and the other says, "Twenty-five plus ten plus four is thirty-nine." The latter child's speech responses parallel the actual events, and the behavior that is mediated —putting away the coins—is thus adjustive. The first child's speech responses are not isomorphic with the actual events and the behavior that is mediated —asking for more change—is not reinforced, but rather leads to an unnecessary and unrewarding social interaction. This child's word associational sequences in not paralleling the actual events produces a "maladjustive" behavior.

It may be added that the actual responses do not have to be the same. Identical behaviors could be mediated by different specific verbal responses, as would be the case in the above example if two children made the correct verbal responses, each in a different language. Whether different verbal sequences are actually functionally different will depend upon the experiential history of the individuals involved. On the other hand, the same verbal sequence of responses may mediate entirely different behaviors. For example, one child, alone in the home standing before a delicious chocolate cake, will say, "Mother told me not to touch the cake," and then proceed to take some of the frosting. Another child subjected to different training with respect to being under the control of language stimuli, including his own, will have withdrawing responses mediated by his sequence of verbal responses. The difference in this case will depend on the extent to which the child's overt behavior has been brought under the control of the verbal stimuli through his past training. Thus, depending upon the training of the children involved, different language responses may mediate the same concluding behavior. Or, the same language responses may mediate different behaviors.

To begin another example of the importance of language in reasoning, the statement of the linguist Benjamin Whorf may be considered in the present conception. The Whorfian idea was that different languages led to differences in thought. Some languages, it was said, contained terms that others did not, and this was said to produce a different view of the world. An example can be cited that will translate this observation into the explanatory principles employed herein, and that will further illustrate the importance of language to reasoning.

The Jivaro Indians of South America are said to have no concept of death from infection or disease. The Jivaro man, on learning of the death of a relative, is likely to say, "This is the result of evil spirits set into the body of the relative by a Shaman (religious leader) at the instigation of so and so." He has no term for virus infection or disease, no sequences of words that relate such terms to other terms referring to death. Thus, as a result, his behavior (usually violence toward the supposed instigator), as mediated by his language-reasoning sequence, will be different from the fundamentalist Christian who says, "It was the will of God, Who moves in mysterious ways." And both behaviors will be different from that which is mediated by the reasoning sequence of a third man who says, "It was the result of a flu virus infection complicated by bacterial pneumonia because he got out of bed too soon." Rather than say that the same physical occurrence may give rise to a different picture of the world, we may say that different learned language-reasoning sequences, with differing degrees of isomorphism with the world, will mediate differing behaviors toward the same physical occurrence. Moreover, the different behaviors will vary in their adjustmental (reward) value to those physical occurrences.

Whorf, while noting the differences in language, maintained a linguistic relativity—which was to say that while different, languages are equally good. The present author would suggest that prejudicial evaluations of other people's cultures are inappropriate, certainly. However, it must be indicated that languages of *different groups and different individuals vary in terms of their functional value* in reasoning, thinking, problem solving, planning, and the like. Real differences in personal and group languages in the various characteristics presented herein should mediate behaviors of varying appropriateness for the situation, depending upon how isomorphic the language sequence is with the worldly events involved.

Certainly, a language without terms for disease, as in the example, will not be isomorphic with empirical events involving this process. It would be equally certain that languages containing terms that have no counterparts in empirical events (such as evil spirits, nonexistent psychological processes, mystical forces, deities, and so on) would contain language sequences that do not parallel empirical sequences of events. Although it cannot be elaborated here, it is suggested that a child who is many times reinforced for using imaginary terms in situations calling for terms that actually label real events, will learn nonfunctional speech to that extent. While it may be no drawback to learn such imaginary terms as Santa Claus, and so on, at some point the expansion of this repertoire may have deleterious effects upon the adjustment value of the child's language. The functional value of language inheres in the types of characteristics that have been enumerated herein. The individual who has language that does not have these characteristics has a repertoire less functional for him in adjustment to his social and physical environment. The less isomorphic the individual's language is with these events—that is, the less the individual's language is under the control of actual events—the less functional it will be. It is suggested that individuals within the same language community may, through their training, acquire different language sequences, and these differences will be involved in different thought sequences that mediate different behaviors. It may be suggested that many cases of psychopathology involve idiosyncratic language not isomorphic with social, or physical, events of the world, and thus mediates behavior inappropriate to those events. (Illustrations will be given further on.)

Differences will also occur within one language as it develops in historical perspective. Terms that occur in a language at one time and that control certain behaviors will occur less frequently at a later date, and in their place will be other sequences that control other behaviors. Thus, languages may improve in the extent of their isomorphism with reality, and as a result mediate more appropriate behavior. For example, at one time in our language community, when a person behaved in an unusual way people would have said, "He behaves that way because he is possessed by the devil." The language-reasoning sequence mediated the inappropriate behavior of beating the person, immersing him in water, and so on to drive out (exorcise) the "devil." The then accepted language sequences were not isomorphic with the events of people afflicted with abnormal behavior and thus, as thought and reasoning processes, could not mediate appropriate behaviors. Presumably because of this nonfunctional characteristic, at a later time in the history of our language community the language sequence elicited by the same abnormal behavior would be more likely to be, "He behaves that way because he is mentally ill." This sequence of thought would mediate behavior appropriate to sick people—solicitous treatment, indulgence in unreasonable behavior, and so on. While this sequence mediates behavior more appropriate to the abnormally behaving individual than the first example, this treatment is actually very inadequate, because there is little isomorphism here either. For there is no actual process of mental illness.

Let us say, using the same example, that the language system is then developed to the point where the same unusual behavior evokes the language sequence, "He behaves that way because his parents rewarded only more and more extreme cases of crying and raging as he grew older, and now he has extreme temper tantrums." This language or thought sequence, let us say also, then has a superior isomorphism with the actual events. This last example of reasoning could mediate behaviors with respect to the person with the unusual behavior that would be most appropriate in terms of correcting the behavior. Moreover, the reasoning sequence would allow one to avoid "training" a child to have temper tantrums. It is to provide such reasoning sequences, those that are isomorphic with the events of child development, that the present book is written.

Reasoning Components

It has been suggested that the various types of language-intellectual learning described herein provide some of the elements for thinking and reasoning sequences that will contribute to mediation of adjustive, or maladjustive, behaviors in the individual. For discussion purposes, three components of reasoning sequences can be abstracted that include some of the aspects of language learning already described.

Labeling and Reasoning

To begin, it has been suggested that important language-intellectual repertoires of the child involve learning labels or names to different events. It may be added that labeling events is frequently the beginning of a reasoning sequence. The mechanic must "listen" to the engine of a car (with his naked ear or with various instrumentation) and label the defect in some way before beginning to repair the difficulty. The physician makes his observations also which, depending upon their nature, will elicit a learned label (diagnosis). If, for example, the observations elicit the label of pneumonia in contrast to lung cancer, they will commence quite different reasoning sequences culminating in very different medical actions. As the examples indicate, many times solution of a problem will depend upon whether or not the individual has learned to label correctly the event involved.

The labeling of the events in a situation may vary from individual to individual in several ways. For example, the individual may simply have learned no term for the event, in which case his reasoning and problem-solving behaviors may never commence. On the other hand, the individual may have learned the incorrect label to the event, in which case an inappropriate reasoning sequence may follow. The physician who makes an incorrect diagnosis reasons incorrectly, and treats the patient incorrectly also. Examples have also been given in which the individual labels events that do not exist, in which case the reasoning sequences are again likely to be discordant with real happenings. There are many cases in the history of every area of thought of labels, concepts, that have no empirical reality, and of the errors in reasoning and action engendered. It is because of this that the philosophy of science has made such an important item of the definition of terms by observations. This emphasis concerns not only scientific language, however, and should be considered to pertain to the language the child learns, since his language is his theory, by which he will guide many of his actions.

Another type of irrational reasoning arises in idiosyncratic variations in the use of terms. For example let us say that the child says, "You promised to take me to the movies today (Saturday)," and the parent replies, "Yes, but I made the promise on Thursday and today is Saturday, so the promise does not count." The parent's behavior may be reinforced by escape from an unwanted duty, but to the child it would represent an example where a word, "promise," would be employed in a different way, depending upon what was reinforcing to the user. With many such examples, the child could learn such an "irrational" characteristic of language that would negatively affect his own reasoning as well as his interactions with others. Many people follow different "rules of logic" when their own interests are involved than when someone else's interests are involved. This is not always disadvantageous in social interaction, if the discrepancy is not too great. When discrepancies in labeling are too large, the nonparallelism of the individual's reasoning with reality may be too wide and have adverse effects upon his social interactions and upon his own reasoning. Again, it is interesting to note that the invariant use of terms has been of concern in logic and science, as would be expected where one is interested in theory (language) that parallels actual events.

Reasoning Sequences

There is more to reasoning than the labeling made to the events, however. The language sequences that connect the events involved must also parallel the relationships of the events. One may be labeling actual events in a consistent manner, yet not state the *relationships* correctly because one has not learned the appropriate sequences. For example, it is commonly said about another group that "These people will only do what you say through using force on them." The people *doing* what is ordered may be an actual event, and the *force* may be observable also. That is, the labels may be correct. However, the above simple statement of the relationship does not adequately parallel the principles of behavior involved, and thus if the reasoning is followed the action is likely to disagree with actual occurrences.

There are various relationships between events that are possible; for example, "If A then B," "If A then no B," "The greater the A the greater the B," "The greater the A the lesser the B," "B increases directly as does A, inversely as does C, and geometrically as does D," and so on. For the reasoning sequence to parallel the events involved, the events have to be labeled correctly and completely and the various *relationships* between the terms must parallel the relationships between the actual events. It may happen that events are labeled correctly but their relationships are not. The statement "A ring around the moon indicates fair weather tomorrow," is not illogical in its labeling of actual events, but in the statement of a relationship that does not exist.

There are many statements regarding the relationships of human behavior to various things. Some of the statements have some kind of codification. For example, the statement, "Do unto others as you would have them do unto you." At least by implication, this states that if you treat others well they will treat you well. Of the many such statements of the principles of human behavior that are commonly learned by the child, some are accurate and some are not. The child who learns a repertoire of more accurate reasoning sequences, in either the physical or social realms of events, will be better able to respond appropriately to these events.

One point may be added here. It has been suggested a number of times that there is an incompatibility between traditional learning theories and psychological theories that consider man's cognitive (or mental) processes to play a part in the determination of his behavior. Thus, for example, one controversy has concerned whether or not the individual has internal "rules" that determine how he behaves—or whether he must directly learn his overt behaviors. This discussion of how sequences of learned language responses mediate overt behaviors indicates that there is no incompatibility between the present learning conception and cognitive theories of human behavior. The individual who has acquired the language repertoires described herein does behave according to his own internal reasoning. Moreover, he is prepared to acquire new rules (language sequences) easily, through being told them or through his own experience, and these will also affect his overt behavior. In the present approach, however, it is necessary to stipulate what the language sequences (reasoning) consist of, how they have their effects, and how they are learned. This is the type of knowledge necessary to understand and do something about human "nature."

The Behaviors Mediated by Reasoning Sequences

In addition to the labeling and relating of events, actual or supposed, reasoning sequences can vary in their ability to elicit the consequent behaviors in the individual. The individual may say, "The enemy overwhelms our forces, I must retreat or die." The reasoning may be entirely isomorphic with actual events and the relationships between them, but the word "retreat" may elicit such negative emotional responses that the individual avoids the action of retreating—and thereby suffers the "negative reinforcement" predicted.

Many reasoning sequences are significant for the behaviors—overt motor behavior, additional language (reasoning) behaviors, or emotional behavior—that they elicit. There is also great room for variation here through the individual's learning. The important point is that the individual's self-direction consists not only of his reasoning sequences but also in the vast repertoires of behaviors he will have learned under the control of language and other stimuli.

Illogical Reasoning

Several additional examples of defective social reasoning will be given in the next section. It is interesting, however, to first consider some examples of illogical reasoning patterns. These were once followed by the most learned of men, and are still learned by different individuals in advanced societies as well as employed widely by less advanced groups of people. In addition, the examples may be considered, as some already presented, to suggest an evolutionary development that occurs in language; that is, movement from the misuse of words to a progressive use of reasoning isomorphic with the realities of the world. These examples, which lend themselves to that interpretation, were taken from A. D. White's history of the conflict of scientific and religious thought.

> Philo had found for the elucidation of Scripture especially deep meaning in the numbers four, six, and seven; but other interpreters soon surpassed him. . . . Josephus argued that, since there were twenty-two letters in the Hebrew alphabet, there must be twenty-two sacred books in the Old Testament; other Jewish authorities thought that there should be twenty-four books, on account of the twenty-four watches in the temple. St. Jerome wavered between the argument based upon the twenty-two letters in the Hebrew alphabet and that

suggested by twenty-four elders in the Apocalypse. Hilary of Poitiers argued that there must be twenty-four books, on account of the twenty-four letters in the Greek alphabet. Origen found an argument for the existence of exactly four gospels in the existence of four elements. Irenaeus insisted that there could be neither more nor fewer than four gospels, since the earth has four quarters, the air four winds, and the cherubim four faces. . . . (1899, Vol. II, p. 296).

These examples show errors in labeling objects and events, as well as in the utterance of reasoning sequences that have no isomorphism with actual events. Another case from history, of which there are many, that especially shows the role of poor *logical* sequences is given in the following quote from the same source.

In the mystic power of numbers to reveal the sense of the Scripture Augustine found especial delight. He tells us that there is deep meaning in sundry scriptural uses of the number forty, and especially as the number of days required for fasting. Forty, he reminds us, is four times ten. Now, four, he says, is the number especially representing time, the day and the year being each divided into four parts; while ten, being made of three and seven, represents knowledge of the Creator and creature, three referring to the three persons in the triune Creator, and seven referring to the three elements, heart, soul, and mind, taken in connections with the four elements, fire, air, earth, and water, which go to make up the creature. Therefore this number ten, representing knowledge, being multiplied by four, representing time, admonishes us to live during time according to knowledge—that is, to fast for forty days. . . . (1899, Vol. II, p. 298).

The nonfunctional nature of such reasoning sequences are very clear to us today. For the most part, we would have to find institutionalized psychotics to see such examples. And that is the very point. A child who is trained to illogical language sequences will have a generally nonfunctional language that will mediate inappropriate behaviors, not mediate appropriate behaviors. His language (reasoning) will in general be nonadaptive. This may occur to the extent that the child is grievously handicapped. A child raised with much experience in the inappropriate and illogical use of language will learn in kind. Many individuals with personal disturbances labeled neurotic and psychotic are such because they have learned language systems awry in these respects. Their reasoning is awry and their behavior inappropriate. There are many individual differences here that have not begun to be explored.

Social Reasoning

It has been said several times herein that the conceptions we hold contribute to the social decisions we make. It has also been suggested here that our language (reasoning) sequences with respect to others mediate our behaviors toward them in the same manner as this occurs toward physical phenomena. Several illustrations in this realm will help in clarifying the principles.

The author (1963, pp. 387–389) described a hypothetical case in which over a period of time an individual acquired a complex constellation of language (reasoning) sequences that were not isomorphic with reality. The reasoning sequences in the example finally prompted the individual to extreme and maladjustive overt behaviors. The example was that of an individual who suddenly one morning takes out a revolver and shoots several men standing together talking in a group. The individual, let us say, later admits that he did this because the group of men were "plotting" against him, that they have been watching him and were part of a plot to kill him.

This behavior and the delusional system of reasoning that prompted the behavior might be considered to be senseless by the objective observer. As a final result of the individual's experiences, however, his behavior could be seen as the lawful working of learning principles in a set of experiences that in their unusual nature produced the unusual behavior. Thus, a conceivable history that could lead to such bizarre behavior could be suggested. Involved in this history would be experiences by which the individual had come to label the group of businessmen as "part of the group who were after him," experiences by which the individual had come to learn such reasoning sequences as, "They are going to kill me but I will kill them first." Moreover, the manner in which the individual had learned the actual motor behaviors of the violent act would be an important aspect.

It may be difficult to see how such unusual constituents of behavior could arise. Consideration of possible learning histories that could produce the behaviors is thus necessary. Let us suppose in the example that the individual as a child had learned behaviors aversive to others—perhaps selfish, unreasonable, demanding, aggressive, bossy behaviors. The child learned these because they were reinforced in the home. However, these same behaviors would be aversive to other children and adults outside of the home (even though the child might continue to be partially reinforced for the behaviors by getting what he wanted). As a consequence, the child's associates would respond aversively to him. Let it be added that when the child described his aversive interactions with others to his own parents they did not "objectively" describe either his own actions or the actions of the others. Rather than describing his behavior in negative terms, the parents described the others' behaviors negatively. Moreover, they gave the child illogical reasoning sequences by saying that the others were mean to him because they were jealous of his high ability and because he was better than they were. Let us say that the child had many experiences in which he was trained unrealistically to describe his own actions in a positive direction and learned to label other's behavior unrealistically in negative ways—both of which would be reinforcing to the individual in his many situations of unpleasant interpersonal experiences.

In addition, let us say the child also learned other reasoning sequences of the type "people are basically evil and are restrained from taking advantage only by force," "you can't trust people to treat you well," "you have to protect yourself from people and beat them to the punch if they try to take from you or do you harm," and so on. This experience could include observation of the parents' in their own difficult interactions with other people. It also might include the experience of being reinforced for aggressive behavior with others who "did not treat him fairly." In such training the child would learn not only to fight with others to "protect" himself, but would also learn additional social-reasoning language sequences, such as, "You must be ready to fight to protect yourself," "The best way to handle anyone who treats you unfairly is to give them back better than they gave."

On the basis of this type of training it would not be unusual for the individual to have many aversive interactions with others throughout his history. Later, as a young man, the individual might begin to experience further the group response to his disliked behavior. As a consequence of his unpleasant interactions, he might not be promoted as expected, for example. In this case he would be likely to respond with aversiveness to the person who got the promotion as well as to the general organization. This would add to the developing vicious cycle. Because he is aversive to a number of others, people would tend to "organize" against him, to talk about him unfavorably, to get him assigned to unwanted responsibilities, and to get him fired from jobs. This would constitute a general picture of aversiveness in his social relations. Moreover, his poor adjustment would result in the loss of other reinforcers such as a good-paying job, social approval, and so on.

As has been described, however, this individual could continue to label his aversive social experiences in terms of the fault of others—while continuing to describe his own behavior in positive and unrealistic terms. And, in a sense, the individual would now be correct, at least in part. For if he is aversive to everyone—his landlady, his grocer, his casual associates of various types—they will respond in kind. Moreover, since more than one individual would be involved, they might talk about him in a group, planning group retaliations against him, giving him group derision, and so on. This could be more aversive to him than he could return. In the process, at any rate, the person would acquire very intense negative emotional responses to people.

All of these things, however, would confirm his maladjustive social reasoning. With such a history, it would not be unreasonable that the individual would label his cumulative social experience as, "Everyone is against me," "They are out to get me," "They hate me and want to harm me," "They are plotting to harm me." In any event, at the point that the individual began to label innocent gatherings of people in the street as plots against his life, the reasoning stage would be reached for the final violent action to occur.

This example is cited to indicate that unusual behaviors can be learned. These unusual behaviors can consist of unusual reasoning sequences that can mediate unusual overt behaviors. There are many examples of an actual nature. The newspaper, for example, recently reported the arrest of a band of young men and women who allegedly had committed a number of violent murders. The rationale given by one of the implicated members was that the leader of the band had indicated that everyone in the world was a part of every other person, that when you killed someone you were really killing part of yourself. Since you were the one that was hurt, it was all right to kill others. So the reasoning went.

Such a reasoning sequence in its unreality could, and apparently did, lead to a great deal of unrealistic violence and brutality on the part of the leader of the group and his followers. The behavior mediated by the bizzare reasoning was bizzare.

Another example may be taken from other recent newsreporting, namely the reported massacre by American soldiers in South Vietnam. The instance reported is one involving from 300 to 500 civilians, mostly women and children, shot by the soldiers (see *Life,* Dec. 5, 1969). Again, it is difficult to see how such actions could occur in "normal" men. When one follows the nature of the men's experiences and the reasoning sequences they have acquired, however, the acts become understandable in a scientific sense—if unacceptable in a social sense. The fault of such behavior, as in the other examples cited, is in part in the unusual and unrealistic circumstances the men have experienced—for example, the general context of killing of civilians and the inappropriate labeling and reasoning sequences they have learned. The following quotations illustrate this aspect.

> One U.S. battalion commander . . . dubbed his helicopter a "Gook-mobile" and recorded his kills on its fuselage with a neatly painted row of conical hats. . . . But the use of such devices as free-fire zones and random H & I (harassment and interdiction) artillery fire inevitably create the unintended impression that Vietnamese life is cheap. . . . (**Newsweek,** Dec. 1, 1969, p. 37).

Moreover, there are unusual reasoning sequences involved in the mediation of unusual behavior of the U.S. soldiers toward the Vietnamese, as is no doubt the case in all wars, but more so in this one.

> Although the full truth about the massacre at Song My may never be known, even the details that have emerged so far point up a distressing fact about the Vietnam war: many U.S. fighting men, under the stress of combat, display a profound contempt for the people of South Vietnam. With hearty distaste, GI's commonly refer to the South Vietnamese—allies and enemies alike—as "dinks" [or "wogs," "chinks," "slopes," or "gooks"]. And in the view of many long-time observers of the war, it is not unreasonable to conclude that the strong antipathy underlying such epithets . . . sometimes plays a part in the casual killing of civilian bystanders. 'Psychologically and morally,' says a U.S. civilian official, 'it's much easier to kill a 'dink' than it is to shoot a 'Vietnamese. . . .' " (**Newsweek,** Dec. 8, 1969, p. 37).
>
> In Vietnam there is a tacit condoning by those in authority who may not explicitly order you to kill everyone in the village but who subtly convey to you that it is okay. . . . (**Newsweek,** Dec. 8, 1969, p. 35).

The first example includes the use of labels—"dinks," "gooks," and the like, that are inappropriate (not isomorphic with reality) in the emotional responses they elicit. When such a label is attached to members of a group of people—a label that elicits strong negative emotional responses—this will ensure that those people will now elicit "striving against" behaviors on the part of others who have come to use that label. Reasoning sequences that specifically mediate violent behavior towards others, as the reports of the massacre indicate (including the second example), may act as a further determinant of behavior that is uncondonable in the context of more appropriate reasoning. This, of course, is the consequence of "prejudiced" labeling and reasoning in general, whether involved in the bizzare thinking of one psychotic person, or in the bizzare thinking of a whole group (or society) in considering another group. The danger of such reasoning, and of the sources that supply such reasoning, is of equal gravity with the violent acts they mediate.

Self-Reasoning
or Self-Concept

The preceding examples have indicated that the words one learns to other people and their behavior, as well as the emotional responses elicited by those words, have an important function in determining how these people and their actions will be responded to. It may be added (as was mentioned earlier) that the words that the individual learns to label himself, and his actions, also constitute an important part of the individual's reasoning sequences. That is, the individual constitutes a stimulus to himself. He sees himself in the mirror as a social stimulus that he can compare with others. He observes himself winning or losing in competition. He observes himself in social groupings where he can be vivacious, witty, talkative, shy, or what have you. He observes that in comparison to others he is strong, fast, agile, courageous, and so on.

It has been suggested in general that the child learns the behaviors he displays; learning is centrally involved in his characteristic behaviors. It has also been noted, however, that the child learns to label his own behavior—and it may be added his own physical characteristics. The child thus learns, let us say, to describe himself as being hardworking, courageous, strong, capable, athletic, intelligent, and handsome; or on the other hand, lazy, timid, weak, incapable, awkward, mentally slow, and plain-looking.

Since the child learns what he describes himself as, it would be expected that there would be several determinants of his self-labeling behavior (his self-concept). That is, to the extent that the child has been trained to label himself and others realistically, when he has experiences of various kinds he will label himself and in this manner "accrue" (learn and retain) a number of realistic self-descriptions. What his self-concept will be in this case will depend upon his physical and behavioral stimulus characteristics.

In addition, however, as has been indicated, there will also be great differences between people in the manner in which they have been trained in social labeling. Thus, as in the prior example, some children are trained to label their own physical attributes and behaviors in a different manner than they are trained to label the attributes and behaviors of others. The child may be given social approval for making statements about himself that exaggerate his physical attributes, ability, social reasonableness, agility, strength, and so on. Or, conversely, the child may be socially reinforced for making statements that deprecate his physical attributes and behaviors.

Thus, independent of what the individual actually is, he may receive learning experiences that train him to an unrealistic self-concept. Everyone has had experience with people who label themselves unrealistically. The terms rationalization and projection in the field of abnormal behavior are categories of such unrealistic labeling of one's own actions in contrast to the actions of others. That is, what the individual says may be a function not only of the events that occurred but also a function of what he has learned to say because he has in the past been reinforced for saying such things. If the individual has had experience in the past in which he has been reinforced for saying positive things about himself even when these things are unrealistically exaggerated, then his verbal behavior will be a function of that training as well as the actual occurrences. To some extent most people have received training in saying things about themselves and their actions that are more positive than reality. However, there are great individual differences here occasioned by wide differences in the training received.

Thus, the individual will learn to label his physical self, his actions, his past history of successes, and other's responses to him. It is suggested that this constellation of self-descriptions will constitute the individual's self-concept. Many of the labels will be ones of "value," that is, will be emotional words, and thus the individual's self-concept will heavily include emotional or attitudinal components. The individual will have emotional responses to his physical and behavioral characteristics.

As with conceptions of other aspects of human behavior (for example, intelligence), it is important not only to describe what the "self-concept" is and how it comes about, but it is necessary to indicate something about the *functions* of this type of learned behavior. This may be summarized by indicating that one's statements about himself affect other people's behavior toward him, and his self-statements (and the emotional responses they elicit in him) also are a factor in determining what his own behavior will be.

To elaborate, what the individual says about himself will help determine how the individual is responded to. The individual who describes himself in negative terms, other things being equal, will be responded to differently than the individual who describes himself somewhat (but not unrealistically) positively, or the individual who does not talk about himself at all. As an example, take the case of several individuals in an organization who have equal behavioral skills but who speak of themselves in positive or negative terms in two cases, and not at all in the third case. If a job arises that calls for high skill, perhaps a promotion, it can be expected that, other things being equal, the individual who speaks positively about himself will have provided statements that in the decision-making processes (verbal reasoning) of his superiors will slant the advantage toward himself. It is a common occurrence that one's "self-concept" will be thrown into the balance in responding to the individual in an evaluative way. This may be spoken of as the individual's self-confidence.

It should be noted, moreover, that the individual's "self-concept" also will determine his own actions. The individual who describes himself as not exceptionally capable or bright, who considers himself to lack creativity and initiative, who describes himself as fearing positions of leadership, who considers many others to have a more positive effect when dealing with people, and so on, in reasoning whether or not to accept a position that involves those behavioral skills will be likely to reach a negative conclusion. He may have the same behavioral skills as another individual who because of a positive self-description goes through a reasoning sequence that culminates in a positive conclusion. It may also be noted that an individual who has a long history of such positive reasoning processes ordinarily will engage ultimately in many challenges, jobs, and activities that will later make him behaviorally more skilled than the individual who began with the same general skill but with a less positive set of self-statements and self-attitudes.

These, of course, are the important functions of this type of language and emotional word learning, the self-concept. Thus, it should be realized that the child learns not only his overt behavioral skills, he also learns to evaluate himself verbally and to respond to himself emotionally. These types of language-intellectual-emotional skills will be a function of what he is reinforced for saying about himself, how he is responded to in comparison to other children, and the types of models he observed in his parents (that is, how they describe themselves). Moreover, these aspects of his learning will help determine how he himself will behave and how he will be responded to by others, and what he will experience in his further life situation.

In concluding this discussion of reasoning it may be said that a child who is trained to a "principled" use of language that coincides (is isomorphic) with the events of the physical and social world (including himself) will in these respects have a functional language. The logic of the terms in his language repertoire must follow the principles that abide in the relations between the events in the physical and social worlds. Otherwise his sequences will not parallel these events and his sequences will poorly serve to predict and to control those events—his reasoning sequences will be awry. This is a topic that demands further extensive analysis and elaboration, which cannot be given here. It is important, however, to consider the general principles in the context of child learning. Before leaving the present topics, it is important also to mention the originality that the child *acquires* through learning his basic behavioral repertoires.

ORIGINALITY

It has been suggested in this chapter, in the process of correcting one of the weaknesses of past learning conceptions of human behavior, that man to some extent directs his own behavior, upon the basis of previously acquired skills. Another objection to traditional learning theories that must be dispelled in introducing the present learning conception of man concerns originality and creativity. For it is said that the conception that human behavior is learned necessarily implies that there is no originality or creativity in human behavior. For how can behavior be novel and original if it first has to be learned?

This is a paradox that must be resolved, for no conception of human behavior can be credible unless it accounts for originality. The most important behaviors in man's continuing advancement are those that involve new behaviors, hitherto not made by others. Such novel behaviors are ones the individual has not been specifically trained to make.

It is suggested, to state one of the important principles in accounting for original behaviors, that we learn *component* behaviors under the control of particular stimuli. However, when we are faced with new combinations of stimuli—when we are faced with a novel situation—the stimuli call out novel *combinations* of responses from us.

As an example, let us say that a child has learned to label a "man" stimulus through direct training of the type already described. Let us also say that the child has also had the same training with respect to the speech response "running," which is a label for a rapidly moving object with alternating legs. Let us also add that the child has never been trained to say "running" in the presence of a man running. Nevertheless, when presented with the visual stimulus of a man running, the child who has learned the component speech responses is likely to say, "Running man," or "Man running." In this case the speech act as a totality would be novel, original, creative, since the child would never before have been trained to make the speech combination, would never have heard the words combined before, and would never have uttered them before.

This is a simple example, involving only a two-word repertoire. It must be realized that in each class of words, noun and verb labels, there are repertoires that number in the thousands. Moreover, there are other classes the individual learns in which there are many component words. The number of different combinations that can be elicited by different combinations of external and internal events is thus infinite in number. We ordinarily emit many original combinations of speech responses each day. Most combinations do not have great social value and are not significant contributions. However, in principle, the mechanism by which this type of originality takes place is the same as that by which significant and socially valuable original behaviors are emitted by some people. Such cases usually include the individual having learned component behaviors that few people have, as well as being subjected to novel stimulus combinations that few people experience. The result is a combination of behaviors quite different from those made by most other people. When the combination has high social utility it is viewed as an act of creativity.

It is not germane to the present discussion to go into examples of such creativity in any detail. It may be noted that the author has made analyses in these terms of various creative behaviors; for example, original geometric proofs (Staats, 1963, 1966, 1968a). One example from science may be discussed here in general terms to indicate the manner in which sequences of creative behaviors may be involved. That is, once original behaviors have occurred they may then serve as stimuli to elicit further original behaviors, and once these have occurred they may serve themselves as further stimuli. These sequences may occur within one person, or the sequences may involve groups of people, sometimes interacting in this fashion over a long period of time. The history of science may be considered to involve such interactions, where one individual encounters new combinations of stimuli that elicit novel behaviors in him. When his "behaviors" are published, other individuals are presented with new sources of stimulation that then elicit novel behaviors in them. These individuals then produce stimuli that affect later individuals, and so on, in a vast sequence of originality.

Let us take the periodic table of atomic weights that students learn about in high school chemistry. Early chemists were interested in finding the constituents of matter and in describing these constituents (elements). They found, for one thing, that different elements had different weights (mass). Looking for the elements involved skills the chemists had learned and elaborated. Recording the findings also required learned repertoires. The listing of atomic weights, however, as the elements were discovered, constituted a new stimulus circumstance. That is, the weights when listed could be responded to by appropriately trained individuals as having certain systematic features. Not only were there a number of different elements, but the weights of the elements increased in magnitude, with certain characteristics of order. This constituted a new stimulus. The response, let us say, was that the elements increased in a systematic manner. Nevertheless the order was not perfect. There were gaps. That was also a stimulus. The response was that perhaps there were elements not yet discovered that would fill the gaps and preserve the ordered system. This verbal conclusion then served as a stimulus to the behavior of other chemists looking further for new elements.

Furthermore, Mendeleyev's resulting periodic table, taken as a whole, served as a novel stimulus to other men to attempt to speculate concerning what it was in the elements that made them increase in weight in an ordered manner. This led to the response, for example, that there must be commonality in all the elements, in all matter. Perhaps the elements themselves were composed of common constituents in varying amounts. This reasoning response sequence then elicited additional theoretical and observational behaviors.

This, of course, is only a loose and general description. However, it does suggest that individuals with certain repertoires of behavior, faced with certain novel stimulus situations, will come up with certain novel responses and products of those responses (discoveries, findings, and so on). These products will then serve as new stimuli that then produce additional novel responses, which then serve to elicit yet other creative behaviors. *It is suggested that a detailed history of such long-term acts of creativity, analyzed in terms of the learned skills of the men involved, and the manner in which their findings served as stimuli to later individuals, would give us a more profound view of human creativity.*

Original Combinations in the Basic Labeling and Verbal-Motor Repertoires

It is the intent of the present book to deal with everyday behaviors, however, not specialized types of activity such as those of science. Thus, examples from everyday language are very relevant. Language may be described as a system because it offers the possibility of making novel combinations of its components under the press of new combinations of stimuli. The components of one's language repertoires can combine and recombine in various ways that produce new combinations of behavior in additional ways than those that have been mentioned. As one example, it has been said that a child learns a repertoire of motor responses under the control of various *verbs,* as well as a repertoire of labeling responses for various objects that we call *nouns.* New combinations of components from these types of words will elicit new responses to the objects in the listener. Once verbs such as *push, pull, close, open, squeeze, touch, rub, lean, kick,* and so on have come to control the appropriate motor responses, and once the child has come to respond to labels for objects such as *door, chair, dog, board, car, ball,* and so on, the combinations of a verb with a noun can be applied to elicit a very large number of different responses. Thus, for example, the child may have learned the "pushing" motor response through being told, "Push the tree," "Push the button," "Push the carriage," and being shown how to push these objects. He may never have had experience with pushing doors, chairs, dogs, boards, cars, balls, and so on on verbal command. If, however, he has learned the pushing response under the control of the word "Push," and he has learned to label doors, chairs, and so on and to look for them on verbal command, the very first time he is instructed to "Push the door," he will behave correctly. When the combinations of verbal stimuli are novel—and there are an infinite number of possibilities—the verbal stimuli can elicit novel responses, ones the child has never yet emitted.

The same is true with other learned behavioral skills. For example, a series of verbs (or verbs and nouns) may be put together in a way that an extended sequence of motor responses may be elicited that is original or novel. This happens everyday when someone gives geographic directions to a stranger and the sequence of verbal stimuli elicit in the stranger a sequence of motor responses novel to him. The verbal stimuli will bring the stranger into contact with new geographic stimuli—the ones the stranger desires, if the directions are isomorphic with reality.

The same principle is involved when a choreographer emits a novel sequence of verbal responses which then controls a novel sequence of movements in the dancer who has a special repertoire of skills learned under the control of the verbs the choreographer employs. The same principle is involved when the individual reads a manual that includes instructions for performing some complex sequence of movements. The novice automobile mechanic, the novice golfer, and so on may acquire new skilled sequences in this manner.

This is one of the sources of the power of words. Novel language combinations, elicited by novel stimulus circumstances, may elicit novel sequences of responses in the individual himself. Or the novel language combinations can yield novel behaviors in the listener or in the reader. One of the vastly important products of a reading repertoire in the child is that it enables him to gain the speech products of preceding originators, and thus to respond overtly in ways that would be impossible without those verbal sources of stimulation. It should be noted that the child's ability to learn an almost infinite number of new behaviors through such new verb-noun combinations depends upon having already learned a basic repertoire in each area. That is, the child must have learned a large number of verbal-motor response units (verbs) and a large number of noun-labeling responses.

Originality in Learning
to Read

One final example will be given of the mechanisms by which original behavioral combinations can arise from the past learning of constituent behaviors (basic behavioral repertoires). This will indicate that such occurrences are important also in the learning of the child. As an example, a primary aspect of learning to read depends upon the type of originality that has been described —the child cannot be trained directly on every word with which he will be confronted in reading. If he had to receive formal training on each word, the training task would be extremely formidable. (Reading in Chinese has to be learned in part in this way, and it is a most difficult learning task.)

In our language the child actually learns to make partial speech responses to the constituent stimuli of which whole words are made. In common-sense terms the child learns to read single letters and syllables. These single letters and syllables as stimuli thus control appropriate *unit* vocal responses. When such a repertoire has been acquired, the child is in a position to read words upon which he has never received training, each case constituting an act of originality. Let us say that the printed stimulus word *man* has through training come to control the appropriate speech response in the child; as have *i* (the sound *i* in pig), *pu* (the sound as in *pew*), and the word *late*. Let us say that the child then encounters the word *manipulate* for the first time while reading a book. The word is thus a novel stimulus combination. The child has had no training in reading the word. He may never have said the word before. Nevertheless, the word stimulus will in this child elicit a sequence of vocal responses constituting a novel word response, a combination of previously learned constituent responses. Moreover, in sounding out the new combination, the child will be training himself, for after having done this sounding-out task a few times, the child will respond immediately to the whole word stimulus when it is presented—he will read it readily.

Additional Repertoires
for Originality

Not all constituent skills that go into original behaviors are of a verbal nature, however. There are other constituent skills for artistic, scientific, mathematical, athletic, acting, and musical creativity—for example. There are general skills of a motor and sensory-motor type that allow the individual to put together novel combinations in various areas. They may be specific skills, but they carry over to new instances. As an example, a parent who teaches the child to observe people carefully will provide the child with attentional skills that will generally bring him into informational contact with human behavior more closely than would otherwise be the case. The present author had such tuition through a parent who found observing people to be interesting. The same type of special and general skill can occur in any realm.

In essence then, the individual learns specific skilled repertoires. These are strictly learned repertoires, but they interact with each other and with the new sources of stimulation that result. That is, when the individual who has acquired these learned repertoires meets later situations, new combinations of behaviors are called out. These behaviors provide new sources of stimulation that lead to yet other behaviors, which in turn provide additional sources of stimulation. These sequences of interactions may be long-term and complex and involve more than one person, as has been described.

Creativity, Inborn
or Learned?

This analysis indicates that a learning conception of man does not suggest in any way that man is an automaton. Furthermore, the learning conception of human behavior has implications for better understanding originality and creativity. Moreover, the learning conception leads to different conclusions concerning originality than those derived from our common-sense notations.

There are prevailing conceptions of originality and creativity that determine some of our currently accepted training and teaching procedures. The most common conception, contemporary as well as historical, is that there is an in-born creativity in children. Although children are thought to have this quality in varying amounts, all normal children are considered to initially have a fund of creativity. It is also generally considered by many people that structured training destroys this natural fund of creativity. Thus, as an example, in art many people do not wish to teach copying or representational drawing be-cause this may destroy the child's creativity. It has also been said that the child should not learn such "rote" skills as counting or the addition and multiplication tables. The same is true of other fields as well, where the acquisition of specific skills has been eschewed by many, including educators.

The author suggests, however, that there is no inborn entity or process within the child which has been found to determine the child's originality or creativity. There is no reason to believe that such an entity or process exists. Thus, the whole conception of an inborn creative process—including the related injunction not to stiffle inner creativity through learning specific skills—is entirely misplaced. This conception, where it is strictly followed, can lead to disastrous results. In lesser form it may lead to training and education for the child that is less than maximally good. Fortunately, most people who have the view in its strict form deal with children from advantaged homes that so well prepare the child in his basic behavioral repertoires that any shortcomings in education that would otherwise spring from the misconception do not become quite so evident.

Whether or not training in a specific skill, such as copying in art, or learning multiplication tables by rote, and so on, will result in less creativity later on cannot be established by reference to some supposed internal creativity of the child that can be destroyed. There is absolutely no evidence for that supposition. The value of a particular type of training can only be established by fact—by the value of the skill in the later behavior of the child. It is not only conceivable but apparent that for many artists the complex visual motor skills of reproducing (copying) three-dimensional visual objects in a two-dimensional medium is very valuable. Certainly, the usual child has to learn to copy letters, and the writing skills acquired thereby are basic to other types of learning and achievement. The child must also learn to count, to employ the addition and multiplication tables, and so on. Effective training procedures in any basic behavioral skill will in no way stiffle the child's creativity.

Another current fallacy is that the child's internal fund of creativity can increase by exposing him to circumstances specificially intended to increase his creativity—not his skills. Thus, there are short-term training programs for children of the "brain-storming" variety that attempt to enhance his "creativity." It may be suggested that a short-term attempt to increase the child's inborn creativity will have little lasting affect. This is not to say that there are not general skills that a child can learn that will make him respond to many different problem situations with a greater quantity of novel combinations of behavior. That is, a child who is trained to make a large number of responses—to try anything and everything—in a problem situation may very well be a better problem solver or innovator. The same is true of a child who is trained to observe better, to scan everything, in a problem situation. However, we are now talking about learned skills, and the implications of this conception are quite different from those that stem from the "inborn creativity" conception. Moreover, the training program constructed from the opposing conceptions of creativity would also differ.

It may also be indicated, as was described in the context of learning logic and grammar, that general statements or rules may be learned that produce general skills. Thus, once the person has learned to respond to complex verbal instructions, he may learn general skills of originality and inventiveness simply by learning rules. One such rule could be, "When in a problem-solving situation, look for all the relevant elements." Another might be, "Try various solutions (responses) until a solution is reached," or "Think of events, principles, and theories that may be similar to the present one." Such rules of search for original behavior to solve problems, once learned for an area of study, may themselves constitute a set of higher-order skills that contributes to originality. Moreover, the individual's own experiences may lead to his own formulation of such rules by which his own later behavior is guided.

Thus, it is suggested that originality, creativity, inventiveness, and so on are built upon basic repertoires of learned behaviors. For example, the creative physical scientist acquires basic repertoires ranging from his early language learning, motivational learning, positive work-learning attitudes, reading, and so on, through counting, multiplying, mathematical skills, and so on, to the theories, facts, and experimental methods in his science—and many more besides. The professional writer, as another example, has to have an exceptional language repertoire, to have read copiously, to have life experiences of various kinds, and observational habits that take advantage of them, to have written a great, great deal, and so on. In both cases, the development of these skills begins at the very early ages included in the present book. The various basic behavioral skills treated herein must be considered to be prominent parts of the foundation upon which the later accomplishments, including those of originality, are built. There are no cases of extreme skill that are not built upon basic components—whether the skill is artistic-intellectual, social-intellectual, athletic-intellectual, or any of the commonly accepted specific intellectual areas such as writing, mathematics, scientific creativity, or what have you.

The "creative" person is typically the person who has a very high level of the constituent skills in the problem field with which he is concerned. He is also a person who confronts persistently the problems in that field—that is, performs work behaviors that systematically provide him with the necessary stimuli for his original behaviors to be elicited. This means that he will evidence, ordinarily, highly developed work behaviors, attentional behaviors, and knowledge-seeking behaviors. Ordinarily, these activities and their products will be highly reinforcing to him—or his behavior will not be maintained. In the course of this endeavor he will emit a great many behaviors that will serve the purpose of improving his skills. Many of these behaviors will also be "solutions" or original contributions.

It is suggested that the conception suggests that we can produce a greater incidence of creativity in a group of children by increasing the efficacy of our training methods for producing the various constituent skills from which original behaviors are constructed. We must accept that the child must acquire basic behavioral skills to be creative. Many of these basic behavioral skills are learned in the home. Many of them are learned out of school—

such as the vast amount of pleasure reading that an appropriately trained child will complete, in itself a source of experience that can contribute to variation in children amounting to many millions of learning trials. Many other basic behavioral skills are learned in school. We should take the emphasis away from trying not to suppress creativity and put the interest into discovering what the learned behavioral skills are that produce original and socially important behaviors and behavioral repertoires. We must learn to train the child in these skills through the use of rewards so that he also learns positive emotional responses to such activities. Only in this way will he continue to work when he is on his own.

PERSONAL FREEDOM
AND SCIENTIFIC DETERMINISM

According to science, all events are determined by other material, natural events. Nothing is spontaneous, capricious, uncaused, or supernaturally caused. This is true of a scientific approach to human behavior, as well as any other events studied within science. If we are interested in the study of human behavior, we look for the laws of causation involved. The principles of learning are such laws. It is suggested that the individual is what he has learned, as affected also by the present conditions to which he is subjected.

The personal freedom, self-direction, creativity, and spontaneity aspects of human behavior are given by the way we extend our past learning—for example, to original combinations of behavior we have not learned, and so on. In addition, however, freedom, self-direction, and spontaneity are *what we experience*. Our repertoires are *us*. They are our personalities, our "being." We do not and could not recall the infinitely complex set of learning experiences that molded our repertoires. What we experience are our own repertoires. For us our behavioral skills are original causes—they are the givens. We experience our decisions, our plans, our reasoning—all complex repertoires of learned responses—as the causes of our behavior. And these *are* the causes, in the sense discussed, although they themselves are composed of previously learned repertoires of skills and are affected by current stimulus conditions.

Moreover, the individual "causes" his own behavior in another sense. He does things because he decides to do so. The way he decides will be a function of his past experience—*but this past experience will also have been affected by many of his past decisions*. Before the time an individual has become an adult his own decision-making behaviors will have affected his experience, and the experience in return will affect his later decisions, and so on, to a very large extent. The combinations are so many and so complex the individual himself with his common-sense knowledge could not trace the original causal sequence. The contribution of the individual's own behavior will have been so large that in adulthood he can be considered in many ways to be under his own direction, to be unique and spontaneous.

It may be suggested that this conception allows a rapprochement between "cognitive" and "personality" approaches and behavioristic approaches to human behavior.

It should finally be noted that although the present view indicates the contribution the parent makes in producing a child supplied with rich basic behavioral repertoires, the conception also shows that the child more and more learns from other experiences. Many of these experiences are ones that the child's behavioral characteristics will select for him. Thus, parental training only goes so far. Then the behavior of the child himself begins to dictate more and more what his further learning, and further behavior, will be. More will be said of these points in the next chapter.

chapter 14/ Hierarchical Learning and the Cumulative Acquisition of Personality

The most influential conception of human development up to the present time has been that the child goes through stages of development. These stages of development are generally considered to be based upon the biological maturation of the child. Thus, for example, Freud suggested that the child's "personality" was formed as he moved through four stages of biological development. The first stage was considered to be the "oral" stage. In this the child's biological energies were concentrated in his oral regions—and his satisfactions and frustrations occurred in these regions. Depending upon how his oral activities were handled, the child might develop a normal or abnormal personality. In the next stage of the biological development, the energy investment was in the anal region. Depending upon how the child fared in his anal activities—largely toilet training—the child's personality would develop or be held back. The next stage was called the phallic stage to indicate that biological energy concentration was now in the genital region. Stimulation of the genitalia would satisfy the impulses of this instinct. At this time the Oedipal situation was thought to exist. That is, the mother would become the object of the instinct for the boy and the father for the girl. Depending upon how the situation was handled, the child's personality would develop normally or abnormally.

In the last stage of development, thought to occur in adolescence, the instinctual energy of the child was supposed to be directed toward other people. At this biological stage of development the individual would thus become interested in other activities and objects important to adult adjustment. He should also acquire the capacity for loving others, doing things unselfishly, and so on.

Another more recent stage theory of human development has been presented by Jean Piaget. This theory is especially relevant to the present one because it deals with the intellectual development of the child. According to Piaget's conception, intellectual functioning advances in four stages, with each stage serving as the foundation for the next. The infant enters first into the sensorimotor period, which extends up to two years of age. He is thought to have a simple system of reflex responses at the beginning but then progresses in this stage to the development of more skilled sensory-motor responses to environmental stimulation. The child develops such skills as reaching for and grasping, standing, walking, and the like. His intellectual functioning also develops in that at first when objects are out of sight, they exert no effect upon the infant. Toward the end of the stage, however, the child will continue to look for objects that have been placed behind obstacles. Piaget sees such changes in behavior as being due largely to maturational processes rather than specifying the specific training and learned skills that produce the changes.

Piaget describes the nature of the child's skills in the next period and calls the stage the preoperational stage. Thus, some of the language skills of the child between two and seven years—the period involved—are listed. Piaget sees certain of the child's incompletely developed skills, however, as an indication of incomplete organic-mental maturation. That is, the fact that the child does not respond to the size of a clay ball, for example, as remaining the same no matter what shape it is made into is seen by Piaget to indicate a mental (largely biological) immaturity in the child.

In the next stage of development, the concrete operation period of seven to eleven years, the child's "cognitive" organization is more complete, according to this view, enabling the child to make more "consistent" and "logical" responses to such concrete problems. Not only can he see the conservation of matter, irrespective of how it is manipulated, as in the clay ball example, but he also reports the volume of liquid as being the same although it is poured into different shaped containers, and so on. He also displays other rudimentary concepts of time, number, space, and rules of logic. But it is said by Piaget that the child is still tied by the nature of his mental (biological) development to concrete situations. He cannot yet indulge in hypothetical thinking, for example.

The final stage of development in Piaget's theory is that of formal operations, which occurs when the child is between eleven and fifteen years of age. At this time the child can think abstractly, test hypotheses, and the like.

Piaget does not exclude the effects of learning in the manner in which these develop (nor did Freud). Piaget indicates that the manner in which the environmental experiences are assimilated by the child are important. However, the conception is highly biologically oriented. There is no systematic study of learning principles. There is no utilization of the basic learning principles that have been discovered and systematically elaborated in laboratory experimentation. There is no systematic and detailed observation of the learning conditions that the child experiences in developing his intellectual skills. Moreover, the method of study—that is, simply observing what the child can do at different ages—is the normal method of study of those who are quite sure that it is the internal development of the child that is the prime determinant of behavioral development. This type of method can never systematically investigate the learning conditions that produce behavioral development. The mental-biological nature of Piaget's conception can be seen also in the following quotation: "When adults try to impose methematical concepts on a child prematurely, his learning is merely verbal; true understanding of them comes only with his mental growth" (1953, p. 2). As will be indicated in the next section, biologically oriented conceptions of child development have always cautioned us against attempting to train the child to skills before he "develops them on his own," one of the important drawbacks to such conceptions.

INADEQUACIES OF STAGE DEVELOPMENT THEORIES

Inadequate Evidence for Stage Development Theories

This section need only be brief, since the inadequacies of organic-mental conceptions of human behavior in general also apply here. Thus, for example, there has never been evidence of biological changes in development that correspond to the stages that have been posited—changes in biological structure or function. There are no such personality processes or structures that can be found. With respect to the Freudian conception, each of the behaviors of the stages of the supposed development of the child could be learned. Thus, we gain no information whatsoever from the conception that there are instinctual energies that shift as the child ages—nor from the conception that biological personality structures are involved.

The same is true of Piaget's theorizing concerning mental structures or processes. The contribution of Piaget's or Freud's theories, or similar works, actually lies in the observations made of the developing behavior of the child. Since they did not observe the conditions that give rise to that development, however, they should have nothing to say about such causes, about how or why the behavior development occurs.

Oversimplification of Stage Development Theories

Another major weakness of such conceptions, moreover, is that they are so oversimplified. The events that affect the child's behavioral development are much more complex than suggested in such theories. For example, as in Freud's theory, taking care of the child's feeding (in the oral stage), his toilet training (in the anal stage), his sexual training (in the phallic stage), and so on do not by any means fulfill the responsibilities of the parent. Certainly toilet training is an important training problem for the parent. If he handles it poorly—for example, if he tries to train the child using punishment as the means—the child will have toilet problems, and also learn negative attitudes toward the parent. If the parent does not utilize the positive reinforcers of feeding to good purpose, as has been proposed herein in a detailed way, the parent will also have lost important training opportunities. Although pointing to these few potential areas of difficulty are certainly productive, even without specifying the casual conditions, this does not begin to provide the information about the *various* aspects of child learning that is needed. If the child must develop a complex of skills, it is necessary that we describe what these behavioral skills consist of as well as the manner in which they are acquired. Stage theories of child development simply do not do this.

Methodological Weaknesses
of Stage Development Theories

Moreover, one of the primary drawbacks to such conceptions is that they constitute a closed system. There is no opening, really, for introducing other concerns about other important behaviors and their causes. Such conceptions are oversimplified, and in their closed system features they do not encourage a developing set of principles, investigations, or procedures for dealing with child problems. Another sense in which they are closed has been in lacking an experimental method to continue to progress—one of the strongest points of the learning approach.

As the present book has shown, there are many different types of learning that are important to adjustment. And this has been shown even when restricting attention to only child development—and then primarily the language-intellectual aspects of personality development. The child has to acquire many, many, many skills, and it is important to know what they are and how they are learned. It should be emphasized that the present conception is not a closed system. It presents principles that can be extended to behaviors not treated herein. The most important task is to provide a general conception that can be used in considering various aspects of child development and human behavior.

The "Fixed Development" Assumption
of Stage Theories

Perhaps the primary weakness of stage theories, however, is in what they suggest about child-rearing practices. In their biological orientation they completely miss the fact that the behavioral characteristics of the children they observe are a function of cultural child-rearing practices. The similarity that is found in children's behavioral development occurs, it is suggested, because of the similarity of child-rearing practices in the culture. The stage theorists assume, on the contrary, that what the child is behaviorally at any age is largely a function of his internal biological development. There is little to be derived from this conception in terms of what is to be done to the child to produce desirable behaviors or to treat undesirable ones. The stages of behavioral development are accepted as givens.

Such conceptions have thus told us that the behaviors usually displayed by children are fixed features of the individual's and the specie's development. Thus, when it is observed that a child of four attends for only short periods, the biological developmentalist says as a principle, "Four-year-olds have only a five-minute attention span." He does not look to the learning history of the child, the difficulty of the task, the conditions and schedule of reinforcement, and so on. As the author has shown, the attention span of the child is a function of these several types of variables. If we want to understand and deal with the child's lack of attention, we must understand the learning principles involved.

Here is another example of this type of drawback to the biological stage development approach. When Piaget observed that children had certain number skills at a certain age, he implied that this level of skill was fixed by the biology of children.

> A child of 5 or 6 may readily be taught by his parents to name the numbers from 1 to 10. If ten stones are laid in a row, he can count them correctly. But if the stones are rearranged in a more complex pattern or piled up, he can no longer count them. . . . [H]e has not yet grasped the essential idea of number (Piaget, 1953, p. 75).

The present author has shown that this view is entirely misleading. In work with his daughter, the present author has shown that a child eighteen months of age may begin to be trained to important aspects of number skills such as the discrimination of numerosity. Moreover, building upon this skill, the child may then learn more advanced aspects of the "concept of number," including the skills Piaget says the child will not develop until after he is five or six years old. The author trained his daughter to count objects, regardless of the order of the objects, before she was three.

Moreover, the author has generalized these findings to other children, with other adults performing the training. Thus, children of four years of age were trained to these number skills, which a Piagetian conception would not expect to develop until after age six. This could be done with the learning procedures regardless of whether the children were those who would be considered to be advanced or those who would be considered to be retarded. Thus, in the study, culturally deprived children with IQs ranging from 89 to 130 all learned to discriminate numerosity, to count objects in series as well as in any arrangement, to read numbers, and so on. Moreover, these children showed the general results of this skill acquisition in the advances they made on standardized intellective tests (see Staats, 1968a; Staats, Brewer, and Gross, 1969). Other investigators have also begun experiments showing that skills described by Piaget are indeed learned (Gelman, 1969).

It has also been said by stage-oriented conceptions that if training is presented to the child too early—supposedly before he is biologically ready— great harm may be done the child. This conclusion has acted as an injunction preventing potential investigators from studying methods of training young children to skills before the time when they usually develop them. For example, one of the specific injunctions of this misconception has been that children should not be trained to read early, and so on. No such conclusion is suggested by the learning conception. Thus, the present author began training his daughter to read at the age of two. There were no harmful effects. The training was conducted within the types of principles suggested here, and the child with no awareness of effort or difficulty began to acquire a reading repertoire in the most desirable way—a gradually introduced training program. It is interesting to note that she entered school a year early, has always been happy in school, and when in the second grade was reading at the 99 percentile (that is, better than 99 percent of children on national norms). These same procedures have been validated with other children, as with the culturally deprived children already described. In the latter case, not only did the children acquire important, functional intellectual skills, but their intelligence measures increased an average of 11.6 points.

Stage Development Theories Have Obstructed Understanding of Child Learning

It is certainly true that a young child may be introduced to training that is inappropriate for him. Ways in which this may be done have been mentioned herein. However, it should be noted that one of the reasons we have lacked knowledge by which to produce benign learning in young children is because organic-mental conceptions have oriented investigation away from the necessary research.

The fact is, as has been indicated, the child is capable of complex learning from the beginning. It is only necessary to provide training on the more basic learned skills before introducing the more advanced skills. Rather than trying to avoid presenting the child with learning situations, it is advantageous to the child to be presented early with appropriately conducted training—on intellectual tasks as well as on social tasks, and so on. Thus, one of the most important findings in the author's work on the early learning of children has been that the rate of learning *accelerates* as the child is trained. For example, it takes about four times as many learning trials for the young child to write the first several letters he attempts as it will take after he has already learned to write a dozen or so. His rate of learning to write new letters accelerates. This is true in various types of intellectual learning. The child not only learns important specific skills when he participates in well-conducted training, he *learns how to learn* intellectual material more rapidly. In one study a three-year-old child took more trials than five-year-olds in beginning to learn to read letters. But after ten or so hours of training he was learning at a faster rate than the five-year-olds had when they commenced training. Thus, the ten hours of intellectual training was seen to advance the stage of the child's development by two years—at least this is what one would have to conclude from a biological maturation conception.

In concluding this section it may be suggested that we have to generally cast aside the handicapping injunctions of the organic-mental view. Such a view does not provide the positive information we need, nor does the view allow us to gain such information. There is little direct evidence for such conceptions, and the implications are widely misleading. It is suggested that *the child is what he learns,* and this depends upon the training experience to which he is subjected. This is not to suggest that each parent start advanced accelerated learning with his child, for it takes information of the type presented here with which to appropriately conduct such training. It may be suggested, however, that ideally each parent should become acquainted with the learning conception and be sensitive to his child's learning, and be prepared to add to the child's learning in areas where he is informed of the possibilities. The scientific areas involved should also develop procedures for the parent to apply in adding to his child's learning, as has been illustrated herein, and as will be elaborated in later volumes. These points also apply to institutions other than the family that deal with the child. That is, one of the strangest phenomena that could exist is the almost monolithic acceptance in the field of education of a biological conception of child development. Although education is concerned solely with the manipulation of learning conditions—and has nothing to do with biological conditions—it has not adopted a learning conception. Rather, it securely holds the biological approach. So much progress could be made if the learning conception was accepted and utilized in the redesign of school practices and in the treatment of learning problems (see Staats, 1968a, in press a).

At this point it is now appropriate to return to consideration of the learning conception of intelligence and to the elaboration of a few additional points in this conception.

DEVELOPMENTAL STAGES AND LEARNING

The preceding discussion has indicated the weaknesses of the conception that behavior development in the child occurs through maturation into successive biological stages. This is not to say, however, that the child is not generally capable at one age of behaviors that he could not learn or perform at an earlier age. It is quite clear that the child can be successfully introduced to training at one age that would have been highly unsuccessful earlier. However, the biological conceptions of child development recognize this in the grossest way. Thus, they simply observe a lot of children and then give an estimate of when the average child develops a particular type of behavior; that is, of about when the average child may be successfully introduced to a particular type of training. Aside from the grossness involved here—since there are wide variations in behavior development in children—such biological approaches do not tell us the behavioral skills that a child has to have before he should attempt a new learning task. We need a better conception than the biological-stages conceptions that have been the traditional mainstay of psychology and education. It has been the intent of the present book to present a learning conception of development. One of the central principles in this conception is that there is indeed a hierarchical advancement of the child's behavior. However, there are sharp contrasts between this learning conception of development and the biological conceptions.

Thus, for example, the present account has attempted to show that the child's intellectual quality, his intelligence, is acquired through learning. His "intelligence" does not develop in simple biological stages, but it is learned as a set of repertoires of behavioral skill. These repertoires are in some circumstances distinctly separable, but are ordinarily rather inter-dependent. Moreover, it is easy to see, when the various repertoires that are important to intelligence are outlined, that there is a hierarchical type of learning. This hierarchical type of learning does not indicate an advancement in the learning principles involved in the child's development as has been suggested (Gagne, 1965). In contrast, it is suggested, the learning principles are the same elementary principles throughout human development.

Rather, the hierarchical learning conception advanced herein is that the child in many instances must acquire one repertoire of skills—if not several—before he is able to move on to the learning of a more advanced repertoire. At any time, it is suggested, *the child's intelligence consists of the various repertoires of skills that he has learned.* These repertoires determine how well the child will do in any performance situation, or in any learning situation. How well the child will learn ordinarily is determined not by the child's internal organic-mental quality but by the basic behavioral repertoires that he brings to the task. There is no evidence that there are organic-mental differences that determine the child's learning rate. It is suggested that learning rate is determined by the child's basic behavioral repertoires (which here are considered his intelligence). The child learns skills that determine how rapidly he will learn new skills.

It may be added that the dimensions of behavior acquisition are complex. A few simple stages will not suffice in describing this complex acquisition process. Moreover, the simplistic stage conceptions do not provide the framework with which to work with the child as a practitioner—such as a psychologist, pediatrician, psychiatrist, or teacher—or indeed to work with the child as a parent. The specific skills that make up the child's intelligence must be specified. The conditions that can be manipulated to produce those skills must be specified. This is then information by which something can be *done* to deal with the problems of child learning.

It may be added that the conception of intelligence presented herein, and the process of the hierarchical learning of one's behavioral skills (intelligence), has been based upon principles that apply to all of the learning. These principles in each case may be simply and straightforwardly stated. They have been corroborated in basic, laboratory research with various organisms, including children engaged in the learning of complex intellectual repertoires. Because of this characteristic, because each learning principle specifies the types of conditions necessary to produce the behavior, each analysis of the child's complex intellectual learning in terms of the principles tells one what to do to produce the behavior in the child. ·This is true whether one's purpose is a research study with the child or the training of the child in the home, in the clinic, or in the school.

What is suggested in the hierarchical learning conception of human development is that the child is involved in a progression of learning that moves from the acquisition of basic repertoires of skill to the acquisition of more advanced skills based upon the earlier learning. Each of the basic behavioral repertoires of skill that has been discussed herein is given that term because such a repertoire will be important in the acquisition of more advanced skills. And the more advanced skills are then necessary to the acquisition of more advanced skills. Any complex, highly skilled repertoire must be considered to be the resultant of such a hierarchical learning process that involves years of cumulative experience. There is no direct evidence that there are biological structures or processes that account for the varied talented behaviors displayed by humans. However, there is much evidence that no such skill arises without such hierarchical learning.

Thus, it is suggested, for example, that the child learns such basic behavioral repertoires as attention and discrimination, imitation, motivation, language skills, and so on. These are repertoires that enable the child to adjust at a level commensurate with his age. Moreover, such skills will constitute basic behavioral repertoires when the child, for example, is later introduced to reading. On the basis of his past learning of basic behavioral repertoires, he will acquire a very complex repertoire of skills that make up being able to read and to profit from the activity. This complex repertoire will then be basic to the acquisition of even more advanced skills in science, mathematics, foreign languages, and so on. *This* is the manner in which we can consider human behavior to develop hierarchically, or in stages. In the present book the emphasis has been on aspects of intelligence. The conception pertains, however, to other aspects of personality. Thus, it is important that complex social, emotional, sensory-motor repertoires, and others, also be treated within the learning conception.

Characteristics of the Hierarchical Learning Conception

At this point, however, a few general characteristics of the hierarchical conception of behavioral development will be mentioned. First, the learning of the infant begins very early—one can say right after birth. There is thus much opportunity for acceleration or retardation to occur as a function of early childhood training with its great variability. This becomes clear when one considers the implications of the hierarchical (or cumulative) nature of behavioral development. A child who more quickly has developed a good attentional repertoire, has learned to follow directions, and so on can be given training in other skills sooner than a child who has not learned these basic repertoires. Then, having acquired the additional skills, he can again be trained to the next type of skill. The general statement here is that acceleration in the acquisition of one repertoire accelerates the acquisition of the next. Because of this cumulative effect, vast differences in the level of behavioral skill of different children can be produced. The same is true also of the quality of the training given the child. The better, as well as the more quickly, a repertoire is acquired, the more quickly will the next repertoire be acquired.

It may be suggested that this is what explains the "learning how to learn" phenomenon that has already been discussed. Specific behaviors that will accelerate the child's learning in many situations have been described in discussing the various basic behavioral repertoires. There are many basic behavioral repertoires that, once acquired, accelerate the rate and increase the quality of learning in further tasks the child faces. Although not all areas have been dealt with here, it is suggested that such learning-how-to-learn acceleration occurs in addition in the *various* areas of human behavioral personality development—in senory-motor skills, athletic, artistic, social, and other intellectual skills.

It is this *cumulative* effect of behavioral development that has led to misconceptions. For example, when one deals with a group of children, there will be included those who have reached different levels and qualities of learning. At this point, even though comparable training is given to all the members of the group, there will be great differences in the learning produced. This will occur because the different levels of previous learning will determine how the children will do in the new learning. Since at this point the children will all be given access to equal treatment, it is easy to conclude erroneously that there must be personal differences in the "ability" or "capacity" of the child to learn—in the "innate" intelligence of the child. It is thus important to suggest that gigantic differences in behavioral skill can be expected on the basis of the great differences in the cumulative, hierarchical learning of the children. Thus, it is to be expected that there will be different *rates* of learning for children, purely upon the basis of their past learning histories.

It is also because of the cumulative nature of the child's learning that many of the short-term studies conducted to show the unimportance of learning in the development of the child have been inadequate and erroneous. The vast differences in skill that can be produced by learning can be shown *only* when the study is of sufficient length and when the behaviors studied are of sufficient complexity to allow large individual differences. To give one twin special training for a short period on some simple skill and then compare his skill to that of an untrained twin—a favorite type of study to show the insignificance of learning and by inference the importance of heredity—will not produce large differences through learning. The short-term training in a skill that is basic to the development of no other skill—where there is no hierarchy of learned skills, each being basic to the next—is actually an inconsequential test of the importance of learning to human behavior and child development. Thus, for example, a few weeks of special training in climbing stairs, as has been shown, will produce relatively little lasting increase in the skill of the specially trained child relative to that of the untrained child. Why should it?

However, if a child was presented with systematic training in learning to walk at an early age, and then in running, swimming, riding a bicycle, throwing and catching a ball, jumping—in short, training in many basic sensory-motor coordinations—and then was introduced to special training of long duration in some sport or physical art form, and this was done in a progressive manner, differences could be produced that would clearly throw the twin without special training into the category of duffer, and the trained twin into the category of skilled athlete or performer. Variations in life circumstances produce for some individuals just such possibilities for long-term, cumulative skill acquisitions of many different types, while others miss such opportunities almost completely.

It must also be realized that these special training circumstances can take place without some parent's guiding hand. For example, once a child has acquired a skill that is a little out of the ordinary, there are many factors that will tend to ensure that he gains even more skill. For one thing, he will receive much extra reinforcement for the behavior involved. This will have the effect of ensuring that this child will receive many more future learning trials than will a child who receives an ordinary amount of reinforcement for the behavior—or even less than the ordinary amount. It should be remembered that such conditions of reward can produce differences in the number of learning trials that probably mount into the millions. On that basis alone great differences in human skill can ensue.

To understand the tremendous effects of learning in the development of all types of human activity, we must consider the case where the acquisition of one repertoire in rate and quality affects the acquisition of the next skill learning, and this in turn affects the acquisition of yet another skilled repertoire—a snowballing effect that can have a positive or negative final result. The very able person is the fortunate one who has had an advantage in his training that has cumulated. He is highly skilled as a result and will be called intelligent, able, talented, and so on. The retardate—excluding in this example those who have detectable physical defects—is the person who has suffered the cumulative deficits of poor training. The retarded individual is one who for one reason or another has not acquired the basic behavioral repertoires, cannot emit them in a new learning situation, and thus cannot respond in a manner that will enlarge his repertorial skills.

It must also be remembered that most cognitive training past school age will be aimed at the average level of the group, not at the child's individual level of learning. Thus, once he falls behind, the retardate's life circumstances will usually guarantee that the cumulative effect will produce a snowballing low level of behavioral development. Ordinarily, a home environment is likely to have a constant rate and quality of training. As a result, the child who has an accelerated or retarded behavioral development because of his early training is likely to continue to receive the same "boost" in later experiences in the home—in a manner that will enhance the cumulative effects of the child's training. There are exceptions, of course; conditions may change in some way, or the parent may be a better trainer at one age level of the child than he is at another. In these and other variations there is room for infinite variability in the parent and thus in the child. More will be said in the next chapter of how the cumulative effects of training can result in problems in the child's cumulative development.

Resolution of the Self-Direction
Versus Environmental-Direction Controversy

A major, perhaps primary reason for the argumentation and controversy in conceptions of man has been that some people see human behavior as coming from within—usually from personal qualities of a biological source. In contrast, environmentalists (or empiricists) have been concerned with considering the ways that environmental events mold human behavior. The strategy of the latter persuasion has been to explain differences in human behavior in terms of gross environmental circumstances to which people have been exposed. The environmentalist treats human behavior not as something spontaneous, from within, but as a result of things that have occurred to the person.

One of the purposes of the present book is to emphasize that in taking sides in these grossly stipulated, antagonistic views, we have allowed ourselves to get locked into positions that are conflicting—when this is not a necessary outcome. The nativists (biologically oriented) are indeed correct. That is, people do contribute "causes" to the determination of their own behavior. Two children in the very same learning situation will acquire different levels of skill—because of what they bring to the situation. Evidence of such individual differences is incontrovertible.

On the other hand, the environmentalist is also correct. *The child (or adult) is what he learns, for the differences in learning ability that we see in children are themselves learned.* Yes, two children faced with the same situation profit differently, but that is because they bring to the situation different repertoires of learned skills. Some of these learned behaviors are propaedeutic to further learning. A child who has these behaviors in good measure for the particular situation will benefit more from the tuition possibilities than will the child who has these behaviors in lesser measure. On the other hand, learned behaviors exist that will interfere with further learning. The child who has more of these behaviors will benefit less well from the same contact with a learning situation.

In this sense, even as a child, and more so later, the individual is *responsible* for what he makes of his life opportunities. If he behaves in a certain way in a situation he will progress, and if he does not behave that way he will not progress. But it must be remembered that whether or not the individual possesses the necessary behavior will be a function of his previous learning history. At any moment in time his behavioral skills depend upon his past history, but these behavioral skills, these personal qualities that set him off from other people for good or bad, are also a determinant of what further will happen to the individual.

Thus, the behaviors that we acquire are learned. But these behaviors then contribute to the quality of our adjustment and learning in later situations. Our total behaviors, personality, if you will, is an effect. But it is also a cause of how we will later do, and how our later behavior (personality) will be formed. Personality, including the individual's intellectual characteristics, may be considered to result from the long-term accretion of behavior, each acquisition dependent upon previously acquired behaviors, in a cumulative manner. This is a concept of cumulative, hierarchical learning.

INTELLIGENCE TESTS
AND HIERARCHICAL LEARNING

It has been suggested that one can never assume from measurements of the child's behavior whether there is any biological defect involved. Certainly, there could be retardation through injury, illness, or birth defect. However, without direct evidence that this is the case, such a factor cannot be assumed.

For the great majority of people, for whom there is no evidence of biological defect (and this constitutes over 90 precent), an explanation of retarded intellective—or other—skill development must, in this author's view, be sought in learning conditions. The concept of intelligence as measured by tests may be considered to refer to a wide sample of the basic behavioral repertoires, and more advanced skills, which the child or adult has learned. When we consider intelligence (and also readiness and aptitudes, talents, and so on) to actually consist of such basic behavioral repertoires, it can be seen that we must have specific analyses of what these skills are and how they are learned. On the basis of such analyses, procedures for producing such skills can be designed—as exemplified herein. The task of measuring or assessing the basic behavioral repertoires (intelligence) may be considered to be very important. Measurement of such repertoires would indicate the level of development of the individual child, what aspects of learning he needed, and so on.

Tests based upon the measurement of the child's behavioral skills necessary for more advanced learning to which the child would be exposed would be very useful tools in composing effective programs of training for children. They would serve as measurements of behavioral skills in indicating how much and how well a child had progressed up to that point. Furthermore, the tests constructed upon the basis of such learning analyses would also better serve as measurements of behavioral skills necessary for further learning of more advanced skills. That is, such tests would indicate what training materials the child was prepared to work with, and so on. These are developments that await the further acceptance of the learning conception and its application to the construction of both curriculum materials and the psychological tests of the child's learning. And this advancement will depend upon our general ability to cast aside the present conception of human behavior that is holding back such progress.

THE ONTOGENY AND PHYLOGENY
OF INTELLIGENCE DEVELOPMENT

In 1963 the author wrote the following in a passage entitled, "Adaptiveness and Reinforcement, Extinction, and Scheduling Principles."

Organisms, including humans, function according to principles that allow for a great deal of modifiability and consequent adjustment to environmental occurrences. It was seen that behavior which is followed by certain consequences (positive reinforcers) increases in strength, that is, is more likely to reoccur. It is not surprising that organisms have evolved in this manner, since a species of organisms which did not function according to this principle would not be likely to survive. An organism that took one branch of a winding path and found water and became less likely to make that same response might not live to reproduce its kind. It seems that it is only because the consequences of an organism's behavior affect its later behavior in a certain way that an organism adapts to its environment and survives.

Sometimes, however, the environment changes. Although a certain type of behavior may have been reinforced at one time, later this type of behavior may no longer be reinforced—the water hole may dry up. It is, therefore, also important for the adaptibility of the organism that, even though a response has become strong, it is not immutable. When a response ceases to be reinforced, it becomes weaker. After the response occurs a number of times without reinforcement, it will return to its original level of strength.

Further, the adaptability of the organism to the conditions of reinforcement in the environment can be seen perhaps from the effects of intermittent reinforcement. Different schedules of reinforcement have specificially different and lawful effects upon the behavior of the organism. It is important to see that behavior makes very sensitive adjustments to the reinforcing contingencies in the environment. As the reinforcing contingencies in the environment vary, distinct and lawful effects are imposed on the characteristics of the emission of a response and the extinction process.

It has been pointed out that the principles by which organisms behave are those of adaptability to environmental events, and that this adaptability must have been necessary for the survival of individual and species—thus, perhaps, the learning characteristics of living organisms arise in biological evolution (Staats, 1963, p. 69).

Skinner has developed a similar thesis, using the terms phylogenetic for species and *ontogenetic* for individuals.

> Another apparent characteristic in common [between evolution and learning] is 'adaptation.' Both kinds of contingencies change the organism so that it adjusts to its environment in the sense of behaving in it more effectively. With respect to phylogentic contingencies, this is what is meant by natural selection. With respect to ontogeny, it is what is meant by operant conditioning [actually, learning in general would be more appropriate]. Successful responses are selected in both cases, and the result is adaptation (1966, p. 74).

At any rate, what is suggested herein is that all men inherit the principles of learning by which they function, as well as a mechanism for the acquisition of many, many stimulus-response coordinations that vary from the simple to the exceedingly complex. In the inheritance of a structure that functions according to learning principles, man is like the lower animals. In inheriting as a member of the human species, a much more complex mechanism than any other animal, man is quite distinctly set apart from other animals. Moreover, as has been indicated, man's learned language-intellectual skills provide him with self-direction, spontaneity, and originality in ways that make him qualitatively different from any other organism.

It may be added that there are additional parallels between individual development and the nonbiological development of the species. Man *develops intelligence* as he learns in an historical or phylogenetic sense. That is, we may look upon the history of man as a species as the acquisition of a great variety of behavioral skills through the principles of learning. The original acquisition of any skill may be seen as a laborious, time-consuming, imprecise process—like the trial-and-error learning that Thorndike investigated. One can see, historically, this slow and uncertain development in any area of complex behavioral development—music, athletics, religion, business rules, government, language, science, and so on. As one example, in the author's lifetime the athletic skill of high-jumping has gone through distinct developments. At one time the skill consisted of the "scissors" jump. Later the jump was performed by a side roll. From there the variations in the behaviors tried produced a more effective jump, one where the bar was crossed as the individual was face down. The winner of the 1968 Olympic Games, on the other hand, trotted up to the bar, swung around, and catapulated himself over backwards, going over directly with his back to the bar.

It is important to note that the refinement of such skills involves the advances of the individuals involved at any one point, plus the general or group advancement that has preceded them. A youngster learning to high-jump today does not go through the various stages in the development of the contemporary skill that were necessary in the historical development, which involved the successive learning of many men. He begins with the maximal point of development that has been achieved to that point. The variations in the skill that he makes are made from a higher point of skill than a youngster in the preceding generation. As a result, the picture we get of such a progression is one of systematic advancement.

The major point here, however, is that man develops his skills phylogenetically—as a species or group, over the generations. The principles of learning are involved for the species development as for the individual. Since man's learned skills are his intelligence, it may be said that man develops his intelligence in this manner. At any point, however, what man has so laboriously learned he passes on to the individual child. The child then receives in his learning the learning of the human race—as provided by its representatives in the form of parents, family, peers, teachers, and so on. The child learns in his lifetime, in the areas of skill he acquires, the learning that has taken his people to learn from the beginning.

Of course, the child does not have to go through the trial-and-error discovery process. He can be directly trained to the skill. It may have taken centuries before a germ theory of disease was developed by man, as another example. But it composes part of the general language skills of the present generation of our children—imparted with relative ease in the language learning of the child. Thus, the intelligence of the individual advances as does the intelligence of the "phylum." The present learning conception is thus a theory of social evolution or change—but that is a topic for later development.

INDIVIDUAL AND GROUP INTELLIGENCE

If, as is proposed, the performance of the child on intelligence test items is a function of his previous learning experience in these areas, the presence of group characteristics would also be expected. To elaborate, it has been suggested herein that the intelligence of man (his various skills—intellectual, artistic, social, and so on) has increased markedly while he has remained unchanged as a biological organism. It was said that early man did not write poems on the walls of his caves, or mathematical formulae, because he did not receive training of the sort that provided these skills (or training that would allow him to "originate" those skills).

Historically, we can see that man develops skills over time, within one individual as he continues to develop through experience, and over succeeding individuals, since the successor begins with a higher level of skill than did his predecessor—because he receives much of his predecessors skills via training. It must be noted, however, that the individual does not receive the benefits only of one predecessor, but of many. In his own family he has plural family members who provide him through learning with many behavioral skills of various kinds. He associates with other children, and through them he receives some of the benefits of the training they have received. For example, if the children with whom he spends a great deal of time speak a high level and grammatical English, then in the many language interactions he will have with them he will be learning very good language skills. These skills will give him a higher score on various kinds of tests, including intelligence tests, and will allow him to read various materials more easily and to learn other language skills more easily.

Children in our culture receive other types of experience—at least most middle-class children do. They receive toys of various kinds, and dolls, and puzzles that have to be put together. And they drive in cars and they travel on airplanes and they visit various places and participate in many activities. These and other activities provide them with different skills than a Bedouin child, for example, who may have had practically no experience with mechanical, motor-driven objects. As a consequence, considerable difference would be expected in the rapidity with which a middle-class boy from our culture will learn to operate military aircraft in comparison to a Bedouin boy.

The child thus "inherits" through learning, it is suggested, the intelligence of his group. He can acquire the special skills of his family, his playmates, his neighborhood, his social and occupational and educational classes, his mass media sources, his society. If his inheritance from these various sources is poor, then barring other interventions in the usual course of events, his intelligence will to that extent be poor. A group that has a lesser development of skills is less in position to produce members of the group who excel in those skills. From a learning analysis, it would be expected that there would be large differences in the "intelligence," "talents," "abilities"—that is, the behavioral skills—evidenced by different groups of people. These types of differences, it should be indicated, can occur within a differentiated society as well as between societies.

Thus, it is suggested that the child acquires through learning the "individual intelligence" that his home is prepared to give him. He also acquires through learning the "group intelligence" his group or culture is prepared to give him. It would be expected that subgroups within a society would continue to display large variations in the general level of skill of their members. There are concepts in genetics to indicate how populations that are isolated may develop "genetic pools" different from other populations. "Behavioral pools" (behavioral characteristics), it may be noted, would be expected to differ between isolated groups on the basis of learning. Moreover, even though the groups were in close proximity within a society, unless the learning between groups was equalized there could be persisting, but learned, group differences.

A highly skilled group will produce learning conditions that result in highly skilled children. The poorly skilled group will not be able to provide high-level learning experiences to its children in the home, or in interactions with peers, and the like. Considered in these terms, it would be expected that general skills, like those labeled intelligence, as well as specific skills, could be part of the group's characteristics. To give examples other than intelligence skills, some groups may have developed special business, scholarly, or artistic skills. And members of the group will to a larger extent than other groups produce members who excel in those specific skills. In any event, it would seem that behavioral skill can be part of the heritage that the group passes on to its progeny through learning. Consequently, the fact that some groups excel and others do not need not be considered in terms of the biological qualities of group members, but in terms of the learning conditions the group supplies.

chapter 15/ Learning and Behavior Disorders: The Downward Spiral of Hierarchical Learning

It is impossible in one chapter to deal in any detail with the broad problems of children. Several additional general points can be made, however, about the acquisition of abnormal behavior in the young child, which are especially relevant to the present concerns. For it is important to have a general conception of abnormal learning as well as normal in a learning conception of human behavior and in dealing with children.

It is suggested that the professional areas concerned with abnormal behavior (clinical psychology, psychiatry, and so on) have always tended to focus upon the abnormal behavior of the child itself—to the exclusion of noting the importance of the child's normal learning. Actually, the abnormal behaviors of the problem child are frequently simple behaviors, whose analysis and treatment may be handled relatively easily. The child's problems in normal repertoires, on the other hand, may necessitate complex understanding as well as long-term treatment procedures. The view taken here will be that the focus on abnormal behavior has been an unfortunate overemphasis in understanding and treating behavior problems. Frequently, the primary problem of the abnormal behavior is the effect it has upon the child's normal learning. The problem then is not solved by attempting to reduce the abnormal behavior alone. In these cases what may seem to be problems of abnormal behavior have at a more basic level a problem of deficits in normal behavior.

To continue, however, the scientific and professional areas that deal with problems of human behavior have been largely oriented toward the development of concepts and methods whose aim is to remediate abnormal behaviors once they have arisen and cause trouble. The psychology of normal development of behavior has not been seen to be as central to such professions. One of the reasons is that abnormal behavior in its bizarre nature attracts attention—and leads to popular as well as professional interest. The normal behaviors are more commonplace, and thus less interesting, even if they are more central and basic to human adjustment.

This misdirection of interest is also tied up with the conceptions of human behavior that have been widely held. For example, the author when still an intern in clinical psychology observed that it was the abnormal behaviors of patients that attracted the attention of the professional staff. This was the case because it was felt that the patient was expressing his repressed internal dynamics through his abnormal behaviors. Thus, one could come to understand profoundly the individual's internal psychodynamics through observing and understanding his abnormal behavior, or so it was thought.

This conception is a legacy of Freud's psychoanalytic theory of abnormal behavior. The present author saw clearly, even at this time (1954), that from the standpoint of his learning approach this theoretical conception translated into treatment of patients that was encouraging their abnormal behavior, rather than treating it. One example that the author pointed to in the literature (Staats, 1957) concerned a schizophrenic patient whose language was abnormal. One of the prominent aspects of this abnormal language was that it was opposite; the patient said "yes" where "no" would be appropriate and vice versa. The doctors were very interested in this behavior—for the signs it could give of the patient's internal problems. This interest, however, meant that the patient got attention when he spoke in this confused manner. When he spoke normal language the doctors were less interested. It was clear that the social reward of attention was maintaining the abnormal behavior. This analysis was verified clearly by Ayllon and Michael (1959) in a hospital study with psychotic patients. (Michael, as a fellow graduate student, had earlier become interested in the present author's behavior modification approach to abnormal behavior as well as his criticism of traditional views.) This study, in turn, was very influential in getting yet other investigators interested in the possibility that learning conditions determined abnormal behavior. Thus, the present conception of abnormal behavior, and the attendant naturalistic observations of hospital treatment of "mentally ill' patients, contributed to the development of the present field of behavior modification. In addition to the analysis of the schizophrenic's opposite speech, the author in more general form showed how various clinically relevant normal and abnormal behaviors may be considered in terms of learning principles. (See, Staats, 1963, especially Chapter 11. This outline of behavior disorders has recently been presented with slight modifications as a social learning approach (Bandura, 1968).

At any rate, the psychodynamic conception of abnormal behavior constitutes another case where the cause of the behavior is displaced from external environmental events to supposed processes internal to the individual—processes that are never observed. Because of this conception, and the practices that stemmed from it, the environmental events that lead to abnormal behavior have largely been ignored. As usually occurs, moreover, once a tradition has been established it tends to persist, even when the determinants relevant to its establishment are no longer present. In the present case, even though many psychologists now take a learning view of abnormal behavior, some of the concomitants of the earlier psychodynamic view still persist. Thus, for example, one of the outgrowths of the psychodynamic view of abnormal behavior was a special interest in abnormal behavior—the assumption being that these were the individual's most significant behaviors. They were thought to reveal more about his nature than more mundane behaviors. Now, even though the rationale for the interest in abnormal behavior is no longer part of a learning conception, the interest has been maintained in a disproportionate amount. The professions concerned with problems of human behavior still show that great disinterest with normal human behavior acquisition.

The present chapter will briefly attempt to indicate that the normal psychology of human behavior and its development should actually be considered primary to an understanding of abnormal behavior. The understanding and ability to produce normal behavior in the child is actually preventive treatment of abnormal behavior. Moreover, the normal psychology must also serve as the basic theory even in cases of remedial treatment procedures aimed at dealing with the problems of abnormal behavior after they have arisen.

It is thus suggested that the primary approach to the cure of behavior problems in children (and thus adults) concerns the presentation of learning experiences to the child that produce normal, adjustive repertoires. This conception involves several points that should be made explicit. First, it has been suggested that the repertoires of skilled behaviors that the child has to acquire to adjust to his present circumstances, and to continue to learn further adjustive skills, are learned in long-term, cumulative acquisition processes. The same may be said for the acquisition of abnormal behaviors. No matter how bizarre the behavior, no matter how it seems to contravert principles of normal behavior, it is suggested that the person has to learn the behavior. Many abnormal behaviors can be considered to be skills in the sense that much "training," inadvertent to be sure, was involved in the acquisition of the behavior. Many learning trials have to be involved in acquiring some abnormal behavioral repertoires. Thus, for example, as many learning trials will be involved in the acquisition of illogical, psychotic social reasoning behaviors as in the acquisition of normal, adjustive social reasoning sequences.

(This conception does not suggest that abnormal behaviors cannot also be produced in the individual through physical deterioration as in age, through disease, injury, drugs, or toxic conditions such as alcoholism. The fact that such conditions may produce undesirable behaviors in the individual that he formerly did not display, or the loss of skills that he did display, does not contradict the conception that the complex behaviors of any type are ordinarily learned.)

One of the important points in the learning conception is that in various ways we may consider that the processes of learning abnormal behavior are in competition with those of learning normal behaviors. The abnormal and normal behaviors are in many instances mutually incompatible. Thus, for example, inappropriate negative emotional responses to a situation will "propel" the individual away from the situation. If the behavior is unusual and maladjustive it will be considered to be abnormal. On the other hand, the person who had learned a positive emotional response to the situation would have learned a behavior incompatible with the abnormal behavior.

As another example, a child may have learned tantrums in situations in which he has been refused something he wants. This behavior may be effective, at least in its learning phases, in that it is rewarded. However, circumstances that result in the learning of this behavior will, if continued, prevent the learning of other, more desirable, competitive behaviors—such as requesting things, working for them, adjusting to delays in rewards, and so on.

There are various interactions between the learning, or not learning, of normal behaviors and the resultant learning of abnormal behaviors. Some of these relevant to the consideration of the present conception of learning will be summarized in the next several sections. The focus of this discussion will be in illustrating how hierarchical learning can work in a negative direction as well as in a positive direction. That is, it has been said that the acquisition of the basic behavioral repertoires, the constituents of personality, aid in the child's later learning in a cumulative process of behavioral skill acquisition. There are circumstances in which the converse is produced—a cumulative failure in child learning, where the *inappropriate learning at one level produces inappropriate learning at the next level, and so on, in a cumulative, hierarchical learning process that results in markedly unusual (abnormal) behaviors of a maladjustive nature.* Several principles involved in such downward spirals will be described.

DEFICITS IN BASIC BEHAVIORAL REPERTOIRES AND ABNORMAL BEHAVIOR

Severe deficits in any type of complex human behavior that is necessary for everyday human adjustment will be seen as abnormal. We may ordinarily think of the abnormality as being within the individual, as is the case with mental retardates, but it is actually in the severe deficits in the behavioral skills of retardates that the problem lies. That is, for he moment disregarding the cause, the primary aspects of so-called mental retardation are that the child does not have the usual sensory-motor skills, the language-intellectual skills, the emotional responses, or the social interaction skills, and so on, that we consider to be normal. It is perhaps in the language-intellectual skill deficits, such as the basic behavioral repertoires that have been described herein, that the central aspects of mental retardation are to be seen. These will be the areas upon which the child will be tested by intelligence tests, for example.

Ordinarily, a child will be diagnosed as a mental retardate if he has severe deficits in these basic behavioral repertoires—and if he does not evidence inappropriate and undesirable behaviors of other types. That is, if the child scores very low on intelligence tests, he will be diagnosed as a mental retardate, provided he does not display bizarre or uncontrollable behaviors of other kinds. If the child also displays bizarre behaviors, and is self-destructive, and so on, he may be considered to be an autistic or schizophrenic child. If he is combative, aggressive, runs aways, and so on, in addition to his language-intellectual deficits, he may be considered to be emotionally disturbed. If he is hyperactive and misbehaves as well as having language-intellectual deficits, he may be considered as brain-damaged—although this conclusion will probably be involved in all of the other diagnoses.

The primary point, however, is that straightforward deficits in the various types of learning that have been described in the present book, depending upon their severity, will be considered to be cases of mental retardation. It should be noted that such cases of language-intellectual deficits may occur purely on the basis of the deficient learning history of the child. If the child has not had any of the training circumstances that have been described, then he will not acquire any of the basic behavioral repertoires that are important to his present adjustment as well as to his learning of other more advanced language-intellectual repertoires.

The downward spiral of the hierarchical learning of intelligence is likely to occur if the deficits in the child's basic behavioral repertoires are severe enough. This can occur in an uncomplicated manner, not involving the acquisition of other undesirable behaviors. That is, the child who has not acquired his basic behavioral repertoires in good quantity and quality will find it more difficult to acquire additional language-intellectual behaviors. Thus, when the child goes to school he will display a lower level of skill than most of the other children of his age, and he will learn new skills more slowly and more effortfully. As a consequence, he will receive less reinforcement for his behaviors than do those other children. This condition, produced by his low level of skill, will in turn produce an even lower rate of acquisition of new skills in this child. If we were able to plot the rate of this child's acquisition of new learning, we would see that it would be very low. Moreover, if it is low enough it will probably decelerate. Thus, for example, we find that "culturally disadvantaged" children—children who have not received the necessary training in their basic behavioral repertoires because of the depressed socioeconomic conditions of their parents—on entering school will score lower than more fortunate children on intelligence tests. It is noteworthy, in addition, that such children will progressively fall behind other children on such intelligence tests. Since the tests are only a reflection of what the child is learning, it would be expected that the child's classroom learning would also be progressively deteriorating in relationship to more advantaged children. And that also occurs.

The final product of such a downward spiral of the cumulative learning of the child is an adult who is markedly less skilled in his intelligence behaviors and in his accomplishments than occurs with children who have had the advantage of a better learning environment. An early deficit in intelligence learning will result from poor quality of home circumstances. It is not compensated for when the child enters school. The present analyses would suggest that extraordinary conditions of training would be necessary for these children to make up for the deficits they have. These compensatory conditions would be necessary until the child has fully made up his deficits. In all likelihood, actually, they would have to be continued even then to compensate for the characteristics of the home situation.

It should also be noted that the common biological conception of lack of intelligence skills has led to circumstances that actually ensure in many cases the downward spiral of the child's learning. That is, if the child's intelligence deficits are severe enough, he will be placed in an institution that in most cases will present even less effective learning circumstances than he had before. Many institutions for the mentally retarded simply afford custodial facilities for the child. At this point, where the child is then in a group of other children who have the same types of behavioral deficits, and thus cannot provide much training experience for the child, his cumulative development through learning will largely cease. To some extent this is also the situation when the less severely deficit child is placed in special education classes in the public school system. In this situation he again associates with other children who have intelligence deficits. Moreover, he receives training that moves at a much slower rate than is usual—for the same number of public school years as children moving at a faster rate. At the end of such training, the child who began with deficits is bound to be even farther behind other children who have had the advantages of the more rapid rate of learning experience.

Motivational Deficits

The preceding section has dealt with the case where the child's deficits have been in the language-intellectual aspects of his basic behavioral repertoires. It should be noted that the focus of the child's problems may begin with deficits in his learned motivation system. For example, ordinarily the rewards for a child in school will largely involve the approval of the teacher and other proficient students, as well as the reward value of learning new skills (achieving). If these sources of reward have not been learned by the child, his attention and work behaviors in school will not be maintained in the same strength as for a child who is more suitably rewarded by the available reinforcers. As a result, the child with the deficit motivational system will learn a good deal less than the other child. As a further consequence of the poor learning, there will be even less reinforcement, this child's attention will deteriorate further, and the result will be a vicious cycle that will produce a downward spiral of cumulative learning. Frequently, of course, the child may have deficits in motivation learning as well as deficits in the intelligence skills themselves.

It is interesting to note one experimental example in deficit motivational systems in such children. The author and associates (Staats, Minke,

Goodwin, and Landeen, 1967) in a study with backward children gave the children an intelligence test as it is usually administered in a school situation. No extrinsic form of reward was provided for taking the test. At a later time, another form of the same type of test was given to these children. This time the children were rewarded (with two pennies) for each intelligence item they responded to correctly. A penny was taken away for each item they responded to incorrectly. Under these conditions of extrinsic reward, the children on the average responded to seven *fewer* items on the intelligence test. However, the children made significant increases in IQ scores— an average increase of 4¼ IQ points. The results, of course, indicate that the children under the usual reward conditions of the class were not attending to the items, but were responding haphazardly. When they perused the items closely under the reward condition, they answered fewer items, but answered more correctly—and they showed themselves to be more intelligent.

This is not to say that any permanent changes were effected in the children. But the results show clearly how motivational variables—especially in a deficit sense—can affect the intellectual performance of the child. Many children are probably diagnosed as retarded, as a matter of fact, and sent to special learning situations because of such lack of motivation. One can also imagine how such lack of attention and work behavior, multiplied by the countless hours these particular children spent in school, would have cumulatively thrown them farther and farther behind other children who displayed better attention and work behaviors.

Thus, it is suggested that sometimes the problem behavior of the child, and his downward spiral of learning, are functions of original motivational or behavioral deficits which themselves affect conditions so that additional deficits occur. The latter then result in further deficits in the acquisition of behavioral skills, and so on. When considered in these terms, it is possible to see how extremely severe cases of "retardation" can occur, and how there can be very, very large differences in the abilities of individuals based upon their learning—not their biology.

It is also suggested that unless the child has a detectable biological defect of some kind it is inappropriate to conclude that he has such a defect. The retarded child is a child who does not have the behavioral skills of other children—including those skills that make him a good learner in many situations. This lack of skill, however, may be a straightforward result of lack of training circumstances that would produce the desirable skills. A child who has not learned to speak, a child who has not learned to respond appropriately to a wide number of verbal stimuli (instructions), a child who has not learned to attend to appropriate stimuli (including verbal directions), a child who does not make learning responses on demand, a child for whom words do not elicit images and serve as rewards, and so on, will not learn even very elementary skills. He will be totally incapable in the formal educational situation, for example. The earlier the deficits begin to "accrue," it may be suggested, the more serious the retardation the child will evidence. *It may also be suggested that successful training in the basic behavioral repertoires that have been described herein would rule out severe cases of retardation.* Moreover, such training, as will be indicated, can be employed to treat such cases of "abnormality."

COMPETITION IN LEARNING: NORMAL OR ABNORMAL LEARNING

The case has been described where the child is called abnormal because he has gaping deficits in his language-intellectual behavioral skills. So-called mental retardation is one of these "abnormalities" in which learning deficits are the central and almost only problem (in cases not complicated by known biological defect or injury). Frequently, however, abnormal behavior is not limited to deficits. A deficit may also occur because the child has learned an undesirable behavior that does not allow the learning or expression of the desirable behavior. The concept is that sometimes behaviors are mutually exclusive—if one is learned and exhibited, the other cannot be. Sometimes the child will learn a competitive abnormal behavior that displaces the normal, adjustive repertoire. Or the abnormal behavior may preclude the opportunity for learning the desirable repertoire. The "replacement" behavior may be undesirable on its own—if it is destructive or is considered to indicate an internal abnormality. The more important disadvantage of the abnormal behavior, however, may be that it displaces the desirable behavioral skill necessary for adjustment. Several examples are relevant here.

We may sometimes see a mother who is solicitous about the welfare of the child and who feels that a primary part of being a mother is to see that the child does not suffer want or frustration. The mother in this case is also likely to feel that the child develops behaviorally through the maturation of his biological being. With this orientation, let us say, when the mother sees the child reaching for some object and grunting or whinning, the mother will obtain the object for the child and give it to him. This type of interaction, of course, if it is general in the child's history, will produce the type of behavior that has previously been discussed. Instead of learning an adjustive speech repertoire, the child will learn the grunting-whining-gesticulating repertoire.

This is thus an example of a child "acquiring" deficits in important adjustive behaviors. At the same time, of course, he is acquiring a replacement behavioral repertoire that may continue to be elaborated. To continue, at some point the mother will become concerned about the child not developing appropriate language and may attempt not to respond to the child's more primitive responses. Then the child will become more insistent through increased amplitude of oral responding, through gesticulating, and through tugging at the parent. If the parent then responds, the child will learn a more intense form of these undesirable replacement behaviors. Furthermore, the child may learn an extensive set of skills that involve how to get the mother's attention, how to get the mother to do things for him, how to use social pressures when he and his mother are with others, and so on. When the skills attain this level of development, they may be quite effective for the child. While they may be considered at this point to be abnormal because they are unusual and not generally adjustive, they have been learned in the home because they actually are adjustive (that is, reinforced).

The important point here, however, is that such behaviors may be considered to be competitive with the repertoires of skill the child should acquire to adjust to society outside the home. Once a child has acquired an extensive replacement (abnormal) repertoire, it is easier for him to employ this behavior than it is to learn a new normal repertoire—even though the new repertoire would be even more effective once it had been acquired. There is no doubt that a speaking repertoire is generally more effective than one of grunting, whining, gesticulating, pulling, having temper tantrums, and so on. However, to the child who does not have the speaking repertoire, such is not the case. The situation is analogous to that of the person who has learned well the hunt-and-peck style of typing. Although he would be more effective if he learned the touch system, learning the touch system would require abandoning a relatively well-learned skill for a more effortful, slower, less precise skill. The ineffective, nonadjustive, replacement behavior is in such cases more reinforcing, and as a consequence *it prevents the person from learning the repertoire which, when acquired, would be much more rewarding.*

Many other undesirable behaviors in children fall into the same category. Take the child for whom the attention of the parent is a positive reinforcer— the usual case. Once the parent is a positive reinforcer, it must be expected that the child will learn behaviors that will be followed by the receipt of the parent's attention. If one were to observe a young child in the home, it would be seen that the child would seek the attention of the parent from time to time. The mother in the home may recognize this and systematically go to the child and give him a few moments of approving attention while the child is engaged in a desirable behavior. Many mothers who are unaware of the principle do so because they have themselves been trained in this manner.

Frequently, however, a mother is busy and involved in her own responsibilities. As long as the child is playing nicely (behaving appropriately), she will leave well enough alone. She may not even respond to requests for attention that are appropriate. Only when the child does some undesirable act will she feel that the child needs her supervision, and in the act of giving him that supervision will actually be providing the attention that serves as a reinforcement. If this is the case, the child will learn undesirable behaviors to gain her attention. This learning may be elaborated into a very extensive repertoire of undesirable attention-getting behaviors. When that occurs, of course, it means that the undesirable behaviors will compete with other desirable behaviors—appropriate play and self-care, social behavior with peers, achievement behavior, learning behavior, work behavior. The latter behaviors should be the ones that are rewarded by the parent's attention, and as a consequence learned by the child.

It is thus important to point out that learning the undesirable repertoire may prevent the learning of more desirable repertoires of skills. As another example, we could describe a whole repertoire of what we might call "dependent" behaviors. These would be behaviors of helplessness and need, which would get the parent to help the child, to support the child, to do for the child what the child should do for himself, to allow the child to avoid social situations with others who are not so solicitous, and so on. By means of the rewarding circumstances of being helped, supported, and so on, the child may learn a wide variety of dependent behaviors. These may range from pleading, crying, acting afraid, remonstrating and threatening to get one's way, and the like. A well-learned repertoire of this kind will be functional for the child in producing immediate avoidance of new, demanding, and effortful situations. However, the repertoire will by its success ensure that the child does not learn the social, intellectual, and emotional skills that he would if he had experienced those situations he avoids. At the end of a history of successful dependent behaviors, thus, the child will be a much less skilled individual in general. The undesirable behaviors in the competition will have emerged as the more dominant—at the expense of the child who has learned them.

INTERACTION OF BEHAVIORAL DEFICITS AND ABNORMAL BEHAVIOR IN THE DOWNWARD LEARNING SPIRAL

It has been indicated that some of the serious problems of child development can reside in not acquiring various aspects of the basic behavioral repertoires—that is, the "acquisition" of behavioral deficits. This may occur because the child simply has not been presented with the necessary training circumstances, or the training circumstances may be very poor in quality or quantity. In some cases, however, it is not a simple case of absence of the training circumstances. The process of acquiring behavioral deficits may centrally involve the acquisition of competing (abnormal) behavior that displaces the learning of the basic behavioral repertoires. The child then has deficits in normal, desirable, behavioral repertoires because his conditions of learning have instead provided him with abnormal, nonadjustive repertoires—at least from the standpoint of society—which have been learned because they have been inadvertently reinforced in the home (or other institution).

The usual circumstance in the downward spiral of hierarchical learning is for the two processes to interact. In many cases the child who has acquired behavioral deficits, if they are severe, will have social experience as a consequence that results in learning abnormal behaviors. On the other hand, many times the abnormal behaviors that a child learns will result in deficits in his later learning in various ways. Examples that demonstrate this interaction between behavioral deficits and abnormal behaviors will be helpful. Thus, as the author has suggested (Staats, 1963) the child learns his toilet habits. In order for a child to be "toilet trained," he has to be presented with appropriate training circumstances. The "repertoire" of being toilet trained, as it turns out in our society, is a central one if the child's learning in other spheres is to take place normally. Thus, in most public school systems the child must be toilet trained to be accepted into regular kindergarten. Because of this stricture, an incontinent child will not receive the normal learning opportunities. This deficit in learning will later lead to deficits disadvantageous to the child.

This example has been employed to demonstrate simply the principle involved. The principle is that deficits in behavior may create social situations that result in further abnormal learning. This may occur even though the behavior involved is not complex, or itself significant. Elaboration of this example illustrates also the types of circumstances that can occur when an important behavioral skill is not learned by the child at the usual time. That is, after the child reaches a certain age and is not yet continent, the parent and child become the target of social censure. The parent becomes aware that something is wrong. Usually the parent, with his conception of biological development, will conclude that the child is at fault. In any event, the parent will be moved to attempt to solve the problem by some teaching method. Since the parent is not informed about the appropriate training methods, it is likely he will fail when he explicitly tries to train his child.

Whenever a parent makes a concerted attempt to teach a child something —which appears to be a simple learning task—and meets with failure, this is very aversive to the parent. This is especially true if the failure meets with social censure. As a consequence, the parent is likely to resort to a commonly used training method, punishment. The punishment may not even be physical, although frequently it will be. The punishment may simply be admonition to try harder, to not behave like a baby, and so on. Other reprimands may be employed, the child may be restricted as a punishment, rewarding activities and objects withdrawn, and so forth.

The fact is that punishment should not be involved in toilet training. Punishment elicits negative emotional responses incompatible with eliminatory responses. Such training will thus be unsuccessful. Furthermore, it will produce other behaviors that are undesirable. For one thing, the more the parent administers punishment of whatever kind, the less the parent will be a positive reinforcer for the child. The child thus will learn negative social attitudes, one aspect of which is to make adults ineffective in future training of the child, leading to further deficits in the child's learning. In the specific case the child will many times also learn to avoid the toilet-training situation. Once he has learned a fear response to the situation, he will avoid going into the bathroom with the parent, he will stay out of the parent's way at times appropriate for elimination, and so on. This, of course, will ensure that the child has more accidents, receives more punishment, and avoids the toilet-training situation even more strongly.

This is a simple example, but it is suggested that this type of interaction can be multiplied until it covers many aspects of the child's life. An example of the interaction of abnormal behavior learning and behavior deficits of a more complex kind—including intelligence deficits—will further indicate the principle of the downward spiral of cumulative learning. The case will illustrate how deficits in some of the more complex intellectual skills can result in further learning of unfortunate abnormal behaviors, and vice versa.

The example concerns a preschool child who, because of severe deficits in his early training, had developed vast deficits in some of the basic behavioral repertoires that have been described herein. His behavior was not under the control of words. You could not give him even a simple verbal direction and expect him to respond appropriately. He had no functional speech himself. He could imitate some words, but as is characteristic of children with such behavior problems, he imitated inappropriately, in a manner technically called echolalia. In short, he had no language repertoire that he could use in interaction with other children or adults. It was obvious that words as stimuli did not elicit appropriate meaning responses in the child; thus the words could not serve as rewards for the child. The child did not score at all on an individual-administered intelligence test. These deficits are severe enough to get him the label "mental retardate." The child was also largely not toilet trained, nor did he have a repertoire of social interaction skills.

On the opposite side of the ledger, the child had already acquired repertoires of "skilled" abnormal behaviors. He had learned "uncontrolled" motor behaviors of getting things for himself, such as in ransacking the refrigerator and food shelves to secure things that he wanted but was not supposed to have. He had also learned a number of abnormal behaviors that would get him out of situations aversive to him. Thus, when he was taken places that were boring to him—such as the grocery store, shopping tours, sightseeing excursions, and so on—he would behave in ways that the parents thought indicated he had "gone out of his mind." He might scream, look and act wildly, run around in a frenzy, go lifeless, and so on. When he behaved in a sufficiently "crazy" manner, convincing them he was indeed in a crazy spell, his parents would take him home, thus rewarding him by taking him out of the aversive (boring) situation. He would also go into these "crazy" behaviors when put into other situations he did not find rewarding. Thus, he would not go to sleep at night, he would not allow himself to be trained in any manner, and so on. As a matter of fact, as soon as a situation took on any of the flavor of training, he would escape the situation. (This indicated that training situations had been aversive for him in the past.) The parents would let him have his way once they were convinced he was "out of his head," that is, was crazy. They thus were teaching him, inadvertently, to behave more and more bizarrely, since they only gave him what he wanted (reinforced him) when he behaved that way. He also employed these bizarre behaviors when he was being punished, because he could avoid the punishment when it was thought he was "out of his head" and not responsible.

(This is a brief analysis of how a child comes to acquire behaviors that will lead him to be diagnosed as psychotic, autistic, or emotionally disturbed. It should be noted that there should be no implication that the parents involved were morally reprehensible in some way. Their problem was one of lack of knowledge—and it is interesting to note that standard professional advice in this case did not help in the solution of their child's problems. Their persistent search for help, however, indicated their good intentions.)

At any rate, it is easy to see how this combination of deficits in desirable behaviors, and repertoires of abnormal behaviors, would result in further difficulty for the child and prevent his continued behavioral development. Let us take his intellectual deficits as the example. The fact that the child had not learned a repertoire of behaviors under the control of words (as in following directions) strictly limited and distorted the further social, intellectual, and emotional learning of the child. It was quite evident that the child could receive little tuition from a teacher in nursery school whose major training contact would have been on a verbal level. Moreover, his deficits prevented him from gaining normal social learning with classmates. A child might say to him, "Let us play cars. You go get the red car." Such a verbal stimulus would elicit no appropriate response in him. Or a group of children might ask him to play house and suggest that he be the father. When this elicited no appropriate behavior, the children would get someone else. Much of even four-year-olds' play takes place through the use of language. This boy was unable to participate, to gain the social rewards of play, and in the process to learn important new intellectual and emotional responses.

In addition, the boy himself could not speak to obtain the things he wanted from other children. He also could not indicate his displeasure with things and thereby control appropriate behavior from other children. Children are quick to learn the handicaps of another child at this age, and to take advantage of these handicaps. This child was thus the butt of many hazing actions of other children.

These deficits in behavior, plus the abnormal behaviors the child would display (such as screaming bizarrely from time to time), also made the other children respond to this child atypically in other ways. The children, when they would play with him at all, would play with him in unusual ways that could be described as hazing or baiting the child. Moreover, he would encourage this—it being his only source of attention—and he would play the fool in other ways for the social reward involved. This, of course, trained him additionally to undesirable behaviors. These and his other unfortunate interactions with the other children would at a later time surely have the effect of training him to negative attitudes toward other children. Without some type of benign intervention, it would be expected that this negative attitudinal learning would have been greatly increased in the child's future.

In addition, because words as stimuli elicited no imaginal-meaning responses in the child, nor any emotional-meaning responses, there were other ways that this child could not profit from the school program. Most children learn a great deal from stories the teacher tells them in preschool. To this child, however, the verbal stimuli of stories were so much nonsense stimulation. While the other children sat and listened to the teacher, their attentional behaviors reinforced by the imaginal and emotional responses elicited by the words, this child would be in a situation where he was receiving no reinforcement of any kind. The other children were not attending to him or playing with him. The teacher was not attending to him or rewarding him in any way.

The manner in which deficits in behavior can produce abnormal behaviors can be well exemplified in this one situation; for if this particular child in the above situation sits quietly, he is in a state of deprivation for attention or any other rewarding event. While the other children are reinforced by the story, he has no source of reinforcement. Let us say, however, that he gets up and begins to wander about the room—which in itself is inappropriate in this situation—and finally bangs on the piano, or begins to run around in a frenzy, or does something else to attract attention. When this has occurred and he has disrupted the story telling time, the child is rewarded by removing the aversive situation and by gaining attention for his disruptive behavior. Thus, again, the one sure source of reinforcement for this child is through the display of some type of disruptive behavior. He will as a consequence learn new "abnormal" behaviors to this school situation. These behaviors will keep him from learning adjustive behavioral skills, however. Moreover, in the usual situation it is this type of behavior that will result in the child being placed in a class for emotionally disturbed children, where his opportunities for normal learning will be reduced and his opportunities for learning abnormal behaviors from other children through imitation will be increased.

In conclusion, it may be suggested that the four-year-old child who has been described would ordinarily as a consequence of his grievous behavioral deficits encounter a continued social experience that would cumulatively add to his nonadjustive, abnormal behaviors. Moreover, he would cumulatively acquire behavioral deficit piled on top of behavioral deficits. After a long history of this kind, the character of the individual's behavior may be so different from normal that one could not easily see how it could have been acquired according to normal principles of development. Long-term analysis of the complex learning circumstances, in the context of the concepts of hierarchical learning, can indicate how such circumstances occur. Moreover, such analyses—because they are based upon empirical principles—can be employed to avoid such circumstances, or to treat such problems once they have arisen.

One additional case will be cited to further illustrate the concepts involved, as well as to indicate the generality of the concepts. The child was a juvenile delinquent, from a family that had already produced three older brothers who were also delinquent. The boy in question had severe deficits in his intellectual repertoires. As a fourteen-year-old, he was reading at the second-grade level, for example. The case may be considered in the following terms. The child had certain deficits in his basic behavioral repertoires on entering school. He was thus not successful enough to merit much positive social reinforcement in the school situation. Moreover, the home situation was one where the means of controlling the children was physical punishment. Lesser forms of admonition thus never become effective controlling stimuli for the boy. This child consequently lacked an adequate motivational system where he had learned positive reward for achievement and negative value for admonition.

Thus, this child went to school but did not attend well and did not do the assigned work. There was no reward for him that would maintain such arduous behaviors. He thus did not learn well. As would be expected, after a few years of school where the conditions of learning were not appropriate for the child because there were no adequate sources of reward, he had not acquired the behavioral skills acquired by more fortunate classmates. The previous experiences of these children had established a more appropriate motivational system. Moreover, their basic intellectual skills gave them a better start in the learning task, so they received more social rewards.

At any rate, after a child's intellectual deficits begin to be evident, the child with the lack of skilled behavior is likely to be treated aversively. That is, as in the present case, the child with a reading deficit (or other evidence of underachievement) is likely to be gibed at and teased when he is still young, and ignored, avoided, and looked down upon when he is older. Moreover, as indicated, he does not receive the same social rewards as other children of more fortunate circumstances. (The absence of approval, in a situation where others are getting such approval, may also be considered to be aversive for humans.) Although the individuals who provide the aversive stimuli, and withhold the rewards, may not intend to be aversive, such actions constitute the presentation of aversive stimuli. Furthermore, this presentation of aversive stimuli by other "successful" children and, as in this case, by teachers who were antagonized by the child, would be expected to result in further learning, but learning of an undesirable nature. For these successful children, teachers, academic materials, and the total school situation can in this way become learned negative reinforcers. This may be translated to say that the child acquires strong negative attitudes toward school. Such attitudes are abnormal in that they are unusual, and also because they will induce behaviors that will be highly undesirable. In the present case there was much evidence of this in that the child baited teachers and students, fought in school, disrupted class, and the like. Later, he participated in vandalizing a school—very direct evidence of his negative attitudes. Such a child will in general also "escape" the school in various ways, such as daydreaming and absenteeism, which further aggravates the deficits he already has. At any rate, as this case demonstrates again, a deficit in behavior, resulting from an inappropriate motivational system, can lead to further development of inappropriate attitudes (aspects of the motivational system) as well as to inappropriate and maladjustive behaviors.

THE DOWNWARD SPIRAL OF
HIERARCHICAL LEARNING

The hierarchical conception of learning that has been presented herein has suggested that learning to be a human is a long-term affair. It involves a process where a repertoire of behavioral skills is learned that is the basis for the learning of additional, more advanced behavioral skills. The acquisition of the new skills, in combination with others already acquired, then enables the acquisition of even more advanced behavioral skills. We can only understand the learning of complex repertoires of great skill in terms of the basic skills upon which the advanced learning is founded.

Following this conception, an analogy will be posed, which while not being recommended or approved, nevertheless seems to pertain. That is, children may be considered to be in a kind of race. The race involves the rapidity and excellence displayed in the acquisition of successively advancing behavioral skills. The race pertains to a large extent all the way through childhood and into and through adulthood.

In this race the child who more quickly acquires certain behavioral repertoires also creates a situation that tends to accelerate his further acquisition of new repertoires. This occurs in two ways. First, the early acquisition of the basic behavioral repertoires will provide the foundation for further skill acquisition. In addition, however, the acquisition of a repertoire of skills at an early time has social consequences. For society in general, and that segment of it which is personal to the child, will provide social rewards to the "winners" of the race at every level of skill acquisition. The informal "competition" involves the various types of skill the child must acquire—ranging from talking first, walking first, and so on, as gauged by the developmental charts, through later acquisition of academic and athletic skills as evidenced by grades, scholarships, honors, intelligence tests, and success in organized sports. The child who is advanced in the acquisition of skilled repertoires will receive social rewards more heavily than the not-so-advanced child. Such rewards will contribute strongly to maintaining the work and learning behaviors of the child for the many learning tasks that remain in the hierarchical task of human learning.

Thus, the child who is more advanced in acquiring skills and thus has the basic skills for the next task will also have created for himself a situation conducive to continued work and learning. When as a result he learns the next repertoire of skills more rapidly than other children, he enhances these salubrious conditions for further learning. Moreover, as has been indicated, there are other conditions that will tend to support the "winners" in the race as they continue. The advanced child will have parents who are able instructors. Ordinarily they will continue throughout to provide the child with superior learning advantages.

In contrast, let us take the case of the child who does not gain his initial repertoires as rapidly as most other children because of poor learning conditions for one reason or another. In this case, in the race we can expect to see a downward spiral of relative performance. The child who acquires his basic behavioral repertoire more slowly than others is not ready as soon to succeed in the task of learning the next more advanced skill. Moreover, at any level, as a consequence of being a laggard in the learning race he will find himself in a less propitious social circumstance of reward for learning. Thus, his attentional and working behaviors will be poor, and his learning will be at a less rapid rate than would be the case in better motivating conditions. Moreover, it can be expected that these conditions grow progressively worse. The less advanced the performance, the less the reward. The less the reward, the less the maintenance of learning behaviors. The less advanced the learning, the greater the decrease in the reward, and so on. The mental retardate can expect to find himself in such a downward spiral of relative progress in learning.

As has already been suggested, the downward spiral may be exacerbated by the conditions that result from retarded learning. The social consequences of being a loser in the learning race can create conditions by which the child learns undesirable behaviors considered abnormal. These behaviors will frequently be such that they interfere with the further learning of the repertoires of skills demanded by society. When this occurs, the downward spiral of relative learning is accelerated. In certain cases the learning of the child can switch almost entirely to the learning of undesirable behaviors that we can conceive of as being basic behavioral repertoires of abnormal behaviors. That is, the acquisition of some abnormal behaviors will enable the acquisition of others. This may include the production of a social situation that is conductive to learning abnormal behaviors. Sometimes the conducive situation for learning abnormal behaviors is an institution, as has been indicated for retardates and as is usually the case also for emotionally disturbed, psychotic, autistic, or delinquent children.

While the concept cannot be elaborated here, it may be suggested that the severity and type of abnormal behavior that the person develops will be influenced by the point in the hierarchical development at which the child falls behind. The most severely incapacitated are those who have widespread deficits in those basic behavioral repertoires ordinarily acquired early in life. If the child has large deficits in any of the basic behavioral repertoires described in this book, for example, it can be expected that the child will be severely handicapped. It may be suggested that the severe mental retardate is a child who has gaping deficits in these basic behavioral repertoires. The autistic child is also a child who has suffered unfortunate circumstances in his early learning of this type—and who has in addition learned bizarre and maladjustive repertoires of behavior that further prevent him from learning the necessary repertorial skills. A child who has acquired the basic behavioral skills to a better extent, but not well enough to do well in more advanced learning, will develop different behavior problems. He will never be so totally incapacitated, but he may nevertheless not learn enough of the more advanced repertoires to do well. And in the process of "losing" he may develop other undesirable behaviors, such as the already mentioned juvenile delinquent child had acquired.

TREATMENT: THE CREATION OF NORMAL REPERTOIRES

It is not the purpose of the present book to indicate how various types of abnormal behaviors are acquired through learning, or to specify in detail how the vicious cycles of progressive deterioration can take place. Furthermore, the present discussion cannot discuss in any detail how abnormal behavior, of types not dealt with herein, can be treated although the principles have wide applicability. Several points may be made, however, that bear upon the statement made in the introduction that there has been an overemphasis upon the abnormal behavior itself and its treatment, to an exclusion of realizing the central role of normal repertoires in adjustment. The creation of such normal repertoires should actually be a focus in the treatment of abnormal behavior. This is especially important in dealing with children, when there is still ample opportunity to repair any behavioral deficits that have arisen.

Thus, it may be suggested that in each of the types of problems that has been dealt with, a heavy contribution, if not the primary cause, was the deficit in learning the child had suffered. This conception leads one to propose treatment procedures quite different from those that might be advised if one focused upon the abnormal behaviors themselves. That is, in the case of the juvenile delinquent, the child's abnormal behaviors consisted of various antisocial acts— he fought with other students, baited the teachers, cursed in the schoolroom, and performed acts of vandalism. If one focused upon these behaviors, one might attempt to decrease them in some manner— through psychotherapy, through rewarding the child for every day during which he made no such behaviors, and so on.

On the other hand, if the problem is analyzed as one that focally has involved behavioral deficits which prevent the child from making normal progress in school, from gaining the social rewards of such progress, and so on, then there are different implications. Then one would be concerned, first, with repairing the child's behavioral deficits. In the present case, treatment based upon such an analysis (see Staats and Butterfield, 1965) was introduced into the child's downward cycle of learning. This was done by instituting an effective system of rewards for the child's learning of reading. The child was given tokens for reading learning in a training program that took place over a 4½ month period. Like money, the tokens could be exchanged for material things the child wanted—a pair of Beatle shoes, a ticket to a movie, fifty cents to give to a brother on his way to a reformatory.

This token-reward system provided reinforcement for normal learning that had formerly been lacking.

Although not sufficient to complete the repair of the child's behavioral deficits, it was clear that the treatment produced solid movement in that direction. The child's reading achievement increased from the second-grade level to the fourth-grade level. He passed his courses in school, for the first time in his life. He reported a change in attitude toward his classes and studies from negative to positive. Moreover, his "abnormal" behaviors, *which had not themselves been treated,* decreased in frequency. For in the first month of treatment he was apprehended in school and was given demerits for acting out misbehaviors ten times. In succeeding months this dropped first to four times, then to two, and then to zero. The indications were that his new skills had begun to bring him more social reinforcement in school— lack of which was one of his primary problems. The results of this case, which have been supported by studies that employed the training methods with additional children, suggest that if this child had not had motivational and behavioral deficits to begin with, he would not have displayed the other undesirable behaviors that were the problem to society.

Another case that was discussed involved the four-year-old preschool child who had not acquired the basic language-intellectual repertoires and avoided learning situations, while he had acquired bizarre behaviors such as hyperactivity, making sudden crazy noises, and so on. This child previously was diagnosed as emotionally disturbed with brain damage, and the focus of interest was upon the child's abnormal behaviors. The treatment stemming from this diagnosis was the administration of drugs to sedate the child and thus diminish the hyperactivity and bizarre behaviors. The author, however, had the child treated in an experimental preschool situation in which rewards were made contingent upon appropriate social behaviors in interaction with other children. The child was also given toilet training. The focus of the treatment, however, was on the repair of the child's basic behavioral language-intellectual repertoires. For this, an effective reinforcement system was again used. This system was based upon tokens that the child could use to get things that he wanted. The child was given training in various aspects of the language-intellectual repertoires that have been described herein.[1] His abnormal behaviors of hyperactivity, silly behavior, bizarre noises, and so on were not dealt with. His mother, on the other hand, was instructed by the author to give the child attention from time to time when he was playing nicely. She was also instructed in methods of training her child in some of the basic behavioral repertoires that have been described; as well as in toilet training, putting the child to bed (a nightly travail), in controlling the child, in playing with the child and, on the other hand in removing some of their harmful interactions.

It was interesting to note as the child acquired the basic behavioral repertoires of language, this provided him with the skills with which to interact with other children in a mutually rewarding manner. As this occurred, the

[1]Carl G. Carlson, as a graduate student, assisted in administering the language-intellectual training to the child.

abnormal behaviors that had formerly gotten him the social reinforcement of attention began to diminish relative to his normal behavior. He got more and better social reinforcement through his normal behavior. After a few weeks the child was taken off the drug treatment. This improvement was extended to the child's home. Besides a marked decrease in his abnormal behaviors there, after some months of treatment he became able for the first time to play with other neighborhood children and to acquire friends. His change in behavior also led to a positive change in the way his parents responded to him, which also contributed to his normal learning. Although the process was not complete in the one school year of treatment, it was evident that the principle of focusing upon the repair of his behavioral deficits was the appropriate strategy.

The last example involves the very central problem of child development that is referred to as mental retardation. In some cases this condition is due to actual physical defect. That is, there is a small percentage of children who by direct observation are seen to have biological deficits. There are mongoloid children, microcephalics, and so on, and those who have suffered actual brain damage extensive enough to impair normal learning functions. Most children who are diagnosed as mental retardates, however, have no detectable physical deficits. It is clear that the diagnosis rests only upon the fact that the child has not acquired the behavioral repertoires acquired by most children. Because the child has not acquired, for example, the basic behavioral repertoires that have been described herein, he is also not able even when presented with additional learning conditions to learn in a normal manner. It thus appears as if the child has a limited learning ability—and there is a general tendency to infer that the child must therefore be biologically defective in some manner.

It follows from the present learning conception that such cases of mental retardation could be effectively treated by appropriate training conditions— especially if they were commenced early enough in the child's history. It may be noted that the four-year-old preschooler with the abnormal behaviors increased in intelligence measurement from zero IQ to one of 50 as he began to acquire the various basic behavioral repertoires. Moreover, in a study previously mentioned, twelve culturally deprived children increased an average of 11.6 IQ points in 7½ months of training. It may be suggested that successful training in the basic behavioral repertoires would thus eradicate the possibility of the many children being severely retarded—if the training was commenced early. Many cases of retardation that we attribute to poor intelligence are actually due to (1) deficits in the learning of the basic behavioral repertoires, (2) inadequacies in the child's motivational system or in the motivational system of the institution (for example, the school) that is responsible for his training, or (3) inappropriate (abnormal) behaviors that interfere with learning. When these conditions are taken care of, we can expect the child's "defects" in learning to disappear.

In conclusion, the primary point of the present discussion is to emphasize that the first line of defense against behavioral deficits and abnormalities is an adequate "offense"—that is, early preventive treatment. The most desirable way of eliminating spirals of deterioration such as have been described lies in providing the positive learning conditions the child requires to acquire his adjustive behavioral repertoires. When this is done, severe deficits and abnormal behaviors will be prevented. We thus need a change in emphasis. It should change from a focus upon abnormal behavior and the direct treatment of such behavior once it has arisen to a focus upon *prevention*. Prevention can be largely achieved through helping disseminate principles and methods that will allow parents to produce the requisite normal behaviors in their children. The presence of such repertoires of normal behavioral skills will not allow the development of abnormal behaviors of various kinds. This prevention, however, depends upon informed parents. The next chapter will consider some additional points in considering the parent's role in the child's vast learning task.

In concluding, a quotation of the author's will be added that can be employed to address the general problem to the professions that work with children with abnormal behaviors.

> Clinical [professions] in following the "[mental] illness model" that has pervaded the field of "mental health" [have] tended to concentrate on the intrapsychic life of the child, his gross social-emotional adjustment, and grossly aberrant behavior, sometimes neglecting consideration of his cognitive learning. If cognitive training is regarded "as it is in many mental health programs, as something that can wait until the child gets better" (Hobbs, 1966, p. 1111), the disturbed child can develop severe cognitive deficits that will preclude later adjustment regardless of any diminution of other difficulties. The complex cognitive skills the child must learn require long periods of training and innumerable training trials. It is suggested that clearing up some other form of behavorial disturbance will not provide the child with those skills as one might erroneously assume from a "mental block" interpretation of cognitive deficit.
>
> "Underachievement in school is the single most common characteristic of emotionally disturbed children" (Hobbs, 1966, p. 1110). It may be added that perhaps the most important significance of emotional disturbance in children is in the manner in which [these behavioral difficulties] prevent normal social learning, cognitive learning, sensory-motor learning, emotional learning, and so on (Staats, Minke, Goodwin, and Landeen, 1967, p. 298).

It may be added that in this sense the present book, in addition to presenting concepts, principles, and procedures by which children can be trained to normal behavioral repertoires, also represents a psychology for dealing with children with problems. That is, as pertained with the four-year-old child who had the severe deficits and the bizzare behaviors, it is suggested that many cases of mental retardation, autism, childhood schizophrenia, and so on involve deficits in the types of basic behavioral skills discussed herein. These discussions can be used as the basis for treating such problems—and in this respect may be considered as behavior-modification theory and procedures by those concerned with such abnormal behaviors.

chapter 16/ Social Implications of the Learning Conception and the Behavioral Interaction Approach

In concluding this book, a few additional words may be said about several implications and extensions of the present conception. One of the important implications involves the role of the parent as a primary agent in the transfer of the accumulated skills of the culture to the child.

THE PARENT AS INSTRUCTOR

Today there are a number of professions concerned with the development of the child. It should be noted, however, that not one of them has had as a central area the systematic study of the child in his task of learning the very complex repertoires of skill that make him into a human being. For example, there are various types of psychologists—some concerned with human learning—but there are very few who have received training or experience in studying individual children over long periods of time engaged in the learning of complex repertoires of functional skills. Skills of the type that have been described herein, as well as the other skills required for individual adjustment, have not generally been studied in psychology—even though the necessary methods and principles may be derived from the basic field. Because of this lack of study, psychology has not heretofore been able to provide the information needed by the parent in the task he faces as the young child's primary instructor.

The field of medicine has much less contact with the study of child learning. Medical doctors have thus had no systematic training in how to work with children engaged in the complex learning tasks involved in development. Medicine, as well as its basic biological and pharmacological sciences, do not have the methods or principles by which to study the child's complex learning. Thus, the field has not dealt with this type of knowledge.

One might think at first glance that the field of education would certainly be concerned with child learning and thus be a source of knowledge concerning the principles of child learning. But a closer inspection of the actual situation reveals the same gap here. The practices of education have been established through the trial-and-error procedures of practical experience, not from systematic methods of research on learning. Thus, basic principles have not emerged from the field of education—nor, indeed, has any special conception of human behavior. It could be said that teachers work with children all the time, and thus must know a great deal about child learning that could be generalized to other situations—such as to the early learning of children. But do teachers actually work with the learning of children in a manner that reveals the principles by which children learn? Actually, no. Teachers never really have the opportunity for the study of individual children engaged in complex learning tasks. There is little chance for the detailed study of child learning of any kind in the practice of education. Moreover, the teacher does not have access to the basic learning principles or methods of research, so is not prepared to profit from the experience that is available. Thus, education cannot tell the parent how to produce the young child's learning, or even what the child should learn in the way of preacademic intellectual skills. The conceptions of human behavior and child learning that one sees in education are exactly the same as those held by the common culture. This is not said in criticism, for it is neither the task of education nor of the individual teacher to discover and to research the general principles of child learning.

What this adds up to, however, is that the professions and sciences concerned with human behavior have not generally studied child behavior within a context that yields the knowledge of child learning that is necessary. There has not been an understanding of how the young child learns his functional repertoires of behavioral skills. There has not been knowledge of the principles involved, of the procedures by which the child can actually be trained, or indeed of the manner and course in which the training should be conducted.

Partially for this reason, the present author began the study of the child's learning of actual, functional, behavioral skills—as part of the general study of human learning. This study of child learning has included work with various children, including the long-term study of his own children. Moreover, the principles investigated in naturalistic circumstances have been verified and elaborated in systematic, controlled study with additional children (see Staats, 1968a).

Actually, the author in 1963 outlined a learning conception of child development as part of his general conception of human behavior. Areas of learning were covered, such as sensory-motor development, feeding problems, toilet training, crying behavior, dependent behavior, socially-controlling stimuli, social reasoning, training involving sex behavior, language and intellectual behavior, and so on. An important part of this conception was that the child developed through learning. Much of this learning was said to take place in the home. Thus, the parent was seen to have an enormous role as a trainer of his child. Moreover, since publishing this learning conception of child development, the work of other investigators has begun to accrue supporting the approach as well as the specific analyses made (Hawkins, Peterson, Schweid, and Bijou, 1966; O'Leary, O'Leary, and Becker, 1967; Wahler, Winkle, Peterson, and Morrison, 1965; Wolf, Risley, and Mees, 1964). The author has also continued his work since that time to gain further knowledge of child learning and to study methods for generally producing desirable child development through learning procedures.

A central point in the author's first outline was that the parent needed a conception of child learning to help him deal with the problems encountered in child rearing. A number of studies since then have begun to corroborate this point also. That is, other investigators have begun working with parents within the context of learning principles and methods. The purpose has been to improve parental training methods and thereby resolve the child's problems.

These studies are only the beginning of the deluge that is needed to provide the information we must have to better understand and deal with various aspects of human development. This understanding is especially important for early child learning, when it is possible to do something about problems of child development relatively easily. It is thus important to continue to emphasize these points, since the importance of the parent as an instructor is not generally recognized and the implications of this conception have not been exercised in science, in education, in the medical or psychological clinic, and in the home, as they should be.

In summary, a learning analysis of the acquisition of behavior by the child leads to a focus upon the parent as the instructor or trainer of the child. Whether the parent intends to or not, he manipulates many conditions of learning that determine to a large extent the behaviors the child will acquire. As has been indicated in the repertoires discussed, the child's behavioral development consists of innumerable training experiences, many of which occur in the home. As a consequence, the parent has in his hands the conditions that determine his child's behavioral development. The parent has this power regardless of his philosophy of child development, and whether or not he wants it.

Thus, the parent faces what is in actuality a formidable task. Not only is he largely responsible for the manner in which the child learns his basic intellectual behavioral repertoires in early childhood, he has a great influence upon the manner of the child's nonintellective learning in social, sensorimotor, and attitudinal areas during early childhood, childhood, and adolescence. Much of the training necessary to produce these repertoires takes place in the informality of everyday living, and we customarily do not realize the tuition that is necessary to produce a normally behaving child. Nevertheless, when the basic behavioral repertoires are described, even when restricted in considering development, it becomes clear that a great deal of the child's basic behavioral repertoires are acquired in the home, and that the parents are primarily responsible for the training.

It must be evident also on the basis of the preceding analyses that our educational system, and our society, depend upon the training that the parent gives to his child. This has only been recognized weakly, however, and the implications and ramifications of this aspect of our educational system have not been delineated. When an analysis of the child's learning is made, however, it can be seen that child learning is an area of fundamental weakness in our whole educational system. When the child's emotional, motor, and social learning are also considered, we may see that problems of child training by the parent are fundamental to other social institutions in addition to education.

What is true from the standpoint of the needs of the society is also true for the needs of the parent himself. The parent is interested in producing a child who will contribute positively to the society. But he is even more personally interested in contributing to the development of his child so that the child will adjust well to life's responsibilities and in general achieve a happy, productive life circumstance.

From the child's standpoint, of course, conditions that will provide him with the various social, emotional (motivational), intellectual, and motor skills that result in his successful negotiation of life's opportunities are of very central importance. The parent's ability to provide the conditions that will produce a child with the requisite learning in these various spheres may be considered crucial to all participants: the individual child, the parent, and to society and the various social institutions that have contact with the child. There are several points that should be made in emphasizing the responsibilities and problems the parent faces in the early training of his children.

First, it appears that a most important part of the child's training—perhaps *the* most important part—is the responsibility of "instructors," the parents, who themselves receive no systematic training in the requisite skills or the knowledge involved in conducting the child's training. The parent's ability as a trainer of the child will depend upon his own individual training history— as well as upon the personal circumstances of adjustment that pertain at the time the child is reared. If the parent is himself the product of a fortunate history, and his life circumstances are benign, he will behave as a successful parent. If the parent is not so fortunate, there is no reason to expect that he will be able to learn the necessary skills and knowledge on his own.

However, not only does the parent not receive through informal societal channels any systematic training to be applied in training his children, there has been no source from whence the individual parent may secure such training or information. With very few exceptions, there has been no provision of materials, procedures, or understanding with which to aid the parent in the prodigious tasks he faces in training a child to become an accomplished human being. The parent can expect no help, regardless of the great complexity of the task that is involved.

It is suggested that the *usual* parent with a *usual* child has great need for understanding what the child is as an organism, especially that the central aspect of humanness is in the things the child will learn—not in his organic development. The parent also needs to know the types of learning essential to the child. The parent must know what his role is in producing the learning conditions that will result in the child acquiring those essential social, emotional, intellectual, and motor skills.

It has been said that the necessary information is not available for the usual parent with the usual child, the cases where no unusual problems arise. However, the parent who encounters unusual problems—some of which arise because of the parent's unfilled need for help—is expected to handle such problems on his own, again without any special information. We presently expect the population of parents to generally treat widely divergent training problems, many of them of a special nature. For the most part, we expect the parents of a deaf child to provide the unusual training necessary to give the child a full basic behavioral repertoire, as we do also for the parents of the child handicapped in other ways, the child who has special illnesses, the child who is a special training problem because of the behavioral deficits from whatever cause, and the child who for similar reasons has developed inappropriate behaviors that interfere with his learning. These expectations are entirely unreasonable. We could only hold such expectations on the basis of an inadequate conception of human development.

At this point it is relevant to quote an excerpt from the author's 1963 learning analysis of child development, indicative of the important role played by the parent in the child's early behavioral advancement.

> In these discussions it has also been suggested that the parent plays a most important role in the training of these complex behaviors. As a consequence, for a parent faced with the task of providing propitious learning conditions, a simple analysis of behavior leading to very general instructions for child care may be insufficient, if not actually harmful. For example, a philosophy of development stages or maturational processes, while it may at times serve various purposes, such as quieting the mother's fears, is not sufficient in the many training tasks where the parent must take positive action.
>
> Or, to take another example, it is also frequently suggested that specific training is unnecessary and that it is the parent's attitude which is crucial to acquisition of behavioral skills . . ., that the parents must be loving and warm and comforting and not rejecting or frustrating. However, it would seem that this is not sufficient as an instruction to a parent, nor would it necessarily provide a good learning atmosphere for the child. Within the pattern of a loving mother, widely different training practices leading to widely different behaviors of the children could occur.
>
> On the other hand, there are aspects of the parents' love for the child that would seem to be affected by their ability as trainers. Much has been said of the cold, loveless, rejecting mother. Little has been said of the fact that there are great differences in the "attractiveness," or positive reinforcing qualities, of the behavior of their children. Some children are "lovable," their behavior has many positive features and few aversive ones. The child whose

behavior has aversive aspects—the whining, crying, complaining child; or the overshy, dependent, nonresponsive child; or the aggressive, cruel, hostile, demanding child, and so on—will not acquire positive reinforcing value (be lovable) as a function of this type of behavior.

The social interactions of individuals and the extent to which they are "attractive" to others depend to an important extent upon the reinforcing value of their behavior. It would be expected that this would hold as well for the parent-child relationship. In order for the parent to be a positive reinforcing stimulus object for the child, the child has to receive positive reinforcement in the presence of the parent. It is suggested that the same is true in reverse, how-ever, and that one of the important sources of reinforcement for the parent is the behavior of the child. It would be expected that the degree to which the parent is loving will depend to some extent upon the behavior of the child.

Thus, the fact that a mother cares for a child as a duty without enthusiasm, or is cold, loveless, and rejecting, may be secondary. That is, her behavior may be a result of the fact that she does not have the skills as a trainer with which to produce behavior in her child which is reinforcing to her and to others. As a consequence she receives relatively little positive reinforcement from the child, as well as relatively little positive reinforcement from other people concerning her child.

In summary, a learning analysis of the acquisition of behavior leads to a focus upon the parent as a **trainer**. . . . This suggests that the parent could be an active participant in arranging circumstances to most efficaciously produce an abundant, rich, adjustive, behavioral repertoire using a minimum of aversive stimulation and a maximum of positive reinforcement. Good working behaviors, good studying behaviors, the ability to work without immediate reinforcement; reasonable, cooperative, not overselfish behavior; a good language system about the world, his own behavior, and that of others; a good system of reinforcers, including words of positive and negative reinforcement value; social stimuli that appropriately control striving and nonstriving behavior; social behaviors that reinforce other people as well as oneself; these seem to be some of the behaviors that the parents help determine by the conditions they present to the child. Thus, to a large extent the learning conditions that occur in the home would seem to determine whether the child will grow into a "well-adjusted," "happy," "productive" individual (pp. 411–413).

When one realizes the very complex repertoires of behavioral skill that the child has to acquire, simple instructions to the parent to establish a loving, accepting, home are inadequate. The parent needs a detailed understanding of what the child has to learn, how the child learns, and how the parent holds in his hands the conditions which will or will not produce that learning. The parent needs to know how to produce desirable behaviors in the child, and how to eliminate undesirable behaviors benignly. The present conception of basic behavioral repertoires, the way such repertoires are developed through learning, and the hierarchical form of more advanced learning provide such a view of child development. When we look at the parents as the trainers of complex basic behavioral repertoires, we can realize the extent of the knowledge the parent should have available. The preceding chapters have dealt with some of these repertoires of behavior and with the role of the parent in producing such skills in the child. The next sections will indicate some of the additional implications of the learning conception of child development.

EMOTIONAL OBSTACLES
TO THE LEARNING CONCEPTION

It should be noted that the lack of scientific and professional understanding of child development through learning has several explanations. Some of these have already been indicated. For one thing, it has taken time for the science to develop its methods, principles, and procedures to a point where they could be applied to human problems of the world. Not until there was this foundation could a general conception be formulated that would influence many people away from their common-sense notions.

It is important to realize ,however, that the competition among conceptions is not an emotionally neutral contest. We have only to look at the history of science to find issues that drew the most poignant involvement. It is interesting to note the title of A. D. White's history of the development of some of the basic scientific conceptions, *A History of the Warfare of Science and Theology* (1899). The term *warfare* tells us something about the intensity of the antagonism that can occur in the competition of ideas. It should be noted that the emotional investment in conceptions cannot be stronger than that which occurs in considering the nature of man himself. In fact, most of the other controversies were so bitterly contested because they had implications for the manner in which man was to be considered. Thus, in the present case, it is not just a matter of marshaling the facts to show that behavior is learned —many people will fight against such a conception because it seems to attack their central values. A moment should be spent in considering what some of these values are.

The Moral-Biological Conception
of Man's Differences

As a general conception, the suggestion that the child *learns* the behaviors that make him a person, that the parent contributes a great deal to this process, and so on, is repugnant to many people. The related suggestion that principles and procedures should be used to provide learning experiences that will ensure that all children will acquire similar levels of basic behavioral skills is also repugnant. The following is excerpted from an article in which the goal of providing all children with similar intellectual skills is considered in very negative terms.

> American educationists often have been repelled by the hetero-geneity that distinguishes American culture; they have long sought to establish what Horace Mann, the prototype of American educa-tionism, called the "common culture"—i,e., a socially and intel-lectually integrated and egalitarian society. . . . The egalitarianism of the common culture is, in Professor Cremin's phrase, 'a radical proposition that flies in the face of two thousand years of Western wisdom to the effect that true culture demands an elite." Indeed, conservative educators, from Cardinal Newman to Russell Kirk, have argued that the democratization of education adds up to nothing less than a vulgarization of the school and the destruction of true culture, which is anything but common (Witonski, 1968, p. 93).

Implicit in conceptions such as the preceding is the premise that the wide differences we see in the quality of human behavior are just and natural to man's state—to be expected and actually valued. In essence, excellence of be-havior and social and economic position may be considered to involve per-sonal and moral virtue. Basically, from this view, the individual is thought to be what he is because of divine gift, gained according to his and his people's level of righteousness.

When this type of conception is examined, it is clear why there is opposi-tion toward progress in finding methods and principles that will be univer-sally successful in producing accomplished children and accomplished human beings. Such methods are considered to be *artificial* means of producing ac-complishment in people who were not actually destined to be so rewarded. It is as though the true aim is being defeated. The biological-divine conception *begins* with the premise that men are different. This difference is assumed to come from biological and moral inheritance—this includes inheritance from family, social class, race, and in some cases religion or other social grouping. Any circumstance that attempts to disrupt this order is considered repugnant. If it is shown that methods can actually be successful in making accomplished individuals of people who formerly were not accomplished, and were con-sidered inferior, this is not considered as contraindicative for a biological-divine conception. The idea that man *is* what he learns is still rejected. The evidence is taken to suggest that human qualities are biological-divine in origin, but that there are illegitimate (and essentially evil) means by which these biological qualities can be circumvented. Evidence that *should* lead to a change in conception is thus negated. In doing so the evidence, the learning conception that the evidence suggests, and the methods of training emanating from these two, are rejected—in fact, all of these elements are considered to be morally condemned in some way.

This biological-divine conception of human behavior thus retards the de-velopment of a more socially productive conception. The biological-divine conception also holds back the development and use of methods by which to effect more adequate training procedures that would more widely produce accomplished humans. This is not said in specific criticism, for the biological-divine conception of human behavior is one common to our cultural background. It is thus, to varying degrees, part of the emotional belief systems of most of us. Nevertheless, at various points it conflicts with a learning conception of human behavior. It may be suggested that the learning conception is not only superior as a basis for dealing with individual children, it is superior as a social philosophy as well.

WE ARE WHAT WE LEARN: A HUMANISTIC
SOCIAL PHILOSOPHY

It may be suggested, thus, that the learning conception of human behavior that is being developed herein provides a more benign approach, and one that has more positive social implications than previous views. The learning conception says that there is no biological excellence that has been found in persons who are behaviorally superior. Moreover, there is no evidence that behaviorally superior persons are more favored by any divine force. Nor can such persons be considered morally superior in any way verifiable by evidence. *The learning conception suggests that people are what they have learned.*

It should be quite evident that a great deal of behavior that we see in favored individuals is what we should want to see in everyone. For example, we should wish everyone to have basic language-intellectual skills such as those the present book has begun to describe. We should wish everyone to have good emotional and motivational development, adequate work-learning attitudes, social behaviors, and so on. We should thus have no fear of the development of knowledge and procedures that would allow people in general to provide conditions for their children that would ensure the developmen of such behavioral skills. In this sense, means by which we would gain homogeneity in the behavior of children would not be condemned because they were producing automatons. To adjust and make one's way independently in our society demands a rich supply of skilled behavioral repertoires. No one would want conditions to be retained that produce individuals whose deficits and inappropriacies of learning make them dependent upon society for care.

Learning and Conformity

Several points may be added to allay any anxieties that standard principles of learning and standard procedures for producing certain behavioral skills may be too mechanistic. The use of such principles and procedures would not be expected to produce an objectionable conformity in the behavior of all children. Actually, the learning of the child is quite complex. The influences upon a child's learning are so multitudinous and variegated that no parent will put his "stamp" upon the child to the exclusion of other influences. The parent does have great influence. He, more than anyone else, is responsible for the rate, quality, and extensiveness with which the child acquires many of his basic behavioral repertoires. However, it has also been said that these basic behavioral repertoires are but the foundations upon which more advanced behavioral skills are constructed. And these more advanced skills are to a larger and larger extent the result of agencies, individuals, and occurrences that develop outside the home and over which the parent exercises a lesser and lesser amount of control as the child grows older. The hierarchical conception of human behavior gives the parent the function of the "starter" of the child's behavioral development. In addition, the parent is in a special position to guide the child through learning conditions he provides throughout childhood, in ways that will not be discussed herein. However, this guiding influence must be expected to diminish as the child grows older, until finally the parent has not much more influence than that of other individuals in the child's social environment, and in some cases much less influence than many other individuals.

Not only are there contributions to the child's learning from many sources besides the parents, but in addition the child himself begins to help determine the circumstances that he meets. It has been suggested that the behavioral skills the child acquires are not merely the effects of past learning conditions. In addition, the nature of the child's learned behaviors will determine to an important extent the types of learning conditions he will meet in the future. This is true of the interaction of parent and child. The parent is to a large extent the agent of the original learning conditions the child meets. But these conditions will produce behaviors in the child that will determine later behaviors of the parent with respect to the child. This is not an area that can be broached now. However, it should be understood that the parent himself behaves according to the same principles as does the child. As the child acquires behaviors, he becomes capable of being rewarding or being aversive to the parent. This circumstance will affect the way the parent treats the child. Such interactions between parent and child go much past the present statement of principles by which to effect the personality learning of the child, and are a subject for later discussions. At this time, however, it is important to realize that the complexity of the learning situation for the child is very great and does not lend itself to the conception of providing a mold by which a certain type of child can be stamped out exactly according to plan. There is a great deal that a parent can do in producing a child who will display general behavioral repertoires desired by the parent. However, this does not suggest that the conditions the parent controls are so exact as to produce such behavior in fine detail.

Moreover, even parents following the same conception of child development and the same training procedures will differ widely in how they deal with their children. This is nowhere more evident than when one sees children of parents who have themselves some type of learning orientation. The author is acquainted with a number of psychologists who have a general understanding of learning principles and the manner in which these principles function in the development of the child. Yet, even though the principles employed are quite similar, one can observe that there are wide differences in the manner in which the principles are applied. The parents will still provide widely different learning experiences for their children. It may be expected that these differences in conditions would result from the differences in experiences that the parents themselves have had. Thus, although there is a good deal of similarity in the practices of these parents in some areas, and these similarities would be expected to result in gross behavioral similarity in the children, there are also wide differences that would produce wide behavioral differences in the children involved. This can be expected to be the general case. Knowledge of learning principles should cut down the incidence of undesirable behaviors in children. However, the individual differences that differentiate children can be expected to remain in large part.

PARENTAL AND SOCIETAL
RESPONSIBILITY

In the context of the learning conception of child development, several implications arise concerning the responsibility for the child's behavior—especially when the child has problems. Some biological conceptions of human nature suggest that a person should just naturally be a good parent to his child. The mother is in common-sense conceptions supposed to have some sort of bond with her natural child that enables her to behave as a good mother. The mother of a child with behavior problems, or the cold mother, may be considered to be deficient in some personal, instinctual, or biological sense.

It may be noted, moreover, that there are protective aspects of the biological conception of children's behavior problems. Our culture has provided a forgiving rationale for the parent, the teacher, and society itself by the concept of biological-mental illness. If the child behaves in *very* atypical and undesirable ways, it lessens one's responsibility if the determinants for the problems are considered to reside in the child rather than in the home, the. school, or other societal institutions.

This is another reason the biological conception of child development continues to be held by some. It removes the aversive qualities of accepting the child's experiences as being responsible for his behavior. For the parent it can be devastating to think that parent-child interactions have been causal in the development of the child's severe behavior abnormalities. The same is true of the school. It would be devastating for the school to consider that large numbers of school failures had nothing to do with the children's biological learning incapabilities. Moreover, the suggestion to society itself that behavior problems result from the nature of the child's experiences has straightforward implications of responsibility—especially in cases of general social problems arising from poverty and repressive discrimination. If the poor are morally and biologically inferior, and have achieved their own personal level, then it is easier to enjoy self-righteously one's own provident conditions. It is thus not an accident that when one finds a society in which some humans are treated as subhuman beasts of burden, there is always an attendant social philosophy that declares that is what they actually are. Such conceptions release those who profit from the arrangement from otherwise aversive implications.

Thus, the biological conception of human nature provides some very strong rewards itself, in various ways. It allows us to avoid responsibility for unpleasant conditions. The learning conception, on the other hand, brings home some implications that are not entirely pleasant. Some of these implications, it may be suggested, *should* be unpleasant—because the unpleasantness provides impetus to change practices that are undesirable. Thus, a learning conception of human behavior, if generally held in our society, would help us in our task of solving social problems through legislative enactment. Specifically, the learning conception of human behavior would remove the rationalizations that help people to evade the responsibilities for improving conditions of poverty and discrimination for wide segments of the human population. The learning conception would also establish an atmosphere within which educational advancement could markedly accelerate, especially for children who do not now profit from school. In these areas it would be good to remove the hindering rationalizations of the biological conception. The same is true with respect to parents and the professionals they consult for advice concerning their children's problems. It may be aversive to consider the child's atypical behavior as a result of home learning. But this aversiveness is very scant in comparison to what the parent will suffer if the child continues with his severe behavior problems.

Actually, however, it is suggested that the need for parental rationalizations is only necessary when there is no information concerning what to do to help the child. The parent will not wish to avoid the learning conception of his child's problems if he can be given information from the learning conception with which to begin to deal successfully with those problems. Moreover, although it has been clearly suggested that the parent is largely responsible for the learning conditions that produce the child's early development of behavioral repertoires, and to a lesser extent the more advanced learning he encounters, this is not to suggest that the parent bears some moral responsibility. The central point of the present approach is that we are what we learn. This applies to the parent as well as to the child. The conditions that the parent's behavior imposes upon his child even in cases of failure cannot be attributed to the parent's moral weakness. The parent, after all, follows the same principles of behavior that have been described for the child. The parent is a function of his past experience and present environment to no lesser extent than the child.

Blame and responsibility for behavior are derivations from a conception of human behavior that considers one's behavior to be a result of one's inner moral quality and up to the will of the person himself. A learning conception of human behavior does not accept that system of causation and thus personal responsibility. Rather, we have to expect that when conditions of learning have been deplorable for the parent, then the conditions of learning the parent provides for his child will also be deplorable. This is true for individuals, and it is true for groups. When groups of people have deplorable learning conditions, their behavior will be deplorable, and it will be perpetuated in their children.

If society is interested in improving the behavior of the children of any generation, then a central place to begin is in improving the learning conditions parents can provide for their children. For example, today there is a widespread acceptance of the fact that the Afro-American population has been subjected to deplorable learning conditions to the point where many parents are not able to provide either the appropriate physical conditions or the appropriate learning conditions for their childrren. If there is no intervention in the process whereby deficits in one generation are passed on to the next, this crucial social problem can be expected to continue.

The preceding would suggest that one way to break into this vicious cycle would be through training and support of the disadvantaged parent so that he could improve the physical conditions and the parental training his children will receive. It is suggested that following the type of principles and procedures that have been outlined herein, such parents could receive training that would enable them to markedly improve the manner in which they would themselves provide training for their children in the basic behavioral repertoires. Rather than giving inadequate welfare payments, it is suggested that society provide a suitable living to the parent who undertakes training to make himself a more accomplished parent and in so doing also to make himself a more accomplished individual. Instruction in child-training principles and methods of the type described herein would be productive. However, in addition the parent himself should receive intellectual training of various sorts. It is quite evident from various sources that the language-intellectual training of disadvantaged adults has left them with gaping deficits that are then passed on to their children. For example, the disadvantaged parent's language is very poorly developed. It is ungrammatical, ungainly, sparse, and minimally functional. This is shown vividly in Hersey's *The Algiers Motel Incident* (1968) which includes abundant quotations from ghetto residents of Detroit. Only with great difficulty and inexactitude can these disadvantaged individuals describe events of everyday life. Individuals with such poorly developed language would have great difficulty with most academic learning. They would also be incapable, without some additional input, of training their children to better intellectual skills than they themselves have.

Such programs of parental training should not be conducted as a charity. They are no more charitable than free public education, or the education provided by state universities to middle-class students, which is largely publicly subsidized. The parent is the sole educational institution for the child in the very early years, and to some extent throughout childhood. It is sheer waste to provide school facilities for the child but not provide him with the basic behavioral skills with which to profit from the school. It is in society's interest to break into the vicious cycle of disadvantaged parents providing disadvantaged training for their children. It is in society's interest to help prepare the parent to assume his role of instructor of his child so that the child will be able to adjust to and contribute to society.

This is proposed because the present attempt at solution of contemporary inadequacies in child learning is to provide some type of limited compensatory education for disadvantaged children. Programs such as Headstart are certainly in the right direction. However, they are not based upon an adequate understanding of early child learning and they are thus not adequate in conception (not to mention in procedures and technique). Programs that begin when the child is three or four years of age and that only include an extra year or two of preschool for the child will not prove to be adequate. For one thing, such a program does not recognize the fact that the child has much to learn before he is three. For the disadvantaged child, there are great deficits in the learning of the basic behavioral repertoires during those first three years. Moreover, learning that requires three years in the usual circumstance is not going to be made up in a year of remedial work. It should take at least three years in propitious training circumstances—a higher standard than classes for culturally disadvantaged children could hope to meet. That is, the learning in the advantaged home is conducted when the child has most of the attention of an adult, the parent. In a preschool program for disadvantaged children, the ratio is not remotely as advantageous.

To some extent this could be remedied by having compensatory education for the child begin at a much earlier age. Thus, it is suggested that nursery school participation that included training experiences for aspects of the basic behavioral repertoire should commence with children one, two, and three years of age. Procedures should be utilized whereby the nursery school situation could be used to produce basic behavioral learning in the child (see Staats, 1968a), unlike the usual situation that is devoted entirely to free play where the supervising adult is largely baby-sitting. The most complete type of remediation of our poverty and cultural-deprivation problems, however, would include the adults as well as the children, the general environment for both, and would be of long duration.

In concluding, a return may be made to the primary purpose of the book. It is not only the culturally disadvantaged parent who needs an understanding of human behavior and of child learning. All parents need that type of information. And the professionals who deal with the problems parents present and with parent-child interaction problems also need such information. Moreover, in a democratic society where the ideal is to have everyone contribute to the solution of social problems, all of us require a conception of human behavior that serves as a better foundation for making social decisions. People will make social decisions on the basis of whatever conception they hold—it behooves us to ensure that the conception is the best available.

Our equanimity in designing our educational system with little regard for the foundation upon which it must rest could only be a result of an inadequate conception of child development and human behavior. That conception of human behavior, it may be suggested, is erroneous in considering the parent's role to be only that of providing a benevolent environment—rather than that of being an active trainer who is largely responsible for the basic behavioral repertoires so important to the child's further learning. It may also be suggested that part of this inadequate approach to human behavior is derived from the conception that the development of the basic behavioral repertoire takes place through physiological maturation rather than through complex experiences.

The present conception of the basic behavioral repertoires and the ways that they are developed through learning suggests an alternative view. When we look at the parents as the instructors of the repertoires that are crucial to the child's later learning, we have to expect large divergences in the parents' ability to teach their children and hence in the ability of the children to profit from later training. Furthermore, we would expect that many parents would not be able to do as good a job of training children as could be done based upon systematic knowledge. Nor could we expect parents to be able to handle special problems of learning that require knowledge and competencies with which they would ordinarily have no experience.

It is to commence the task of providing the necessary principles, procedures, and general conception of human development—for science, the relevant professions, and social institutions, as well as for the parent—that the present work has been begun.

IMPLICATIONS OF THE BEHAVIORAL INTERACTION APPROACH TO PERSONALITY

It has been suggested herein that human behavior is a complex subject matter. It is important to realize in the study of human behavior that one cannot, in many cases, go directly from the basic learning principles to an explanation of the complex act. Generally, it is not the present learning principles and conditions that will differentiate the actions of the individual from someone else's. The differentiation lies in what the individual brings to the situation. What he "brings," moreover, may be involved in his behavior in many situations. So the individual's behavior may have general characteristics that ubiquitously identify him as unique from others.

It has thus been suggested that many times the explanation of individual differences in response to various situations, across time, resides in the individual's enduring complexes of behavioral characteristics—his personality. An outline has been presented of some of the principles by which the individual's previously acquired personality characteristics interact with each other and with the environment to produce the individual's characteristic ways of adjusting and adapting to the environmental conditions he faces. The conception has also indicated that the acquisition of personality complexes begins with certain repertoires that in combination form more complex repertoires. The child, for example, learns repertoires as part of his language learning that can be separately identified but which in linkage with other repertoires become larger, functional complexes. The combinations of language and other repertoirial complexes, as an illustration, were seen to give him the general behavioral or personality characteristics that are labeled his intelligence. No one of the repertoires, complex as it might be, is alone the basis of his intelligence characteristics. The *various* kinds of repertoires contribute towards his personality characteristics of intelligence.

Some of the repertoires, like those of the child's word labeling and word meaning vocabulary, are of a cognitive or symbolic sort and traditionally are more likely to be considered in the intellective realm. However, there are motivational repertoires and attitudinal repertoires that additionally compose and affect the general behavioral characteristics of intelligence. Thus, in the present book, even with a focus upon dealing with the behavioral repertoires that compose the traditional conception of intelligence, it was necessary to deal with aspects of personality usually considered in the emotional, the sensory-motor, and the social realms—not only with the intellectual realm. This indicates that the traditional categories of human personality—based as they are upon outmoded theories—do not realistically divide up the events in which we are interested. We cannot expect to find clean cut divisions of the behavioral repertoires that compose one's personality characteristics by following the traditional personality divisions. The complex behavioral repertoires that compose such traditional personality categories as the super-ego, achievement motivation, the self, the ego, abilities, intelligence traits, emotional maturity, and so on, may be expected to overlap and be intertwined in behavioral interaction and to be important in more than one category. It is also suggested that we will only see, understand, and be able to deal with the composition of the traditionally described personality characteristics when the relevant complex behavioral repertoires and their interrelationships and behavioral interactions have been analyzed.

Thus, the present work was intended to suggest a general method or strategy. Some of the important aspects of personality were dealt with herein, especially intelligence. However, as was also indicated, there are other important personality characteristics that were not considered or were not considered in depth. *It is suggested that the task that lies ahead is to identify these various personality repertoires and to subject them to analysis.* This must include theoretical analysis of (1) the personality repertoires in terms of their acquisition (learning), (2) what the personality repertoires are composed of in terms of the complexes of interrelated behavioral skills involved, and (3) the varieties of ways the personality repertoires play their role in the individual's characteristic behavioral identity, his self-direction, his adjustment, and his further learning (personality development).

This task is not an armchair task, however. It demands observations as the basis for the personality theory. Some of the principles and analyses demand laboratory experimental verification. Others may be noted in naturalistic or clinical circumstances. As in the present case, experimental-naturalistic study is also very important. There were many examples herein of this method, where learning conditions and principles were employed to produce the particular behavioral skill in the child in the natural situation. Each positive instance where the child's (or adult's) behavior development takes place according to the principles and the analysis helps verify the personality theory and its learning theory foundation.

In this level of theory construction the general principles of behavior-behavior interaction, and behavior-environment interaction, in their long-term, cumulative, hierarchical and cyclical relationships, also must be elaborated. For example, the personality repertoires play their role in (1) directly determining future behaviors, (2) making it possible to respond and learn in new situations, and (3) altering the individual's social and physical environment in other ways that affect his development.

It is suggested that the contemporary strategy of conducting psychological science by theoretical combat is unproductive. A strategy by which the field of personality comes to grips with its real subject matter, that of the analysis of the actual behavioral components of personality characteristics—their acquisition and function—will unleash a great deal of productivity. The basic theory is there, as are the methods of theoretical analysis, and methods for experimental and naturalistic investigation and clinical treatment. The analysis of the *various* aspects of personality can be expected to constitute a long step forward in the understanding of human behavior and in dealing with problems of human behavior.

One of the most central aims of the present book, as an elaboration of previous statements of the author (Staats, 1963, 1968a, 1968b, 1968c), has been to work toward the necessary rapprochement between the behavioral approach and the empirical concepts and rich observations of personality and social theory stemming from naturalistic study and clinical activities. The present "behavioral interaction" conception is part of a general attempt at the theoretical unification the author has called *social behaviorism*. Generally, the naturalistic observations and conceptions of man arising in personality and social theories are not couched in empirical princicples that are precisely stated and "causative" in the sense that variables are indicated by which to *affect* or produce human behavior. The laboratory-established principles of learning, on the other hand, are relatively precise, detailed, and of a cause and effect nature. When the two are combined, based upon the empirical principles, the result is a theory concerned with significant, functional human behavior, but with the potential for making empirical predictions and producing control of (solutions to) important problems (Staats, 1968b; 1970, pp. 119).

In the present case, a central point of the approach has been to resolve the conflict of determinism that haunts psychology as well as other social and behavioral sciences. There has persisted in all fields concerned with man's behavior the conflicting attempts to explain his behavior by what he is, and contrastingly by what happens to him. This basic schism can be resolved by realizing that what the individual is at the beginning depends upon what has happened to him. But what he *is* then determines what will happen to him, and therefore what he will further become. The individual's behavior is determined. But his behavior determines what he becomes. The interaction even at an early point becomes so involved, and continues in such a complex, cyclical and reoccurring way, that in a very real sense there is self-determination. Moreover, because of the personal experience of self-determination in reasoning, deciding, planning, self-reinforcement, and so on—and the observations of other behavioral interactions—personal freedom, personal causation, and spontaneity have become concepts entrenched in our cultural conceptions (or world view) of human behavior. The *behavioral interaction* explanatory conception of the determination of human behavior is in harmony with a scientific (and behavioral) determinism as well as with the traditional "personality" views. It is hoped that the resolution of the age-old "objective" versus "subjective" schism helps join the very important contributions of the two heretofore separate traditions in psychology and the social sciences, leading toward the unity of science that harbors such great potentiality in the study of man. But this "unity of sciences in the study of man" is a topic requiring separate development—the concern of the next book in the conception.

References

Ayllon, T., and Azrin, N. *The token economy: A motivational system for therapy and rehabilitation.* New York: Appleton-Century-Crofts, 1969.

Ayllon, T., and Michael, J. L. The psychiatric nurse as a behavioral engineer. *Journal of Experimental Analysis of Behavior,* 1959, **2,** 323–334.

Azrin, N. H. Time out from positive reinforcement. *Science,* 1961, **133,** 382–383.

Baer, D., and Sherman, J. Reinforcement of generalized imitation by reinforcing behavioral similarity to a model. *Journal of Experimental analysis of Behavior,* 1967, **10,** 405–416.

Bandura, A. Social learning through Imitation. In Jones, M. R. (Ed.), *Nebraska symposium on motivation.* Lincoln: University of Nebraska Press, 1962.

Bandura, A. A social learning interpretation of psychological dysfunction. In London, P., and Rosenhan, D. (Eds.), *Foundations of abnormal psychology.* New York: Holt, Rinehart and Winston, 1968.

Bandura, A., Ross, D., and Ross, S. A comparative test of the status envy, social power, and the secondary reinforcement theories of identification learning. *Journal of Abnormal and Social Psychology,* 1963, **67,** 527–534.

Bostow, D. E., and Bailey, J. B. Modification of severe disruptive and aggressive behavior using brief time-out and reinforcement procedures. *Journal of Applied Behavior Analysis,* 1969, **2,** 31–37.

Brown, R., and Fraser, C. The acquisition of syntax. Paper delivered at the Second ONR-New York University conference on verbal learning, Dobbs Ferry, N. Y., June 1961.

Brown, R., and Lenneberg, E. H. A study in language and cognition. *Journal of Abnormal and Social Psychology,* 1954, **49,** 454–462.

Carmichael, L. A further study of the development of behavior. *Psychological Review,* 1928, **35,** 253–260.

Carter, H. D. Over- and underachievement in reading. *California Journal of Educational Research,* 1964, **15,** 175–183.

Chomsky, N. Language and the mind. *Psychology Today,* 1968, **1,** 48ff.

Coleman, D. E. The classical conditioning of attitudes toward selected educational concepts. Unpublished doctoral dissertation, University of South Dakota, Vermillion, 1966.

Crook, W. G. Child care. *Honolulu Star-Bulletin.* Feb. 27, 1970, p. D-2.

Crook, W. G. Child care. *Honolulu Star-Bulletin,* Oct. 31, 1969, p. C-3.

Crook, W. G., and Harrison, W. W. Child care. *Honolulu Star-Bulletin,* Nov. 15, 1967, p. D-4.

Dawe, Helen C. A study of the effect of an educational program upon language development and related mental functions in young children. *Journal of Experimental Education,* 1942, **11,** 200–209.

Death at Song My: A U. S. Atrocity? *Newsweek,* Vol. 74, Dec. 1, 1969.

Diamond, I. .T, and Hall, W. C. Evolution of neocortex. *Science,* 1969, **164,** 251–262.

Dysinger, D. W. A comparative study of affective responses by means of the impressive and expressive methods. *Psychological Monographs,* 1931, **4,** No. 187, 14–31.

Etzel, B. C., and Gewirtz, J. L. Experimental modification of care-taker maintained high-rate operant crying in a 6- and a 20-week-old infant (Infans tyrannatearus): Extinction of crying with reinforcement of eye contact and smiling. *Journal of Experimental Child Psychology,* 1967, **5,** 303–317.

Finley, J. R., and Staats, A. W. Evaluative meaning words as reinforcement stimuli. *Journal of Verbal Learning and Verbal Behavior,* 1967, **6,** 193–197.

Freeman, F. N. *Mental tests: Their history, principles, and applications.* Boston: Houghton Mifflin, 1939.

Gagne, R. *The conditions of learning.* New York: Holt, Rinehart and Winston, 1965.

Gelman, R. Conservation acquisition: A problem of learning to attend to relevant attributes. *Journal of Experimental Child Psychology,* 1969, **7,** 167–187.

Gewirtz, J. L., and Baer, D. M. Deprivation and satiation of social reinforcers as drive conditions. *Journal of Abnormal and Social Psychology,* 1958, **57,** 165–172.

Goldman L. The Kwakiutl Indians of Vancouver Island. In Mead, M. (Ed.), *Cooperation and competition among primitive peoples.* New York: McGraw-Hill, 1937.

Harris, F. R., Johnston, M. K., Kelley, C. S., and Wolf, M. M. Effects of positive social reinforcement on regressed crawling of a nursery school child. *Journal of Educational Psychology,* 1964, **55,** 35–41.

Hart, B., Allen, K. E., Buell, J., Harris, F. R., and Wolf, M. M. Effects of social reinforcement on operant crying. *Journal of Experimental child Psychology,* 1964, **1,** 145–153.

Hawkins, R., Peterson, R., Schweid, E., and Bijou, S. Behavior therapy in the home: Amelioration of problem parent-child relations with the parent in a therapeutic role. *Journal of Experimental Child Psychology,* 1966, **4,** 99–107.

Hersey, J. *The Algiers motel incident.* New York: Knopf, 1968.

Hobbs, N. Helping disturbed children: Psychological and sociological strategies. *American Psychologist,* 1966, **21,** 1105–1115.

Hull, C. L. *Principles of behavior.* New York: Appleton-Century-Crofts, 1943.

Hyman, J. D. I. Q. and race. *New Republic,* Vol. 161, No. 17, Oct. 25, 1969, pp. 30–31.

Jensen, A. R. How much can we boost I. Q. and scholastic achievement? *Harvard educational Review,* 1969, **39,** No. 1, pp. 1–123.

Kagan, J. Personality and the learning process. *Daedulus,* 1965, **94,** 558–559.

Kaplan, D. The super-organic: Science or metaphysics. In Manners, R. A., and Kaplan, D. (Eds.), *Theory in Anthropology.* Chicago: Aldine, 1968.

Killings of Song My, The, *Newsweek,* Vol. 74, Dec. 8, 1969.

Lipsitt, L., Kaye, H., and Bosack, T. Enhancement of neonatal sucking through reinforcement. *Journal of Experimental Child Psychology,* 1966, **4,** 163–168.

McCandless, B. R. The effect of enriched educational experience upon the growth of intelligence of very superior children. Unpublished masters thesis, University of Iowa, 1940.

Maccoby, E. E., and Gibbs, P. K. Methods of child-rearing in two social classes. In Martin, W. E., and Stendler, C. B. (Eds.), *Readings in child development.* New York: Harcourt, Brace & World, 1954.

Marshall, G. Toilet training of an autistic 8-year-old through conditioning therapy: A case report. *Behavior Research and Theory,* 1966, **4,** 242–246.

Massacre at Mylai, The. *Life,* Vol. 67, No. 23, Dec. 5, 1969.

Miller, N. E. The influence of past experience upon the transfer of subsequent training. Doctoral dissertation, Yale University, 1935.

Money, J. Two cytogenic syndromes: Psychologic comparisons I. Intelligence and specific-factor quotients. *Journal of Psychiatric Research,* 1964, **2,** 223–231.

Murray, A. A. *Explorations in personality.* New York: Oxford University Press, 1938.

Mursell, J. L. *Psychological testing.* New York: Longmans, Green, 1949.

Newsweek, Vol. 72, July 8, 1968.

O'Connor, R. D. Modification of social withdrawal through symbolic modeling. *Journal of Applied Behavior Analysis,* in press.

O'Leary, D., O'Leary, S., and Becker, W. Modification of a deviant sibling interaction pattern in the home. *Behavior Research and Therapy,* 1967, **5,** 113–120.

Osgood, C. E., and Suci, G. J. Factor analysis of meaning. *Journal of Experimental Psychology,* 1955, **50,** 325–338.

Peters, C. C., and McElwee, A. R. Improving functioning intelligence by analytical training in a nursery school. *Elementary School Journal,* 1944, **45,** 213–219.

Peterson, J. Intelligence and its measurement: A symposium. *Journal of Educational Psychology,* 1921, **12,** p. 125.

Piaget, J. How children learn mathematical concepts. *Scientific American,* 1953, **189,** 74–79.

Pintner, R. *Intelligence testing: Methods and results.* New York: Henry Holt, 1931.

Rheingold, H. L., Gewirtz, J. L., and Ross, H. W. Social conditioning of vocalizations in the infant. *Journal of Comparative and Physiological Psychology,* 1959, **52,** 68–73.

Rosen, B. C. The achievement syndrome: A psychocultural dimension of social stratification. *American Sociological Review,* 1956, **21,** 205–211.

Ryback, D., and Staats, A. W. Parents as behavior therapy-technicians in treating reading deficits (dyslexia). *Journal of Behavior Therapy and Experimental Psychiatry,* in press.

Simmons, M. W., and Lipsitt, L. P. An operant-discrimination apparatus for infants. *Journal of Experimental Analysis of Behavior,* 1961, **4,** 233–235.

Skinner, B. F. Philogeny and ontogeny of behavior. *Science,* 1966, **153,** 1205–1213.

Staats, A. W. Learning theory and opposite speech, *Journal of Abnormal and Social Psychology,* 1957, **55,** 268–269.

Staats, A. W. (with contributions by Carolyn K. Staats). *Complex human behavior.* New York: Holt, Rinehart and Winston, 1963.

Staats, A. W. An integrated-functional learning approach to complex human behavior. In Kleinmuntz, B. (Ed.), *Problem solving: Research, method, and theory.* New York: John Wiley, 1966.

Staats, A. W. *Learning, language, and cognition.* New York: Holt, Rinehart and Winston, 1968a.

Staats, A. W. Social behaviorism and human motivation: Principles of the attitude-reinforcer-discriminative system. In Greenwald, A., Brock, T., and Ostrom, T. (Eds.), *Psychological foundations of attitudes.* New York: Academic Press, 1968b.

Staats, A. W. Social behaviorism, human motivation, and the conditioning therapies. In Maher, B. (Ed.), *Progress in experimental personality research*. New York: Academic Press, 1970.

Staats, A. W. Motivational (reinforcer) systems in the solution of human problems. In *Behavior modification in the classroom*, G. A. Fargo, C. Behrns, and P. A. Nolen (Eds.), New York: Wadsworth, in press. (a)

Staats, A. W. Linguistic-mentalistic theory versus an explanatory S-R learning theory of language development. In Slobin, D. (Ed.), *The ontogenesis of language*. New York: Academic Press, in press. (b)

Staats, A. W. A learning-behavior theory: In programmatic outline. In Gilgen, A. R. (Ed.), *Contemporary Scientific Psychology*. New York: Academic Press, in press. (c)

Staats, A. W. *Complex child learning and behavior modification,* in preparation.

Staats, A. W., Brewer, B. A., and Gross, M. C. Learning and cognitive development· Representative samples (reading, number concepts, writing) and experimental-longitudinal methods. *Final report of child learning project,* Contract No. OEO 4121, November 1969.

Staats, A. W., and Butterfield, W. H. Treatment of nonreading in a culturally deprived juvenile delinquent: An application of reinforcement principles. *Child Development,* 1965, **4,** 925–942.

Staats, A. W., Finley, J. R., Minke, K. A., and Wolf, M. M. Reinforcement variables in the control of unit reading responses. *Journal of Experimental Analysis of Behavior,* 1964, **7,** 139–149.

Staats, A. W., Finley, J. R., Osborne, J. G., Quinn, W. D., and Minke, K. A. The use of chain schedules in the study of reinforcement variables in a reading task. *Technical report no. 25,* between the Office of Naval Research and Arizona State University, 1963.

Staats, A. W., Minke, K. A., and Butts, P. A. token-reinforcement remedial reading program administered by black therapy-technicians to problem black children. *Behavior Therapy,* in press.

Staats, A. W., Minke, K. A., Goodwin, W., and Landeen, J. Cognitive behavior modification: "Motivated learning" reading treatment with sub-professional therapy-technicians. *Behavior Research and Therapy,* 1967, **5,** 283–299.

Staats, A. W., and Staats, C. K. A comparison of the development of speech and reading behavior with implications for research. *Child Development,* 1962, **33,** 831–846.

Staats, A. W., Staats, C. K., and Crawford, H. L. First-order conditioning of meaning and the parallel conditioning of a GSR. *Technical Report Number 6,* Contract Nonr-2305 (00) between the Office of Naval Research and Arizona State University, 1958.

Staats, A. W., C. K., Heard, W. G., and Nims, L. P. Replication report: Meaning established by classical conditioning. *Journal of experimental Psychology,* 1959, **57,** 64.

Staats, A. W. Staats, C. K., Schutz, R. E., and Wolf, M. M. The conditioning of textual responses using "extrinsic" reinforcers. *Journal of experimental Analysis of Behavior,* 1962, **5,** 33–40.

Sten, W. *The psychological methods of testing intelligence,* translated by G. M. Whipple. Baltimore: Warwick and York, 1914, p. 14.

Terman, L. M., and Merrill, M. A. *Measuring intelligence.* Boston: Houghton Mifflin, 1937.

Tharp, R., Gallimore, R., and Kemp, B. Positive reinforcing function of "negative attention." *Journal of Experimental Child Psychology,* 1969, **8,** 140–146.

Thomas, D. R., Becker, W. C., and Armstrong, M. Production and elimination of disruptive classroom behavior by systematically varying teacher's behavior. *Journal of Applied Behavior Analysis,* 1968, **1,** 35–45.

Wahler, R., Winkel, G., Peterson, R., and Morrison, D. Mothers as behavior therapists for their own children. *Behavior Research and Therapy,* 1965, **3,** 113–124.

Weisberg, P. Social and non-social conditioning of infant vocalizations. *Child Development,* 1963, **34,** 377–388.

White, A. D. *A history of the warfare of science with theology in Christendom.* New York: Braziller, 1899 (1955 ed.)

White, R. (in collaboration with Fallaci, D.). The dead body and the living brain. *Look,* No. 24, Nov. 28, 1967.

Witonski, P. P. The federal schoolmaster.*The University Bookman,* 1968, *VIII,* p. 93.

Wolf, M., Risley, T., and Mees, H. Application of operant conditioning procedures to the behavior problems of an autistic child. *Behavior Research and Therapy,* 1964, **1,** 305–312.

Zimmerman, D. W. Durable secondary reinforcement: Method and theory. *Psychological Review,* 1957, **64,** 373–383.

Index

71 72 73 74   7 6 5 4 3 2 1